THE DYNAMICS OF
HUMAN COMMUNICATION

A LABORATORY APPROACH

please Understand me.

Coming Alive
Some nine to Five

Realistic
Investigative
Artistic
Social
Entertainment
Conventional

THE DYNAMICS OF HUMAN COMMUNICATION

A LABORATORY APPROACH
FOURTH EDITION

GAIL E. MYERS
MICHELE TOLELA MYERS
Trinity University

McGRAW-HILL BOOK COMPANY
New York   St. Louis   San Francisco   Auckland   Bogotá   Hamburg
Johannesburg   London   Madrid   Mexico   Montreal   New Delhi   Panama
Paris   São Paulo   Singapore   Sydney   Tokyo   Toronto

This book was set in Optima by University Graphics, Inc.
The editors were Marian D. Provenzano and Susan Gamer;
the designer was Anne Canevari Green;
the production supervisor was Marietta Breitwieser.
The photo editor was Inge King.
R. R. Donnelley & Sons Company was printer and binder.

THE DYNAMICS OF HUMAN COMMUNICATION
A Laboratory Approach

234567890 DOCDOC 898765

ISBN 0-07-044221-5

Cover photograph credit
Vasily Kandinsky, *Accompanied Contrast,* March 1935.
Collection, The Solomon R. Guggenheim Museum, New York.
Photographed by Carmelo Guadagno.

Chapter-Opening Photograph Credits
 1. Hugh Rogers — *Monkmeyer*
 2. Owen Franken — *Stock, Boston, Inc.*
 3. Charles Gatewood — *Stock, Boston, Inc.*
 4. © David R. Frazier
 5. © Jim Anderson 1980 — *Woodfin Camp and Assoc.*
 6. Owen Franken — *Stock, Boston, Inc.*
 7. Richard Kalvar — *Magnum Photos*
 8. © David Hurn — *Magnum Photos*
 9. © Thomas Hopker 1980 — *Woodfin Camp and Assoc.*
10. © Hazel Hankin — *Stock, Boston, Inc.*
11. © Christina Tomson 1983 — *Woodfin Camp and Assoc.*
12. © Burt Glinn — *Magnum Photos*

Library of Congress Cataloging in Publication Data

Myers, Gail E., date
    The dynamics of human communication.

    Includes bibliographies and index.
    1. Interpersonal communication.   2. Interpersonal
communication — Problems, exercises, etc.   I. Myers,
Michele Tolela, date   II. Title.
BF637.C45M9   1985   153.6   84-11286
ISBN 0-07-044221-5

To Erika and David

CONTENTS

PREFACE

This textbook grew out of our need to combine *information about communication* with the essential *practice of communication.* When the first edition of *Dynamics of Human Communication* came out in 1973, it was certainly a pioneer in the field, as it put theories together with the skills of applying them to our human interaction. Over the years since its introduction (and its very warm reception), many thousands of students have used this text and have been encouraged to share their reactions with their instructors and with us. Feedback from students and teachers has prompted each new edition as we have heard from many friends in the field how they were able to use this text, how they found it clear to read, and how it helped them apply the principles of communication. Wide acceptance not only of this textbook but of the principle of "laboratory learning" has meant a very significant change in the way many communication courses are taught. It has never surprised us that we apply chemical principles in a chemistry laboratory, that we test out biological theories in a biology laboratory, or that we develop greater understanding of energy or motion in a physics laboratory. It is logical to assume that a communication laboratory, as established by this text and reinforced by others like it, can be a place where communication theory can be brought to first-person experiences in a safe and controlled environment.

Besides feedback from instructors and their students, the development of new theory has also compelled us to revise this textbook, as new ways of viewing the human communication condition emerge from research and new writings. You will find reference to classical studies in human communication dating back scores of years; these we feel must be included to help you gain a historical perspective on communication. These references also pay tribute to the earliest researchers, thinkers, and leaders in the field of interpersonal or speech communication. But you should also recognize the enormous amount of current and creative research and writing which is published each year; and it is to that end that we watch the communication journals (*Human Communication Research, Quarterly Journal of Speech, Journal of Communication, Communication Education, Communication Monographs,* and many others in speech communication and related fields) to bring to this book recent examples of scholarly observations. Both the number and the quality of publications reporting on interpersonal communication scholarship indicate how strong this field has grown. We encourage you to dig more deeply into those journals for even more current reports than we can include in each edition.

ORGANIZATION OF THIS BOOK

In Part 1, you are introduced to some of the more popular, more interesting, and more useful theories about how people communicate with one another and with what effect. We give you a working definition of *interpersonal communication,* and we also tell you what this kind of communication is *not.* From the various ways of viewing communication, we encourage you to follow our model of the transactional view, which is currently the most widely researched as well as one of the most clearly explained systems of interpreting how people interact. We include theories of perception, of how we develop a self-concept, and of how we formulate and act on our values and beliefs, as well as some of the more familiar theories about cognitive dissonance and consistency.

In Part 2, we extend those theories to demonstrate how our communication is related to language and meaning. Because language has the power to build or to destroy, we propose some ways of looking at the use of language — by you and by others around you — which may help you detect unhealthy use of language in others and make your own words more effective. The field of general semantics, which is part of the material of this section, is enjoying a resurgence among departments of philosophy and linguistics in our colleges as well as retaining its recognized place among students in communication and the social sciences. Listening is included as part of the "interpersonal tools" in Chapter 8; the fascinating and ever-present forms of nonverbal communication are discussed in Chapter 9.

Part 3, "Interpersonal Strategies," brings to a focus the applications, or methodologies, by which people can actually use the principles and theories discussed earlier. Roles and rules are two such methodologies of building a place in the communication society. We take a new and enlightened view of conflict as a potentially healthy and useful communication interaction. Negotiation, closely related to conflict theory, is suggested as part of effective management of our interpersonal transactions. Traditional ways of solving problems, leading others, and performing in groups, and some more innovative looks at trust and risk taking, are all treated in Part 3. You will enjoy the lists of communication styles and will find yourself part of the predictable moves made by people within the "dynamics of human communication."

ACKNOWLEDGMENTS   Previous editions of this text, as well as our own professional lives, were deeply influenced by Dr. Elwood Murray, teacher and scholar. We want again to give credit to Dr. Murray, as we have done in the first three editions. He is an inspiration to many generations of students at the University of Denver and was a man well ahead of his time: at least three decades before the rest of the speech discipline had accepted the human transactional view of communication, Dr. Murray was writing, arguing, organizing, and probing this set of then revolutionary formulations. Many of our colleagues who have had a continuing effect on this book are also friends, if not disciples, of Dr. Murray.

Our editors at McGraw-Hill, especially Marian Provenzano, have had a long-term interest in our keeping this textbook both current and readable. We are jointly impressed by the reports from students who say they enjoy reading it, and from grateful instructors who say the same. That makes editors and authors very happy. This book is written to be read, and we are pleased when the response from so many students and teachers confirms that purpose.

When we wrote above that the new work in the field prompts us to make revisions, we were responding to the needs of colleagues whose judgment both the publishers and the authors respect highly. Three such persons, selected by the publisher to be reviewers and critics, were of great value from the first plans to bring out a new edition. This latest edition reflects in many ways their critical evaluations and their good advice; we owe them much. It is small recognition to list them here, but each knows how personally grateful we are for the excellent suggestions and the continuing confidence in this work. Our sincere thanks to Sue Griffiths at Atlantic Community College in Mays Landing, New Jersey; to Jimmie D. Trent at Miami University in Oxford, Ohio; and to Eugene Rebstock at San Francisco State University.

Gail E. Myers
Michele Tolela Myers

THE DYNAMICS OF
HUMAN COMMUNICATION

A LABORATORY APPROACH

Part 1

INTERPERSONAL THEORIES

Chapter 1

YOU AND
YOUR COMMUNICATION

In
a
Nutshell

This chapter develops an overview of the term "communication" and how that concept relates to our lives. We compare the views of communication as technology, as mass media, as skills and tools, and as human interaction. Although the focus of this book is on the dimension of *interpersonal* communication, there are many implied references to and acknowledgments of the importance of other dimensions: intrapersonal, group, and even mass communication, as the growth of interactive systems moves this area closer to the interpersonal one.

In developing a definition of interpersonal communication, we refer to a set of dynamic characteristics rather than static ones. Four communication "rules" are suggested: (1) You cannot *not* communicate. (2) Communication is a "chicken-and-egg" process. (3) Communication occurs at both a content level and a relation level. (4) Communication transactions are either among equals or up-and-down.

In explaining how this book emphasizes the transactional approach to communication study, we review two earlier theories which we call the "bulls-eye" theory and the "Ping-Pong" theory.

INTRODUCTION

This is a book about communication — the specific behavior which sets humans off from other species. Communication, the use of symbols to influence and move ideas, is at the very core of your humanness. It is the essential process by which you *become who you are* and through which you *establish and maintain relations with others.*

Without communication you would be in a desolate landscape of vague and unidentified shapes, noises, colors, and movements, not understanding what is going on around you and not knowing how to find out. Sensory data coming to you would not be compared, interpreted, or understood. People around you would be ambiguous figures, threatening and flailing about in seemingly disorganized, uncoordinated, and random actions without purpose or direction.

In other words, you would be without the symbolic systems you use to make sense out of your world and out of your own place in that world. You would be overwhelmed with confusion and would have no way to get out of it.

Communication helps reduce the ambiguity and confusion in your world and increases the possibility that things will happen according to understandable and useful patterns. When people talk about "communication," they refer to a great many different things. In this chapter we will develop some of the ways this term can be defined. We will also discuss the limits we place on the term when we use it in a textbook on interpersonal communication. Very important, we will also show how theories about communication are related to what people do to each other.

Communication as Technology

If you tell people that you are studying communication, there is at least some chance that they will think that you are going to work as a radio announcer, or a telephone installer, or a person who knows about the electronic wonders of satellites, multidistribution systems, or microwaves. Many people confuse the *act* of communicating or the actual *communicating behaviors of people* with the machinery, devices, physical systems, or technologies of communication. So much emphasis today is placed on robots, computers, and mass information distribution systems like television cables and satellites that we almost automatically think of these technical developments as "communication." However important these devices may be to moving information and entertainment around the world, they are not what we consider as communication in this textbook.

Communication as Mass Media

Another common misconception of the word "communication" is the assumption that it refers only to widespread dissemination as practiced in the mass media — newspapers, radio, television, magazines. While these media may be a very important part of our lives, influencing the way we live, buy products, or vote for candidates, the mass communication industry is only one special case of communication. Professional media people refer to themselves as "communicators" quite honestly. Theirs is a very formidable task—to inform and entertain vast audiences with a wide range of interests, likes, needs, beliefs, and levels of understanding. Another reason we may confuse these two types of communication is that many of the same principles and theories about communication can be applied quite consistently to both mass and interpersonal communication.

Communication as Speaking and Writing Skills

You may have had courses in your school which were called "communication" and were primarily concerned with spelling, grammar, punctuation, typing, handwriting, giving prepared speeches, writing essays, or other tools of human symbolic exchange. We have no quarrel with learning the proper skills of speaking and writing. There is, however, a tendency among some people to think that if they can just spell correctly or put margins and headings in the correct places on letters or reports, then they are communicating effectively. Mistaking the tools of communication for the essential human elements of cognition and emotion are common errors. The reason we need to spell correctly and form our letters clearly is not just for the sake of correct form or orthography. The reason is to make it easier for others to *make sense out of what we want to say* as well as to help us to *reduce the ambiguity* of our relations with others and our entire surroundings. We believe you should learn communicating skills as well as the implications of your communicating efforts. We also believe you should master the tools of communicating—spelling, voice control, writing, typing, reading, listening, effective habits of outlining, projecting, organizing, to name a few. But too often learning the tools absorbs so much of your time and energy that you neglect other very significant aspects of communicating: (1) making sense and (2) reducing ambiguity, thus increasing predictability.

Communication as Human Interaction

As you study communication, you will be impressed by how many different fields of study—subject matter areas or disciplines—are involved. You will learn that nearly all our human contacts involve communication, from our internal state of thinking and feeling to the broad scope of international (and perhaps even interstellar) exchanges. You will also be impressed by how many different ways we have of talking about communication. We call it "discourse," we call it "rhetoric," we call it "speaking," we call it "interacting," we call it "transactions." Whatever name we give it, the practice of interacting symbolically has a long history and a broad application today in human enterprises.

For your further information about the origins of communication theories, there is an interesting chapter by Littlejohn in *Human Communication Theory* in which he writes:

> *Any serious communication scholar must recognize that our understanding of this phenomenon stems from the work of many disciplines. Communication lies at the heart of just about all human affairs. We cannot fully probe individual behavior, social structures, political activity, artistic creation, language and culture, or a host of other human concerns without including investigations of communication processes. This is why communication is such a ubiquitous theme.[1]*

Littlejohn shows how the fields of philosophy, sociology, psychology, anthropology, mathematics, linguistics, English, literature, media studies, psychiatry, management, and others have contributed to the theories which we use in writing about interpersonal communication. Beyond these essential relations is the realization that communication is evolving its own discipline, its own body of literature, and its own researchers. Another interesting treatment of the word "communication" can be found in a report by Katriel and Philipsen,[2] who examine the term as a cultural concept. They suggest that differences in how people use the word relate to rituals, including how people give each other support and how they develop closeness to others.

Communicating does not, therefore, involve only the *information* or *data* which people exchange with one another. Studying discourse means looking at the actual behaviors of people as they create meaning for themselves, which not everyone does in the same way. People may refer to "real communication" as deeper and closer than some other kinds of "small talk." This distinction is suggested by Hart and others, who, in addition, introduce a term, "rhetorical sensitivity," which refers to an attitude people have about communicating:

> *[Rhetorical sensitivity] represents a way of thinking about what should be said and, then, a way of deciding how to say it. Rhetorical sensitivity is not a behavioral guideline for measuring one's interpersonal competence but is a mind-set which some persons apply usefully in their everyday lives.[3]*

---

[1]Stephen W. Littlejohn, "An Overview of Contributions to Human Communication Theory from Other Disciplines," in Frank E. X. Dance (ed.), *Human Communication Theory,* Harper & Row, Publishers, Inc., New York, 1982, p. 244.

[2]Tamar Katriel and Gerry Philipsen, "What We Need Is Communication: Communication as a Cultural Category in Some American Speech," *Communication Monographs,* vol. 48, no. 4, December 1981, pp. 301–317.

[3]Roderick P. Hart, Robert E. Carlson, and William F. Eadie, "Attitude toward Communication and the Assessment of Rhetorical Sensitivity," *Communication Monographs,* vol. 47, no. 1, March 1980, pp. 1–22.

We discover that how people communicate relates to what they think the word ''communication'' means. They not only choose what to say or write according to ''rules'' they have learned, but also choose to speak or not to speak, to act in specific ways, to look for ways to tell others their ideas or feelings or to conceal them. All this is involved in communication as human interaction, probably the broadest definition of the word we can find.

DIMENSIONS OF COMMUNICATION

Before developing the definition of communication which we will use in this textbook, let's look at some more aspects of communication which will be included in our text. It is not unusual to look at communication according to where it goes on (e.g., inside people versus over broadcast airwaves) or how many people are involved at a time (just your own personal, private self or small groups or masses of people).

Intrapersonal Communication

You will read a great deal in this book and other textbooks about what goes on inside people as they think, feel, value, react, imagine, dream, etc. The dimension known as ''*intra*personal'' has been the subject of psychological and cognitive studies which attempt to learn how people respond to symbols and how they make decisions or store and retrieve data in their brains. There has also been much concern about how people's biases, loves, hates, or even apathy can affect human interaction. How people handle information about their world goes on inside their heads, but the interactions show up in behaviors.

In developing a theory of meaning, Cronen and others write about what they call ''coordinated management of meaning,'' which necessarily starts inside people's symbol-processing centers — intrapersonally. ''The locus of meaning is intrapersonal, while the locus of action is interpersonal.''[4] It is not possible to study one without the other. While we do not call any single chapter ''Intrapersonal Communication,'' there is much material related to the intrapersonal level in the sections dealing with perception, values, self-concept, styles, general semantics, language, meaning, etc.

Interpersonal Communication

As we will discuss later in this chapter, the definition we find most appealing treats interpersonal communication as a transaction between people and their environment, which includes other people such as friends, family, children, coworkers, and even strangers.

---

[4]Vernon E. Cronen, W. Barnett Pearce, and Linda Harris, ''The Coordinated Management of Meaning: A Theory of Communication,'' in Frank E. X. Dance (ed.), *Human Communication Theory,* Harper & Row, Publishers, Inc., New York, 1982, p. 71.

Communication is now seen as a transaction in which both parties are active. The parties are not necessarily equally active — that is more likely in the case of interpersonal communication, less so in the case of mass media and their audiences — but to both parties the transaction is in some way functional. *It meets a need or provides a gratification. To a greater or lesser degree information flows both ways. Like other transactions, this one is likely to be guided by rules or agreement or ''contract,'' as we see when a teacher communicates with a student, a parent with a child, or even a driver with a traffic light — in which latter case the light is contractually designed so that the driver can be sure the color* will *change and drivers will therefore not have to wait forever.*[5]

Most people who write about interpersonal communication appear to insist that the more communication you have, the better off your relations will be. More may not always be better, however. As Sillars and Scott point out, how people see each other (''interpersonal perceptions'') may have a significant effect on how those persons will interact.[6] They find that couples, for example, tend to make up their reality about each other and then communicate in terms of those beliefs. Another study of married couples' adjustment suggests that a complex pattern of relating to each other has the greatest effect on how well couples get along.[7]

In effect, what happens in interpersonal communication involves so much more than words that we must pay careful attention to people's *habits of relating to each other* if we are to be effective in either studying about or participating in these transaction.

Group Communication

Not all communication theorists agree on a definition of small group communication — how many people make up a group, what differences there are between dyads and other numbers of people in communication, etc. The field of group dynamics, however, represents a very interesting and special case of communication. It involves theories of leadership and management, small group discussion, and decision making. ''One consistent finding [of management research] over the years has been that management style and communication are inextricably linked.''[8] There are many excellent books and journals about groups,

[5]Wilbur Schramm, ''The Unique Perspective of Communication: A Retrospective View,'' *Journal of Communication,* vol. 33, no. 3, Summer 1983, p. 14.

[6]Alan Sillars and Michael D. Scott, ''Interpersonal Perception between Intimates,'' *Human Communication Research,* vol. 10, no. 1, Fall 1983, pp. 153–176.

[7]Stella Ting-Toomey, ''An Analysis of Verbal Communication Patterns in High and Low Marital Adjustment Groups,'' *Human Communication Research,* vol. 9, no. 4, Summer 1983, pp. 306–319.

[8]Linda McCallister, ''Predicted Employee Compliance to Downward Communication Styles,'' *The Journal of Business Communication,* vol. 20, no. 1, Winter 1983, p. 68.

group process, and leadership. We cannot begin to do justice to that important field in the limited space of this textbook. You will note, however, that many of the examples we use and a number of the exercises and activities involve group dynamics, group discussion, and leadership and management principles. There is no way you can interact in your class without applying or taking into account the principles of group interaction. If you wish, you can undertake formal study of that field by consulting the bibliography on groups or by finding courses in which group dynamics, leadership, or discussion are the main topic.

Mass Communication

One of the most popular areas of study in our colleges today is that of the mass media — or "communication," as the term is used in some places — to indicate a broadened view of what once was called simply "journalism." At one time it was believed that audiences were a sort of homogenous blob which could be reached through a "magic bullet" shot from a media source. This very simplified view of audiences was useful to some mass media practitioners but did not explain how complicated are both the process of communicating and the character of audiences. While mass media study is beyond the scope of our book, there are many ties between interpersonal and mass communication. As the mechanical and technological limits to communicating disappear, there will still be the human limits — different meanings in different people with different needs and desires and levels of understanding. "Interactive" systems[9] now being put into use in mass media include computers linked by modems and other long-range systems, teletext information systems, banking or shopping by television-supported devices, and a wide variety of ways in which people can "talk back to" their mass media sources. One-way transmission over mass media is no longer the only way to view information and entertainment access. As the significance of two-way (or interactive) communication grows, people studying and working in mass media will have to take into account many of the theories and principles of interpersonal communication; and we can predict a further merging of such fields of study.

DEVELOPING A DEFINITION OF COMMUNICATION

In this section we will develop a series of descriptions of human communication. They include the assertions that communication is everywhere, that it is continuous (or that it keeps going on into the future after it comes from somewhere in the past, and that it is important how we decide when it starts and when it ends), that it involves sharing

[9]Everett M. Rogers and Steven H. Chaffee, "Communication as an Academic Discipline: A Dialogue," *Journal of Communication,* vol. 33, no. 3, Summer 1983, pp. 24–25.

meaning, that it has many predictable elements in it, that it occurs at more than one level, and that it occurs among equals or unequals.

For a more detailed treatment of defining interpersonal communication, see Miller and Sunnafrank in *Human Communication Theory*,[10] in which they propose a "developmental" definition as being more dynamic than some earlier "situational" definitions. They propose two main assumptions about interpersonal communication, which are important for you to know about — basically the same assumptions we use in this textbook

> *Our first major assumption is that the basic function of all communication is to control the environment so as to realize certain physical, economic, or social rewards from it. . . . We do not invoke the term* control *in [a] narrow, marketplace sense; rather as we use the term, communicators have successfully controlled their environment when at least some degree of correspondence exists between their desired and their obtained outcomes.*[11]

> *The second fundamental assumption stems directly from the centrality of control to our conceptual perspective. . . . We assume that whenever people communicate with others, they make predictions about the probable consequences, or outcomes, of their messages. . . . Stated differently, messagemaking is not a random activity. . . . Nevertheless, predictions underlie the most casual, commonplace interactions. Typically, communicators remain blissfully unaware of the predictions they are making until such predictions are disconfirmed.*[12]

Interpersonal communication can be defined, then, in relation to what you do with it. First, you use communication to have an effect on your "environment," a term which means not only your immediate physical surroundings but also the psychological climate you live in, the people around you, the social interchanges you have, the information you want to get or give in order to control the questions and answers of your living. Second, you use communication to improve the predictability of your relations with all these environmental forces, which act on you and on which you act to make things happen. Much has been written about reducing ambiguity in our lives, which is simply another way of saying increasing predictability.

In the following pages we will take you through a series of state-

---

[10]Gerald R. Miller and Michael J. Sunnafrank, "All Is for One but One Is Not for All: A Conceptual Perspective of Interpersonal Communication" in Frank E. X. Dance (ed.), *Human Communication Theory,* Harper & Row, Publishers, Inc., New York, 1982.

[11]Ibid., p. 233.

[12]Ibid., pp. 224, 225.

ments about communication. Each will become part of the definition of communication used in this textbook. These sections will also include some "communication rules," presented in Boxes 1 through 4. We hope you will pay particular attention to these rules, or axioms, as they will be an important part of our later discussions.

Finally, we will compare our approach—the transactional view—with two earlier approaches to communication. In a way, this will explain why we use the word "dynamics" in the title of this book. From its first edition to the present one, we have been presenting the idea that communication is not a static or linear or one-sided activity. Communication is an ever-present, continuous, predictable, multilevel, dynamic sharing of meaning for the purpose of managing our lives more effectively.

Communication Is Everywhere

People may be only vaguely aware of the things which are closest to them in their lives. They often pay very little attention to familiar things. Just as a fish takes for granted the water around it, people living in a communicative world take their communication for granted. And just as the fish will miss the water when taken from the lake or stream, people will miss communication if they are suddenly cut off from it.

The universal human characteristic, using symbols, is highly developed in some societies, less developed in others. But whether you are in the heart of our greatest city or in a small village in some primitive area of the world, the use of symbols is what will tie you to the people and activities around you. Most human behavior involves the use of a system of symbols. We speak in oral symbols; we write in written symbols; and we make use of a highly structured and rich system of nonverbal signs, gestures, movements, and actions to express much of what we want to convey to others.

Anthropologists tell us that any society will develop the symbol system necessary for its survival. If symbols are only needed for gaining food and shelter, the society will develop those symbols. It is important to note that we should not feel superior to a culture that does not have our mechanical devices for communication, nor feel that our language system is better because it has some words or symbols that another culture lacks. It has, in fact, been argued that there is no such thing as a "primitive" language, because whatever language a society uses will meet the needs of that society. Many spoken languages have the ability to express concepts that are not normally found in English or that English-speaking people may take many different words to express. Symbol systems, and hence communication, arise in relation to people's needs to express themselves within the places they occupy in the world.

Not only do you need and use communication, but you find it all around you. When you start your day, it may be to the sound of an alarm clock, a radio, or someone calling you. But the message gets across that you should get up.

Getting dressed and cleaned up are largely the product of previous communication. You were not born with a tremendous urge to brush your teeth, shower, or comb your hair. If these have become part of your behavior patterns, it is because you learned them and because someone at some age in your life conditioned you with rewards and punishments through an effective communication system called ``child rearing.''

You select some clothes to wear for the day. They will be part of your communication with others. You know through previous communication that some outfits are acceptable in certain situations and some in others, that you can give a pretty strong message by showing up in class too dressed up, or at a formal wedding in a T-shirt. Clothes you wear will communicate much about you: your tastes, your finances, the groups you want to be identified with. This will influence the response of others to you. The jewelry you wear, the style of your hair, any articles you carry will all tell something about you and will bring predictable responses from others throughout your communication day.

By now you are ready for breakfast; whether or not you eat and what you eat will be influenced by previous communication. If you believe ``it is not good to leave the house with an empty stomach,'' you may be listening to the voices of your parents or a television commercial. The cereal you eat, the brand of coffee you use, and the amount you eat have all been conditioned by your communication environment.

Going outdoors brings you into more communication, this time with your natural environment. Noisy and smoky, or quiet and clear, it may well influence you in what you do the rest of the day. Meeting another person lets you select your behavior — to speak or not. If you speak, you make a selection of tone of voice and message: ``Hello,'' ``Hi,'' ``Nice day'' (or a grunt) can all convey an important message.

If you walk to work or to class, you move past people and try to avoid running into them. A radarlike system of communication tells you which way to dodge when you come close to colliding with someone. Sometimes you don't read these signals well and end up in a kind of ``dance'' with strangers as you try to move around them. Research in this field has clearly established the communicative nature of the simple act of walking on a crowded sidewalk even when you think that you are not paying any attention to the moves of others. This hidden dimension of communication was treated by Edward T. Hall[13] and popularized more recently by Julius Fast.[14] Your communication, then, can be silent and so automatic that you are not consciously aware that you are communicating. You are constantly giving off many kinds of messages all the time to anyone who is perceiving you. *You cannot not communicate.* Even your silences or your attempts to show another person you don't want to communicate are actually communication of a very specific kind.

Another example occurs if you drive to work or class. After you have made the trip a few times, your responses to symbols and signals around you become almost automatic. You pull out into the street; watch for cross traffic at the corner, a "School — Slow" sign in the next block, a blind intersection coming up next; wonder whether or not the light will change to green at the next corner; anticipate the 35-mile-per-hour zone which is often patrolled by a radar car; turn into the parking lot; head for the only available place near your work or class and find it occupied by a sports car with the top down; and finally make a few turns around the lot and settle for a place far away from where you want to go. You were responding all this time to symbols and signals from other drivers; from your past experience; from the normal controls placed on drivers by authorities who communicate to you by setting up signs, lights, and lanes; and from their uniformed representatives. Even though the authorities may be many miles away and doing something else at the moment, they still communicate to drivers and pedestrians everywhere in the city.

When you get to class, you begin to see the communication process more clearly. You hear a lecture, you get assignments, you talk about the class with another student, and you agree to meet someone for lunch. You know these acts involve communication, because they involve obvious verbal messages, and because it is your intention to communicate. But all the time these overt or open acts of communication are occurring, there is action at another level going on. What is happening inside you — your thoughts and your seeing and hearing many other kinds of data — is also communication. Writing on the blackboard, noises from the other room, or someone passing by the door will all attract you momentarily. The way a student next to you is dozing off or the way the professor fumbles with lecture notes are all part of communication. The notes you take from the lecture and the items you decide not to write down are important communication decisions. Ask-

---

[13]Edward T. Hall, *The Hidden Dimension,* Doubleday & Company, Inc., Garden City, N.Y., 1966.
[14]Julius Fast, *Body Language,* M. Evans and Company, Philadelphia, 1970.

ing questions and listening to others bring you again into active communication.

The rest of your day will broaden your communication. Do you listen to a radio, watch television, talk on the telephone? These are extensions of your personal contact with people. An advertiser on radio will tell thousands of you at once where to get a bargain in short-term loans, hoping that some of you need money and will respond. The advertiser has paid good money on the assumption that the communication will reach someone. You can find out from newspapers, magazines, and media news reports what has happened in Washington, Moscow, London, Chicago, or Podunk, even though you were not there. Someone is ready to report to you every hour the big news stories of worlds you may not even know and tell you about people you have never met. The mechanical and electronic means of communication have increased for you far beyond your ability to assimilate all their potential. You listen to only one radio station at a time, although there may be hundreds within reach of the instrument you tune in. You may read one or two newspapers out of the hundreds published every day. You see only a few selected programs on television, although the several stations available will broadcast all day and most of the night. A friend telephones you, or you call someone to seek information or perhaps just to keep your personal contact with others.

During your day you will speak, be spoken to, write, read, respond to many symbols. You will be in touch with many people who will tell you things, ask you to remember some others, and ask you to do still others. You may feel satisfied with your day in relation to how successful you feel your communication has been: Did you ignore someone you wished you had spoken to? Did you miss seeing and talking with a friend or not get the telephone call you expected? Did you get confused in class? Out of an entire day of communicating possibilities, you have selected certain things to do and not do. You are like your radio, in a way, as you tune in certain "stations" to pay attention to; you cannot listen to all of them at once. In Chapters 9 and 10 we will develop the idea that *communication is everywhere and inevitable,* and also the idea that because you select and choose your communicative behaviors, *communication is not random.* The view that you cannot *not* communicate may make you more aware of the many ways communication takes place and may make you sensitive to the communicative aspects of all human behavior.

Communication Is Continuous

Your communication comes from the past and goes into the future. It does not have a clear-cut beginning and end. It is part of your life, which flows and changes as your environment changes, as you change, and as others change. Your communicative needs are never static and

BOX 1. **The First Rule:**
You Cannot *Not* Communicate

Communication truly does not have an opposite. There is no way for
human beings not to behave, and all behaviors have communicative
value. Whether you speak or are silent, whether you act or do not
act, in one way or another you will affect others who in turn cannot
not respond to your behaviors and thus are communicating also. If
you intently read your book as you sit next to someone in the library,
you are in effect communicating that you do not wish to speak or be
spoken to. Usually your neighbor "gets the message" and leaves you
alone. You are no doubt familiar with the experience of waiting at
some counter while the clerks on the other side of the window
occupy themselves with paperwork and thus communicate to you
that they are busy and you'll just have to wait. As you wait in silence
for a while, you indicate that although no words were spoken, you
understood their message.

     Communication does not take place only when it is planned, con-
scious, or successful. You communicate many things you may not
intend to communicate. You are not always aware of what indeed
you communicate, and you may not always be understood. Yet, communicate you do, and in many ways. You use spoken and written
words. You use the inflections of your voice and the stresses you put
on certain words or parts of words. You use the intensity of your
voice, as when you whisper or yell. Your facial muscles form a smile
or a frown, or express a host of different feelings. You use your body
postures, and you gesture. You use the many contexts of your communication—space, time, objects, etc. All these communicative
behaviors are used simultaneously, and each qualifies in some way the
meaning of the other. A moderately loud "hi," a smile, and a wave of
the hand at ten o'clock in the morning in the company coffee shop
are all communicative behaviors which fit together, reinforce one
another, and communicate one kind of message, A "hi" whispered in
a raspy voice over the telephone at four o'clock in the morning communicates something else. A simple "no" may mean "yes" or
"maybe," depending on how it is said and the context of the communication, which includes not only the present space and time
dimensions but often past history. All these elements of communicative behaviors can be organized in highly complex ways and can be
congruent with one another, as when a friendly comment is spoken
in a friendly tone of voice and is accompanied by friendly gestures; or
they can be *incongruent,* as when verbal and nonverbal behavioral
cues "say" opposite things.

therefore require adjustment based on your previous experiences and your future expectations. Communication is a process. We agree with Don Fabun when he writes that all stories should begin with the word "and." "It would remind us that no experience ever begins; there was always something which preceded it. What really began, for us, was our awareness of something going on."[15]

Any communicative behavior has roots in the past. You are conditioned to talk in a certain way about things and to think in ways your habits have taught you. Similarly, you plan what you think should happen, and your communication affects the outcome. A simple-sounding phrase such as "Will you marry me?" has a history of past association and many future implications. It is not merely a flow of words in the present. In very simple messages such as "Phone me tonight," or "Read the next chapter," or "What do you want to eat?" one can trace a history of past associations with the other person and can realize that there will also be effects in the future if the friend does or does not phone, if you read or do not read the chapter, or if you eat something you don't like.

When you advise a friend about what kind of movie to see, or what clothes to buy, or whom to date, it will be on the basis of the values you have developed about movies, clothes, and members of the opposite sex. In most cases you will have an opinion based on your previous experience and be perfectly willing to share that opinion. Your values, then, make up part of your present communication, and the long-range effects of this communication will be felt by the participants. You bring to any communication a lifetime of attitudes, values, experiences, and assumptions. You carry along with you after the communication the consequences of your behaviors.

Feedback is essential to the continuous process of communication. You guide your future communication by using a rearview mirror of your own past. You direct your communication by finding out from others how things are working out. You observe what you do and compare it with what you intended to do.

The term "feedback" refers to that part of your communication behavior which pays attention to the effect of a message so that you can know what to do next.

Examples of feedback in your communication might include tests by a professor who wants feedback on what you are learning and the feedback he or she in turn provides you by giving you a grade. This feedback is a report on how you are doing in the course.

[15]Don Fabun, *Communication: The Transfer of Meaning,* Glencoe Press, Beverly Hills, Calif., 1968, p. 4.

BOX 2. **The Second Rule:**
Communication Is a "Chicken-and-Egg" Process

You seldom perceive communication as an uninterrupted flow of exchanges. Your habitual thinking in linear causality trains you to look for cause and effect, stimulus and response, action and reaction, sender and receiver, beginning and end. Although the concept of feedback adds the notion of circularity to an otherwise linear process, feedback is often conceived as little more than a reaction to an action. The chicken-and-egg process in communication refers to the grouping and sequencing of communication events in order to organize these events into meaningful units. How this organizing is done depends very much on who does it. What you might see as the cause of a communication event may well be the effect of a preceding event. So what you may choose to focus on as the beginning of a communication series may not be at all what I may choose to regard as the beginning of the series.

Take the example of a department chief, a woman who likes to ride herd on her employees. She might describe the situation to you as one where she feels she has to supervise the employees' work closely *because* they take no pride in their work, are careless, and therefore make errors unless she is on their backs all the time. According to the department head, the employees' carelessness is the cause of her strict supervision. If you were to ask the employees how they see the situation, you might get a different picture, not because the events themselves are perceived differently—everyone may agree that the employees are indeed careless in their work and that the department chief is a martinet—but because the sequence of communicative events are perceived differently. The employees may tell you that it makes them nervous to have the chief stand over their shoulder all day long; that she expects them to make mistakes; that they are left with no opportunity for initiative and thus do not feel inclined to take pride in their work. In other words, they may see the chief's behavior as a cause for theirs. In brief, the chief is strict because the employees are careless, and they are careless because she is strict.

Communication Is the Sharing of Meaning

In describing communication, it is important to emphasize that it has a purpose. Although most communication scholars agree that communication is related to symbol manipulation, there is not always agreement on the aims of communication. Some may view communication as designed to transmit information and to transfer ideas, but we agree with those scholars who have developed the view that *creation of meaning,* rather than transmission of information, is central to the study of communication.

Yours is a world of booming and buzzing confusion in which you are assailed from all directions with messages and stimuli. Yet this world becomes understandable to you, full of beauty or ugliness, because you assign significance to what you perceive. It is like walking into a vast supermarket of noise and sights without any organization. From your experience you begin to sort things out — the vegetables are there, the canned goods over there, meats are back there, and so on — and you can find with the help of signs the order in the otherwise chaotic world or disorganized store.

In the supermarket you get help from a classification system known to you from your past experience and from the arrangement of signs and aisles. You don't expect to find the canned string beans next to the fresh string beans just because they are beans. Would you expect to find milk with the other beverages such as colas, coffee, or tea? In fact, the classifications used by most supermarkets are not the only way things could be arranged; but they reflect some needs for displaying and preserving the goods, which is why fresh vegetables are not found with canned ones of the same name and why milk is located in a cooler with dairy products rather than with other beverages.

As Dean Barnlund writes, "Communication, then, is an 'effort at meaning,' a creative act initiated by man in which he seeks to discriminate and organize cues so as to orient himself in his environment and satisfy his changing needs."[16] To communicate is to process stimuli from raw data into meaningful information. This creative act of generating meaning performs the function of *reducing uncertainty*. The cues you select out of your internal, physical, and social environment all serve the purpose of clarifying what an encountered situation is all about so that you can adapt to it.

Meaning may not be the same in two individuals because they may select different areas and may have different classification systems; and thus they may have different experiences. Communication is an attempt to call up inside yourself a meaning which has a close relationship with what is going on around you and to share meanings with others by providing them with stimuli or cues to which they will assign meaning, and which you hope will be similar to yours.

As Wilbur Schramm has written:

> It is illuminating to think of communication as a relationship built around the exchange of information. . . . For example, recall how important a goodnight hug can be to a parent-child relationship, or how a good-morning greeting can improve a neighborhood or a workplace relationship, or how the satisfaction of seeing one's candidate do well in a debate or a television appearance can reinforce one's party relationship.[17]

[16]Dean C. Barnlund, *Interpersonal Communication: Survey and Studies,* Houghton Mifflin Company, Boston, 1968, p. 6.

[17]Wilbur Schramm, "The Unique Perspective of Communication: A Retrospective View," *Journal of Communication,* vol. 33, no. 3, Summer 1983, p. 15.

BOX 3. **The Third Rule:
Communication Occurs at Two Levels**

In the words of Watzlawick and his associates, "Communication not only conveys information, but . . . at the same time . . . imposes behavior." (Paul Watzlawick, Janet Beavin, and Don Jackson, *Pragmatics of Human Communication,* W. W. Norton and Company, Inc., New York, 1967, p. 51.) The information conveyed through communication is the *content* level of communication and refers to *what* is said. However, more than conveying content information, communication of any kind always implies a definition of the relationship between the two communicators and always contains instructions about how to interpret the content of that communication. This other level, the relationship level, refers to how the message or content is to be taken and how the relationship between the people involved is defined. Statements such as "I was only joking," "I mean it," and "This is an order" are verbal examples of the relationship level of communication. This level of communication need not be expressed in words, and in fact, more often than not, it is expressed nonverbally. When I speak to you, I give you information, the content of my communication, and simultaneously I give you information *about* that information; I tell you in some way whether this is a serious conversation, a friendly one, a stern lecture, a put-down, a tease, a joke. Nonverbal and contextual clues will often help you determine which it is and thus will tell you how to behave toward me. A woman who is a clerk in a store does not need to preface her "May I help you?" with an elaborate description of her relationship with the customer. She does not need to state that she is a salesperson here and that her job is to help customers find and buy things. Nonverbal and contextual clues, such as a name tag, a uniform, her demeanor, all contribute to your understanding that she will help you purchase what you need.

The distinction between content and relationship levels is not just a theoretical one dreamed up to satisfy the intellectual needs of fuzzy-headed academicians. The distinction has enormous implications for an understanding of your communication behavior. In Chapter 10 we will discuss at length the practical implications of this distinction.

Communication Is Predictable

In this textbook we will attempt to provide you with the means of understanding more about your communication, and hence to help you better predict the outcomes of your communication. For many years research has been conducted on the effects of communication on others, and more recently scholars have focused on what happens inside a person during a communicative act. Some results of these studies provide the basis for other chapters of this book. The experience of many years of research has led communication scholars to believe that what happens when a particular kind of message comes from a particular kind of source and reaches a particular kind of audience can generally be predicted.[18] With all the uncertainties of human association, we still can make our sending and receiving of messages consistently more accurate if we know more about the process of communication. Communication is not random. It appears random only when we do not understand the parts of the process and how they are related to one another.

You are all familiar with the polls taken on the popularity of political candidates and on social issues. This guidance offered by poll takers gives some advance information on how a candidate may come out in an election or how a political move may be accepted. In a smaller way, you tend to conduct your own "poll" when you talk with others and when you are sensitive to the feedback from your messages. You continually adjust your communication in relation to what you find out.

By further study of the factors involved in communication behavior, you can become more adept at this adjustment. This book, then, will deal with factors which seem to affect communication — your own perceptions and assumptions, language itself and the classification systems it provides, other aids and barriers to communication. The following chapters will provide information about communication and what you should expect from it, and the exercises in the laboratory manual will give you a chance to find out for yourself how these ideas come out in your everyday experiences. By understanding the material in this book, you may become better at predicting the outcome of your communication.

Let us emphasize here that communication begins inside you. We believe that *no one but you can do anything to improve your own communication*. People do not learn by being told; they learn by discovering for themselves. If you can discover how your own communication behaviors work, you can understand the communication inside others and your communication with them.

---

[18]See Carl I. Hovland, Irving Janis, and Harold H. Kelley, *Communication and Persuasion*, Greenwood Press, Westport, Conn., 1982. See also Edwin Bettinghaus, *Persuasive Communication*, Holt, Rinehart and Winston, Inc., New York, 1980.

BOX 4. **The Fourth Rule:
Communication Transactions Are between Equals or Up-and-Down**

You can relate to people either as equals or as nonequals. The most typical example of a nonequal relationship is that of the mother-infant pair. The mother clearly takes care of the baby, and the baby is clearly taken care of. The two cannot exist without each other, and this is not just a biological truism. There can be *no taking care of* if there is *no one to be taken care of.* Nonequal relationships include two different positions. One communicator is in the superior, one-up position while the other occupies the one-down or inferior position. It is important not to equate the words ''up'' and ''down'' with ''good,'' ''bad,'' ''strong,'' or ''weak.'' Nonequal relationships are often set by social or cultural factors as in the case of doctor-patient, student-teacher, and parent-child relationships. The one-up person usually defines the nature of the relationship, while the one-down person accepts and goes along with the decision.

In equal relationships, communicators exchange the same kind of behavior. Mutual respect and a feeling of partnership exist. Friends, peers, and colleagues are usual examples of relationships among equals.

Because you learned to communicate in an informal way, beginning by imitating your parents and older children, you have picked up some unhealthy habits. Very little formal training has ever been offered you on how you perceive, or how language affects your behavior, or how your habits of thinking can make you more or less successful in communicating. You manage to erect barriers in your communication inside yourself and with others, barriers which may not be necessary. You get confused and may confuse others when you really don't have to. By being aware of the barriers and the confusions and how they happen, you should be able to avoid many of them. In Chapters 5 and 6, we will summarize how your relations with your language and thinking may make your communication unsatisfactory and will give you some possible ways to avoid pitfalls of communication.

One study of how children ''get their way'' may also relate to how adults succeed in influencing others in somewhat common or predictable ways.

As children become competent communicators, they learn . . . how to comfort a good friend, how to refuse someone a ride on their Big Wheel, and how to join a game of frisbee. Children learn to adapt their commu-

nication strategies to the particular situation. . . . Just because children are small does not mean that they are powerless with each other or with adults. Just as adults assume dominant and submissive roles in their communication, children also communicate in equal and unequal status conversations. . . . Children must acquire a flexibility to alternate between dominance, equality, and submissiveness. With time and plenty of experience with family members and peers, children develop skills in communicating effectively in different communication contexts.[19]

A TRANSACTIONAL MODEL OF HUMAN COMMUNICATION

Many influences have shaped the field of human communication. From the early rhetorical tradition to the mechanistic perspective offered by the mathematical model of information theory to sociopsychological contributions and general systems theory, human communication has continued to pique the curiosity of many scholars and laypeople. Indeed, no other field touches you so deeply, for you are all communicating beings. Communication not only is at the heart of your humanity but is also the vehicle of your intentions toward others. Only through communication can you realize your social potential. Without communication you would all be evolutionary misfits.

Before taking stock of the present understanding of human communication processes, it will be useful to review briefly the major threads that run through the various approaches to the study of human communication.

The Action View: The Bull's-Eye Theory

The rhetorical tradition and information theory perspective share the view that communication very much consists of a one-way act like shooting an arrow into a target. You hit the bull's-eye. You got close. You missed. The whole activity of communication was centered on the one-way action of doing something to someone. How good you were depended mostly on how well you shot the arrow, or how well you made your point. The emphasis was on the sender and his or her encoding skills. This meant that how you constructed a message, organized it, delivered it, was just as crucial as sharpening your arrow, testing its feathers, flexing your bow, and shooting straight would be in target practice. The key questions centered on what a *speaker* must *do* in order to persuade, sell, help, or generally change someone else's behavior.

Another important aspect of this concept — frequently asserted, even if unintentionally — was that words actually had meanings. Therefore if the sender knew the meanings of words, the same meanings

[19]Barbara S. Wood and Royce Gardner, "How Children Get Their Way: Directives in Communication," *Communication Education*, vol. 29, July 1980, pp. 264, 265.

would be sent directly to the receivers — like a pipeline. In this simplistic view misunderstandings would occur only if people did not know what words ''meant.'' Further, if misunderstandings did occur, you would look to the way the speaker performed to find the error. You could learn to influence the world if you mastered the meanings of words and mastered your speaking voice — or so this theory proposed. But if you did not perform adequately, it was the fault of your external efforts only. This view paid more attention to tools and skills than to potentially more important aspects of communicating. It insisted on blaming. It did not spend much time analyzing the reasons except that somewhere along the line you used the ''wrong'' words, did not organize your message well enough, did not possess a good voice, did not possess enough credibility (as though credibility were a quality that a speaker could own); in essence you did not shoot straight at your target and therefore missed a little. This view is still quite widely believed, especially among those who sell people on ''speaking success'' and the ''cookbook'' systems which promise to make you an overnight success in your communication if you follow a few simple rules of delivery. It is also still believed by those who say: ''I don't know why she does not understand this; I explained it fifty times'' or ''How come they didn't know that? I told them.''

The Interaction View: The Ping-Pong Theory

Another favorite way to look at communication is to compare it with taking turns in a table tennis match. You say something; I answer. You say more; I reply. I serve; you respond. We take turns at being sender and receiver. This view accounts for more complexities of human communication than the bull's-eye theory. It does include the receiver by adding the concept of linear feedback, which permits the sender to exert more control over his or her communication. Yet, the communication process is still oversimplified by being treated as a process of linear cause and effect: I speak, you answer.

The weakness in this view is that communication is not divided into ping and pong, stimulus and response, shot and return, action and reaction. Senders and receivers do not simply alternate in sending and receiving, and the simple linear model of cause and effect is inadequate to explain the complexities of communication.

The Transaction View: The Spiral Theory

By ''transactional communication'' we mean that there is more than a simple interaction between senders and receivers. A transaction implies interdependency and mutual reciprocal causality among the parts of a system. Human communication, like any dynamic process, is best understood as a system where senders are simultaneously receivers and receivers are simultaneously senders. Communication is not the static, picturelike view of still photography. It resembles more the continuous flow of motion pictures. Communication viewed as a process is characterized less by the actions of a sender and the subsequent reactions of a receiver than by the *simultaneity of their reciprocal responses.* Who starts the process is an irrelevant question, since processes have no specific beginnings or ends.[20] Human communication comes from somewhere and is going somewhere. Any communicative behavior we want to isolate for the purposes of analysis has a history and a future. It has been born in the mind of the speaker and relates to the mind of the receiver, and these minds are not simply appearing in front of each other as the words are spoken. They have lived in many places; they have said many things before, possibly to each other. In a transactional view of communication you are both cause and effect, stimulus and response, sender and receiver. Not only are you the product of your previous communicative behaviors; but — very important — what you see yourself to be is in a large measure affected by how you perceive others to behave toward you, that is, how you perceive others' communication. Your perception of other people's responses is itself the product of previous perceptions of previous responses, a lifetime of previous communication. To isolate a communicative act is to ascribe an arbitrary beginning and an arbitrary end to an unending process. Perhaps you need to do this to understand the process, but stopping the process is really distorting the richness of the communication flow between people.

To view communication as a transaction does more justice to the complexities of the process than any other conceptualization we know.

BIBLIOGRAPHY Barnlund, D. C.: *Interpersonal Communication: Survey and Studies,* Houghton Mifflin Company, Boston, 1968.

Bettinghaus, E.: *Persuasive Communication,* Holt, Rinehart and Winston, Inc., New York, 1980.

Dance, F. E. X. (ed.): *Human Communication Theory: Original Essays,* Holt, Rinehart & Winston, Inc., New York, 1967.

Fast, J.: *Body Language,* M. Evans and Company, Philadelphia, 1970.

Fabun, D.: *Communication: The Transfer of Meaning,* Glencoe Press, Beverly Hills, Calif., 1968.

Hall, E. T.: *The Hidden Dimension,* Doubleday & Company, Inc., Garden City, N.Y., 1966.

[20]For an early discussion of spiral learning in communication, see: Frank E. X. Dance (ed.), *Human Communication Theory: Original Essays,* New York, Holt, Rinehart & Winston, 1967, pp. 293–303.

Hart, R. P., Robert E. Carlson, and William F. Eadie: ''Attitude toward Communication and Assessment of Rhetorical Sensitivity,'' *Communication Monographs,* vol. 47, no. 1, March 1980.

Hovland, C. I., I. Janis, and H. H. Kelley: *Communication and Persuasion.* Greenwood Press, Westport, Conn. 1982.

Katriel, T., and G. Philipsen: ''What We Need Is Communication: Communication as a Cultural Category in Some American Speech,'' *Communication Monographs,* vol. 48, no. 4, December 1981.

Littlejohn, S. W.: ''An Overview of Contributions to Human Communication Theory from Other Disciplines,'' in F. E. X. Dance (ed.), *Human Communication Theory,* Harper & Row, Publishers, Inc., New York, 1982.

McCallister, L.: ''Predicted Employee Compliance to Downward Communication Styles,'' *The Journal of Business Communication,* vol. 20, no. 1, Winter 1983.

Rogers, E. M., and S. H. Chaffee: ''Communication as an Academic Discipline: A Dialogue,'' *Journal of Communication,* vol. 33, no. 3, Summer 1983.

Schramm, W.: ''The Unique Perspective of Communication: A Retrospective View,'' *Journal of Communication,* vol. 33, no. 3, Summer 1983.

Sillars, A., and M. D. Scott: ''Interpersonal Perception between Intimates,'' *Human Communication Research,* vol. 10, no. 1, Fall 1983.

Ting-Toomey, S.: ''An Analysis of Verbal Communication Patterns in High and Low Marital Adjustment Groups,'' *Human Communication Research,* vol. 9, no. 4, Summer 1983.

Wood, B. S., and R. Gardner: ''How Children Get Their Way: Directives in Communication,'' *Communication Education,* vol. 29, July 1980.

Chapter 2

PERCEPTION:
THE EYE OF THE BEHOLDER

In
a
Nutshell
What you know about reality and the world in which you live comes through perception — a process of selecting, organizing, and interpreting sensory stimulations into a coherent picture of the world.

Your perceptions are *theories* about "reality" and should be taken as *predictions* about the nature of the real world.

Your perceptions are determined by (1) the physical limitations of your senses and (2) the psychological limitations of your interests, needs, and past experiences.

You give meaning to your perceptions by treating them in relation to their context. The more ambiguous the context is, the more likely you are to project yourself into what you perceive.

To the extent that your perceptions of reality are different from those of other people, you will experience difficulty communicating with them. To the extent that your perceptions are similar to those others, you are likely to understand them and they are likely to understand you.

INTRODUCTION   In Chapter 1 we took you through a brief tour of the field of interpersonal communication. In the past, many communication scholars made a distinction between intrapersonal and interpersonal communication. "*Intra*personal communication" referred to processes which go on inside a person, such as perceiving the world and acquiring information, creating meaning, and "learning and using language." *Inter*personal communication referred to the processes which take place when two or more people trade the currency of language with each other. The distinction was arbitrary at best and posed more questions than it answered. Because of the transactional nature of communication it is very difficult to separate what is internal to the individual from what belongs to the environment. For example, perception is an internal process, but much of what determines how you perceive comes from what you have learned in the social-cultural context in which you live. Perception is both internal and transactional. Is self-perception an internal affair? Or do we treat self-concept as an interpersonal process, since we learn who we are as we see others seeing us? Rather than using the old dichotomy intrapersonal versus interpersonal, which holds little theoretical value,[1] we will focus our analysis on two basic elements of the communication process: meaning and transaction.

How you perceive the world and how each of you constructs your own experience of events you attend to will be the subject of this chapter. How you develop a sense of self, how you use language, and how language molds your sense of reality will be described in this chapter and Chapters 3 through 6.

> *Nature gets credit which should be in truth reserved for ourselves; the rose for its scent, the nightingale for his song, and the sun for its radiance. The poets are entirely mistaken. . . . Nature is a dull affair, soundless, scentless, colorless: merely the hurrying of material, endlessly, meaninglessly. (Alfred North Whitehead)*

You rely on your senses to tell you what is happening in the world around you. You see things, people, situations, happenings. You hear noises and words. You taste food and drink. You smell odors and scents. You feel and touch objects and surfaces. You are generally excited by something outside your skin and react to this stimulation by becoming aware of something you were not aware of before. Then you say you perceived something — a sound, a taste, a sight, a touch. Because you do not live in a vacuum, you are constantly being bom-

---

[1] Gerald Miller, "The Current Status of Theory and Research in Interpersonal Communication," *Human Communication Research,* vol. 4, no. 2, 1978, pp. 164–178.

barded by sensations. You are surrounded by things, people, odors, tastes, and happenings. There are sights to be seen, words to be heard. Asleep or awake, you are in the center of noises, smells, and a multitude of stimulations.

You have a great tendency to consider yourself only a passive receiver of all this stimulation coming to you from the world "out there" — the "empirical world," as we will call it. You think these things "just happen" to you. You have a sort of resigned "I can't help it" attitude. You act as if you were being hit randomly by all the marvelous and not-so-marvelous things of the world, as if you were a helpless victim. This is the "I am a camera" attitude — the film simply grinds away, taking in the events around it; or the "tape-recorder" attitude — the recorder turns and turns, slowly accumulating recorded bits of sound with no selectivity or discrimination.

Human perception is much more complicated than such passive attitudes, as can be seen in the following conversations:

"Hey, did you see that John Wayne movie? Man, was it good, I really
    liked it. . . ."
"Yeah, I saw it. Hated it. Can't stand John Wayne. . . ."

"Beautiful, absolutely beautiful. Now that's the kind of art I really relate
    to. . . ."
"Art? You call that art? That's trash, friend, trash."

"See, I talked to him and he said I could leave early. He's really a won-
    derful teacher. . . ."
"You mean Jones? Not Jones? Jones is a great teacher? He's a creep.
    Couldn't teach even if he tried. . . ."

"I know it happened like that. I was there. I saw it."
"My friend was there and she said it was different."

Conversations like these are familiar to most of you. They sound like the kinds of remarks you've heard someplace before. All of them show that the same thing, person, or event may not have been perceived the same way by different people. You look at a painting and it's art; I look at it and it's trash. You like Professor Jones; I despise him. You like John Wayne movies; I don't. Why is it that two people looking at the same thing may not see the same thing? Who is right about the painting? Is there a right or wrong? What makes you so sure, just because you were there and saw something happen, that the report you give on it is accurate? Are your senses always reliable? Do you see things *as they are* or perhaps as you want them to be, or perhaps as *you* are? Is beauty in the eye of the beholder? If so, what are you really communicating about when you tell someone about the merits of Professor Jones, or of a painting, or of a movie?

How you experience the world is in some ways unique and in some ways commonly shared with others. It is the purpose of this section to unravel what is unique in your experience of reality and what are shared elements common to the people around you. Communication is essentially a process of structuring reality through perception and symbolization. How you do this structuring shapes the information you gain from all the stimulations you get and thus shapes your image of what the world is like. This is a fundamental statement, because your behavior is based on your *image* of what the world is like; on how you *experience* events, people, and things; and on your *perception* of reality.

We believe that perception is not something that randomly happens to you. You are never the passive receiver of information, you are not a nonparticipating, zombielike recipient of unselected stimulations. In fact, you are a major actor in the perceiving process and an active partner in what is going on ''out there.'' You actually *select,* choose what you perceive, what you look at; you *organize* sensory stimulations; and you *interpret* them into a coherent and meaningful picture of the world.[2] You do this rapidly, automatically, and often unconsciously, but you do it nevertheless. You literally create what you see.

You may find this a startling statement, since, like most people, you probably experience a reality out there and you are pretty sure that you don't just make up what you see. If you see something, it must be there. After all, you are a reasonably normal person, and you don't make a habit of hallucinating. Yet, we maintain, you do create what you see. Let us explain this seeming paradox and discuss *what* it is you do perceive when you respond to stimulations from your environment.

WHAT YOU PERCEIVE[3] You are probably well entrenched in your conviction that the world is full of things, objects, and people which are separate from you. You know what they are like, what they do, and what you can do with them. You do not expect things to change suddenly or disappear into thin air. Were that to happen, you would suspect that a magician had tricked you.

Your knowledge of what things ''are,'' their ''identity,'' and their ''permanence'' is indeed most valuable. It not only gives you a feeling

[2]Bernard Berelson and Gary A. Steiner, *Human Behavior, An Inventory of Scientific Findings,* Harcourt, Brace & World, Inc., New York, 1964.

[3]This discussion is based on M. D. Vernon's exciting book, *The Psychology of Perception,* Penguin Books, Baltimore, 1962, pp. 11–15.

of security but also allows you to react to things quickly and usually appropriately, since you can make fairly accurate predictions based on your previous experiences with these things. But ask yourself for a moment how you know what objects are and how you know they will remain the same. Of course, you can see them and notice that they do not change, except slowly over time. But your eyes, or your other senses, play only a part in your perception of things. Let us examine that part.

When you look at the world, those objects toward which your eyes are directed reflect light to your eyes. Light comes to those objects from the sun or from a source of artificial light. These radiations vary in wavelengths, and the wavelengths of the reflected light vary. The reflecting power of the surface of the object also varies. This is how the differences in color and brightness which you see are produced. The light which reaches the eyes is then focused by the lens in that part of the eyeball sensitive to light, called the "retina." The cells of the retina react and send nerve impulses to the nerves of the eye. These impulses are then transmitted by the optic nerve to a specific area of the brain. What happens is a transfer of vibrations or radiations. What reaches the brain, however, is a pattern of electrical impulses where frequency corresponds more or less to the brightness of the light reaching the eye. It is a pattern of moving light, shade, and color. There is nothing there like the solid object in space. What is recorded in the brain is no more the real event than the picture on your television set is the real cowboy or news commentator. Vision alone cannot account for the picture you get of the world as you know it. Complex mental processes convert the patterns recorded on the brain into the perception of the world as you know it.

Add to this the fact that the visual patterns which impinge on the brain are far from being static. They move and change, since light radiations are in constant motion and since what appear to you as solid objects are also made up of particles in constant motion. Yet you do perceive constancy, immobility, and permanence. These impressions of constancy, immobility, and permanence are a *product of the mental processes which take place in your brain*. What you see is a private creation of your brain. Permanence is not in the objects out there, but in your mind.

Fortunately, however, a curious order runs through your perceptions. Although you can never know whether your perceptions of red or E-flat are exactly the same as another person's, *you can, and do, act on the assumption* that most people see colors and hear tones more or less alike. You assume that others create a world out there similar to your private world. In a large measure the assumption proves true (though not invariably; see Box 5). But you must not forget that your

BOX 5. **The Blind Men and the Elephant**

It was six men of Indostan
To learning much inclined,
Who went to see the Elephant
(Though all of them were blind),
That each by observation
Might satisfy his mind.
The *First* approached the Elephant,
And happening to fall
Against his broad and sturdy side,
At once began to bawl:
"God bless me! but the Elephant
Is very like a wall!"
The *Second,* feeling of the tusk,
Cried, "Ho! what have we here
So very round and smooth and sharp?
To me 'tis mighty clear
This wonder of an Elephant
Is very like a spear!"
The *Third* approached the animal,
And happening to take
The squirming trunk within his hands,
Thus boldly up he spake:
"I see," quoth he, "the Elephant
Is very like a snake!"
The *Fourth* reached out an eager hand,
And felt about the knee
"What most this wondrous beast is like
Is mighty plain," quoth he;
"'Tis clear enough the Elephant
Is very like a tree!"
The *Fifth* who chanced to touch the ear,
Said: "E'en the blindest man
Can tell what this resembles most;
Deny the fact who can,
This marvel of an Elephant
Is very like a fan!"
The *Sixth* no sooner had begun
About the beast to grope,
Then seizing on the swinging tail
That fell within his scope,
"I see," quoth he, "the Elephant
Is very like a rope!"
And so these men of Indostan
Disputed loud and long,
Each in his own opinion
Exceeding stiff and strong,
Though each was partly in the right,
And all were in the wrong!

(John Godfrey Saxe)

perceptions are no more than theories or guesses about what the world is like. A good deal of the time your theories work and your perceptions of reality are reinforced. However, when someone challenges your view of the world, a great sense of uneasiness and dissonance is created. You may experience some anxiety when you discover that not everyone perceives objects, people, and events exactly as you do. The experience may be more or less unsettling, depending on who challenges you and whether the perceptions challenged are particularly important to you. Discovering that there is no Santa Claus is often a traumatic experience for little children, who must then realign their whole sense of what is real and what is fantasy. Discovering that you have been deceived by a close friend can also be a shattering experience and may result in a rather drastic reevaluation of your perceptions not only of that particular friend but of other people as well. Once ''burned,'' you may resolve never again to trust another enough to risk emotional involvement.

In summary, *what* you perceive is exclusively yours. It may or may not be shared by others. To the extent that it is — to the extent that many of your perceptions are common to most people — you stand on validated ground and feel secure in your belief that what you see is indeed there just as you see it. You may then forget that all you really have are consensually validated perceptions, that is, simply perceptions which many people agree they have. The ''reality'' on which you stand firm is no more than a consensual reality. You created it, others created it, and you simply happen to agree. You are betting that if many people create alike, it is worth acting upon. And most of the time you are right.

Let us repeat: what you perceive is a construct of your mind, a creation, indeed stimulated by external events. Yet you can never know these external events as they really are. The best you can do is guess and assume what they are like and then test your guesses by acting on them and by finding out whether they approximate other people's guesses. The reality you take for granted is no more than an agreed-upon reality, a consensual reality. What you do is based on your perception of reality. What others do is based on their perceptions of reality. If you ever want to understand why people act the way they do, you must be prepared to understand first how they see the world, what their reality is like. We do not all live in the same world.

HOW YOU PERCEIVE

Now that we have discussed *what* it is you perceive, let us turn to *how* you perceive and how the mental processes work that account for your vision of the world.

You Select

At any given moment you pay attention to — notice, are aware of, perceive — only very little of what is going on around you. When you pay attention to something, it means that you are not paying attention to something else. Why you select what you do is usually the product of several factors, some environmental, some internal.

Environmental factors

The environmental factors include influences such as intensity, size, contrast, repetition, motion, and familiarity or novelty.

INTENSITY
The more intense a stimulation, the more likely you will perceive it. A loud noise in a silent room, or a very bright light in a dark street, usually commands your attention. Advertisers capitalize on this when they use particularly bright packaging or television commercials slightly louder

than regular programming. The army sergeant shouts commands, and many a teacher finds himself or herself yelling at an unruly class to get the students' attention.

SIZE

The principle of size is quite simple. The larger something is, the more likely it will capture your attention. A full-page newspaper spread is more catchy than the fine print of the classified ads. Toys are often packaged in large boxes containing a lot of cardboard fillers to give children the impression that the actual toy is bigger than it really is. Although toy manufacturers are now obligated to print the actual dimensions of the toy on its box, few children notice the fine print and most are lured by the sheer size of the box. To most of us, bigger is better.

CONTRAST

Things that stand out against a highly contrasting background are usually quite noticeable. Safety signs with black lettering against a yellow background, or white lettering against red, catch your attention. A woman manager stands out in an all-male executive meeting.

REPETITION

A repeated stimulus is more attention-getting than a single one. This is particularly true in dull contexts where your attention may be waning. An interesting story may be remembered after one telling, while non-sense words or just dull material need to be repeated several times to be remembered. Advertisers know well that a repeated short message is more effective than a longer message with a one-time exposure.

MOTION

You will pay more attention to a moving object in your field of vision than to the same object when it is stationary. Again, advertisers use this principle when they incorporate moving parts into otherwise still signs. The flashing or rotating lights of the police cars or of ambulances are designed to command attention.

FAMILIARITY AND NOVELTY

The principle of familiarity and novelty may simply be an extension of the contrast principle. New objects in familiar surroundings are likely to draw your attention, just as familiar things in an unfamiliar environment will stand out. The idea of job rotation is based on this principle. Changing jobs periodically may do much to increase a worker's attention otherwise dulled by routine and familiar activities.

The environmental factors we have just described represent only a small part of what goes into selective perception. Internal factors of a physiological and psychological nature are extremely powerful in determining not only what you do perceive and how you perceive it but also what you cannot perceive.

Internal factors   PHYSIOLOGICAL FACTORS – HOW YOU ARE BUILT

As you probably know, you are stimulated by what is going on outside of you through your five senses. You see, hear, smell, taste, and feel. However, these five senses are not all-powerful. Human beings are built in such a way that there are sights you cannot see, sounds you cannot hear, tastes you cannot distinguish, smells you do not sense. Your sense of touch does not give you much information if you do not use your eyes to help you determine what you are touching. Many animals have much sharper senses, which enable them to see better, hear better, and smell better than humans can. Most other animals, of course, rely more on their senses than you do and have thus developed them more than you have. It's a little bit like the blind, who cannot rely on their eyes to find out what's going on and develop their sense of touch and hearing to compensate for their lack of sight.

The human nervous system is built in such a way that you cannot register with your senses much of what is going on around you. You cannot hear certain sounds – those below 20 cycles per second and those above 20,000 cycles per second. Dog whistles are great to call a dog from a distance, although, to you, they sound silent. You do not hear the sound because it is at a frequency higher than the ones you can perceive. You can see only one-seventieth of the total light spectrum. You do not see x-rays or infrared or ultraviolet rays. The human eye is sensitive only to a narrow band of radiations which fall between the red and the violet. A difference as small as a few hundred-thousandths of a centimeter in wavelength makes the difference between what you can see and what you cannot see. Naturally there are many radiations you cannot perceive. Infrareds have a wavelength of 0.00008 to 0.32 centimeters and are too long to give the retina the impression of light. The ultraviolet rays are too short to be perceived (0.00003 to 0.000001 centimeters). The even shorter x-rays, gamma rays, and cosmic rays, and the longer heat waves, radar waves, and long radio waves, differ from visible light only in wavelength. What you can perceive of the reality around you is determined by the limitations of your sense organs. Think what the world might look like to you if your eyes were sensitive to x-rays or gamma rays.

Most of you cannot distinguish between fine differences in delicate taste sensations. Part of your food selection is thus made for you. You do not pay attention to certain things simply because you are not built to perceive them.

These sensory limitations are shared by every human being. In addition to our limitations as a species, there are individual physiological differences which affect what each of you can and does perceive. Not everyone has 20/20 vision, and not everyone hears perfectly well. The finely tuned ear of professional musicians permits them to hear tones in a much more discriminating manner than nonmusicians. The wine connoisseur distinguishes extremely fine variations in taste that most people could not begin to experience.

PSYCHOLOGICAL FACTORS

Motivation. All of you differ in terms of your needs, motives, interests, desires, etc.; and each of you will tend to perceive what is in accord with your needs, motives, and interests. If you are hungry, you will notice restaurant signs and you will detect food smells which might otherwise go unnoticed. In this culture, visual stimulations dealing with sex are powerful attention-getters. Here again, advertisers, who make it their business to get your attention, know that if they play on your needs, particularly basic sexual and social needs, they will succeed. It may be hard to get your attention about toothpaste, but when toothpaste is linked with sex-appeal, the task of getting your attention becomes easier.

You tend to pay attention to what interests you. Sometimes you distort things so they will fit what you want. You see what you want to see, and sometimes you hear what you want to hear. To a person who feels very threatened or insecure, everything will appear to be a potential source of danger. If you are in a house alone at night and suddenly you feel uncomfortable or nervous, every little noise will reinforce your fear, although the same noises in broad daylight would sound perfectly normal and harmless if you paid any attention at all.

Past experience and past learning—Perceptual set. People are more likely to pay attention to aspects of their environment they anticipate or expect than to those they do not anticipate or expect. And people tend to expect or anticipate what they are familiar with. You may, for example, vaguely hear people talking behind you without really identifying anything they are saying until they mention your name. You will usually hear your name distinctly. That word will stand out from all other words they were saying because you are familiar with it.

When you have followed the directions given for Figure 1 and Figure 2, the following comments will be of interest. If you counted three F's and read "Paris in the spring time," "once in a lifetime," and "bird

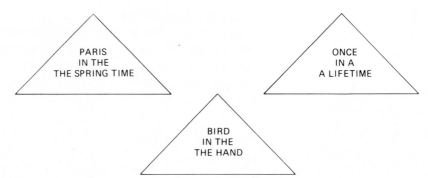

FINISHED FILES ARE THE RE-
SULT OF YEARS OF SCIENTIF-
IC STUDY COMBINED WITH THE
EXPERIENCE OF MANY YEARS

FIGURE 1. Count the F's in
the statement in the box.

PARIS
IN THE
THE SPRING TIME

ONCE
IN A
A LIFETIME

BIRD
IN THE
THE HAND

FIGURE 2. Read aloud the
phrases in the triangles.

in the hand," you are wrong. There are six F's in Figure 1. Because the F in "of" sounds like a V, it seems to disappear; most people will count only three F's in the sentence. Read again the sentences in the three triangles. Perhaps you need to read them aloud to realize that in two of them the word "the" was repeated and in one of them the word "a" was repeated. Habit makes us fail to perceive things as they really are, and learning affects your perceptual set by creating expectations to perceive in a particular way. You see what you expect to see. Have you ever bought a car only to find that the whole world seems to be driving the same kind of car? It is not that the sales of these cars have dramatically increased overnight. You were simply cued to noticing this type of car; it is familiar to you. Also, you were unconsciously looking for it in the street in an attempt to reinforce your buying decision. Much of the time you look not just "at" but also look "for."

Your particular training has a great deal to do with what you perceive. Education is at best a process of differentiation, of learning to make discriminations. What to the untrained eye looks all the same is full of significant differences to the specialist. If you do not know engines, chances are that when you look under the hood of a car you see an engine — black greasy parts connected to one another — and to you an engine is an engine. Engines are generally all alike. For a mechanic, engines are far from alike. All the little parts can be differentiated; differences can be noticed. A jeweler will perceive the differences between two seemingly identical diamonds. A physician will notice the differences between seemingly identical symptoms. An English professor will perceive differences between two student essays which to others would seem very much alike. Your particular training definitely affects what you perceive. A physician, a mechanic, and a police officer reporting on the same accident will comment on the things which stood out for them. The physician is likely to notice the people, the mechanic will comment on the conditions of the cars, and the police officer will look for causes. Each selected from the total event the aspects he or she thought were significant. You see what you are trained to see, and you bring to any perception a lifetime of past learnings and experiences: your perceptual set.

If you were given the task of reporting on the size of the fish in a local river and had a 2-inch-mesh net, your report might include the statement, "The fish are 2 inches or bigger." If you repeated the task with a 4-inch-mesh net, your report might read, "The fish are 4 inches or bigger." Remember, you are reporting on the same fish in the same river. Which report is accurate? Each? Neither? What are you reporting on? The size of the fish? *No.* You are reporting on the size of the net you used. The size of the net determines the size of the fish you catch.

In a way, you all have nets in your heads. These nets of course are made not of threads but of all the things that make each of you a unique individual: your physiological makeup, your motivations, aspirations, needs, interests, fears, desires, past learning, past experiences, training, etc. These nets act as a filter. The stimulations from your environment have to pass through that filter before they are perceived. Each of you has your own individual filter. Even though you may share the same environment with others, chances are that you will filter different aspects of that environment and perceive a somewhat reality than the others do.

Some people have defective filters—filters that are so clogged up that they see very little of what is going on. Some people have filters that distort the stimuli which come to them from the environment. To the extent that your filters are similar to those of other people, you will select out of your environment pretty much the same kinds of things they do. However, the engineer, the sales representative, and the production manager may all be part of the same organization yet perceive and work in three very different companies.

It is important to remember that *whenever you make a comment about something, you are describing not the thing but rather your net, your filter.* (See Box 6.) When you report that Sam Jones is a conscien-

BOX 6. **What Kind of People?**

Drove up a newcomer in a covered wagon: "What kind of folks live around here?" "Well, stranger, what kind of folks was there in the country you come from?" "Well, they was mostly a lowdown, lying, gossiping, backbiting lot of people," "Well, I guess, stranger, that's about the kind of folks you'll find around here." And the dusty grey stranger had just about blended into the dusty grey cotton-woods in a clump on the horizon when another newcomer drove up. "What kind of folks live around here?" "Well, stranger, what kind of folks was there in the country you come from?" "Well, they was mostly a decent, hardworking, law abiding, friendly lot of people." "Well, I guess, stranger, that's about the kind of people you'll find around here." And the second wagon moved off and blended with the dusty grey. . . . (From *The People, Yes,* by Carl Sandburg, copyright 1936, by Harcourt Brace Jovanovich, Inc.; renewed, 1964, by Carl Sandburg. Reprinted by permission of Harcourt Brace Jovanovich, Inc.)

tious fellow, you are commenting not so much on Sam Jones as on yourself and your value system. This is not a trivial point. Much of the trouble people experience in communicating with one another stems from two misguided assumptions: (1) What they see is what everyone else sees. (2) They have direct access to reality. Access to reality is at best indirect, filtered by your own observations and your built-in physiological and psychological limitations.

In most scientific reports (or talks about scientific experiments) the researcher-scientist takes great care to describe the conditions under which observations were made and particularly what kinds of instruments were used to make the observations. Most of you, on the other hand, do not carefully describe how you made the observations you talk about to others, nor do you tell much about what "instruments" you used in making the observations — such as firsthand vision unaided by glasses, or secondhand reports from friends, or deductions made from seeing something after it happened and the action was over. A scientist will generally report on the size of the net used, although most of you go around glibly ignoring net size in your reports to others. It is true, however, that it is very important that others know the net size — or more scientifically, the conditions and equipment involved in making observations — if they are to understand what you are saying.

The scientist is also generally aware (and this may be hard for most people who do not have scientific training to grasp) that the "qualities" of things such as color, sound, taste, and even space and time have no objective reality completely independent of our senses, which are the instruments we use to measure these qualities. Color is not inside or intrinsic to the things we look at. Color is merely a reflection of a tiny portion of radiations of a particular visible wavelength. Color is a product of our own nervous system – our own insides.

Furthermore, the physicist Werner K. Heisenberg in his famous ''principle of uncertainty'' (reported in 1927) removed hope for determining the ''real'' nature of the microcosm. There is a basic indeterminacy about the atomic universe which no refinement of measurements and observation can ever dispel. Heisenberg demonstrated that determination of the position and speed of an electron is impossible, for the very act of observing its position changes its speed. This demonstration shook traditional science, which was based on causality and determinism, and ''probabilities'' replaced the previously held notion that nature exhibits a determined sequence of cause and effect between events. Another tremendous implication of the Heisenberg principle is that whenever you attempt to observe the ''real'' objective world, you change it and distort it by the very process of your observation.

When we talk about selecting among the stimuli in your environment, we refer not only to the various kinds of sounds and sights you select from. Much of the time you are also selecting from among the different sensory stimuli, so that you ignore sights to pick up sounds, etc. You develop habits of watching or listening or touching, and so your selecting process is actively sorting out a whole barrage of sounds; but it is also flitting back and forth between seeing intently and listening acutely. Selecting not only is always part of your communication habits, but is a combination of physical choices and psychological preferences all woven together.

You Organize   Once you have ''selected'' what to perceive, you usually organize it in some fashion. Even the most simple experience requires that you impose order on a series of disconnected elements. The way you order or organize what you perceive is not random nor arbitrary; you follow certain ''rules.'' According to gestalt psychologists, these rules are innate. Behavioral psychologists, however, claim that these rules are learned through social experience. There is evidence to support both views, and we will not try to settle this argument here. What is clear, though, is that these rules have important effects on how you perceive.

Look at Figures 3, 4, and 5. What do you see? Perhaps at first just some white and black shapes. Perhaps one shape will stand out. In that case you have organized the shapes into a picture by visually putting some of the shapes in the background and some in the foreground. Of course, you may not organize shapes in the same way everyone else

FIGURE 3. Which do you see — the goblet or the famous twins?

FIGURE 4. Describe the woman you see in this drawing. How old is she? Is she attractive? What kind of covering is on her head? Etc.

FIGURE 5. In these patches of black and white, do you see the face of Christ?

does. Some of you fail to organize certain visual stimuli into some coherent picture. Many people do not see the face of Christ in Figure 5. Some cannot see the old woman or the young woman in Figure 4. Yet every line or shape you need to organize the particular configurations is in the picture. Organization of the lines and shapes into a specific design depends solely on the perceiver.

You usually organize by giving priority to what is striking or outstanding. In figure-ground relationships you tend to identify figures by their usually more dominant color. When there is not enough contrast between figure and ground, it is more difficult to decode which is which, as in the picture of Christ.

You also tend to organize what you perceive into whole figures. If what you look at is incomplete, you fill in the gaps, a process called "closure." Look at Figure 6. You see a dog, not twenty different spots. Look at Figure 7. You see a completed square even though the lines do not touch.

Sometimes we tend to organize what we perceive in misleading ways, as the optical illusions in Figures 8, 9, and 10 prove.

FIGURE 6. This collection of twenty discrete blotches is a picture of a dog.

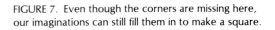

FIGURE 7. Even though the corners are missing here, our imaginations can still fill them in to make a square.

FIGURE 8. Are the long lines in this drawing parallel?

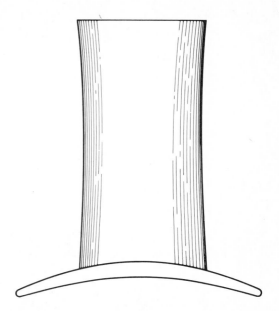

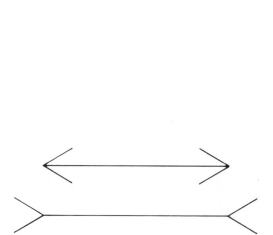

FIGURE 9. Are both of these lines the same length?

FIGURE 10. Is the hat higher than it is wide?

You Interpret What you look at or hear is often ambiguous. Sometimes you may not see distinctly because a room is dimly lighted or because you are looking at something that goes by very quickly. "Now you see it, now you don't," says the magician, who capitalizes on distraction and speed of movement to create visual illusions. But even when what you look at is very clearly delineated, there is no automatic conclusion about what the object is. Even the simplest objects can produce a variety of visual stimuli (for example, a cup and saucer seen at different angles), and different objects can produce the same stimuli (for example, an orchestra and a 12-inch high-fidelity speaker). Consequently, it is necessary to interpret what object the thing you are looking at actually represents. This interpretation is not always easy, and it is rarely conscious. The greater the ambiguity of the object, the more room there is for interpretation. This is the theory behind what psychologists call "projective tests," such as the test in which you look at an inkblot like the one in Figure 11 and tell what you see. Usually what you see reveals what you project into it, and this comes from your personal experiences, motives, needs, interests, etc.

You usually interpret what you see by looking at the context of the object. For example, the shape I3 will be read as the letter B if it is preceded by the letter A. However, if it is preceded by ihe number 12,

FIGURE 11. The inkblot projective test assists our minds to shape meaning.

then it will be perceived as the number 13. (See Figure 12.) It is often not the facts themselves that are the basis for different perceptions of the same event. Rather, it is the interpretation of those facts in the light of differing contexts which creates most of the communication difficulties in interpersonal encounters.

Another very important factor which affects how we perceive things in context is age, or maturity. Just as we learn how the world works by experience in it, and as we learn our language by a special

FIGURE 12. An example of the effect of context. The middle figure can be either the letter B or the number 13, depending on what kind of sequence it appears in.

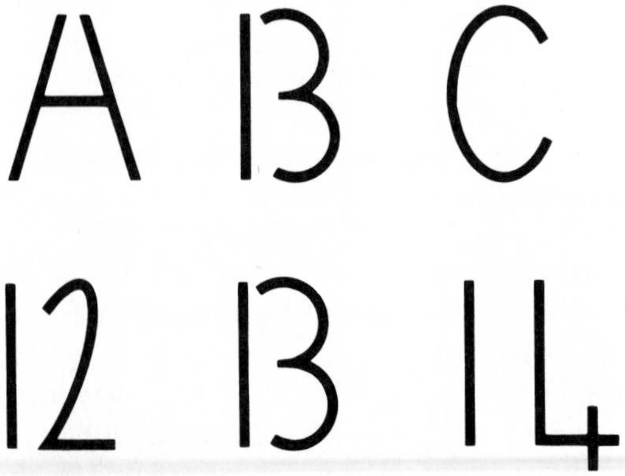

A B C

12 13 14

imitative developmental process, we also develop habits of perception of the environment. Television advertisers of products appealing to young children are conscious of the effects of showing toys, prizes, or candy "blown up" to make them look larger than they actually are. Some adults also can be fooled by camera tricks and by distortions of perspective. A study by Acker and Tiemens that compared "preoperational" children with older children and adults determined that younger children responded differently to images of a candy bar shown "normal size" and in close-up.[4] The younger children believed that the candy bar actually had "more candy in it" when the image was larger. Most older children and adults perceived a trick of the camera rather than a candy bar that was "growing."

What we have been saying all along in this section is that your world, the environment in which you live, is uniquely yours. Your view of the world belongs to you because you created and constructed it as you selected, organized, and interpreted bits and pieces of stimulations which originated outside of you. How you do this selection, organization, and interpretation is largely based on how you have done it in the past, and in a very real sense, you are the product of your past perceptions. Much of what you perceive stands against the backdrop of a lifetime of previous experiences which have permitted you to develop expectations about how the world goes around. Your "frame of reference," as psychologists call it — or your "nets and filters," as we have referred to it — permits you to make sense out of all the stimulations you experience. A person who grew up in the center of a large city does not respond to the outdoors the same way a rural person does.

PERCEPTION, LANGUAGE, AND CULTURE

Your selection, organization, and interpretation of the cues available in your environment are to a large degree related to your ability to symbolize; that is, to use language. We will discuss the relationship between language and perception later, in Chapter 5. At this point, however, a simple experiment will demonstrate our point.

Read the following sentence:

YOUR SHOES ARE FULL OF FEET.

You may have suddenly become quite aware of your feet. A few seconds ago, unless your feet hurt or for some reason stood out in your

---

[4]Steve R. Acker and Robert K. Tiemens, "Children's Perceptions of Changes in Size of Televised Images," *Human Communication Research,* vol. 7, no. 4, Summer 1981, pp. 340–346.

consciousness, you were probably quite unaware that they were there. After reading the sentence, you probably have begun to ''perceive'' your feet and to feel them. Language influenced your perception by directing your attention and thus cueing into something that had not registered before.

Language and cultural factors influence perception in even more direct or subtle ways. In the late 1800s, for example, the use of lipstick and cigarettes by women was restricted very much to prostitutes, and rouge was so scandalous that no self-respecting woman would dare to wear it. It is likely that the perception of women wearing makeup was colored (no pun intended) by the taboos imposed by the culture of the time. For another example, giving names for human tendencies related to animals has been an interesting way of describing good or bad traits. If someone refers to you as a ''snake'' or a ''cat,'' you are likely to be offended. ''Sheep'' and ''wolf'' connote other qualities which seem to have much the same meanings in many different cultures. Are all mules stubborn? What do you see if someone says ''an old crow''? Are bats really blind? Are owls wise?

As we shall see in Chapter 5, language is also a special way of looking at the world and interpreting experience. Language is more than just a vehicle for exchanging ideas and information, for reporting about your world, for expressing yourselves and your feelings, or for getting people to do what you want. Hidden in the structure of your language are unconscious assumptions about the world; up to a point, you see what the language system has made you sensitive to and trained you to look for in your experience. Experience may be organized in a number of different ways, and language is a major force in that organization.

In a language in which the person speaking is an active participant in any occurrence (because of the way a grammar is constructed) anyone speaking that language will assume a kind of basic blame for what happens: ''I missed my bus.'' Other languages may construct the person speaking as a victim of the other events or actors and thus without conscious blame for what happens: ''A bus missed me'' or ''The bus passed me by.'' Some languages have a variety of names for relatives for which there is no equivalent in English; therefore, native speakers of that language will pay attention to some facets of families which don't interest English-speaking persons. For example, an uncle could be related (in English-language structures) to you on your mother's side or your father's side; the word ''uncle'' does not describe a difference. Amazonian Indians would be astonished that we make no distinction, as is done in their language, between male-related uncles and female-related uncles. Another example involves the way you refer to animals you eat. The bird is a duck both when it is swimming in the pond and when it is on the table. But what happens to the Anglo-Saxon word ''steer'' when it is made into steaks for the table? It turns into "beef," from the Norman-French *boeuf.* An Anglo-Saxon name was given to "calves," but the meat was again Norman-labeled "veal." These samples of historical language development come from the time when Anglo-Saxon farmers took care of the cows, steers, and calves, but the meat was served to the aristocratic Normans, whose language was French.

A PROCESS VIEW OF THE WORLD

Ours are the days of relativity and uncertainty. Since Max Planck, Albert Einstein, and Werner K. Heisenberg, a new era of scientific thought has begun — one much less in agreement with your everyday perceptions of the world based on imperfect instruments such as your senses and moderately powerful microscopes. "The certainty that science can explain *how* things happen began to dim about twenty years ago," Lincoln Barnett wrote originally in 1948, "and right now it is a question whether scientific man is in touch with 'reality' at all — or can ever hope to be."[5]

Much of what is talked about, even by scientists, is only guesswork. Even aided by powerful electron microscopes, scientists cannot view the subatomic functioning of our world so perfectly that they can conclusively say what is going on so far below the threshold of our ability to perceive directly. Questions arise when astronomers indirectly measure streaks on a photographic plate and infer celestial activities which took place billions of light-years ago. Consider, then, how difficult it is for most of you to report on your world when you are inexperienced in making carefully controlled observations and not in the habit of asserting carefully circumscribed statements about the observations you make. It is a humbling thought that even with the training, the instruments, and the rigor of the scientific world, there are problems of accuracy and meaning. Think, then, what you face in the majority of communicative situations when you think and talk about events and people that are not amenable to the scientific method.

Although a discussion of relativity, uncertainty, and quantum physics theories is clearly beyond the scope of this book (and of its authors), their impact on your view of the world and the implications of this view for your daily communication should not be ignored in attempting to understand how and what you perceive.

What modern science tells you about the world is that it is an ever-changing, dynamic, moving pattern of radiations or energy transformations; that what appears solid and unchanging to the naked eye is merely a construct of your brain; that you cannot know reality as it is,

[5]Lincoln Barnett, *The Universe and Dr. Einstein,* Time, Inc., New York, 1962, p. 6.

since your act of observing it changes it; that by dealing with happenings in the world in terms of probabilities, you abandon the idea that nature exhibits an inexorable sequence of cause and effect among individual happenings; that physical events are indeterminate and the future is unpredictable; that neither you nor scientists know what the "real" world is like; that mathematical equations are all you have to use in describing the "real" world; and that the equations of quantum physics at the present time define phenomena beyond the range of your senses more accurately than the Newtonian mechanical model.

A process view of the world tells you that what you might see as a static, solid thing like a table or a chair actually consists of continuously moving particles which keep a relative degree of constancy in terms of the whole, but whose individual parts change and move in unpredictable ways.

An important comment on this subject comes from Rogers and Kincaid in their book *Communication Networks:* "Most past discussions of communication have not stressed: (1) that the creation of information occurs at a physical level of reality, (2) that interpretation occurs at the psychological level, and (3) that perception bridges the physical and psychological levels of reality."[6] Their term "interpretation" also includes the organizing function we referred to earlier. Perceiving provides the link between us and the ongoing buzz of events, noises, sights, smells, and other stimuli of the world around us. It is a dynamic process, subject to change as we change, subject to personal whim and individual tendencies and habits.

It should be evident by now that perception is by no means a simple process. Perceptual variations are caused partly by the great complexity of the world making up your surroundings and partly by your own limitations. You can view only a small part of your environment at any one time; even when you look deliberately, there is much you tend to overlook, or to perceive incompletely or inaccurately. During the course of your lives, however, you learn to perceive more and more accurately, particularly when you are interested in the object perceived or when you acquire some special training. But as we said earlier, the effects of knowledge and experience also tend to produce selective perception. Thus two observers may either perceive a scene in the same way or totally disagree about its nature or content.

Fortunately, many perceptions are common to many people; to that extent their "reality" (their theories about reality) will be mutual,

[6]Everett M. Rogers and Lawrence D. Kincaid, *Communication Networks,* The Free Press, New York, 1981, p. 52.

and they are likely to understand each other when they communicate about it.

But individual differences do exist. You as people resemble others in many ways, yet you each retain your unique qualities. So it is with your perceptual world. Much of it is shared with others; much of your "reality" is theirs. Yet parts of your world are unique, and in that sense you may act as an island unto yourself.

This raises some important questions. If reality as you know it is shaped by your filters, and if your filters are different from other people's, how do you evaluate perceptions and decide that some perceptions may be better than others, that is, represent more closely what the world is like out there? Are some filters better than others? How do you check your own perceptions?

IMPLICATIONS FOR COMMUNICATION

What you communicate about is your perception of what the world is like. Having created for yourselves a perception of people and events, you then go on to *recreate* for others, through the medium of language — oral, written, or nonverbal — what you perceive.

You always hope that the people you communicate with will translate your language into something similar to what you originally perceived. To the extent they end up with about the same conclusions you make, you say you have communicated successfully.

The process of communication among people can be said to include two phases. First, it consists of the perceptions someone (maybe you) has of something; second, it consists of descriptions through symbols (language) so that someone may recreate in the other person's mind the original perception.

Let's examine the first phase and ask some important questions: How do you evaluate your perceptions or someone else's? How do you know if you perceive something as it "really is"? Do you know if you distorted what you saw or heard, and how much you distorted it? On what basis can you trust your perceptions or someone else's? How reliable are the conclusions you draw from your observations by your senses or the reports you get from someone else's senses?

Any perception or observation involves some distortion. You can never be absolutely certain that you have perceived something the way it is. Reports from others are most likely to contain additional distortions.

Checking Perceptions

In practice, then, how do you go about checking perceptions to try to get along better in the world? How do you test your theories? One way is by finding out that others seem to have perceived something the way you do. If you get support from others, you feel confident that what you perceive is accurate. You depend on others to help you sort out what is real and what is not. There is some danger in this dependence on others. For one thing, if you only check your perceptions with those whose distortions may agree with yours, you may not get any nearer to the actual "truth" of an event or object. For another thing, you can be tricked by others who may want to fool you. If everyone around you said they saw a book on the table and you did not, but they insisted it was there and appeared to be quite serious about it, you might begin to doubt your own sanity. If all those around you swear that aliens from Mars have infiltrated the leadership of the city council and act very serious about it, you may begin to wonder.

Here you begin to get a clue for figuring out how you normally check your perceptions. If enough people agree with you about a given perception, you tend to trust that perception. This process is known as "consensual validation," which simply means other people agree with you that they perceive what you say you perceive.

You also tend to trust a perception that you experience repeatedly. If it happens over and over again, it builds confidence. If, for example, you see a tree in the front yard once, then look again and don't see it any more, you may think you had a vision, But if you look and see the tree time and time again, you are pretty confident that it's there.

Another way you check your perception is to use more than one sense to determine what it is you perceive. If you saw that tree in the front yard and then walked toward it and went right through it, you might question your eyesight. If, on the other hand, you see the tree and touch it, you get a confirmation from the sense of touch that your sense of vision was not playing a trick on you.

Still another way you check your perceptions is by comparisons. If you see somthing that is a lot like something you saw before, you tend to believe in what you saw. Because of your storing capacity, you have the ability to accumulate data about past experiences. Because of your symbolizing ability, you can classify, categorize, and otherwise organize your experiences. Storing and classifying allow you to *compare* new perceptions with old ones. When you perceive a new experience, you can usually find in it some elements similar to those in previous experiences conveniently stored in your brain. You can thus assign the new experience to a known category. In other words, you compare the present to the past by checking for similarities.

This is related in some ways to the "repeated perception" idea but with a small difference. The new experience (or person, or thing) may not be in the same place, or may have some differences. That's where you can get into trouble — by treating the new event as if it were exactly like the other ones. As Wendell Johnson wrote: ''To a mouse, cheese is cheese. That's why mousetraps work.''[7]

The mouse, by focusing on the similarities it perceives — cheese is cheese — fails to notice a rather significant difference in its environment, the trap. In this case it means life or death. You behave like the mouse if, for example, you treat an empty gasoline drum as not dangerous because it is empty, operating on the assumption that a container emptied of its dangerous content is itself safe. In this case the comparison process would lead to an explosion if, as a result, you were to throw a lighted cigarette into the ''empty'' gasoline drum (which still contains gasoline fumes, much more explosive than liquid gasoline itself). The warning here is to make sure that the similarities are genuine and that the differences are not more important than the similarities you have perceived.

The comparison process and repetition process are similar in that they are both based on your ability to store up and classify information. They differ, however, in that the comparison process is based on *perceived similiarities* between the past and the present and not on exact duplication of identical experiences.[8]

Finally, you test your theories by putting them into practice and by checking whether the results obtained match the guesses you made. For example, you perceive a room and its furniture. You make a theory about how the furniture is spaced in the room. You then navigate in the room *as if* your theory were correct. If it is, you do not bump into things.

In summary, then, you usually validate your perceptions in these ways:

Validation type	*Method*
1. Consensual	By checking with other people
2. Repetitive	By checking with yourself by repeating the observations
3. Multisensory	By checking with yourself by using other senses

[7]Wendell Johnson, *People in Quandaries,* International Society for General Semantics, San Francisco, 1980.

[8]We are indebted to Dr. John W. Schmidt of Central Michigan University, who read this manuscript, for pointing out that opportunities for repetitive validation are relatively few in our experience. In a world of process and constant change, experience does *not* repeat itself. As Heraclitus pointed out 2,000 years ago, the same man does not step in the same river twice. The man changes and so does the river. In the absolute, repetition is an illusion. In a relative sense, we perceive repetition when similarities between two events outweigh the differences between them.

Validation type	Method
4. Comparative	By checking your past experiences with similar but not necessarily identical perceptions
5. Experimental	By acting on the basis of your perceptual theories as if they were correct and checking the consequences of your actions by comparing them with what you guessed would happen

When you get the same results from these checkpoints, you have something solid to communicate about. You see the tree, touch it, look at it several times, touch it several times again, get others to agree that a tree is indeed there and that it is endowed with a kind of "treeness" that other trees in your experience have all had. You climb it (if there is a tree and it is big enough, then one can climb it, says the theory). Now you can be sure that the tree is really there. For all practical purposes, the tree is in your field of communication with yourself and others.

Checking Communication

Checking communication, the second phase in the process of communication, deserves some special attention. Once you have established a perception inside you about something, you may say something about it. How do you know you have communicated successfully; or, to put it another way, how do you know the other person has recreated the same perception you had? Did you manage to "get across" enough so that the other person could translate your message about your perceptions?

Your communication may be written, oral, or nonverbal. You may write something, say something, or act out by gestures and signs. Then you watch and listen to see what happens. You may get a written message in return, you may hear a response in words or grunts, or you may simply observe something happen. When you do that, you are getting *feedback*.

To find out what part of your message was translated accurately by the other person, you make use of your senses to perceive again. At this point it is impossible not to communicate, because if the other person does absolutely nothing, you still learn something about your communication. Being ignored is a very clear kind of feedback; it says that the other person didn't hear or see, or didn't want to make a response.

Whenever you communicate with others, you are making public reports of your private perceptions. The reactions of others to what you say (feedback, again) not only tell you something about your own perceptions and the perceptions of others but actually let you know how the communication is going. You can get agreement, disagreement, or doubt, and you can even get tuned out. Each of these responses tells you something about the way you are heard by others, as well as something about your perceptions.

What Does This Have to Do with You?

What does all this have to do with you? Here are a few comments which should point out what this discussion of perception has to do with the way you communicate and relate to other people.

There are many ways to experience "reality." No two people experience it in exactly the same way. To the extent that many perceptions are common to most people, their "reality" — that is, their theories about reality — will be common, and they are likely to understand each other when they communicate. To the extent that your perceptions of reality are different, because each of you is unique, you may have difficulty sharing them with others.

Because validation methods ultimately involve additional perceptions which also have to be validated (a vicious circle), you can never be 100 percent certain that what you perceive is identical to what is out there. You can only have probabilities of fit between your perceptions and reality. Although absolute certainty and absolute objectivity are impossible, some people's predictions about the world are more often correct than other people's. Although people are all biased, some are more biased than others, and some may not even be aware that they are biased. To increase the probability that your perceptions will yield accurate information about your world, (1) you must become aware of the part you play in perceiving; (2) you must realize that you have biases and that your filters shape, limit, and distort the information you take in; (3) you must interpret your perceptions in light of your biases and correct for them whenever you can; and (4) you must realize that simply perceiving something does not give you, or anybody else, a corner on the truth of the matter. Perception, or how you experience reality, is a concept fundamental to the understanding of interpersonal communication. Because you experience the world subjectively and give it meaning, there is always a difference between the messages that are sent and the ones that are received. Managers who assume that other people simply *should* understand what they say and write are simply naive. The fact that you told someone something is no guarantee that what you said has been heard or understood the way you intended it to be.

The "same" event is not "read" the same way by different people. A memorandum explaining a new policy will be read differently — that is, will be understood and interpreted differently — by the people to whom it is addressed. This does happen, not out of malicious intent, but simply because of the different frames of references and filtering systems which come into play as people experience their world. You need to understand that people's behavior is actually based on their perceptions, their mental image of what the world is like to them at a given moment. If your task is to get things done through other people, it behooves you to thoroughly understand the factors that influence human behavior.

BIBLIOGRAPHY   Acker, S. R., and R. K. Tiemens: ``Children's Perceptions of Changes in Size of Televised Images,'' *Human Communication Research,* vol. 7, no. 4, 1981.

Barnett, L.: *The Universe and Dr. Einstein,* Time, Inc., New York, 1962.

Berelson, B., and G. A. Steiner: *Human Behavior, An Inventory of Scientific Findings,* Harcourt, Brace & World, Inc., New York, 1964.

Johnson, W.: *People in Quandaries,* International Society for General Semantics, San Francisco, 1980.

Miller, G.: ``The Current Status of Theory and Research in Interpersonal Communication,'' *Human Communication Research,* vol. 4, no. 2, 1978.

———, and M. J. Sunnafrank: ``All Is for One But One Is Not for All: A Conceptual Perspective of Interpersonal Communication,'' in F. E. X. Dance (ed.), *Human Communication Theory,* Harper & Row, Publishers, Inc., New York, 1982.

Rogers, E. M., and L. D. Kincaid: *Communication Networks,* The Free Press, New York, 1981.

Sandburg, C.: *The People, Yes,* Harcourt Brace Jovanovich, Inc., New York, 1964.

Vernon, M. D.: *The Psychology of Perception,* Penguin Books, Baltimore, 1962.

Chapter 3

SELF-CONCEPT:
WHO AM I?

In a Nutshell

You learn about who you are and how to feel about yourself through a process of interpersonal communication. How you see yourself is the product of how you see others seeing you.

You maintain your self-concept and change it through a process of interpersonal communication.

Other people may either confirm or disconfirm your image of yourself. When you feel confirmed by others and when what you do matches your self-image, you may derive a sense of self-esteem. You feel good about who you are. Self-esteem is usually maintained through self-disclosure and feedback.

Self-disclosure permits you to improve your relationships with others, when you learn to do it appropriately.

AN INTRODUCTION TO YOURSELF

In Chapter 2 we discussed how you develop your view of reality, your perceptions of what the world is like, and the meaning you attach to your experiences. In this chapter we are going to look at a very important feature of the filter system that you use to make sense out of your environment: your perception of yourself. We hope to convey to you the excitement we feel about this inquiry into self-perception. Few areas of study hit closer to home than interpersonal communication and self-concept. After all, you live among people who in many ways shape you and whom you influence. We all need one another to conduct the business of our lives; ultimately your interpersonal communication is the only source of validation for what goes on inside you and in your world.

Much has been written about alienation and loneliness. We strongly believe that the misery you sometimes experience springs from your inability to develop and sustain meaningful and satisfying relationships with others. The key, we believe, lies in developing healthy interpersonal communication habits. We hope this book will help develop and strengthen the best in all of you: your ability to relate to others in a mature, independent, and responsible way.

In your study of interpersonal communication you must first explore the most important agent in the process — you. Who you are, how you see yourself, how others see you, what roles you play for the various audiences of your life, what your needs and values are. These are fundamental questions because who you think you are determines so much of what you do and which roles you choose to play. And who you think you are is to a large degree determined by responses you get from others to your behaviors. These responses shape in many ways how you see yourself, and so you are already in another loop of that ongoing, spiraling, transactional process called "communication."

Your behavior is also the product of complex feelings about who you *should* be, what role you *should* play, and what your interpersonal transactions *should* be like. All these *shoulds* represent the values you hold. In Chapter 4 we will also look at how you form, maintain, and change your values and, more particularly, how these values affect your self-image and your communicative behavior.

What you do is partly determined by who you think you are. Who you think you are is influenced by how others respond to what you do. Therefore, your ways of relating to others play an important part in how these images of yourself are developed.

Your behavior is not influenced only by the accumulations of your past experiences. More important, it is influenced by the very *personal meanings you attach to these experiences*. What you do is not just a function of what happens from the outside; it is very much a function of how you feel about yourself on the inside. You organize your environment so that it has personal meaning for you, and how you perceive the world is dictated in a large measure by your self-concept and your symbolic background.

"Who am I?" is a question you may have asked yourself at some time. How you answer this question determines to a great extent whether you will describe your life as productive and happy or unfulfilled and frustrating, and most important, how you will relate to other people. The question "Who am I?" is not just an adolescent query. It is a question which will face all of you daily and which takes on greater significance as you go through life crises and important decisions.

A psychologist friend of ours is fond of telling the story of a young woman who came to him for counseling and told him she was planning to quit school in order to go to Mexico and live in a commune. When he asked her why she intended to follow such a course of action, she replied: "I want to find myself." He queried facetiously, "But what if you go all that way and then you are not there?"

Perhaps for many of you, as for this young woman, the concept of self-identity elicits a vision of some creature living inside you that you need to become acquainted with at some point in your life. Of course, there is no such mysterious person; and even though you may be initially puzzled when you must answer the question "Who am I?" the fact is that you do have a great deal to say about yourself because you do hold pictures of what you are like in your head. It is those pictures that form your *self-concept*.

HOW YOUR SELF-CONCEPT DEVELOPS

How the self and the self-concept develop has been the subject of much speculation and research. What psychologists and sociologists tell us basically revolves around the key assumptions that the self-concept is learned, maintained, and changed through interpersonal communication processes. Let us look at how this process works.

You Learn Your Self-Concept through Interpersonal Communication

A fundamental assumption shared by sociologists such as George Herbert Mead and Charles Horton Cooley, and by psychiatrists and psychologists such as Harry Stack Sullivan, Karen Horney, R. D. Laing, Carl Rogers, and Abraham Maslow, is that the self-concept is learned through interpersonal communication.

What this means is that how you come to see yourself is the product of how you see how others see you. Cooley, for example, writes about the "looking-glass self" as the process of imagining how the self appears to be for another person.[1] The concept of self is but a reflec-

---

[1]Charles H. Cooley, *Human Nature and the Social Order*, Transaction Books, New Brunswick, N.J., 1983.

tion from the minds of others. For George Herbert Mead, people develop the ability to see a situation as they imagine other people would see it.[2] Through the socialization process you learn what is good, how you should behave, how to view the world, and how to view yourself. A baby girl's definition of herself as good or bad is totally dependent upon the interpretations that other people in her world make of her behavior and the responses they have toward her as a result of these interpretations. The way you think you are is to a great extent shaped by how people treated you when you were growing up.

When you were born you did not have a sense of self. The way you were treated began to lay the foundations upon which you developed feelings and thoughts about what kind of person you were. If you were lucky, you received messages of warmth and love, you were fed when you were hungry, you got attention when you cried, you were cuddled and held, and you learned that you were cared for — the roots of a basic sense of worth. Some children are not so lucky and go ignored and untouched for long periods of time. The tragedy of such children is that they learn at a most impressionable stage of their lives that they do not matter, that no one cares for them, and consequently that they must be no good.

From the first months of your life until you reach your second birthday, language begins to introduce some degree of permanence into the objects around you as you begin to be able to generalize from discrete experiences. Smiling mother, angry mother, quiet mother, loud mother, busy mother are no longer separate people but are merged into a generalized "mother." What was perceived previously as different experiences (all the different mothers) is now perceived as one person in different roles. Mother is the same person but assumes different roles in her interaction with you. This personification process occurs also in your perceptions of your "self."[3] All the "you's" develop as a result of your interactions with the people around you based on their interpretations of your behaviors. They get thrown together, and you begin to experience yourself as a collection of roles that you assume in the variety of interpersonal situations which make up your life. This is the stage where how people talk about you and to you makes a great impression and literally shapes the way you begin to feel about yourself. You may learn traditional role expectations, such as "Big boys don't cry"; "You are too old to potty in your pants"; "You are the brains of the family"; "Little girls should mind"; "Boys don't play with dolls"; "Girls help their mommies in the kitchen." The way you begin to view yourself is a function

[2]George Herbert Mead, *Mind, Self and Society,* University of Chicago Press, Chicago, 1967.
[3]Harry Stack Sullivan, *The Interpersonal Theory of Psychiatry,* W. W. Norton & Co., New York, 1968.

of how other people want you to be and how well they reinforce your learned identity.

From the time you are about 10 months old to about 18 months, you go through a phase of simple *imitating* without understanding the actions and words of the people around you.[4] Some of these behaviors and words will be reinforced and will remain in your repertoire of roles and in your developing vocabulary. As you get a little older, you go through a phase of *role playing* which simply consists of trying on roles that you are familiar with, patterns of behaviors that you have observed around you and that you now associate with specific meanings. Watch a 3-year-old playing house. A child is extremely skillful in playing the role of the father or mother with a doll or another child. Eavesdropping on little kids can be a revelation for many parents, allowing them to see themselves as they come across to their children.

Between the ages of 3 and 5, children begin to understand the dimensions of the roles they play. This role-playing ability is directly related to the degree of language development achieved by the child.[5] As they role-play, children develop the capacity to imagine how others behave in certain situations. When the little girl plays mommy, she is in effect imagining how her mother would act in a given situation. This is a most crucial skill, which ultimately permits children to imagine their own behavior in relation to other people. If a little girl can imagine what her mother will do in a given situation, she can then develop expectations about her mother's behavior in relation to her should that situation arise. Interpersonal transactions are based upon your ability to imagine what other people think and expect of you in a given situation, how they are likely to respond to your behavior.

Finally, you reach a phase when you no longer need to actually play the role of another person to figure how that person might respond to you. You simply go through the process symbolically, in your head. The process of *symbolic role taking,* as Berlo describes it, permits you to behave on the basis of what you believe other people think of you.[6] You become accustomed to classical questions like "What will people say?" or "What would daddy think about that?" You incorporate all the roles that you imagine others expect of you in any situation you can think of. As your capacity to imagine increases, as the situations you imagine get more complex, and as the number of people you are capable of imagining increases, you do not simply think of the role behaviors

[4]Mead, op. cit.

[5]Dennis R. Smith and Keith Williamson, *Interpersonal Communication,* Wm. C. Brown Company, Dubuque, Iowa, 1977, p. 146.

[6]David K. Berlo, *The Process of Communication,* Holt, Rinehart and Winston, Inc., New York, 1960.

a specific person might expect from you, but you think in terms of other people *in general.* Mead's *generalized other* is at the root of all your transactions.[7] As an adult, you behave in a given situation not just on the basis of how you perceive the situation but on the basis of *how you imagine other people in general expect you to act.* The generalized other is very much related to your self-concept. How you view yourself influences to a great extent how you will imagine that others in general view you. If you think of yourself in positive terms, you will tend to imagine that others perceive you in a positive light. If you think of yourself in negative terms, you will anticipate negative reactions from others. The important thing to remember here is that in both cases you act on the basis of *how you think other people view you* and not on the basis of *how they actually view you.*

Perhaps you begin to get the idea of the transactional nature of the self-identity merry-go-around. How you view yourself is largely determined by your perception of how others see you; and your perception of how others see you is largely a function of your self-concept, acting as a filter which shapes your perceptions of other people's reactions to you. This entire cycle frequently turns into a self-fulfilling prophecy. Your expectations of how others perceive you leads you to act in such a way that ultimately you may help develop in others the kind of perceptions you thought they had; and you find in their behavior toward you the final evidence that you were right in the first place.

The example of the shy young man who feels inadequate and believes that others, particularly women, are keenly aware of his inadequacies illustrates the self-fulfilling prophecy. The young man, believing that he is inadequate, anticipates being rejected by women and seldom musters courage to ask anyone for a date. By retreating into his personal shell and acting withdrawn, he communicates to others, women in particular, that he is not interested in social communication. Few people will invite him to parties and few will seek him out for social occasions. That he remains a kind of social isolate reinforces his view of himself as inadequate and unattractive, and he continues to believe that others reject him, stronger in his conviction because he finds evidence for it in what he perceives and interprets as rejection from others. "No one pays any attention to me; I am unattractive, and I knew it all along," becomes his entrenched philosophy, making it more and more unlikely that he will break out of the vicious circle he helped to create. The fact is that it is quite possible that he reads other people's reactions accurately. They might indeed find him socially withdrawn, and they may not seek him out; but as is often true in self-fulfilling prophecies, the behav-

---

[7]Mead, op. cit.

ior of other people is a response to the young man's unwillingness to make social contacts. Had he been willing to act in a more outgoing fashion, he might have elicited much more favorable responses, thereby increasing his feeling of confidence that he was socially acceptable and enhancing his chances to act more and more outgoing and to find proof in his popularity that indeed he had effective social skills. This self-fulfilling prophecy would work in his favor. This brings us to a second key assumption about the self-concept.

The Self-Concept Is Maintained or Changed through Interpersonal Communication

The view that you hold of who you are is by no means static. Because the self-concept develops through interpersonal communication, it also is maintained and changes through interpersonal communication. Each person and each new experience that you encounter to some extent confirms, but may also change, how you view the world, other people, and yourself. The impact of new people and experiences in your life may be tremendous and obvious at times, but more often it is quite subtle and may go unnoticed for a while. Yet, as you experience new behaviors in new environments and as you meet people whose response to you is different from what you expect, your sense of self and identity may change. The story is told of a graduate student, a young and rather plain woman, who went quietly through all her classes and who seldom interacted with any of the other students. She never approached anyone, hardly ever laughed, and generally appeared quite self-conscious. No one ever talked to her, and she was never included in the groups that met for coffee or to study for exams together. After a lecture on self-concept a group of five male graduate students decided to experiment and began to treat the girl as though she were important and very attractive. They made it a point to talk to her whenever they could. Although she did not know how to handle their attention at first, she began to loosen up a bit and, after a few weeks, even began to initiate such contacts. One by one the men asked her for dates, and after a couple of months a noticeable change occured in the young woman. She started wearing more attractive clothes, she did her hair in a more becoming style, she smiled more, and she talked more in class and outside of class.

The Pygmalion effect

We do not know whether the story is true, but the Pygmalion effect is a very real one.[8] What this young woman experienced was consistent and sustained positive reactions. At first it is doubtful that she paid much attention to this positive feedback, since her negative self-concept probably acted as a filter that rejected positive strokes and would admit

[8]See Robert Rosenthal, "The Pygmalion Effect Lives," *Psychology Today,* vol. 7, 1973, pp. 56–63.

only what would be reinforcing to what she already believed about herself. Yet, after a while, it became more difficult to ignore or filter out the consistent and frequent positive reactions she was getting. As these reactions kept coming, she slowly began to alter the image she kept of herself, and in doing so she became able to *act differently*. She talked more, smiled more, started to take better care of her appearance. The reactions she was getting were not just verbal. The male students *behaved* toward her as if they perceived her as attractive and important. In the process she became so. Since your self-concept is developed as a result of interpersonal experiences and communication, such experiences will continue to mold how you view yourself. Your life experiences will act as a way to confirm how you see yourself and in some cases change how you see yourself.

Confirmation and disconfirmation   Your image of who you are needs verification and support from other people, and much of your communication will in many indirect ways contain subtle demands to have your image confirmed. Virginia Satir, Paul Watzlawick, Don Jackson, and others contend that just about every message you send includes a request: "Validate me." You seek confirmation not only of the way you view yourself but also of the way you view others and the way you experience the world around you. The process of confirmation and disconfirmation has been described by several authors. Sieburg writes:

> Communication with others is a basic human need, for it is through communication that relationships are formed, maintained, and expressed. It was theorized that in attempting to establish relationships, individuals engage in behavior which involves the formulation of messages with the expectation of a response. If this expectation is met — if response is direct, open, clear, congruous, and relevant to the prior communicative attempt, the persons involved are likely to experience the benefits of genuine dialogue as well as the advantages of "therapeutic interpersonal communication". . . . If response is absent, tangential, unclear, ambiguous, or otherwise inadequate, the participants are likely to feel confused, dissatisfied, misunderstood, and alienated.[9]

Further clarification of confirming and disconfirming responses is provided by the following examples.

CONFIRMING RESPONSES
Confirming responses include (1) *direct acknowledgment,* when you respond directly to another person's message and thus indicate that you

---

[9]Evelyn Sieburg, "Dysfunctional Communication and Interpersonal Responsiveness in Small Groups," unpublished Ph.D. dissertation, University of Denver, 1969.

heard what was said and that the person is included in your perceptual world; (2) *agreement about content,* when you reinforce or support the opinions and ideas expressed by another person; (3) *supportive response,* when you give assurances, express understanding, or somehow attempt to make the other person feel better or encouraged; (4) *clarifying response,* when you try to get the other person to express more, to describe more feelings or information, to seek repetition or make past remarks clearer; (5) *expression of positive feelings,* when you share positive feelings about what the other person has done or said.

DISCONFIRMING RESPONSES
Disconfirming responses include the following: (1) *Impervious response,* when you do not acknowledge or ignore what was said, when you give no indication that something has been said. (2) *Interrupting response,* when you interrupt or cut off something that is being said, or begin a new thought while the first person is still speaking. (3) *Irrelevant response,* when you introduce a new train of thought or a new topic, or in some way indicate that what the first speaker said is so inconsequential that it is not worth commenting upon. (4) *Tangential response,* when you make a slight attempt to relate a new thought to what was said previously, but when in fact you take the discussion in a new direction. The "yes, . . . but" ploy is often the mark of a tangential response; and so is "by the way, this reminds me of . . ." when the subsequent story has little relationship to the previous discussion. (5) *Impersonal response,* when you use generalizations, clichés, pronouncements, and intellectualizations abundantly. (6) *Incoherent response,* when you ramble, when you use words in special idiosyncratic ways that are unclear to your listeners, when you leave sentences uncompleted, or when you reword and rephrase so much that your main idea gets lost. (7) *Incongruous response,* when your nonverbal communication is completely at odds with your verbal statements (for example, when you are red in the face, bang your fist on the table, and shout, "I am not angry!").

WHY STUDY SELF-CONCEPT? Who you think you are is confirmed or denied by the responses others make to your communication with them. Unless you get clear and supportive messages, you are not likely to have effective communication experiences. Early in your lives you learn how to give each other many different kinds of responses, and you should recognize that what you do to each other has an effect on your feelings of worth, on your self-esteem, and also on how well you can get the job done, because without some internal support for your activities the outside work you do will not get done.

The reason we have gone into this lengthy discussion of the formation of the self-concept and of the ways it is maintained and changed through interpersonal communication processes is that self-perception is a major filter mechanism. As such, it plays a significant part in how you generally perceive the world and hence how you behave.

Much of the development and maintenance of your self-concept is intimately related to your work and the roles you learn in the formal organizations you participate in. Much of your sense of inner worth comes from performing the roles that society provides. You learn to see yourself as a lawyer, an engineer, a professor, a secretary, a coal miner, an accountant; and you learn the expected behaviors of a "good" lawyer, engineer, professor, secretary, coal miner, or accountant. When what you do matches the standards you have learned to accept, you feel good, competent, and worthwhile. And you often know that you have achieved those standards when other people give you confirmation. "Good job on that report, Jones," an A+ on a paper, a promotion, inclusion in a highly select group — these are examples of the messages which confirm your sense of adequacy.[10] The anxiety you experience in a new job or when meeting new people is closely related to the fact that you do not know whether you will measure up. The situation is ambiguous. You may be a top student in your class, but will you cut it in your first job? Will you be able to perform as you think you should or as you think others think you should? If not, the risk is not simply that you may lose your job but — more important — that you will lose some degree of self-esteem. Protecting the self-concept in the face of disconfirmation and potential failures is for most people a very strong desire. Like most people, you tend to act in ways that are consistent with your self-concept. If for some reason you are faced with evidence which suggests that the way you see yourself is inaccurate, you first tend to look for ways to defend that concept rather than modify it. By using a variety of *defense mechanisms* you are often able to explain away the inconsistencies between your behavior and the way you wish to think of yourself. How you protect and defend yourself is discussed in more detail in Chapter 12.

SELF-ACCEPTANCE AND SELF-ESTEEM

In the process of developing a self-image, you develop feelings about who you think you are and you tend to look to other people for confirmation of those feelings. That confirmation, when you get it, makes you feel that you are entitled to have your image of yourself. Let us look at how we build a sense of self-esteem.

Self-esteem is the feeling you get when *what* you do matches *your self-image* and when that particular image approximates an *idealized version* of what you wish you were like. For example, you might see

[10]For an interesting fable about giving praise, see Kenneth Blanchard and Spencer Johnson, *The One Minute Manager,* New York, William Morrow and Co., Inc., 1982.

yourself as an ''outdoor type'' (self-image). You may imagine yourself as a successful forestry engineer (idealized self-image). You may go and register in a forestry school (action). That action matches your self-image and your idealized self-image. If you are accepted in the school and subsequently earn high grades, you are confirmed by others (peers and professors), and this confirmation will validate your feelings of self-worth and your self-esteem.

Maintenance of self-esteem is complex. Many times your attempts at maintaining positive feelings about yourself are successful. Yet some of your attempts are self-defeating.

You sometimes try to hide parts of yourself from others, fearing that if they knew these parts they might reject you. In his excellent book *Why Am I Afraid to Tell You Who I Am?* John Powell relates a poignant and real answer to that question:''I am afraid to tell you who I am because if I tell you who I am, you may not like who I am, and it's all I have.''[11]

You hide parts of yourself, for example, when you cover up feelings. You store up anger or frustration and keep a cool facade. Half the time you don't really deceive others because your nonverbal behavior gives you away. But when you succeed in hiding, you tend to ''gunny-sack,'' that is, to collect angry feelings inside you (generally in the stomach — a sure way to get ulcers) until the time when a trivial incident will ''make you'' explode — the staw that breaks the camel's back.

Sometimes you try to put on masks to appear something you are not. You give off false cues to the people around you and erect walls of intended impressions. This little game, a full-time job for many people, consumes much energy and concentration; to pay off, it must be carried off well. Most of you, however, are not professional actors, and thus your masks, deceptive as they may be for a while, are usually seen through by others. The more you pretend to be what you are not, the more you tend to believe the phony verbal world you hope to create and to lose touch with the real world and your own reality.

Self-Exposure and Feedback

Effective maintenance of self-esteem is based on a dual process of *self-exposure* followed by *feedback*. You expose to others, through your behavior, some parts of you; others give you feedback about their reactions to your behaviors, thus confirming you in some way.

Your doubts about who you are can be discarded only by checking them out through honest and direct exposure and direct and honest feedback.

---

[11]John Powell, *Why Am I Afraid to Tell You Who I Am?* Argus Communications, Chicago, 1969, p. 12.

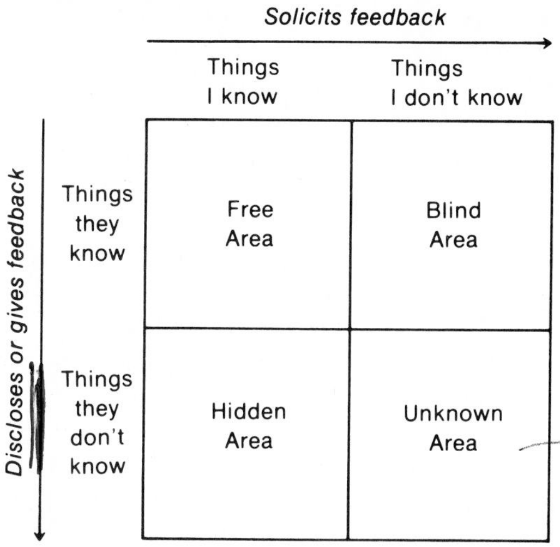

Solicits feedback →

	Things I know	Things I don't know
Things they know	Free Area	Blind Area
Things they don't know	Hidden Area	Unknown Area

Discloses or gives feedback

Quize

FIGURE 13.
Luft and Harrington's "Johari
window."

Gernativit / the area that you dont Know and try to learn and get out of that area.

The Johari Window

In this respect Joe Luft's theory of the Johari window[12] is an extremely useful way to look at the transactional process of disclosure, feedback, and self-esteem. As we stressed in the first chapter of this book, there is an essential relationship between the factors of communication — they affect each other. A change in one factor, such as the sender, means a change in the message. A change in perceptions will mean a change in meanings. The "transactional" nature of finding out about yourselves is demonstrated by the Johari window diagram, where a change in any one of the four quadrants (or "panes" of the window) will mean a change in another. See Figure 13.

The term "Johari window," exotic as it may sound, simply honors the first names of the originators of the model, Joseph Luft and Harrington Ingram. The window represents a way to look at the self, and the quadrants are formed by the intersection of two dimensions of awareness about the self. There are things you know about yourself and things you don't know. There are things other people know about you and things they don't know. When the four quadrants are formed, they represent the various areas of the self.

Area 1, the area of free activity (I know, others know) represents your public self: the shared knowledge and awareness about who you are. It usually includes "name, rank, and serial number" type of information. That information is common knowledge, and thus you feel rel-

---

[12]Joseph Luft, *Of Human Interaction,* National Press Books, Palo Alto, Calif., 1969.

atively free of anxiety if it gets exposed, since other people know about it anyway.

Area 2, the blind area (others know, I don't know) includes information others have about you which you do not have. The sound of your voice, your nonverbal behavior, your mannerisms are examples of things which might fall in that quadrant.

Area 3, the hidden area (I know, others don't know) represents all the things you know about yourself but are not willing to share with others. You usually protect this area by preventing others from invading your privacy. Examples of things that fall into this area are feelings you have and do not share with others, motivations, fantasies, secrets, things you are ashamed of, and things you feel are no one else's business.

Area 4, the unknown area (I don't know, others don't know) represents those things about yourself which have not yet penetrated your consciousness. There is universal curiosity about this area. It covers, for example, your deep needs, your expectations, your unconscious fears, etc.

The beauty of this simple model resides in the fact that it accounts for the dynamism of interpersonal transactions. Through *disclosure,* you can shrink the hidden area, thus opening up the area of free activity to include more shared information about yourself. Through *feedback,* others can shrink the blind area by giving you data only they have, further opening up the area of free activity.

Most new relationships (meeting people at a party, for example) are characterized by a fairly small area of free activity. After all, you seldom trust strangers at first sight and share intimate things with them. You usually restrict conversations to safe topics (the weather, movies, jokes). You tend to relate on the basis of masks or facades to protect your "real self" from dangerous exposure. Others don't give you much feedback either, except in safe areas (your outfit is attractive). A great deal of energy is expended on both sides to keep the walls up. "I am afraid to tell you who I am, because if I tell you, you may not like who I am, and it's all I have."

As relationships mature, the area of free activity expands. The walls slowly crumble through more disclosure and feedback as trust is built, as risks are taken. After all, you can talk about the weather only so long. But we also believe that there may be a universal craving for closeness, intimacy, and relatedness. Although your attempts may be feeble, awkward, and sometimes misguided, most of you would prefer meaningful contacts to superficial encounters.

Following are some points about feedback. More on this subject is included in Chapter 8.

1. Feedback is the kind of information needed to check out whether the actual results of your communication are the same as your intended results.
2. Feedback is absolutely necessary for survival and for growth.
3. Feedback at best is a nonevaluative process of sharing data with another person while respecting that person's right and freedom to accept or reject it, to act on it or not act on it.
4. Feedback is not the kind of gang bombardment pictured in some television stereotypes of groups. It is not sharpshooting, sniping, or blasting.
5. Feedback is not forcing another person into your preconceived mold or expectations.
6. Feedback is not just a request for change in behavior. In human relationships, it may well be the beginning of the process of mutual acceptance.

VERBAL PATTERNS AND SELF-CONCEPT

A study of the verbal patterns of persons with low self-concept and high self-concept shows some tendencies which can be identified. In looking at tendencies, let's not classify people or decide that a person who acts one way will always act that same way. Self-concept may vary with the situation or topic, and the relations of the others with whom a person is communicating. Highly verbal students in the dormitory may be tongue-tied in the classroom because they feel they get along fine with their friends in a social setting but are lousy students. A boy or girl who is deeply sensitive in serious talk with others may become a giggling wreck in the presence of the opposite sex. A youngster may take advice and instruction from a teacher and not be able to listen at all when a parent tries to advise or explain the same items. The way people see themselves in relation to others has a great effect on the changing patterns of communication.

Low Self-Concept

The following are some verbal patterns which may characterize low self-concept.

Frequent use of cliché phrases or a few words (``you know,'' ``like,'' ``young people are like that,'' etc.) which are used not so much to help identify something in common with others as because the person with a low self-concept does not trust his or her ability to be original.

A need to talk about self in terms of criticism, weaknesses (``all thumbs''), and difficult experiences which help explain why he or she is not better.

An inability to accept praise gracefully, often expressed by a superficially worded disclaimer which invites additional proof.

A defensiveness about blame to the degree that the person may be more anxious about who gets credit or blame in a project than about actually getting the project accomplished.

A cynicism about accomplishments or possessions; a hypercritical attitude about those of others.

A persistently whining or sneering tone of voice or posture as assumed in relation to one's own or others' successes, as if to dismiss as luck or special privilege any accomplishments by anyone.

A pessimistic attitude expressed about competition. (In the game of Monopoly ''I always get the cheap properties and end up in jail.'')

High Self-Concept   On the other hand, here are some verbal patterns which may characterize a high self-concept:

Use of original expressions, a rich vocabulary used in appropriate settings, an ability to ''find the right word'' or to use the balanced correct forms of address with others (Mister, Miss, first names, or nicknames, for example).

A tendency to talk about the self less frequently and to talk about others easily in terms of their accomplishments; an apparent ability to get along without constant reassurance of personal worth.

The ability to accept praise or blame gracefully; in working on projects, taking risks and verbalizing positions other than the ''correct'' ones; not spending much time figuring out the ''safe'' way of approaching problems in order to avoid blame.

A willingness to look at accomplishments with a balance of credit to ability and to circumstances and to give credit to others for their part in what is done.

A confident tone of voice; avoidance of a condescending tone or attitude; ability to say ''I don't know'' or ''I was wrong.''

Admission of a wide range of feelings and empathy for others whether or not these are popular.

An optimistic attitude about competition; willingness to try new games, to enter discussions about new topics with questions (to risk displaying ignorance in an effort to learn more).

Lack of dogmatism about beliefs; little tendency to be biased, to stereotype others, or to classify events too broadly.

We want to emphasize that this list is partial and that it does not necessarily describe a person. It describes some verbal patterns which may, in some circumstances or if found persistently, indicate low or high self-esteem for that particular relationship. We would discourage your taking this list and analyzing your friends. We would, on the other hand, encourage your looking seriously at your own verbal outputs in light of these possibilities to find out how often you may act in these ways. Do not then conclude that you *are* one or the other. You may conclude that in some situations you *act* in a certain way. These actions may be changed if you feel like it. Also, you may — and again, only if you feel like it — ask someone who knows you well to tell you if you operate in one way or another (1) never, (2) seldom, (3) sometimes, or (4) frequently. We have left off "(5) always," because no one (including yourself) knows you that well.

RANGE OF SELF-CONCEPT

What have variously been called "modes," "categories," "classes," "dimensions," "groups," or "types" of self-concept, we want to refer to as "ranges." How you see yourself is complex. You are a living, breathing, functioning, human being, and you have a physical presence in the world which others as well as you can recognize on sight. You also have a great number of roles you play in relation to others and the world around you. There are many ways you behave in public or by yourself, many ways you carry on the business of acting like "you." You are even more complicated than that — internally there is a thinking, feeling, reacting, believing you; a sort of mental-emotional-spiritual-metaphysical creature.

The dynamic process of reacting with your self-image means that you can adjust your perceptions. You can decide which of the ranges you will emphasize in any situation. You can choose which "you" is the most significant one as you move through your life. What has been called the "mutable" self by Zurcher and others we will call the "adaptive" self. It is important for you to understand that you are not frozen into one set of responses but can adapt as you feel the need to show a different self or to take another look at yourself in relation to events or people around you.

Your adaptive self will therefore concern itself with the three broad and overlapping ranges described above: first the "physical" range, second the "role" range, and third the "introspective" range, which includes your intrapersonal workings such as intellect, emotions, fears, beliefs, and perceptual sets.

Physical Range

First is the *physical range:* your age, height, weight, hair color, and other such observable and functional attributes which make up your person. Items such as your sex may overlap into the other attributes; and for this reason we prefer to call these dimensions "ranges," to indicate that they are not always clear-cut classifications but may merge and shift back and forth. For example, your physical self-concept may affect the roles you play — if you consider yourself a physical weakling, then you will not attempt the role of athlete or bully. Being male (physical range) will in some ways determine what jobs (role range) you are expected to perform; being female (physical range) may restrict your efforts toward mental or emotional diversity (introspective range). A very significant part of the physical range is the dimension of beauty or attractiveness. Plastic surgeons report that their work in changing the features of a patient actually improves the person's self-concept more than the actual physical appearance. Maxwell Maltz's popular book tells many stories about minor cosmetic changes in patients' appearances which resulted in major emotional improvements based largely on the way the patients saw themselves before and after surgery.

Role Range   Your *role* range, as described in Table 1, in many ways says that what you are results from what you do — a common judgment in our society. Stereotypes of teaching, police work, medicine, law, and other occupations tend to restrict the behaviors of people in those fields. Roles, however, are much more than what people do for a living. Roles include your relationships with others in the environment. You may be a son to a parent, a friend to someone, a student in a university course, a patient in a dentist's chair, a musician in a band, or a pedestrian on a busy city street. Think of the different ways you act as you move from one of these roles to another. (In Chapter 10 we will discuss roles further.) Most of you know what you should do when you interact with

TABLE 1. **Ranges of the Self-Concept**

Range	What you say to yourself	What others may say to you (for good or bad . . .)
Physical	I am quite handsome. I have pretty hair. I dance (swim, run) well. This jacket is expensive.	You are strong for your size. I like that dress. You played that shot well. Don't spill the milk again.
Role	I am a student. I am a lawyer. I am a pedestrian. I'm your friend.	Do you read a lot? You seem to work very hard. Boys don't cry. What grade are you in?
Introspective	I am sensitive to others. I have deep convictions. I'm a natural optimist. I cry at sad movies.	You look as if you are worried. Thanks for your concern. You always seem so happy. Do you really believe that?

parents, sit in a dentist chair, play an instrument in a band, or walk down a street. What do you think you look like when you do these things? Are you satisfied with the way you handle yourself in such situations, or would you like to do something differently? You spend much of your time checking to see if you are acting properly in the role as you have defined it. Others give you feedback which helps direct your future role behaviors. Or, if you cannot get feedback from others, you make a guess about how you are doing and tell yourself whether to continue or to adapt.

Introspective Range   Within yourself are the *introspective* ranges. As you search for the "real you" within your head and heart, you watch others and assume certain attitudes and emotions from what they do. You begin to develop a set of your own private cognitions, emotions, and biases which you then may share with others. You can become a storyteller and inform others about news events, humorous incidents, or car repair — all based on intellectual self. You can share deep feelings of faith with others, or you can talk about your anxieties or phobias — all based on other dimensions of your introspective self. As mentioned before, it will be your behaviors (usually what you choose to talk about) that will give data to others about your introspective self, and from these encounters you will learn how to adapt. What and how much to disclose to others will become an important part of the relations you develop and will affect your self-concept.

Knowing that you are made up of a complex relationship of these factors, can you determine how your self-concept is conveyed? Do you tend to spend most of your time worrying about how you appear to people (physical range)? Is the job you hold a great source of pride or shame to you (role range)? Do you see yourself as a deeply religious person in relation to others (introspective range)? Which of the ranges seems to be one you would worry about and try to make very significant improvements in? Would you like most to be a physically attractive person, or does emotional stability or intellectual power appeal to you?

Before you decide that you can be only one of these, consider the idea that a range exists in each general grouping, and that the ranges overlap to some extent. Even more important, consider that you can adapt to the special circumstances in each range. For example, when playing tennis you may want to see and check how others see your physical self, while in a class recitation your introspective range would become dominant. Before you decide once and for all that you "are" some set of qualities, remember that you (1) are a complex of many facets which make up the total person, (2) can adapt to the different ranges represented in your self-concept, (3) have developed your self-concept over a long period of time, and (4) have considerable control of how you see yourself.

SELF-DISCLOSURE   How easy is it for you to tell others about yourself? What information will you tell others easily? Will others disclose personal information to you easily — are you considered a keeper of intimate secrets, or a shoulder to cry on? Can you be comfortable exchanging quite personal ideas or thoughts with others? How long do you have to know another person before you can easily tell him or her how you feel about your religion, your fantasies, your secret fears? What does it take for you to risk revealing some of your inner thoughts?

Revealing yourself can take many forms. You can share those reactions you are immediately experiencing about an event, the other person, or whatever you and the other person are engaged in. You can also share your thoughts and feelings about things in general: your views on politics, religion, education, etc. You can share values and things that are important to you or that you believe in very much: what you would die for, what you wish to become, what kind of person you wish to be. You can also share those things about you that you like very much and that you are proud of: your accomplishments, your skills, your special talents. You can also share things that you do not like about yourself and perhaps would like to change.

Self-disclosure is usually one of the bases for healthy relationships. When you hide things from another person, your concealment can damage the relationship. In addition, hiding or masking what you are for fear the other person may not like you or may hurt you often leads to loneliness.

There are some interesting ideas about self-disclosure. The more you self-disclose to another person, the more likely that person will like you. The amount of sharing you do will determine the amount of sharing the other person will do. The more you share, the more the other person shares.

Researchers in social psychology have given us a better understanding of disclosure. It has been demonstrated that disclosure is an activity closely related to interaction — not some inborn or stubbornly acquired trait of character which people have or don't have. The dynamics of disclosure are being studied by scholars who look at the relation between the way you disclose, how that depends on who starts, what kinds of information you will disclose early or late in a relationship and in what sequence, and how quickly disclosure patterns develop between people. For example, too much disclosure too soon is viewed as somewhat aberrated, while not disclosing at all is seen as a snub. Personal attraction appears to be related to disclosure — you disclose more to people you like. Other studies suggest that we may also "come to like those to whom we disclose most."[13] It has been suggested that under some conditions intimate disclosure can lead to more attraction between experimental subjects than nonintimate disclosure does. In your own experience, do you think you like people better — and they like you better — when you can talk easily with them about very private matters?

Research on self-disclosure also shows that if you are the kind of person who self-discloses willingly, then you are probably competent, open, and socially extroverted, and you probably feel a need to interact with other people. You are also probably flexible and adaptive, and you may be a bit more intelligent than those people who are not as willing to self-disclose. You also tend to view people as generally good rather than basically evil. These statements, of course, are generalizations, and, as such, they may not hold true for every person who is willing to self-disclose.

Being self-disclosing means that you are open, willing to let other people know who you are, as you are, without masks, fronts, or other protective covers. Self-disclosure is based on honest, genuine interaction with others, and this is why it is such a prerequisite for the building of meaningful relationships. In addition to being open to others, you are also willing to be receptive to the self-disclosures of others. You are interested in other people, willing to hear them, and interested in how they feel and think. This need not mean that you will pry uninvited into their lives; you may be simply willing to listen.

When Is Self-Disclosure Appropriate? Self-disclosure is not always appropriate. There are times and situations when self-disclosing too much too fast or with the wrong persons may have negative consequences for you. It is important that you be sensitive to those situations in which self-disclosure is appropriate and those in which it is not. If you self-disclose when you should not, then you are likely to scare people off and get hurt in the process. Once you have told another person very intimate things about yourself, or shared some inner secrets, that person "owns" a bit of information which carries some responsibility with it. Here are some guidelines you might want to use in determining when self-disclosure is appropriate — remembering that you must decide for yourself when and what to disclose and under what conditions. You may want to disclose:

1. When you have an already developed relationship, and disclosing is not simply an isolated incident, unrelated to your future or past.
2. When the other person is willing to disclose also.

[13]John H. Berg and Richard L. Archer, "The Disclosure-Liking Relationship," *Human Communication Research*, vol. 10, no. 2, Winter 1983, p. 279.

3. When self-disclosure is about what is going on in the present between you and the other person. (Avoid historical references in a relationship, or saving up concerns, slights, worries, or other feelings or thoughts so you can "dump them" on the other at some later time.)
4. When self-disclosure is about positive rather than negative things. (Very often the person who discloses too much negative information about self is considered "poorly adjusted.")[14]
5. When self-disclosure leads to improving your relationship.
6. When you are sensitive to what effects self-disclosure will have on the other person. (Do not make others responsible for all your troubles without making sure they want to be, for example.)
7. When self-disclosure is gradual, a little at a time. (Don't "dump on" the other person by giving him or her too much to handle.)
8. Self-disclose when you trust the other person, and you are confident the other person trusts you. (Both of you should be willing to take the risks associated with self-disclosure.)

What Will You Disclose?

What kinds of things are you willing to disclose to another? An answer to that question will depend on many factors. One factor is how intimately you know the other person. Another factor is the purpose of your disclosing, and still another is your own feelings about taking risks. The level of your disclosing therefore is related to the sensitivity of the information you intend to share, any cultural norms you have between you, the feelings you have about the other person and your perception of the relationship, and the amount of risk you want to take for yourself. Table 2 gives you an idea of the range of material or information you might want to disclose and the conditions under which you might disclose.

What Do You Gain from Self-Disclosure?

We suggest that self-disclosure, appropriately done, can be helpful to your communication. The payoffs include these: (1) Improving accuracy of communication, and adding thoughts and feelings to the already public material you share with another. Example: "I just saw that movie, and it was depressing to me." (2) Getting to know more about another person in a more intimate way. Example: learning from the other what depth of feeling you may share on some issues and thus increasing the predictability of your communication. (3) Getting to know more about yourself. Example: as the other person mirrors back your feelings and

---

[14]T. E. Runge and Richard L. Archer, "Reactions to the Disclosure of Public and Private Self-Information," *Social Psychology Quarterly,* vol. 44, no. 4, December 1981, pp. 357–362.

TABLE 2. **Levels of Disclosing**

Content to be disclosed	Risk level	Conditions of disclosing	Examples
Information available to you and the other; of a general and public nature.	Minimal. Just let the other know you know.	Can be done between persons who are strangers as well as close friends.	Basic neutral data or data of little consequence to the participants: "I just saw that movie." "The President is on television tonight." While the content may be neither very revealing nor very significant *of and by itself,* it may prepare the way for more sensitive disclosing later.
Preferences you have; likes and dislikes.	Some risk.	Used if you want to get your own way or want to avoid doing something you dislike.	"I'd prefer a beer." "Let's play tennis instead of swimming." "Can you shut the door more quietly?" "I'd rather watch the football game on television."
Thoughts or ideas you have about public issues such as politics, books, and movies.	More risk.	Individual differences are likely to occur in ideas, and so people may react negatively to what you think.	"I really hated that movie." "My course in history represented a very global view and liberal ideas." "The President is not helping the poor."
Feelings, emotions, your own values, internal reactions, faith, judgments.	Most risk.	You may be able to argue from data about such matters, but your feelings are so personal that it is most difficult to share them with others.	"What faith do you have?" "I believe that students are less moral today than they used to be." "I'm opposed to drinking any alcoholic beverages." "The thought of dying frightens me."

whatever impressions your own behavior creates, you gain new insights into yourself.

Self-disclosure is an important element in developing close relationships with others and in knowing yourself. However, you must be sensitive to your needs as well as the needs of others. When you are able to self-disclose in a sensitive manner, you have made a giant step toward warding off loneliness, and toward developing high predictability about how you and others will act in a great variety of situations. You are your own tool in learning how to belong, how to care, how to share, and how to communicate your own needs appropriately in relation to those of others.

Another way of looking at the outcomes of self-disclosure is by focusing on what it does to the "self," putting aside any effects on others. First, you are giving of yourself. Second, you learn to recognize more of yourself. And third, you learn to evaluate your "self" more accurately and more predictably.

BEHAVIORS AND SELF-CONCEPT

In this textbook we have been careful to distinguish between the person (as a total entity) and his or her behaviors. This is an important distinction. If we are to treat people appropriately, we need to recognize that we never see *all* that any person is, and that any person will change as experiences accumulate. In other words, it is inaccurate to label a person as dishonest, selfish, bigoted, smart, kind, etc. We will be more accurate if we *describe behaviors* which the person has exhibited and limit our judgment to those.

Behaviors and Self-Disclosure

The question of whether or not to disclose information about yourself may not be a real question. You disclose with your behaviors constantly — sometimes intentionally, sometimes not. However you may try to hide certain things about yourself, there is always a chance that your behaviors will give you away. There is also a strong chance that you will not know the effects of these behaviors unless you remain open to (1) an understanding of the nature of behavior as a part of self and (2) a willingness to adjust behaviors in relation to the feedback you receive. In this way, behaviors help people train each other.

Your behaviors grow out of what you feel about yourself (your self-concept) and which role you elect to play in any circumstance. If you adopt a habitual orientation to your world, it is likely you will exhibit some typical behaviors. It is from this pattern of behaviors that others will judge your "personality." Without some interaction, there is little chance that anyone can develop a picture of you — right or wrong — in terms of behaviors. It is from the established pattern of typical behaviors that you begin to categorize one another and begin to make predictions on how the other will behave. It is then you boast that you "know" someone. In a game of chess it may be more useful to know the other person's style of play than all the strategies of the game. If you can predict which moves the other is likely to make in response to your moves, you will play more effectively. The accomplished chess player will predict many moves in advance because certain logical progressions of play are assumed. If the opponent is playing a person who does not follow a chess logic on moves, the game may be very confusing.

In human interaction you are often caught in a dilemma. On the one hand, society places such high value on dependability, steadfastness, and reliability that it would seem that you should strive to be predictable in your communicative behaviors. On the other hand, novelty, imagination, creativity, and spontaneity are also prized highly, and so you might therefore want to establish yourself as less predictable.

To resolve this apparent conflict you should remember that not only are your behaviors a source of judgment from others, but they are also a testing ground for yourself. If you do not develop some patterns of behavior, you have very little to test; yet if you do not add some novelty to your behaviors, you cannot learn new things about yourself. The answer, then, seems to be to do both — to try to select wisely those events and circumstances in which to make familiar and typical moves and those in which to try some new behaviors. In all this discussion, it is imperative that you remember that your behaviors will not necessarily be "consistent" in all the roles you play, and are therefore not the total you when taken in by any one group you have interacted with.

Your behaviors are, then, only bits and pieces of you, given out a few at a time in selected circumstances to selected people. In closing this chapter on self-concept, it may be useful to note these characteristics of behavior.

1. Behaviors, although only a portion of you at any one time, are still *yours*. They are your responsibility. You invented them. You must take the consequences of them because they belong to you.
2. Behaviors may not always be the same but may vary as your relationships vary.
3. Behaviors may, however, demonstrate tendencies (or habits of behaving) which may force others to label or categorize you, sometimes mistakenly, particularly as the predictability of your behaviors increases.
4. Your behaviors are a testing procedure you use on others.
5. Your behaviors are a source of judgment of you by others.
6. Your behaviors are, for better or worse, an overt expression of your intentions.

7. Your behaviors are subject to change as you may like, and others may give you opportunity to change.

8. Your behaviors are visible tokens of exchange with others from which you can learn more about yourself if you attend to the feedback you get about them.

The "Shoulds" We said earlier that your behaviors grow out of what you feel about yourself and which roles you choose to play in a given situation. Your behaviors are also the product of complex feelings about who you *should* be, which roles you *should* play, and what interpersonal transactions *should* be like. All these *shoulds* point to value areas. In Chapter 4, we will look at how your values are formed, maintained, and changed. More particularly, we will see how they affect your self-image and how your communicative behaviors are a visible display of your needs as well as your values, beliefs, and attitudes.

BIBLIOGRAPHY Berg, J. H., and R. L. Archer: "The disclosure-liking relationship," *Human Communication Research,* vol. 10, no. 2, Winter 1983.

Berlo, D. K.: *The Process of Communication.* Holt, Rinehart and Winston, Inc., New York, 1960.

Blanchard, K., and S. Johnson: *The One Minute Manager,* William Morrow and Co., Inc., New York, 1982.

Bradac, J. J., C. H. Tardy, and L. A. Hosman: "Disclosure Styles and a Hint at Their Genesis," *Human Communication Research,* vol. 6, no. 3, Spring 1980.

Cooley, C. H.: *Human Nature and the Social Order,* Transaction Books, New Brunswick, N.J., 1983.

Fitts, W. H.: *The Self Concept and Self Actualization,* Counselor Recordings and Tests, Nashville, Tenn., 1971.

Luft, J.: *Of Human Interaction,* National Press Books, Palo Alto, Calif., 1969.

Mead, G. H.: *Mind, Self, and Society,* University of Chicago Press, Chicago, 1967.

Powell, J.: *Why Am I Afraid to Tell You Who I Am?* Argus Communications, Chicago, 1969.

Roloff, M. E., and G. R. Miller (eds.): *Persuasion: New Directions in Theory and Research,* Sage Publications, Beverly Hills, Calif., 1980.

Rosenfeld, L. B.: "Self Disclosure Avoidance: Why Am I Afraid to Tell You Who I Am?" *Communication Monographs,* 46, March 1979.

Rosenthal, R.: "The Pygmalion Effect Lives," *Psychology Today,* vol. 7, 1973.

————, and L. Jacobson: *Pygmalion in the Classroom,* Irvington Publishers, New York, 1983.

Runge, T. E., and R. L. Archer: "Reactions to the Disclosure of Public and Private Self-Information," *Social Psychology Quarterly,* vol. 44, no. 4, December 1981.

Sieburg, E.: "Dysfunctional Communication and Interpersonal Responsiveness in Small Groups," unpublished Ph.D. dissertation, University of Denver, 1969.

Simon, S. B.: *Vulture: A Modern Allegory on the Art of Putting Oneself Down,* Argus Communications, Niles, Ill., 1977.

Smith, D. R., and K. Williamson: *Interpersonal Communication,* Wm. C. Brown Company, Dubuque, Iowa, 1977.

Sullivan, H. S.: *The Interpersonal Theory of Psychiatry,* W. W. Norton & Co., New York, 1968.

Zurcher, L. A.: *The Mutable Self: A Self Concept for Social Change,* Sage Publications, Beverly Hills, Calif., 1977.

Chapter 4

ATTITUDES, BELIEFS, AND VALUES: WHO SHOULD I BE?

In a Nutshell

People are motivated by a variety of needs. Although these needs — as well as your values, attitudes, and beliefs — cannot be seen or touched, they are often displayed by your actions or behaviors. From a set of needs you determine what system or sequence will satisfy them, so that your inner motivations are clarified and organized in your system of beliefs, values, and attitudes.

You develop your values, attitudes, and beliefs largely through your interpersonal communication. Your values, attitudes, and beliefs in turn affect how you communicate with others (your rhetoric) and how you act (your behaviors).

Your values are your conception of the relative worth you attribute to things, events, and people in your world. Beliefs represent how you view your world, what you think is true, what you agree with. Attitudes reflect your tendencies to respond to things in certain ways.

Values, attitudes, and beliefs cannot be directly observed. They can be inferred from your behavior. All are learned from the people you associate with, particularly your reference groups. Reference groups consist of those people whom you admire, like, and identify with and whom you use as a source for your goals and aspirations.

Sometimes you may experience dissonance among your values, attitudes, beliefs, and behaviors. You may, for example, have two contradictory beliefs. Or you may believe in one thing and do the opposite. When you experience such dissonance, you try to reduce the resulting tensions by using a variety of rationalizing strategies or sometimes by changing your behavior or your beliefs.

WHAT MOTIVATES YOU?	Human motivation is a complicated matter; but in general it has to do with needs and with values, beliefs, and attitudes. In this chapter we discuss these sources of motivation.

NEEDS	While most behavioral scientists agree that people are motivated by the desire to satisfy many needs, not all agree about what these needs are and how each affects individuals' perceptions of their relative importance. Knowing something about your needs is important, since much of your behavior can be explained by the existence of these needs and in a sense reflects the ways in which you go about satisfying them. What motivates you? What makes you move a certain way? What makes you do the things you do? These are undoubtedly puzzling questions, particularly at times when you are not sure why you did what you did.

Maslow's hierarchy of needs and Schutz's theory of interpersonal needs are discussed in this section.

Maslow and the Hierarchy of Needs[1]

Maslow's theory is based on two fundamental assumptions:

1. People all have basic needs which are arranged into a hierarchy of importance. Only when the first basic level of needs is satisfied can people devote energy to seeking satisfaction of the needs on the next level.
2. Only unsatisfied needs can motivate behavior. Once a need is satisfied, it no longer acts as a motivator.

Maslow identified five basic need levels; these are discussed below.

Physiological needs

First, psychological needs include the most basic necessities which sustain life—the needs for air, water, food, sleep, elimination, sex. They are the most basic of all needs and, if frustrated, take precedence over other needs. If you have not eaten for several days, your behavior will very likely be solely motivated by your desire to get food. It is difficult to lift the spirit of a person with an empty stomach. If you have not slept for a long time, the need for sleep will take precedence over any other need.

Safety needs

The second level of needs in Maslow's hierarchy is the need for safety or the desire for protection from danger, threat, and deprivation. People look to their home as a generally "safe" place to be. From an organizational standpoint, safety needs are manifested in a desire for job security and steady or increasing monetary income.

[1]Abraham Maslow, *Motivation and Personality,* Harper & Brothers, New York, 1970.

Social needs   It is only when physiological and safety needs are relatively well satisfied that social needs — those on Maslow's third level — motivate people's behavior. Social needs are related to people's desire for companionship, belonging, acceptance, friendship, and love. Some people will go to great lengths to belong to particular groups they value. Family reunions, searching for "roots," and keeping in touch with relatives are all related to the social needs of a family unit. The need to belong, formally as well as informally, to a variety of human groups is indeed a powerful motivator for those who derive their sense of identity from their membership in social or professional groups.

Esteem needs   Esteem needs — those on the fourth level — do not act as motivators until the previous levels of needs have been reasonably well satisfied. Esteem needs consist of (1) the need for *self-esteem,* which is characterized by a desire for self-confidence, self-respect, and feelings of competence, achievement, and independence; and (2) the need for *esteem from others,* which includes a desire for recognition, status, appreciation, and prestige. You look to your friends and family members to help you fulfill this need at a very personal level. In most large organizations, there are relatively few opportunities through formal channels for the satisfaction of the esteem needs at the lower levels of the organization. However, one of the functions of the informal system which exists in all organizations is to provide a means for the satisfaction of the esteem needs at all levels of the organizational structure. Respect from coworkers often means more to a person than recognition from the boss.

Self-actualization needs   Self-actualization needs — those on the fifth level — include the need for self-fulfillment, creative expression, and the realization of one's potential. It is not unusual to meet people who are highly respected in a field, whose lower needs are satisfied in large measure, yet who feel restless and experience discontent. The highly successful executive who suddenly turns artist or the eminent scholar who starts a business venture are not uncommon examples of people motivated by the need for self-actualization who shift gears in mid-career.

Some observers assert that the family life of the past provided all these human needs and therefore tend to blame all society's problems on a "breakdown of the family." Whether or not this argument is valid, family, friends, church, community, etc., are all part of your search for satisfaction of your needs. Widespread frustration over unmet needs may be at the root of many global human problems. For example, a nation of starving people is not likely to govern itself well; a generation of people in a nation which has been politically or economically enslaved by another nation is not likely to develop world leaders, great ideas, or highly innovative or creative products.

By and large, organizations in this country have been successful in providing relative satisfaction of the lower needs of their members. Salary levels permit a fair amount of satisfaction of the physiological and safety needs for a majority of the people. Organizations also permit the relative satisfaction of social and belonging needs by providing opportunities for association, interaction, and communication on the job. If this is true, and if Maslow's theory is accurate, these needs are no longer motivators. The implications for the management of organizations are tremendous. More money, more fringe benefits, and more opportunities for socializing will do relatively little to encourage people to produce more or better. If a satisfied need is no longer a motivator, it is clear that managers must make some attempts to satisfy higher-level needs of the organization members.

This is, of course, easier said than done. For one thing, a need is a motivator only if it is felt as a frustrated need by the persons themselves. Only *you* know whether you are hungry, need friends, or would like a pat on the back. Furthermore, only you know the relative importance of a given need for you at a given time. Sometimes you may forgo the satisfaction of a need, even a basic one, for the fulfillment of another, higher-level, need. You may choose to deprive yourself of sleep and social activities for great periods of time in order to have the satisfaction of achieving professional goals which require a great deal of work. The student who works long hours, has little social life, and is thoroughly dedicated to getting through school is motivated essentially by esteem needs at the expense of having social and sometimes physiological needs met. Not all students will make this choice, of course, and ultimately, motivation is a very personal affair. Knowing that *generally* all people have five basic needs, and that *usually* a satisfied need is not a motivator, is helpful but does not provide a specific answer to the question "What should I do to motivate Susie to work harder?"

The problem of how to satisfy basic needs leads back to the communication area because it is through transactional communication that people can let you know what is important *to them,* and it is through your own sensitivity and attention to the messages you get from others that you may be able to determine (1) what their needs are, (2) what needs are particularly important to them at a given time, and (3) whether or not they perceive accurately your attempts to satisfy their needs. You may be doing all the "right" things, but if other people do not perceive what you do in the spirit in which you intended it, they may interpret your actions in a counterproductive manner.

**Schutz and the
Theory of
Interpersonal Needs**

William Schutz, in his book *The Interpersonal Underworld,* has identified three basic interpersonal needs which underlie most of your behavior around other people.[2] These needs can be best represented as dimensions or continuums along which most people fall. Schutz calls these interpersonal needs the ''need for inclusion,'' the ''need for control,'' and the ''need for affection.''

Inclusion

According to Schutz, the need for inclusion is the need to be recognized as an individual distinct from others. A person with a very high need for inclusion needs recognition and attention from others. Such a person likes to be in the spotlight, to be singled out, to be noticed. At one of the extremes of the continuum, we find the prima donna, or the obnoxious little kid who does anything simply to attract some attention, even if it results in punishment. To be punished is better than to be ignored. On the other hand, a person with a low inclusion need prefers not to stand out, would rather not receive too much attention, does not like to be prominent in the public eye.

Schutz holds that people at both extremes are motivated essentially by the same fear of not being recognized as individuals. The people high on the inclusion need will combat the fear by forcing others to pay attention to them. Those low on the inclusion need have convinced themselves that they will not get any attention, but that it is just the way they want it. Most people are probably somewhere in the middle of that continuum. Your needs for inclusion may change as the people you associate with differ, and as the situations you find yourself in change. You may want very little recognition from a professor when you have not done an assignment and do not wish to be called upon, while at the same time you may have a strong need for attention from the person sitting next to you, whom you are interested in getting to know better.

The need for inclusion has some influence on the process of interpersonal communication. Imagine a situation in which two or more people equally high on the need for attention get together to plan something. Much of the energy they are going to spend in that interpersonal context will be spent establishing in the group a position from which they will get the recognition they need. However, if all members are recognition seekers, chances are they will have a difficult time securing attention from one another. Much of the group's time, it can be predicted, will be spent vying for recognition from anyone in authority or from each other. Little else is likely to get accomplished.

[2]W. Schutz, *The Interpersonal Underworld,* Science and Behavior Books, Palo Alto, Calif., 1966.

A group composed of a reasonable balance of people high *and* low on inclusion will probably function in a smoother fashion.

Control The need for control involves a striving for power, for being in charge, for running things, and for influencing one's environment. The need for control is not necessarily related to the need for inclusion. Some people enjoy being in charge of things even if no one is aware that they are running the show. These people are high on control while low on inclusion — power-behind-the-throne types. Some people, on the other hand, may seek leadership or prestige positions not for the power they bring but for the attention they produce. This is why it is not always easy to determine whether a person's behavior is influenced by one need or the other. You should be careful not to play "analyst" with your friends and summarily peg them into one or the other category.

Naturally, some people are quite low on the need for control and are not interested at all in taking initiative, in assuming responsibilities, in making decisions, or in leading a group. As is true for the inclusion need, a mixed group composed of highs and lows on the control dimension has a better chance of getting things done.

Too many "leaders" and not enough "followers" may result in a constant struggle for leadership, and the ensuing climate of competition may not be conducive to accomplishing much. On the other hand, too many "followers" and no "leader" may result in apathy, and not much may get done.

Affection The need for affection has to do with how close people want to be to one another. Some people like to be very intimate and enjoy warm relationships, even with relatively casual acquaintances. They enjoy telling about themselves on a personal level and expect similar behavior on the part of others. They want and need to be liked. Sometimes people high on the need for affection are perceived by others as too friendly or coming on too strong. Affection is closely related to disclosing behavior, which — as we have already seen — can have a great effect on our interpersonal relations.

Some people, on the other hand, prefer to keep others at a distance. They do not like to become too friendly too rapidly. They do not wish to be too personal with others and share too much of themselves with people they do not know well. They may have a strong distaste for closeness and intimacy except with carefully selected people. These people are usually perceived as aloof, cold, or "superior."

In the case of affection, a mixed group is not the best combination for productive interpersonal relationships. Cold people and warm people do not mix well. Each type makes the other uncomfortable, and they find it hard to figure each other out. Neither is able to satisfy the other's needs.

In Summary: Needs

Interpersonal communication is satisfying to you when you manage to satisfy your needs. In the case of interpersonal needs, you depend solely on others for their satisfaction. If others give you the recognition you seek, or give you a chance to exert influence when you wish to, or provide you with the close intimate atmosphere you like, you feel satisfied and you seek these people again in other interpersonal situations. You tend to avoid, when you can, that type of interpersonal communication situation where your needs are generally thwarted.

An understanding of interpersonal needs is essential, not only in facilitating your insights into group processes, but in helping you predict the situations that will be more or less satisfying and productive for you.

VALUES, BELIEFS, AND ATTITUDES

You may often feel that your personal world is unique, peculiar to you, unshared by anyone. You have great difficulties explaining to someone else a feeling or an experience. Even when you manage to describe the feeling or the experience with words, you doubt that others know it as you do. The life of a black person in a ghetto is filled with experiences that no white person can ever understand in the same terms the black person does.

However, people are peculiar. At the same time that you intuitively believe in your uniqueness, you also assume that you live in the same world others do. You assume that what you see is what others see. Despite your feeling of uniqueness, your daily life is usually spent in a world you assume is shared as much as unique.

This may be the vital function of communication. Were it not for human communication or human contact, you would live alone, exclusively in your world of uniqueness, without getting confirmation of your experiences.

Confirmation of your experiences (or disclosing) not only involves the physical world — checking your perceptions with others to test their reliability. It also involves the social world — comparing your ideas about religion, politics, morals, etc., with others to test their validity.

Because human beings are symbol-using creatures, they can create for themselves rules of conduct which go beyond the mere survival needs of the species. When a female animal raises her young, she does so because she is programmed to do so in order for the young to survive and for the species to continue to exist. When human parents raise their children, considerably more is involved — feelings, societal expectations, laws, duty, etc. Human beings create value systems, form beliefs about the nature of their world, and as a result, learn to respond to their environment in some ways more than in others.

In the remainder of this chapter, we will examine how values, beliefs, and attitudes — the ingredients of a person's assumptive system — are formed, held, and changed through *interpersonal* communication.

A Few Definitions

Values

Values are fairly enduring conceptions of the nature of good and bad, of the relative worth you attribute to the things, people, and events of your lives. Values are usually embodied in complex moral or religious systems that are found in all cultures and societies, from the most "primitive" to the most complex and industrialized. Values define for people the parameters of their actions. They indicate to those who share them what is desirable, to what degree it is desirable, and therefore what one should strive for. They also provide people with a guidance system which is supposed to enable them to choose the "right" alternative when several courses of action are possible.

Words you use in making your value judgments, such as "bad," "good," "moral," "immoral," do not stand for any quality of the object or people you apply them to. Value judgments are applied by human beings to objects; they are not "in" the objects. Something is good to a particular individual or group only because it is defined as good.

Were it not for your ability to communicate and to use language, evaluating (that is, making value judgments) would not be possible; without symbols you could not be told by others that something is good or bad. Communication is what makes our system of morality possible. Judgments about beauty or ugliness are in the same category as those about goodness or badness. It has been said that beauty lies in the eye of the beholder. You cannot discover beauty — you can only discover how people define it. It is a dimension created by human beings.

Values grow out of a complex interaction between basic needs and the specificity of a given environment. For example, all humans need to eat in order to survive, but they do not all value the same foods. In America beef is commonly eaten, while in India the sacred cow must not be touched. What is valued in a particular area, region, or country is partly determined by the availability of certain foods. Values thus differ from place to place because of the variety of ways specific needs can be fulfilled.

What people value at a given time is based on the needs they try to fulfill at that particular time. The indictment of "materialism" directed at the generation who lived through the great depression in the United States, by a generation who lived mostly in post-World War II affluence, may reflect a change of need levels. Once people know a certain level of material affluence which satisfies physiological and safety needs, they can reject what they no longer need, since it fails to fulfill the next need level, which has become more prominent.

Values are fairly enduring and resistant to change because they are tied to fundamental human needs and because they are learned very early in life in a somewhat absolutistic way. Thou shalt, and thou shalt not. However, many values that are held by a given group of people can be, and often are, conflicting. In order to act, people must decide which of the conflicting values is more important or more basic, which takes precedence over the other. (For example: Thou shalt not kill; yet it is all right to kill the ''enemy'' in war.)

Beliefs   Beliefs represent the way people view their environment. Beliefs are characterized by a true-false continuum and a probability scale. The existence of ghosts, for example, may be closer to the ''false'' end of the continuum for some people than for others. That humans evolved from apes is still debated by many who place Darwin's theory of evolution closer to the ''false'' end of the continuum and place the story of Genesis closer to the ''true'' end of the continuum. Beliefs represent what you agree with and what you usually think is true. Some things you believe to be absolutely true, some you believe to be probably true, some you are not sure about, and some you think are false, probably or absolutely. According to the social psychologist Milton Rokeach, a belief system ''may be defined as having represented within it, in some organized psychological but not necessarily logical form, each and every one of a person's countless beliefs about physical and social reality.''[3]

You cannot observe a belief. You can only observe a person's behavior and assume that it came about because of a particular belief. Beliefs are not necessarily logical. They are largely determined by what you want to believe, by what you are able to believe, by what you have been conditioned to believe, and by basic needs which may influence you to have a certain belief in order to satisfy those needs.

Some beliefs are more central than others. The more central a belief, the more likely that it will resist change. If it does change, however, the repercussions on the whole belief system will be widespread.

It is not always easy to determine which of the beliefs a person holds are central and which ones are less important. According to

---

[3]Milton Rokeach, *Beliefs, Attitudes, and Values,* Jossey-Bass, San Francisco, Calif., 1968, p. 2. In addition, the discussion of types of beliefs is based on Rokeach's ''Organization and Modification of Beliefs,'' ibid., pp. 1–21.

Rokeach, the importance of a belief depends on how it is connected to other beliefs and what consequences it has on those other beliefs. Central beliefs are *connected* to other beliefs and have deeper *consequences* on this larger number of beliefs than less central beliefs do. Connectedness and consequences are more likely to be strong in the case of beliefs about your own existence and who you are. This is one of the difficulties you will find in discussing the story of Jackson (see page 225) which appears to make you question your existence and identity as a part of your primary belief system. Relatedness to your existence also is evident in your attachment to your own name; you want it pronounced and spelled correctly; in some cases you can hear your own name spoken when nothing else in the conversation can be accurately discriminated. Beliefs learned from direct experience and shared by others are very much connected to you and hence very central. By examining some of your beliefs in relation to their centrality for you, it is possible for you to distinguish among the following five types of beliefs which Rokeach identifies.

PRIMITIVE BELIEFS: 100 PERCENT CONSENSUS
Primitive beliefs are the most central beliefs of all. You learn them from direct experience. They are supported and reinforced by unanimous consensus among the people with whom you associate. They are fundamental, seldom-questioned, taken-for-granted axioms which rarely come up for controversy. It is as though you were saying, "I believe this and I also believe that everyone else believes it too." Beliefs in the existence and constancy of things are primitive beliefs. Even though you see a rectangular table from many angles, you continue to believe that it remains a table and that its shape does not change. Your belief that things remain the same in the physical world and in your social world is extremely important in the development of a sense of self-constancy. If such beliefs are disrupted, you begin to question the validity of your own senses, your competence to deal with reality, and sometimes your sanity. Because so much would be called into question, disruption of primitive beliefs is extremely upsetting and seldom occurs. Primitive beliefs are the most central, the most important, the most clung-to beliefs of all. They are very resistant to change. They include things that your parents taught you and that have been reinforced by teachers, the media, peers, and your own experiences. Day of the week and time of day are verifiable beliefs on which you base much of your day-to-day personal activity. Think of the problems caused when you forget which day of the week it is, or when you change from one time zone to another, or when an area changes from daylight savings time to regular time and people forget to reset their clocks.

PRIMITIVE BELIEFS: ZERO CONSENSUS

Some primitive beliefs are not shared by others and do not depend on social consensus, but arise from deep personal experiences. Because they need not be shared by others to be maintained, they are usually quite resistant to change. Many of these unshakable beliefs are about yourself. Some are positive (what you are capable of); some are negative (what you fear). These beliefs are held on pure faith. For example, you may have always thought that you were totally inept in mathematics, no matter what other people have told you about your mathematical ability. You kept your belief in spite of other evidence. Perhaps you feel you live in a very hostile world; no matter what others tell you, your belief stays unshaken. As a matter of fact, even when you want to change these beliefs about yourself because you are intellectually convinced that they are unfounded, they are still extremely resistant to change. It often takes the help of a therapist, a counselor, or some other professional to really modify these deep-seated beliefs.

AUTHORITY BELIEFS

When you were a child, all your beliefs were of a primitive nature; at the time you assumed that they were shared by the rest of the world. A 3-year-old may not only believe in Santa Claus, but also believe that everyone else holds the same belief. At some point, however, the realization comes that not all beliefs are shared. At that time, the child usually turns to authorities to figure out the issue. As you mature, you wrestle with the question of which authorities to trust and which ones not to trust, which reference group to identify with. You generally worry over the question of how to evaluate information about your world. At first, naturally, your family serves as reference group, but later you diversify your experiences and expand the number of groups with which you identify.

These nonprimitive beliefs do not have the same taken-for-granted character that primitive beliefs have. You learn to expect controversy and differences of opinion when you deal with authority beliefs. You learn that not everyone shares them, that different people have different authorities they trust. These beliefs are somewhat easier to modify than primitive beliefs.

DERIVED BELIEFS

Once you put stock in an authority for a particular belief, you tend to buy other beliefs from that authority, even in unrelated areas. The derived beliefs may not be based on any direct experience, but they may be held simply on the strength of the trust put in the authoritative source. This is the principle behind endorsement practices in advertising. If your favorite actor shaves with a particular brand of shaving cream, you may believe his testimonial and buy the product on faith. Would Joe Namath lie to you?

INCONSEQUENTIAL BELIEFS

Matters of taste are usually considered inconsequential because they seldom have connections with other beliefs. If and when they change, there are usually few consequences on other beliefs that you hold. To say that these are inconsequential beliefs does not mean they may not be held strongly. Nor does it mean that you don't think of them as important. They sometimes are. You may be absolutely convinced that vacations in the mountains are better than vacations at the shore. This belief is inconsequential, however, because if you change your mind, it will not necessitate a massive reorganization of your belief system.

Attitudes   Attitudes are relatively lasting organizations of beliefs which make you tend to respond to things in particular ways. Actually, attitudes are never seen directly. You infer their existence from what people do. If people seem to act consistently in a similar fashion in a particular set of circumstances, you infer the existence of an attitude which predisposes them to act that way. Attitudes include positive or negative evaluations, emotional feelings, and certain positive or negative tendencies in relation to objects, people, and events.

Attitudes are human responses, and they can be examined along three dimensions: their direction, their intensity, and their salience.

DIRECTION

"Direction" of an attitude refers simply to how favorable, unfavorable, or neutral one tends to be in relation to an object, person, or situation. It refers to whether one is attracted to, repulsed by, or simply indifferent to a particular course of action; whether one evaluates a thing positively or negatively. You like someone, or you do not, or you do not much care. You approve of birth control, or you do not, or you are ambivalent about it, oscillating between one direction and the other. You have attitudes on just about everything you know about. You will judge what people communicate to you about in relation to the background of your existing attitudes about that thing. When you do not know much about something, and thus have no particular attitude about it, what people communicate to you will usually help you form one.

INTENSITY

"Intensity" of an attitude refers to how strong it is — to how much you like or dislike someone or something. You may not like science courses very much, but your dislike of mathematics may be stronger than your dislike of biology.

SALIENCE

"Salience" refers to how important the attitude is to the person holding it. As mentioned earlier, you have attitudes on just about everything you know about. However, you do not attach the same importance to everything you know about. There are things in your life that are much more important than others. Salience and intensity should not be confused. There are some objects, people, or ideas you may have a very strong attitude about (high intensity), yet they may not be terribly significant (salient) to you. For example, you may be convinced of the merits of a certain toothpaste and buy only one brand — a strong attitude — yet toothpastes in general do not represent what is most important in your life. There are other things that are more salient, such as your attitudes toward freedom, individual rights, or pollution.

Formation of Values, Beliefs, and Attitudes

The point we wish to emphasize strongly here is that values, beliefs, and attitudes are *learned*. People are not born anti-Semites, conservatives, atheists, or football fans. They are not born fearing God and valuing freedom and human dignity; nor are they born convinced that a steady use of mouthwash will make them social successes. All values, beliefs, and attitudes are learned from the people with whom you live and associate. Because they are learned, they can be unlearned — that is, changed — although change may often be resisted (as we will see later in this chapter).

It is essentially through interpersonal communication that people develop prejudices, assumptions, and outlooks on what life is like or ought to be like. Your values, beliefs, and attitudes were formed through the various human groups you were and are exposed to, which "indoctrinated" or "socialized" you — and still do — in those values, beliefs, and attitudes they hold dear.

To communicate with others is to influence them and to be influenced by them, because any time that you have human contact with others, their behavior and what they tell you affect you. Any time you learn something new, you change and become a little more like those who taught you. This is what makes society possible. Interpersonal communication thus fosters the minimum uniformity necessary for people to live and work together. Sometimes the indoctrination is successful. Sometimes it has a reverse effect; the child of an ultraconservative parent becomes a radical. This common phenomenon may be explained in terms of what social psychologists call ''reference group theory''.[4]

Reference groups

No one is an island. Most of your ties, commitments, aspirations, and goals are related to other people in one way or another. You identify yourself with a lot of different groups of people — your family, your friends, organizations you join, etc. Some of these groups matter more than others in your life. Some may influence you more than others because you have a higher desire to belong, or because you have an especially great admiration for group members whom you want to emulate. Reference groups are those groups to which you relate yourself as a member, or with which you identify, or to which you aspire to belong, or to which you attach yourself either physically or psychologically.[5]

Reference groups are the source of your goals, aspirations, standards, and criteria for judging how you are doing. They are extremely important, since you use them to check on yourself and to evaluate your successes and failures.

Although it may seem like splitting hairs to differentiate between membership and nonmembership reference groups, the distinction is a real one. Being a member of a group does not mean that the group is necessarily a reference group for its members. Some of you find the grass greener in groups other than your own. Some of you belong to groups which do not entirely satisfy your needs; some of you identify with other groups to which you may not even ''officially'' belong. For example, there are social-climbing people who work and play at one level of society, at the same time complaining about its values and desperately trying to emulate another social set. Because of our highly mobile society, you often get caught by circumstances of geography or location in groups not of your choosing. Thus, your membership groups may not necessarily be your reference groups. A radical child in a conservative family apparently identifies more with some other reference group than with the family; a campus roommate who spends all waking hours associating with others besides the assigned partner has chosen another reference group to be with and may follow the behaviors of the other friends more closely than those of the roommate.

[4]T. H. Newcomb, ''Attitude Development as a Function of Reference Groups: The Bennington Study,'' in E. E. Maccoby, T. H. Newcomb, and E. L. Hartley (eds.), *Readings in Social Psychology,* Holt, Rinehart and Winston, Inc., New York, 1958, pp. 265–275.

[5]M. Sherif and C. Sherif, *Social Psychology,* Harper & Row, Publishers, Inc., New York, 1969, p. 418.

In addition, there is another consideration about reference groups which relates to roles you play. In our complex society, in your busy life, you have many reference groups — not just one — and in each you have a special role to follow. In Chapter 10, you will meet Jackson, the man in the middle. He is a father, a husband, an employee, a boss, a golf partner, a member of a church committee, and many other things. In only some of these reference groups does he play the same kinds of roles.

Although not all the reference groups to which you belong or with which you identify will demand that you change your role, there are often conflicting demands as you move from one reference group to another, paying attention to how you are to perform in each group. The multiple values of your multiple memberships may sometimes be incompatible. Usually the group with whom you most deeply identify will be most successful in shaping your values and influencing your behaviors.

You have, however, a strong tendency to strive for consistency in your positions in different reference groups. For example, if you do not find a job in line with your educational level, you are likely to experience great discomfort. Many studies have shown that dissatisfaction with one's occupation is greater when a person is overtrained or overqualified for the job. In part this relates to how you see yourself in relation to your reference groups, and it is explained by the theories of dissonance and consistency.

A radical son may be radical simply to oppose his conservative father, or because radicalism is a view held by the friends he associates with, or because he has derived some satisfaction from his communication with others when he has shown he was a radical. In any event, his belief is shaped by other people, including his father.

Stabilization   Once an attitude is formed, several factors are influential in keeping it stabilized. Many of you resist change and expose yourselves only selectively to new information (for example, when you read a paper which reflects your political, social, and economic views or listen to a political candidate you like and plan to vote for).

Many research studies[6] have demonstrated that people actively seek reinforcement and get involved in those situations which they consciously or unconsciously believe will reinforce their attitudes, beliefs, and values. This has important implications for your interpersonal communication. You tend to seek people who you think hold attitudes,

[6]J. Mills, E. Aronson, and H. Robinson, "Selectivity in Exposure to Information," *Journal of Abnormal and Social Psychology,* vol. 59, 1959, pp. 250–253.

beliefs, and values similar to yours. You choose to stay away from those people who you think differ too much from you.

If you cannot avoid exposure to opposing views, you listen only selectively and thus hear only those things which confirm beliefs you already have; sometimes you may not even become aware that opposing views are being stated.

Considerable discussion has taken place over the reasons which make the television program *All in the Family* and its leading character, Archie Bunker, so popular. One theory (fostered by the sponsoring network and some actors involved) is that viewers enjoy a program which pokes fun at bigots and which displays prejudice for what it is, and that a value in the program comes from laughing at bigotry and helping people understand their own prejudices. Both the reasons for watching this television program and the reasons advanced for its contribution to social change have been challenged in research reported in the *Journal of Communication*.[7] A well-designed American-Canadian study finds that the program may reinforce, rather than reduce, racial and ethnic prejudice. The study also suggests that many persons do not see the program as a satire on bigotry. Those viewers scored high on measures of prejudice. Many viewers (again the highly prejudiced) believe that Archie Bunker is right and that he wins in the end. Not only are some older racial slurs being resurrected and brought into common use by the program, but other researchers indicate that treating Archie Bunker as a "lovable bigot" reinforces the bigotry in many viewers. If you pay attention to information from your world in relation to your predispositions — your presets, or your ways of looking at the world — and if you tend to avoid uncomfortable situations which attack your attitudes, then perhaps your selection of television programs to watch is a significant factor in your continued drive for support for your attitudes, values, and beliefs.

Theories of Consistency and Cognitive Dissonance

As we pointed out earlier, a person can hold many different attitudes, beliefs, and values, and it is quite common for some of them to be in conflict with each other. A group of classical psychological theories[8]

[7]Neil Vidmar and Milton Rokeach, "Archie Bunker's Bigotry: A Study in Selective Perception and Exposure," *Journal of Communication,* vol. 24, no. 1, Winter 1974, pp. 36–47.

[8]F. Heider, *The Psychology of Interpersonal Relations,* John Wiley and Sons, Inc., New York, 1982. T. M. Newcomb, "An Approach to the Study of Communicative Acts," *Psychological Review,* vol. 60, 1953, pp. 393–404. P. Lecky, *Self-Consistency: A Theory of Personality,* The Shoe String Press, Inc., New York, 1961. C. Osgood and P. H. Tannenbaum, "The Principle of Congruity in the Prediction of Attitude Change," *Psychological Review,* vol. 62, 1955, pp. 42–55.

called the ''consistency theories'' (or ''balance theory,'' ''dissonance theory,'' and ''congruity theory'') deal with this phenomenon. These theories say (1) that people need consistency among their values, beliefs, and attitudes, (2) that the awareness of inconsistencies will produce tensions, and (3) that they will usually do something to reduce the tensions.

In his theory of cognitive dissonance, Leon Festinger refers to the same ideas when he states that (1) the existence of dissonance (inconsistency) will motivate people to attempt to reduce it to reestablish consonance (consistency) and that (2) when dissonance is present people will, in addition to reducing it, actively avoid situations or information likely to increase it.[9] According to Festinger, two major factors account for the occurrence of dissonance: (1) New events or information may create dissonance between what a person does and what a person ''knows'' or believes, or between two opposite beliefs. (2) Few things are black-and-white and clear-cut, and so most opinions or behaviors are likely to be to some extent a mixture of contradictions.

An example of a dissonance-producing situation is finding out that a close friend, a man whose opinion you respect a great deal, is politically engaged in a cause you despise. The two facts clash: that the person is a close friend whose opinion you respect and that he is supporting a despicable (in your eyes) cause. The clash will probably arouse some tension in you which you will try to reduce in some way. Dissonance might also occur when you get a low grade from a professor you admire and for whom you worked very hard or when you buy a stereo and find out later that it was considerably cheaper in another store.

Reduction of dissonance   You seek to reduce the tension generated by dissonant situations by use of several ''strategies.'' If you hold two conflicting values or beliefs, you will tend to reduce the dissonance created by conflicting information by changing one of the two beliefs, generally the least salient belief or the one with the least intensity. Let us say, for example, you believe that LSD is really not dangerous and you read a very convincing medical document giving ample evidence to the contrary. If your initial belief in the harmlessness of LSD is very strong, chances are you will reject the medical document. This rejection may take several forms. You may (1) belittle the source (they don't know what they are talking about; they don't really have enough evidence), (2) accuse the source of dishonesty or bias (that's just propaganda), (3) find new information which fits the belief you do not want to change (I read another report that said just the opposite), or (4) escape psychologically or physically (when you

[9]Leon Festinger, *A Theory of Cognitive Dissonance,* Row, Peterson & Company, Evanston, Ill., 1957.

realize that the report goes against what you believe in, you do not finish it, or you skim it in such a way that not much of it will create an impression).

Take the example of your highly respected friend whom you found supporting a political cause you despise. To reduce dissonance you can use one of several strategies. You can mentally change one or the other of the two conflicting elements, the friend or the political cause. If you choose to change the friend, you may decide that this person was really not respectable and admirable after all, and you were pretty dumb to have been fooled, and he no longer will be your friend. Consonance is then reestablished. You now have a person you do not care for working for a cause you do not care for.

However, you can elect to change the other element of the dissonance, the political cause. Here again you have several options: (1) Pretend that the source through which you found out that your friend belonged to the organization was unreliable, lied, or did not know the facts. In essence, you are saying that your friend could not possibly belong to that organization, and so consonance is reestablished. Sometimes, of course, such a strategy cannot be used—when you find out about your friend because he himself tells you. If he tells you, you vaguely make an attempt at reducing the dissonance by saying that he is joking, that he is not being serious, etc. But it usually appears soon enough that the friend is not joking, and you are faced with the conflict. (2) Another way to reduce the dissonance is to find excuses for your friend. You tell yourself he really did not know what he was doing, he got brainwashed in some ways, or maybe early toilet training is the cause of his turning out that way. Essentially, however, the friend is not responsible. (3) Still another strategy is to tell yourself that if a person of the caliber of your friend belongs to such an organization, perhaps the organization is not so bad after all. (4) Another commonly used option is to *compartmentalize* your friendship and the political views of your friend. This process, often used in practice, consists of discounting your friend's political views and accepting him on the basis of certain other merits (his faithfulness as a friend or his sincerity in his relationship with you). Your awareness of his political views is filed somewhere in your brain but is consciously ''forgotten'' or ignored. (5) Finally, you may engage in interpersonal communication with your friend with the hope that such communication might lead to more consonance. The push to resolve the disagreement with your friend will depend on how much you like the friend and how intensely you feel about the conflicting issue. You may discuss the issue until one of you changes your views after learning about the other's arguments and feelings. What can also happen is that you may end up liking your friend a little less and liking his political cause a little more.

The first four strategies are based on *rationalizations*. People have, unfortunately, a great capacity to fool themselves, willingly or unwillingly. You very often believe what you tell yourself simply because you want to believe it so badly. No harm is done when you tell yourself accurate things. Rationalization, however, always involves an element of self-deception. When you depend on this strategy too often, you run the risk of not being very much in phase with reality.

Resistance to change   Reduction of dissonance does not always involve rationalization strategies. There are times when instead of rationalizing away a new piece of information in conflict with one of your behaviors, you will simply change the behavior. For example, if you smoke and find out that smoking is dangerous and may lead to severe health problems, you may simply reduce the dissonance by quitting smoking.

However, it is never easy to change a behavior, an attitude, a belief, or a value. You tend to resist change because it is always difficult. You often regard change with mixed emotions. What you are used to, however unsatisfying it may be sometimes, still provides you with the ease that comes from habits, and a relative comfort from doing what comes easily and is well known. You usually feel more confident toward something you know well because you know how to perform. You also know what rewards you can get and how to avoid unpleasantness. You know the ropes. When a new situation presents itself (it may be a new job, moving, going to a new school, joining a new organization, meeting new people, or being exposed to new ideas), you are faced with a problem. Change *does* have many positive aspects: doing new things is exciting. It is a relief from boredom, an adventure, an opportunity to make new dreams. However, the risks are great because change always represents the unknown. You fear what you do not know well and tend to hang on to the familiar.

As Thelen pointed out, resistance to change can be self-generated and can also be encouraged by the group we identify with.[10]

1. You often resist change out of your need to maintain illusions of expertness — changing a behavior or a course of action might imply that what you did before was not good — something hard to admit. So you may rationalize your failures as successes (you did not accomplish anything today, but you sure had fun) in order to reduce the dissonance.
2. You often feel that a change is too much of a task requiring far more energy than you have. You resist making the effort and rationalize

---

[10]H. A. Thelen, *Dynamics of Groups at Work,* University of Chicago Press, Chicago, 1963.

that you just don't have the time for such major undertakings or that you will start tomorrow.

3. Changes in one aspect of your behavior, you fear, may involve subsequent changes in your role or position in relation to others around you. Even when you might be inclined to try out new behaviors and learn new things, you are afraid to upset other people's expectations, to be given new responsibilities, or to lose your place in the system.

Social judgment theory   In discussing attitude change, Sherif claims that your attitudes are best represented by a three-part continuum, or a range of responses divided roughly into three kinds.[11] The first range is your *latitude of acceptance,* which includes the various positions or ideas about an issue you are ready to accept or agree with. Along the continuum, the next area would be your *latitude of noncommitment,* which includes the range of positions about the same issue on which you are either undecided or neutral. Finally, at the other end of the continuum is your *lattitude of rejection,* which includes all those known positions on the same issue which you find unacceptable. For any idea or issue you may confront, the continuum would look something like Figure 14.

According to this theory, if you hear a communication message which falls within or slightly out of your latitude of acceptance, you will tend to perceive it as closer to your own position than it really is. This is called the *assimilation effect* (Figure 15). As a result of assimilation, your latitude of acceptance expands a little.

On the other hand, if you hear a message which falls in your area of rejection, you will tend to experience it even further from your position than it really is. This *contrast effect* (Figure 16) might even lead to a *boomerang effect* which consists of shrinking your acceptance area in such a way that positions which might have been acceptable or tolerated before will be definitely rejected.

How these effects operate in our communicative lives can be illustrated by a person who is, say, a Presbyterian. The rituals and the dogma of the Presbyterian church are a strong part of this person's acceptance area (latitude of acceptance). Other Protestant denominations are likely to be in this person's latitude of noncommitment. In this person's latitude of rejection are likely to be Islam, possibly Roman Catholicism, and certainly atheism. If this person hears something about another Protestant church activity, it will probably be considered positively because such denominations are close to Presbyterianism (demonstrating the assimilation effect). On the other hand, a message about

[11]C. W. Sherif, *Attitude and Attitude Change,* Greenwood Press, Westport, Conn., 1982.

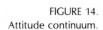

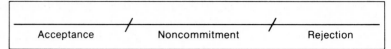

FIGURE 14.
Attitude continuum.

FIGURE 15. Assimilation
effect: A communication
message falls in the "latitude
of noncommitment" near the
"acceptance" area; the
"latitude of acceptance"
moves over to take in the
new material and enlarges the
"latitude of acceptance" on
this issue.

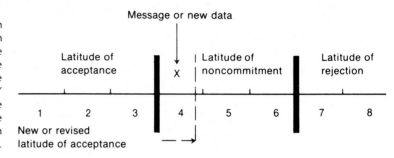

FIGURE 16. Contrast effect
(boomerang effect as
"latitude of acceptance"
shrinks): A communication
message falls in "latitude of
rejection." It is perceived as
more discrepant — more
different — from the original
ideas held and may under
some circumstances actually
narrow the person's "latitude
of acceptance" on that issue
if the message is threatening
or strong enough.

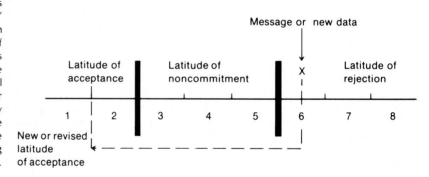

atheism will pull the reaction further away from any neutral possibility, demonstrating the contrast effect. This person is likely to think more positively about other Protestant messages (assimilation) and more negatively about atheistic messages (contrast) than the messages really deserve.

Another example might involve two persons with distinctly different attitudes about marijuana — one in favor of it, the other opposed. They both read the same research report on the effects of smoking marijuana. In the report are tentative findings that dangers may exist with prolonged use, and other findings that occasional use has not been demonstrated to be immediately harmful by itself. Each of the readers will tend to perceive these messages in terms of what he or she already believes, as we have discovered in earlier chapters. The readers also will have their attitudes involved either by assimilation (reading the mildly supportive messages as being more strongly supportive to either argument) or by contrast (reading the messages as being more divergent from original beliefs when they mildly disagree with the original positions held). What happens in many cases like this is that the person who starts reading an article will end up with previously held beliefs soundly reinforced because the reader can either exaggerate the strength of the supporting messages or downgrade the effects of the disagreeing ones.

Implications for Communication: Values, Rhetoric, and Behavior

Who you think you are is largely determined by the reactions you get from other people to what you do. Your choices to do or not to do certain things, as well as other people's reactions, are heavily influenced by how you define the social situations which you encounter. These definitions in turn come from the values and beliefs you share with people and develop through interpersonal communication.

So you come full circle. It is by interacting and communicating with others that you make decisions about what is good and bad, about what is beautiful and ugly, about what type of toothpaste is best for preventing cavities. In turn, these value decisions affect how you define social situations, what you expect from other people, what you think they expect of you, and finally how you choose to act.

Your attitudes, values, and beliefs need to be inspected often, since they affect so much of what you do and so much of what you are.

It is important for you to know what you value and believe in, how you came to hold these values and beliefs, whether they are adequate for your life situations now, and how congruent they are with what you say and what you do.

Perhaps you know the story of the young bride who cooked a ham for the first time and cut off both ends before putting it in the pan. Her husband was surprised but said nothing. When she served ham a second time and both ends of the ham were cut off again, he asked why she did this and she answered that her mother always did it that way. The next time he saw his mother-in-law, the young man asked her why she cut off both ends of the ham before cooking it. She answered that she did not know, but *her* mother always did it that way. When the grandmother was asked why she cut the ends of the ham, she answered plainly, "Oh, because my pan was too small." And so it is with many of your uninspected values and beliefs. You believe certain things and act a certain way, simply because your mothers, or fathers, or teachers, or friends believe and act that way. Perhaps they have a realistic reason to act the way they do, as the grandmother did when her pan was not big enough. But when life situations change and old beliefs and values are kept indiscriminately, you may end up cutting off the ends of a ham for no good reason at all.

This is not to say that all old values and beliefs are no longer useful.

This obviously, as an allness statement, would be inaccurate. We are saying, however, that values and beliefs should be examined, clarified, and chosen to serve a current need rather than blindly followed.

Much of the time you hold certain values, but you *say things* that may or may not reflect these values (your rhetoric). For example, you may talk about human freedom and human equality and yet deep down still hold powerful prejudices.

Furthermore, you often *do things* which may or may not fit either your values or your rhetoric. For example you may value sexual equality. You may reflect this value in what you say (rhetoric) and what you do (behavior). In this case, values, rhetoric, and behavior are in line, congruent with one another. However, it often happens that values, rhetoric, and behavior are not in line with one another. You have heard people say, ''Do as I say, not as I do,'' demonstrating by such a statement that they do not act on the basis of their stated values. This is true of most of you, particularly when your values reflect a striving for perfection. Most of you value honesty and integrity, yet most of you have lied or acted less than honestly on certain occasions. Your behavior was not in line with your values.

For appropriate communication interaction it is important to strive for congruency between what you value and believe, what you say, and what you do.

If your behavior is consistently different from your rhetoric and your values, you probably should wonder whether you do feel strongly about these values or whether you are just paying them lip service. If you say you love sports but play tennis once a year, swim a couple of times in the summer, and never go to a football game, your ''love'' of sports seems weak indeed and you may just be kidding yourself.

Teenagers have long decried the ''hypocrisy'' of their elders who seem unable to live by the principles they preach. Of course, none of us is perfect, and failing to live up to some of our ideals certainly does not warrant throwing out the ideals altogether. Yet if you are constantly caught in incongruency between what you practice and what you preach, the criticism is warranted. Even if you fool yourself, you may not fool others.

One way of looking at the interaction of values (V), rhetoric (R), and behavior (B) is to use an equation system to analyze your valuing, your talking, and your acting. You can look at this sequence in relation to any kinds of systems you are involved in or others around you. Here are three examples:

1. I believe that reading is a great experience and I value it highly; I also talk to others about what I read and encourage them; I also buy books, read them, give them to others. My values, rhetoric, and behaviors tend to be congruent: $V \cong R \cong B$.

2. Suppose I value religion as an important part of life and I talk to others about the importance of religious activities and observances. However, I never go to church or participate in any religious services. The equation would look like this: $V \cong R \not\cong B$.
3. Another example: I have a strong aversion to the use of alcohol, but I tell others that they should do as they please and that it's not important whether or not anyone drinks. I also serve alcoholic beverages to others. The equation would look like this: $V \not\cong R \not\cong B$.

These examples seem to imply that you know and understand what motivates you (your values) and how you send your messages to others (your rhetoric) and how you act (behaviors). It is not true that all the inner needs, values, attitudes and beliefs which you have are clearly known to you. Neither is it true that your words will have exactly the meaning you intended when they reach another person; also, you may not clearly form the message you want to send. In addition, when people observe your behaviors, they may misinterpret them for some reason, accidentally or on purpose. In other words, there are accidents of interpretation occurring at any of these three stages which may make it appear that you are acting inconsistently, when the inconsistency actually comes from how somebody (perhaps you) sees the sequence.

Incongruency of values, rhetoric, and behavior is not limited to one age group. Young and old, we all strive to keep these factors in line. Incongruency is also not limited to one set of relationships. You can act inconsistently among strangers as well as among friends.

Look at your *behavior* in interpersonal situations and check to see if your *rhetoric* follows what you know your own *values* to be. Strive for order in that sequence. Strive also for clear understanding from others by checking to see if they agree with your own evaluation of the balance you have among your values, rhetoric, and behavior.

BIBLIOGRAPHY   Festinger, L.: A *Theory of Cognitive Dissonance,* Row, Peterson & Company, Evanston, Ill., 1957.

Heider, F.: *The Psychology of Interpersonal Relations,* John Wiley and Sons, Inc., New York, 1982.

Lecky, P.: *Self-Consistency: A Theory of Personality,* The Shoe String Press, New York, 1961.

Maccoby, E. E., T. H. Newcomb, and E. L. Hartley (eds.): *Readings in Social Psychology.* Holt, Rinehart and Winston, Inc., New York, 1958.

Maslow, Abraham: *Motivation and Personality,* Harper & Brothers, New York, 1970.

Mills, J., E. Aronson, and H. Robinson: "Selectivity in Exposure to Information," *Journal of Abnormal and Social Psychology,* vol. 59, 1959.

Newcomb, T. M.: "An Approach to the Study of Communicative Acts," *Psychological Review,* vol. 60, 1953.

Osgood, C., and P. H. Tannenbaum: "The Principle of Congruity in the Prediction of Attitude Change," *Psychological Review,* vol. 62, 1955.

Rokeach, M.: *Beliefs, Attitudes, and Values,* Jossey-Bass, San Francisco, 1968.

Schutz, W.: *The Interpersonal Underworld,* Science and Behavior Books, Palo Alto, Calif., 1966.

Sherif, C. W.: *Attitude and Attitude Change,* Greenwood Press, Westport, Conn., 1982.

Sherif, M., and C. Sherif: *Social Psychology,* Harper & Row, Publishers, Inc., New York, 1969.

Thelan, H. A.: *Dynamics of Groups at Work,* University of Chicago Press, Chicago, 1963.

Vidmar, N. and M. Rokeach: "Archie Bunker's Bigotry: A Study in Selective Perception and Exposure," *Journal of Communication,* vol. 24, no. 1, Winter 1974.

Part 2

INTERPERSONAL TOOLS

Chapter 5

LANGUAGE:
TRANSLATING PERCEPTIONS
INTO COMMUNICATION

In a Nutshell

There is really no absolute way of knowing what reality is like. Your perceptions are only predictions — theories — about reality. You need to use language to translate your perceptions into something communicable to others. The relationship between language and the reality it describes is, however, not totally accurate. Language is to reality what a map is to a territory. The correspondence between the two can never be perfect.

When we use language, we classify. We also limit our perceptions by language use, and we say much about our own interests, our values, and our individual cultural heritages. Dialects and languages distinguish one person from another and encourage stereotypical responses in many of us. Recognizing how we respond to language is a first step toward bringing our language and the external world closer together.

LANGUAGE AND YOUR EXPERIENCE OF REALITY

Language is an essential part of your quest to figure out the world. Although you are probably accustomed to thinking that language simply expresses your thoughts and reflects what you see, this is essentially a naive belief. Meaning is largely a function of the system of symbols through which you organize and order whatever you encounter. Language directs your perceptions, and the pictures you create of your world are colored by the symbols you use. *What you say, how you talk, influences what you see.*

Consider how many times human history has been drastically altered and shaped by new ideas. What happened to humanity when someone jiggled things and came up with the radical idea of the wheel? Or when some "nut" had the idea that the earth was revolving around the sun and not vice versa? Or when Darwin had the idea that biological humans were somehow related to the ape through a long evolutionary line? Or when someone came up with the political idea that a person should rule and govern only by the consent of his or her fellows? Or when a white person realized that black people are as much human beings as white people and should thus have the rights to which all individuals are entitled?

Ideas such as these were, and are, not rapidly accepted because people intuitively realize that they will change the order of things. Yet these ideas slowly leave their mark in the history of our civilization. Because of them, none of us is the same ever after.

Language is your medium to think about and talk about such ideas. What you call "knowledge" is language. What each one of you "knows" is the product of your language. Language, or symbolization, is more than a mere naming of the things you bump into in your environment. Language lets you dream of things that never were and perhaps never will be. Language is the major factor in producing your perceptions, your judgments, and your knowledge. Language is the medium through which you organize, talk about, and make sense out of reality. Unless you understand the relationship between language (symbolic world) and your environment (empirical world), you are blind to the relativity and uncertainty which govern your universe.

The study of language is really a study of your way of living, a study of your way of perceiving reality. Although your perceptions are unique to each of you, you need to know if one person's statements about the world are better than someone else's. You need to distinguish between lunatics, careless observers, sloppy thinkers, charlatans, and those whose relations with the observable world are more orderly, more accurately observed and reported, and more honestly evaluated. You need to have a way to know differences. You need to know whether you are deluding yourselves and others in what you perceive and report. You must find out how to tell delusions from accurate representations of what's out there.[1]

In this chapter and Chapter 6, we want to take a close look at the relationship between language and your perception of reality, and between language and your communicative behavior. In this chapter, specifically, we want to describe how language stands in relation to reality and how important it is for the structure of language to fit the structure of your experiences if you are to (1) gain useful information from your perceptions and (2) communicate honestly with yourselves and with others. We want to increase your awareness of how language works and what language does to you. We are not concerned here with diagraming sentences, the parts of speech, the difference between *who* and *whom,* or Shakespeare. Our study will focus on the relationship between language and reality, between the symbolic world and the empirical world.

THE WORLD OF SYMBOLS

You live in two worlds: an empirical world and a symbolic world. The "empirical" world is the world of your actual living. It is the world of your firsthand experiences, your personal observations. It is the world which you get to know directly from your own senses, the one you can personally see, hear, touch, taste, and smell. It is the world of objects, persons, events, and situations, which you can observe outside your skin. It is also the world of sensations and feelings, which you can experience inside your skin.

Then there is the "symbolic" world, the world of language, the world of the words you use to name and refer to the objects, persons, events, and situations you observe outside your skin, and the sensations and feelings you experience inside your skin — the world of "symbols."

What Are Symbols?

A "symbol" is anything that stands for something else. Things can be symbols (a ring is a symbol for marriage; a uniform, a symbol for an occupation; a flag, the symbol of a country). A person may be a symbol (the minister stands for religion or the church; the President stands for the country). A picture is a symbol. Gestures (such as a clenched fist) and expressions (such as a smile) are symbols. A word, spoken or written, is a symbol. The word "chair" stands for or refers to an actual object which we can observe outside our skin. The name "Albert Einstein" refers to the actual person who wrote about the theory of relativity.

[1]Neil Postman and Charles Weingartner suggest, earthily, that we need to know how to "detect crap." See their book *Teaching as a Subversive Activity,* Delacorte Press, New York, 1969, and the references in chap. 1, "Crap Detecting," pp. 1–15.

Symbols in a way are shortcuts. Imagine what it would be like if you did not have convenient shortcuts like words to communicate with one another. if I wanted to tell you something, anything at all, about an object and did not have words to name it, I would have to point at it so that you would know what exactly I had in mind. Our conversation would be limited necessarily to the objects or persons or events actually present to our senses at the moment of the conversation. If you did not have words at your disposal, you would be extremely limited. Actually, you would not be much different from animals, whose survival depends mostly on being able to move around to get food and whose communication is limited to some groans and grunts. Fortunately, our ancestors very conveniently developed, littly by little, a symbolic code in which certain sounds or sequences of sounds have come to be accepted by those living together to refer to certain objects, persons, events, situations, feelings, and sensations.

These sounds and sequences of sounds were given "meaning" by the members of these human groups, and these meanings were shared by the group members. This was the beginning of oral language; and that was our first step into humanity, because oral language made communication step out of the boundaries of the immediate present. It became possible through the symbolic world, through the use of words, not only to talk about the empirical food to eat, present at the moment to the senses of the communicators, but also to talk about the food eaten yesterday and the food needed for tomorrow.

Words have become your link with the past and the future. It has become possible to store experiences in your mind, record them in your memory, and later recall them to yourself or to others. If this sounds quite insignificant, don't be misled. The ability to communicate one's experiences to others is essentially what made human civilization possible. When people became able to transmit their knowledge — the sum of their stored experience — orally to their children, and their children to each new generation of children, human civilization had begun.

Late-twentieth-century people are indeed the product of all the generations that existed before them. As a late-twentieth-century man or woman, you did not need to start your education completely from scratch when you were born. You could benefit from all your ancestors' past discoveries and all the accumulated knowledge which was recorded and preserved through the symbol system. You learned to read, write, and count, yet you did not need to invent the alphabet or the number system. We all have inherited this knowledge from earlier people in the chain of humanity who were able to transmit through spoken words (or written words, when humans became a little more sophisticated) the products of their experiences and their knowledge.

Symbols and Your Communication

What symbols accomplish, then, is to enable you to translate your first-hand experiences from the empirical world into a communicable version of these experiences. What you communicate to one another is *not* the experience itself but a symbolic representation, a symbolic picture, of the experience. The symbolic picture of an experience is *not* the experience itself: the words you use to refer to the objects, persons, events, situations, and feelings from your empirical world are *not* the actual objects, persons, events, situations, sensations, and feelings. It is one thing to experience a toothache and quite another to say, "I have a toothache." The words merely describe or refer to the pain and are a symbolic picture of the personal sensation you are experiencing.

This distinction is not as obvious as it sounds. Let's pursue it a little further.

We said that you communicate to yourself (we call this "thinking") and with others by using symbolic pictures of the experiences you seek to convey. When you communicate to yourself, the process is extremely fast, of course. You feel something that is hot or cold, and as you feel it you label your feeling, you name it, and almost simultaneously you tell yourself, "I am hot" or "I am cold." It is quite difficult to feel something and not immediately name it. Much of the time this labeling process is unconscious. When you communicate to others, the process of using symbolic pictures—using symbols to refer to a felt experience—is necessary and conscious because there seems to be no other known way to communicate a felt experience to someone else. *To be communicated at all, the experience must be translated into a symbolic picture of some kind—oral, written, or nonverbal.* Communication is oral when you speak words to one another; written when you write words to one another; nonverbal when you use gestures, facial expressions, and other symbols instead of words. The three kinds of communication are symbolic pictures, for all three refer to and are not the experience felt. The point here is that communication involves using symbols to represent, describe, or refer to whatever it is we experience, perceive, and remember. Symbols permit you to translate your perceptions into communications.

Symbols as Maps

To make this a little clearer, let's use the analogy of the map and the territory.[2] If you are planning a car trip in a territory you are not too familiar with, what do you usually do? You get hold of a roap map to become acquainted with the area so that when you actually drive through the territory you will not get lost.

Well, what is a map? It is a picture of a specific piece of land drawn

---

[2]Alfred Korzybski, *Science and Sanity,* 4th ed., The International Non-Aristotelian Library Publishing Company, Lakeville, Conn., 1958, p. 58.

by experts. It is not a free picture as an artist might draw it. It is a picture very carefully drawn so that the actual measurements of the territory are accurately scaled down and — the crucial point — the spatial relationships between different points in the territory are maintained within the map. The advantages are great: you get a picture manageable in size yet accurate; a picture which shows you, in miniature, what the territory is like; a picture which helps you predict or anticipate what you will find in the actual territory when you take your actual trip. Let's emphasize here that the map is useful only to the extent that *its structure accurately reflects the structure of the territory it represents.*

A map should not lie. If it lies, it misleads. If you are misled, your predictions don't materialize, and you get lost and confused.

If maps are to be useful — that is, help you make valid predictions — *they must present as accurately as possible the territory they describe.* In the case of communication, words are like maps. Words are symbolic maps. Words refer to and describe the empirical world just as a map refers to and describes an empirical territory. If you tell your little sister that "Columbus discovered America," you are making a symbolic map which describes an empirical territory which existed 500 years ago. If you tell a friend that you're going to quite smoking tomorrow, you are making a symbolic map of a future territory. When you say, "I have a headache," you are making a symbolic map of a territory you alone are able to survey. When you say, "John is 6 feet tall," or "John is a very good student," you are making a verbal map about a real, empirical person.

Just like a map, words can describe the empirical world more or less accurately, more or less precisely. Just as inaccurate maps mislead, words that do not accurately describe the empirical world mislead.

If you see inaccurate symbolic pictures, or inaccurate symbolic maps in your communication with yourselves or with others, you mislead yourself, mislead others, and hence are unable to anticipate successfully events in the empirical world.

Let's look at some examples of inaccurate symbolic maps which often lead to difficulties. Take a young boy whose parents think he would make a good engineer. They tell him constantly how good an engineer he would be and how much he would like it. They have built around the boy a symbolic world in which the boy has to be an engineer and has to like it. The boy is pushed into conforming to this symbolic world. He thus takes courses to actually become an engineer and does very poorly in school. In reality, he passionately hates mathematics and physics and really loves music, and he experiences a deep conflict between what his own feelings are, how he actually performs in class (empirical world), and what his parents' dream is (symbolic world).

The parents have an inaccurate picture of their son. The map they have of him is distorted. They see him as dedicated to mathematics and physics, although he is actually more inclined toward music. The inaccurate symbolic map leads them to push him toward a career for which he is unfit and which will probably make him quite unhappy.

This is not an unusual example of symbolic maps that don't fit the real world, and of the conflicts and grief that are thus generated. Ask any vocational counselor. Counselors' offices are full of students, like our young boy, who are pushed one way while their real talents and inclinations lead them a different way.

Take another common example. Friends of yours tell you about a great film they've just seen that you absolutely must not miss. It is *the* beautiful film of the year. So you go, and it's a flop. You can't see what's so great about this inane movie.

What happened in terms of our map-territory analogy? The film itself is the empirical world, the territory. Your friends' description of the film is the symbolic world, the map. Different people can draw different maps of the same events; film reviewers prove this every week. Which map is accurate? There is no one answer to that question, since it is a value question. However, if you knew *how* your friends came to draw the map they drew, you might be in a better position to evaluate what they were telling you about the film and thus not blindly follow a statement which may be valid for them (they did have a good time at the movie) but may not be valid for you.

One final example. If you make a mistake in your checkbook, so that your balance reads $150 when you really only have $100 in your checking account, some of your checks will bounce. In this instance it is quite important for your map to fit the territory. Repeated errors might lead the bank to question your integrity.

We are making several important points here, many of which are directly related to our discussion of perception.

First, *there is no absolute way of knowing what reality is really like.* There is no way to know whether you have a "correct" picture of the empirical world, since the word "correct" implies that you would know what the empirical world is like and thus could judge whether your perceptions match it. Since your perceptions are only theories—predictions—about the empirical world, the best you can do is test the theories by acting, behaving, and communicating *as if* they were "correct" and then observe the results you get.

Second, *to describe your perceptions of reality (empirical world) you rely on language (symbolic world).*

Third, *language is to reality what a map is to a territory.* The map is useful only to the extent that its structure accurately reflects the structure of the territory.

Fourth—and this is the crucial point—because the structure of our language is relatively static and the structure of reality is constantly changing and in process, *there can be no exact correspondence between language and reality, between symbolic maps and empirical reality.*

So here you are, imperfect human beings, forever encapsulated within your limited sensory equipment and within your even more limited symbolic tool—language—both of which you must use to understand and describe an ever-changing, ever-unknowable reality.

The fact that language and reality, maps and territories, can never completely correspond should not blind you to the fact that a good deal of the time you manage to predict your environment quite adequately. In spite of your perceptual limitations, you seldom bump into walls, furniture, people; in spite of symbolic limitations, you don't usually get the pepper when you ask for the salt.

What we are saying, however, is that there are times when you do delude yourself into seeing what you want to see and into distorting what you see to fit preconceived ideas. There are also times when you do not get the salt when you ask for it. You may buy the right kind of toothpaste or mouthwash only to find out that you still don't achieve the popularity implied by the commercials. We are suggesting that the symbolic world—that is, how you talk about what you perceive—must be treated with extreme caution. Maps are not territories. Words are not the things they represent. One person's verbal map of something may be useful to you but not useful to someone else. Verbal maps need to be examined carefully. Short of firsthand experience, they are all you have to help you in adapting to your environment. That's why you must evaluate carefully the verbal maps you make for others and the ones others make for you. This is why it is so important to develop criteria for evaluating the relative accuracy and usefulness of verbal maps, a point that we will develop more fully in Chapter 7, on semantic traps.

For now, let us describe the relationship between language and reality another way and look more fully at the implications for your communication of the noncorrespondence between the structure of language and the structure of reality. We'll look at the processes of abstraction and classification, and at attitudes toward language and reality.

THE ABSTRACTING PROCESS[3]   The world around you is full of ''stuff.'' There are sounds, smells, and sights—the noise of voices, cars, machines, and nature; the smells of cooking, smoke, flowers, and exhausts; and the sights of people, animals, signs, and objects.

[3]Material adapted from ibid.

This "empirical world," to use our expression, has things happening all around you. You pay attention to some and you miss some. You don't hear or see everything. You can't pay attention to everything at once. For that reason, you select those things you are interested in and pay attention to them.

In this respect you are like a radio. Think about all the different radio stations constantly transmitting music, news, and advertising all day and night. You neither see nor hear all that stuff coming at you — all those bombarding radio waves — without some kind of electronic or mechanical aid. Then you tune in the radio. It selects a station to pick up that frequency of waves, and you get a sound. Certainly the other stations don't stop broadcasting when you tune in only one of them. And when you change stations, what happens to the station you just tuned out? It goes on, beaming its messages of music or promotion in spite of the fact that you don't have it tuned in.

The world is like that. Things go on whether you tune them in or not. But when you decide to pay attention to something, you begin to take in a part — but not all — of what is going on and listen to it. You select — that is, you "abstract" (another word for "select") — only some of the stimuli out of all that are available around you. If you recall our discussion of perception, you are already familiar with this idea. What we called "selective perception" in Chapter 2 is what we now will refer to as the "abstracting process."

It is impossible for any living organism to pay attention to all that is available at one time, and so your responses are always selective. You usually abstract, or select, a very small part of what is going on around you. The term "abstraction process" refers to this selection, which takes place any time a living organism — including you — reacts to its environment.

There is a sequence in this abstracting process. Let us say, for example, that you go to the cafeteria and see hundreds of students moving in and out and sitting around. The cafeteria with its occupants, including a tall, skinny fellow walking with a cup of coffee in his hand, represents the total environment. Let's call that level 1, the level of *what is going on.*

Level 2 is *what you see of what is going on.* As you know, you do not see all; you pay attention only to certain things and not to others, and you may also distort what you do pay attention to.

These two levels are silent. You haven't said anything yet. You haven't even put labels on the fellow with the cup of coffee, and so words don't have to be involved. This fellow is, at level 2, just someone who caught your eye and whom you watched because he moved.

To go any further in abstracting, you'll have to use some kind of language or symbol system. You name the details of this tall, skinny fellow to yourself, and you begin to use language to think in, even if you don't speak to anyone else.

At level 3, you begin to put *labels* on this moving creature — male, tall, skinny, carrying a cup of coffee. But you also leave out details when you put on the labels. You perhaps saw, but did not describe to yourself, his clothes, his eyes, or his hair. You chose the things to notice and to name.

At level 4, you might say that the tall, skinny fellow carrying the cup of coffee is a student, thus *generalizing* from your previous observations.

At level 5, you might say that he is a human being, thus *generalizing even more*.

To summarize our discussion about these levels, we can say that level 1 represents what is going on; level 2, what you see of what is going on; level 3, what you say about what you see, in a descriptive way; level 4 and all subsequent levels, the verbal generalizations you make which are based on the previous abstractions.

Your abstractions are personal. It is one thing to feel pain and quite another to say, "I have a toothache." This statement involves three different levels of abstracting. The feeling of pain is at level 2, where you recognize something happening that is painful out of all the things that are happening (level 1). You tell yourself what it is at level 3. The statement about the toothache is at level 3, the level of interpretation; words about your silent experience are at level 2. Between the feeling of pain and the statement about it there is a reduction, a loss, a simplification which the word "toothache" does not begin to represent. The throbbing, the heat, the dizziness, etc., somehow get lost in the translation.

Remember the map-territory analogy? The territory itself might be considered level 1. That's where things are going on, where actual roads are, where towns are located, etc. The map is a symbolic description of what you abstract from that territory. The map becomes successive levels of abstraction.

When you begin to talk about what you perceive, you make a verbal map. Level 3 is a verbal map of level 2. And what you say about what you perceive can be at various levels of abstraction, depending on your degree of generalization. When you closely describe what you see — when you make reports of observations — you are quite close to level 2, the level of your perceptions. The better you describe, the closer your maps are to the territory. When you start interpreting and generalizing with your language, you get farther and farther from the empirical world, from the territory. When you proceed along the levels of abstraction, you become more and more general and thus convey less information because you have lost more details from the territory.

Example: You want to find your way around your campus, so a

campus map of all the buildings would be quite helpful. If you have only a map of the city the college is located in, it is likely you won't have a very good map of your campus and its buildings and sidewalks. The city map is a higher level of abstraction. It leaves out specific details you want. A map of the state will have your city in it, but not the campus roads (a still higher level of abstraction). A map of the United States will have your state and probably your city, but certainly not the campus (another level of abstraction). A map of the world will include the United States but maybe not your state and city, and certainly not your campus.

What happens as you go from one level to the next? Essentially, the higher the level of abstraction, the more territory that level includes. If you cover more territory, you are bound to leave out smaller details. *You are saying less and less about more and more.*

Another example: We say we own a "means of transportation." That's a very general, high-level term which covers a lot of territory, such as airplanes, cars, bicycles, horses, trains, boats, buses, roller skates, or motorbikes. Those words, "means of transportation," don't give enough information at that level of abstraction to really tell you what we are talking about. You want to know what kind of "means." We tell you, "a car." You eliminate the other things we listed, but even by restricting the territory you still don't have much of an idea of what we are talking about. You are closer to the territory, but maybe not yet close enough for communication purposes. Is it a new car, an old car, an American or foreign car, a station wagon, a sedan, a sports car? What make and model? What year?

The word "car" may be more specific than "means of transportation" but it is still at too high a level of abstraction to convey enough information to you. *To be as descriptive as possible, we would show you the car, and you could experience it at the lowest level of abstraction.* If there were no way to show you the car, then we could describe it in considerable detail, thus moving to a verbal level but still remaining close to the territory with the verbal map we make.

A communication principle emerges from these examples. The lower the level of abstraction — that is, the more descriptive and specific you are — the more effective communication can be. On the other hand, the higher the level of abstraction — that is, the more abstract and general you are — the more chance there is for confusion, accidental or deliberate.

CLASSIFICATION   What happens when you talk? Whenever you use language, even at a very low level of abstraction, even at the descriptive level, you are essentially classifying. Language serves the purpose of organizing the confusion of the multitude of things you observe at a given time into some kind of an ordered sequence of stimuli. When you see a person or an object, you are really exposed simultaneously to a variety of different stimuli. You will experience many different reactions and feelings at the same time. Yet whenever you start talking to yourself about what you are perceiving, your choice of characteristics to describe your perception forces you very subtly, but nonetheless effectively, to order the various sensations into something coherent.

Similarities and Differences

What does the word "classification" refer to? When you classify an object, or a person, or a situation, you are in essence saying that this object, person, or situation fits into a category which comprises objects, persons, and situations similar to the one you are talking about. You focus on *similarities*. Look at the book you are now reading. Take another book from your bookshelf. Look at these two objects. At the level of your perception, they are probably different. Different colors, different sizes, different types — paperback or hardback perhaps — different thicknesses, different weights, different words on the covers, different words inside, different uses, etc. Almost everything about them is different at the level of perception, and even at the level of description. However, when you call both these objects "books," what you are doing is *neglecting* the numerous *differences* and focusing only on the one thing they have in common, "bookness," *however that may be defined.* The important thing here is that the classification process is *arbitrary.* You classify these objects as "books" because you subscribe to a certain definition of "book" such as "a set of sheets bound into a volume" (dictionary definition). The objects you are looking at fit the definition; therefore they belong to the category. The definition of the category is arbitrary. To the U.S. Postal Service a book is twenty-four or more printed pages that are bound and contain no advertising. If you notice the details that show that your two objects have the characteristics that put them in this category, it is a personal matter. In other words, the fact that you noticed that the objects have printed pages and are bound comes out of your personal process of selection. Another person looking at these same two objects might notice only their weight and decide to classify them in the category "paperweight."

The same object can be classified in many different categories, depending on which characteristics you pay attention to.

As you know, you select what you see — the abstracting process — and thus classify things a number of different ways. These classifications are not right or wrong. They simply reflect different sets of criteria on which the abstraction process was based. Classifications are not neutral, however. They do something to you and to the things that are classified. If a woman were classified "guilty" by a jury, consequences would follow that would be quite different than if she were classified "not guilty." Something may be a piece of mail in your mailbox and thus protected by federal law — no one is free to tamper with it — yet it becomes trash when you throw it away, and it may be burned by the trash collector.

We must stress again that whenever you classify, you focus on similarities and neglect differences. "Rose is a rose . . . " may be a nice literary phrase; in reality not all roses are alike. They differ, even though you choose to focus on what they have in common when you put them all in the category "rose." At the empirical-world level, at the first level of the abstracting process, everything is different, everything moves, everything changes, everything and everybody is unique. Whenever you choose to group things and people in neat little categories and pigeonholes, you are simply playing a verbal game, which of course is very useful. You can talk about "houses" in general without referring to a particular house. Categories, at best, are shortcuts. When you say that a person is a "liberal," you are focusing only on certain traits or characteristics that you perceive in this individual. The same person can be classified as a father or mother, a husband or wife, a friend, a customer, a student, a citizen, an American, a taxpayer, a movie fan, etc. In each case you focus on certain characteristics that you perceive.

Classifying permits you to talk about things in general without having to refer to specifics. Classifications are not neutral, however. They help guide your behavior toward whatever you choose to place into the category. Whether an event is classified as an accident, an act of self-defense, or a murder makes a great difference to the person involved and will determine the way that person will be dealt with by the rest of society.

Classification and Language

Language and perception

To talk is to classify. You cannot utter a word without categorizing. How does this affect your behavior? You use language to describe to yourself and to others what the world around you is like. Language influences your very way of looking at this world and the people in it. Your perceptions are filtered through and shaped by your language patterns.

All you know of the world you live in is what you perceive of it, and this perception is colored by the language you use to describe what you see. Language is not just a tool which names what your eyes see and your ears hear. Language acts on your perceptual processes to shape these perceptions.

If we say, "She's smart," it sounds as though she has something inside her called "smartness." What we actually tell you is that (1) we have a category system about a quality we call "smartness" and (2) the person we describe has a place in our categories. If you say, "There's a car," you are categorizing and locating a public event in your language system. But in the real world, a better statement of this perceptual transaction would be for you to say, "I see a car," and thus relate more accurately the fact-of-the-car-out-there and your own report-of-seeing-it.

At one time the devices to restrain automobile drivers and passengers were called "crash belts" and were generally worn by racing drivers and sporting types. In an attempt to widen their use, the devices were installed in passenger cars and were given a less ominous label, "safety belts." But that term was still not entirely acceptable, and the devices have more recently been labeled "seat belts" or "lap belts," much more neutral terms suggesting neither disaster ("crash belt") nor impending danger ("safety belt").

As the anthropologist Clyde Kluckhohn points out in his *Mirror for Man,* language is a "special way of looking at the world and interpreting experience."[4] The structure of each language hides a whole set of unconscious assumptions about the world. Anthropologists and linguists have come to realize that the ideas we have about what happens in the world are not just "given" by external events. Rather, you see what the structure of language has made you sensitive to and has trained you to look for.

Many languages have different forms of address to be used with different people. French use of *tu* and *vous* distinguishes between those most familiar to you and those to whom formal address is appropriate; Spanish makes the same kind of distinction between *tu* and *usted.* While embarrassment may be the only outcome of misuse of these forms, more dramatic incidents have been reported in the news. On July 2, 1983, three seamen from the Korean freighter Tokai Maru entered a bar in Oakland, California, and began speaking in Korean to another patron at the bar. According to a report from the Associated Press, the bar patron took offense at the use of a familiar form of address used by one of the Korean sailors, pulled out a large-caliber pistol and shot the three sailors, killing one of them.[5]

In the Navajo language, there are three different ways to say, "It rains," accomplished by conjugating the verb "rains" differently. There is one form of the verb which means "It rains and I know it because I went outside and got wet." All that. Another form means "It rains and I know it because I am inside and I am looking outside and I see the rain falling." The third form means "It rains and I know it because someone

---

[4]Clyde Kluckhohn, *Mirror for Man,* Fawcett Publications, New York, 1963, p. 139.

[5]San Antonio *Light,* Jul. 3, 1983.

told me.'' This Indian language makes a distinction between the sources of information utilized to find out about an event. In one case, the verb form indicates, *in addition to* the information about the rain, that this information was gotten *firsthand* through direct observations. The second form tells that the information was gotten through *indirect firsthand* observation. The third form tells that the information was gotten through *hearsay*. In Chapter 7, we will discuss the difference between inferences and observations. In this example, you can see that the Indian tribe has incorporated into its language a very nice distinction between observations and inferences. The distinction has to be made before the rain can be talked about to know which of the three verb forms to use. Speakers are practically forced to make this distinction before they talk. In English, of course, there is no such need. You just say, ''It rains,'' and you do not need to know whether you know it firsthand or you just heard someone telling you. Perhaps, if you had to make the distinction to know which verb to use, you might not mix up observations and inferences as much as you do and take for certain what is at best only slightly probable.

Eskimos, who live in a snowy world, have eighteen different words to refer to snow. There are only three in English: ''snow,'' ''ice,'' and ''slush.'' Even when you add an adjective or adverb in front of the word, you get only a few more types of snow: freshly fallen snow, powdered snow, packed snow, and icy snow. This gives you about seven different kinds of snow. Where do Eskimos get their additional eleven types of snow? Each of their words refers to a particular kind of snow, different from all other kinds. Of course, they live in snow most of the year. Snow is a very important part of their lives, and they must know it well, for its consistency may warn them of changes in the weather, storms, etc. Therefore, they are quite aware of tiny differences in consistency that most of you would overlook. And if you have never seen snow, you might not even see the difference between icy snow and packed snow. A skier would. The Eskimos saw all the tiny differences in snow and made up words for them. However — and this is an important point — *the fact that they have all these words helps them see the differences.* Each of these words calls their attention to one little facet of the snow. It is probable that the words were coined originally because they saw differences in the snow, but that after a while the words themselves became pointers, pointing to one particular aspect of the snow. The words made it easier to perceive that particular characteristic, to perceive differences rather than similarities.

In English, there are many different words to talk about ''what we throw away because we don't want it anymore.'' We have words such as ''litter,'' ''garbage,'' ''trash,'' ''rubbish,'' ''refuse,'' ''junk,'' ''debris,'' and ''waste.'' As you know, our culture is one in which cleanliness is very important. So you know all the little differences among things that are usually dirty and that you want to get rid of. Of course, because you pay much attention to these things so that you can get rid of them, you learn to perceive all kinds of differences between them. Garbage is not trash. Trash is not litter. Etc. The more familiar you are with something, the more likely you are to perceive differences and to have a name to call these differences. And the name that is used to refer to something will point to one of its characteristics. Of course, the object has many more characteristics not covered by this particular name; but these other characteristics may not be perceived at all, since the name will not call attention to them. "I am reading a textbook" and "I am reading a book" will convey quite different ideas to the person you are talking to. In the first case you may be drawing attention to the fact that you are doing your homework. In the second, you may be pointing to a pastime — what you do to entertain yourself.

"Each language," Kluckhohn writes, "is an instrument which guides people in observing, in reacting, in expressing themselves in a special way. *The pie of experience can be sliced in many ways, and language is the principal directive force in the background.*"[6]

Language is a means for categorizing and classifying experiences and is not just a tool for reporting them. Your classification of objects into pigeonholes is established by our language through the types of things which receive special emphasis in our vocabulary and in our grammatical forms. To say, for example, "The rose is red" implies by the structure noun-verb-predicate that the rose possesses a quality which you call "redness." Yet redness is not in the rose as much as it is the effect perceived by your eye of that part of the light spectrum reflected by the rose. It may not matter much when you talk about roses, but it hits closer to home when you talk about qualities "possessed" by people, as when someone says, "John is stupid," as if John possessed an objectifiable quality called "stupidity."

Language and culture   Eric Fromm in *Beyond the Chains of Illusion*[7] explains how your linguistic filter permits certain experiences to enter awareness while others are stopped. Some experiences, such as pain, hunger, and sexual desire, and most incidents having to do with individual and group survival, have easy access to awareness. When it comes to more complex experiences, however, such as "seeing a rosebud in the early morning, a drop of dew on it while the air is still chilly, the sun coming up, a bird singing," cultural differences are noticeable. In Japan, this kind of experience

---

[6]Kluckhohn, op. cit., p. 140. Italics ours.
[7]Erich Fromm, *Beyond the Chains of Illusion*, Pocket Books, Inc., New York, 1962, p. 125.

lends itself easily to awareness. In our modern western culture this same experience may not come so easily into awareness, because it is considered too uneventful and too unimportant to be noticed. There are many experiences for which certain languages have no words, whereas other languages may be rich in words which express these feelings. In a language in which different emotions are not expressed by different words, it is more difficult to be clearly aware of what one is feeling. It is difficult to express subtle differences of feelings and emotions with some English words. You can love spaghetti; you can love your mother, you can love a boy (or girl) friend; you can love a husband, a child, a dog, horseback riding, reading, or "pot." The same word, "love," represents a variety of different feelings.

Language provides you with a way to cut up your environment into little categories that make it easier for you to cope with what is around you. But these categories in turn shape your perceptions because they make you more prone to notice the characteristics that make up these particular categories. When you call something a "pen," you are subtly made to perceive the ability of that object to write. If you had labeled it a "weapon," you would notice the fact that it is a pointed object. To call things or people by a name forces us to focus on the characteristics which are supposed to belong to any thing or person which is a member of that category. Thus, the words you have in your language force you to notice certain things and not others.

Language is not simply the means we use to get messages to and fro. Language has been, since recorded history, a force for maintaining power over others, for gaining economic, political, and social advantages. The language spoken by a nation is considered an integral part of that nation's heritage and its present impact on the world. When some languages seem to be "universal," in the sense that most of the literate world uses them, this is an indication more of power than of information exchange. Studies have been made of the number of world radio stations which broadcast in various languages, not just to determine how many potential listeners they have, but also to measure their potential impact on the thinking of people, since the different languages reflect the political, economic, and social norms of the nation of linguistic origin. Researchers find that even if the content of broadcasts is not, of itself, political, the choice of which language to broadcast in is a political choice. Religious and political messages are among the most frequent broadcast content. Transnational broadcasters use shortwave broadcast bands, and the languages which dominate are English first (by a wide margin), French second, Arabic third, and Spanish fourth. German, Russian, and Portuguese follow. On the other hand, the Voice of America broadcasts in thirty-six different languages (the BBC is close with thirty-four languages), while Radio Peking (broadcasting from the

People's Republic of China) broadcasts in forty-three different languages and Radio Moscow in a staggering total of seventy-two different languages.

With so many languages in the world, it is common for Americans to think of languages as the property of nations. That is, in the United States we all speak English of some kind; in Mexico, everybody speaks Spanish; and so on. We have a very oversimplified idea that a language starts and ends at a nation's border. There are, however, many different parts of the world where English is spoken besides England and America; there are also many parts of the world speaking French, Arabic, and Spanish. And there are nations within which several "official" languages exist. Linguistic minorities exist in many nations of the world. "If, however, the minority became large, powerful, or compact enough, it might claim special language rights, ranging from local tolerance for limited purposes to universal and equal status for all purposes under the jurisdiction of the state. Afrikaans in Africa, Flemish in Belgium, French in Canada, and more recently Basque and Catalan in Spain are examples of languages whose speakers have obtained official status within bilingual states."[8] According to the 1970 census, about 15 percent of the population of the United States does not speak English as its native language. Use of languages other than English is a controversial issue in many parts of the country. The debate over bilingual education is only one part of this controversy. The use of languages other than English in work settings has become an issue that involves more than the understanding of words — there is a tendency to divide workers by their language use, to resist promoting non-English-speakers, to find occasions to ridicule members of linguistic minorities. It is not unusual to have courts called on to decide issues of language use and to help determine which languages are appropriate. Laws enacted in Quebec concerning French as the official language are a classic study of a political nation-building mechanism of language planning and policy.[9]

Dialects   In any society it is possible to have codes within the main code, languages within the primary language, that only certain groups are familiar with and really understand. English as it is spoken in the United States may have begun in England, but most British speakers of English will

[8]William F. Mackey, "Language Policy and Language Planning," *Journal of Communication*, vol. 29, no. 2, Spring 1979, p. 49.

[9]In the Spring 1979 issue of *Journal of Communication* (vol. 29, no. 2) an entire section is devoted to "The Politics of Language, Studies of Language Planning and Policy." See particularly William F. Mackey, pp. 48–53, for issues of policy and planning; Allison d'Anglejan, pp. 54–63, for a study of French in Quebec; Alicia Pousada, pp. 84–92, on bilingual education; and Richard E. Wood, pp. 112–123, on transnational radio broadcasting.

hardly recognize what the "colonies" have done to their language. Of course, the original English language was itself a mixture of several languages, and there are many sub-Englishes spoken within the British Isles. Therefore, it should not be surprising that Americans have made some dialectal changes in the original. As English is spoken in the United States, it is really many different languages, too.

The expression "Y'all come back soon, heah?" stereotypes the language of the south. A Bostonian may speak differently from the Mexican-American in the *barrio,* the black in the ghetto, or the farmer from the Indiana prairies. Many of these sublanguages have their own rules, their own structure, their own vocabulary. This is true of such dialects as Chicano, black English, and Cajun. Many of the differences may be geographical, as language develops differently within a region. Differences may also be ethnic, or socioeconomic, or linguistically identified. Two people working side by side on the job, earning the same pay, using the same tools or facilities, may go home to quite different dialects, even though they may communicate on the job in an easy way. In the historical colonial empire of the British, there was usually found a mixture of local languages and the English language which produced a new language common to both cultures called "pidgin." As a spoken language, pidgin was adequate for most working contacts and could hold together those who had to communicate without learning each other's language. At the end of a working day or a communicative encounter, the English speaker would return to that linquistic pattern and the native speaker to the language of family and friends.

In the United States today we are developing a generally used dialect as "standard" for most encounters. It is taught to radio and television announcers and thus becomes part of the speech patterns of most Americans who are exposed to the oral mass media. This dialect is called "general American" and represents the largest of the speech dialects in the country. (Others are eastern speech and southern speech, as listed by most phoneticians who group American speech into these three basic patterns. Within any of these dialects there are many subgroupings which the trained linguist can distinguish.)

General American speech, through radio and television, comes into many homes where other dialects are spoken. And in some cases the listeners do not distinguish between their own speech and that of the announcer who is using quite a different dialect. Is general American, therefore, the "correct" way to speak English? Is it the only "standard" speech in the United States, putting all other dialects in substandard categories? Experts generally agree that no one dialect should be considered "better" than any other so long as it communicates meaning effectively and is appropriate for the situations in which it is used. This pragmatic look at language questions the existence of so-called inferior languages. The only requirements for effective communication are that the speech dialect have an appropriate grammar, useful vocabulary, and consistent phonology (if spoken) and orthography (if written).

It is a fact, however, that many people in our speaking world look at language as an index to a person's level of education, social class, intelligence, and even individual worth. To these "judges" of language, the language they speak is "right" and the others are "wrong." With so many Americans speaking versions of general American, that particular dialect may be the one considered most widely acceptable.

The early Irish immigrants in Boston, the Scandinavians in Minneapolis, the Germans in Milwaukee, all brought speech patterns or vocabulary or inflections which became part of a local dialect, even after the immigrants had learned to speak English. For example, there is only one place in the country where a drinking fountain is typically called a "bubbler" — a person using that term can almost always be identified as from Milwaukee. Substitution of the "y" sound for the "j" sound is typically Scandinavian and persists long after the speakers have become fluent in English. More recently, Puerto Rican linguistic patterns have emerged in some large cities. In the west and southwest, Chicano speech has emerged as a significant Spanish-originated dialect.

In the history of American education, there are many examples of linguistic snobbery and outright attempts to destroy a language system. Some early missionary work on Indian reservations included schools for English in which the native Indian tongue was derided, ridiculed, shut out, and generally subjected to an organized attempt to stamp it out. Children who attended such schools would go back home, where the native language was spoken, and try to understand why the teacher said that the speech of their parents was such a shameful thing. Trying to expunge a native language from an uncertain child was a cruel act of linguistic snobbery, as it removed from the child a real part of his or her young life. In some school systems today, it is not impossible to encounter methodological attempts to deny the usefulness of languages other than English. Some bilingual communities still do not recognize the potential of a person having two language systems, although we may greatly admire European speakers of several languages as learned people. Even the argument that some bilingual speakers handle two languages *badly* does not overcome the loss of personal pride if a young speaker of, say, Spanish, is told not to be heard using any words of that language — such a command cuts the child off from an important part of his or her world.

When people believe that one speech dialect is better than others, more prestigious, or the only way for educated people to speak, the consequences can be quite damaging to those speaking other dialects. This problem was particularly apparent among children from the black ghettos in the late 1950s and the 1960s. Because it was found that black children were not reading and writing at the same rate as nonblack children, some educators contended that the problem was caused by the "substandard dialect" spoken by the black children, which in effect made them live in an "impoverished" culture, inadequate for meeting the needs of schooling. The key to solving the problem, they argued further, was simply to make all black children learn standard general American English. Controversy immediately arose when some other educators took the position that black English was in no way "inferior" to standard general American English. The language of the black ghetto not only was valid but, they maintained, contained subtleties that were missing in standard English. One favorite example cited was the distinction black children make between "He sick," meaning "He is sick today," and "He be sick," describing a continuing or permanent condition. The scholars pointed out that in standard English, the child would have only one, less descriptive, phrase, "He is sick." They concluded that the ghetto dialect should have equal acceptance with standard English in schools attended by black children. These scholars emphasized a growing sense of black pride in black culture. Teaching black children that their language was inferior and holding them back in school, they felt, would damage their pride severely.

The controversy continued when other scholars maintained that the fact that certain language forms were used did not make them generally acceptable. They said that the "everything goes" approach to language was unacceptable because it really implies the racist view that black children are not capable of learning the language that other Americans use. They further argued that continued use of black dialect would hold these children back from success in our culture, where many people who speak the predominantly general American dialect are intolerant of people whose speech is "different."

What needs to be underscored here is the fact that "better" or "correct" language is not "better" or "correct" because of any inherent qualities in the language itself or because of any qualities inherent in the people who speak it. Language is essentially an arbitrary business. Common usage or common agreement is what makes it work. For the people who speak black English, this is a "correct" language, not any less acceptable than any other. For those who speak general American English, this is the "correct" language. Someone who never intends to step out of the black language community has little reason to learn to speak general American English, except perhaps as a curiosity, as some scholars learn Latin or ancient Greek. However, in our complex, changing, and mobile world, chances are that isolation in any one group, to the total exclusion of other groups, is rather unlikely. If you increase your repertoire of "languages," you increase your choices. The more tools you have in a tool kit, the more likely it is that you will find the appropriate tool for a specific job. The more "languages" you are able to master (and we do not mean only "foreign" languages), the more chance you will be able to fit your language to the varied situations you are likely to encounter in a complex society.

SYMBOLIC AND EMPIRICAL ATTITUDES

Let us describe now two basic attitudes people have toward the relation between words and what they stand for, between symbolic maps and empirical territories, between language and reality.

Symbolic and empirical attitudes are not clear-cut dichotomies into which the world can be conveniently divided. They are the two ends of a long continuum, a wide spectrum of human behaviors and responses.

Symbolic Attitude

A symbolic attitude characterizes persons who become so absorbed in verbal maps — in what is *said* about something — that they do not check the territory, the empirical world, to see if the words describe it accurately. Persons with a symbolic attitude are more concerned with their inferences, assumptions, thoughts, suppositions, and beliefs "inside their skin" than with the "reality outside." You behave symbolically when you rely on labels, on words, on verbal maps to guide your behavior *without checking in the empirical world to see whether these words, labels, or verbal maps have any validity and are accurate representations of the territory.* Imagine that you want to buy a used car. You answer an ad in the paper that describes the car as "foreign sports car, excellent condition, top shape, a beauty." If you bought the car without looking at it, driving it, or inspecting its engine simply because you relied on the words you read in the ad, you would be behaving on the basis of an unchecked verbal map, which in this particular case is not likely to be very accurate. Have you ever read an ad that said the car for sale was lousy, beat up, in terrible shape, and a real lemon?

When you respond to a rumor without checking its accuracy, you behave symbolically. When you respond to what you hear and read as if the words you heard and read were the real thing, you behave symbolically. When you are swayed by speeches, slogans, advertisements, and propaganda, you are behaving symbolically. When you respond to people on the basis of stereotypes, you behave symbolically.

Empirical Attitude

The empirical attitude characterizes persons who check in the empirical world the validity of what they hear and read. An empirical attitude is a tendency to inspect the territory *first* and then to make verbal maps to describe it and to correspond with it. The empirical attitude is the scientific attitude. The scientist makes a hypothesis (symbolic) but checks its validity by making observations in the empirical world.

Persons with an empirical attitude will not believe an ad and buy a car without looking at the car, without inspecting it or checking it. Persons with an empirical attitude will estimate the degree of probability of their inferences and will try, when possible, to verify them in the empirical world. Note here that we do not say that the empirically oriented person does not make inferences. We all make inferences. We could not live without making them. Empirically oriented persons are *aware* that they make inferences and are consciously trying to determine their validity by checking them in the empirical world. The empirical attitude is awareness that the abstracting process takes place constantly and that one cannot see all and say all. People who are empirically oriented are aware of different levels of abstraction and rely less on the higher levels (far from the territory) than they do on the lower levels (close to the territory).[10]

The Symbolic-Empirical Continuum

So far, it sounds as if there were only two kinds of attitudes, symbolic and empirical. Actually, most of you have both. You behave symbolically some of the time, empirically some of the time — and you should. There are situations which require a symbolic attitude, and some which require an empirical attitude. Behaving with the appropriate attitude is what is important.

Symbolic behavior becomes creative when done on purpose with frequent returns to reality. Great novelists, poets, and composers; imaginative engineers, businesspeople, and political leaders; people who have visions and dreams — all these operate symbolically in their creative moments. When you make a bold guess, you behave symbolically; and you must make bold guesses about your world. The nature of the abstracting process makes it inevitable for you to make guesses about your environment. If you believed only what you saw and were willing to operate only on the basis of what can be checked firsthand, your world, your reality, would be very limited indeed. A symbolic attitude is very useful and creative as long as you do *some checking in the territory to make sure you are not too far off base.*

A symbolic attitude is dangerous when it is self-generated — when verbal behavior and silent assumptions become split off from reality, from the empirical world. Unchecked, a symbolic attitude leads to habitual daydreaming. Prejudices based on stereotypes and categories can be very misleading. When you react to individuals not on the basis of what they are like in the empirical world, in your real contact with them, but on the basis of what you "know about their kind," you lose

[10]The formulations of symbolic-empirical attitudes are adapted from Korzybski's discussion of intensional-extensional attitudes, op. cit.

the benefit of direct observations which may go counter to public folk-lore and widespread prejudices. The mentally unbalanced man who thinks that he is Napoleon and that the rest of the world is mad is show-ing an extreme case of symbolic behavior. He believes the words he tells himself rather than evidence from the empirical world. Paranoid people are absolutely sure that everyone hates them and persecutes them, and they believe what they tell themselves repeatedly rather than what people actually do to them. Their symbolic attitude is so extreme that they probably distort the data that come to them from the empir-ical world to fit their inaccurate verbal maps. When you act as if the things you say about the empirical world make it so, you act symboli-cally, and these delusions may sometimes be dangerous.

However, most of you are not that extreme. Most of you float along the symbolic-empirical continuum, from day to day, from event to event. Being stuck at any point in the continuum is probably not very useful for your communicative behavior. You usually drift from one end to the other. When you talk about things like whether or not the post office is open, you may have a fairly empirical attitude and call the place up to find out. When you use words like "religion," "freedom," "democracy," and "Texans," you may drift toward the symbolic end of the scale.

At the empirical end of the continuum are the proof-demanding souls. If you say it's 60 degrees outside, they will run to get a thermom-eter and then report that it's really 61 degrees. They are the research-ers, the literal-minded persons, the absolute doubters, perhaps the cyn-ics who cannot accept anything.

There is a story about President Coolidge riding on a train through the Kansas plains. The train passed a flock of sheep. Coolidge's friend, who was riding with him, said, "Look at the sheep; they've just been sheared." Coolidge looked and replied, "Yes, at least on this side."

An empirical attitude is a fine trait in the laboratory, but it can be carried too far, to an extreme of foolish and needless doubting of everything that cannot be touched or experienced directly. When per-sons with this attitude intrude in your day-to-day social communication, their kind of precision becomes a bore. Some call them "nit-pickers." People like these, without some degree of symbolic attitude, some degree of inference making, can cut themselves off from many different things in the world. The important thing is to be aware of what is infer-ential and what is factual. If you cut yourself off from the world of vicar-ious experiences and sensations, you may become a hermit living only on firsthand contact with the world. This is rather limited living.

Language has long been known and respected as a force for mov-ing people to believe or to act. Memorable language has been associ-ated with the great leaders of history. During World War II, Winston

Churchill was considered a great force in maintaining England's fighting strength and determination. His "prose" was so much like poetry that today a series of Churchillian phrases still demonstrate the most carefully constructed use of the language. For examples: "We shall fight on the beaches, we shall fight on the landing grounds, we shall fight in the fields and in the streets. We shall fight in the hills. We shall never surrender."

A contemporary of Churchill, the United States' wartime president, Franklin D. Roosevelt, was a master at language use. One small story illustrates the dedication to the "right" phrase which made his rhetoric memorable. When the Japanese attacked Pearl Harbor on December 7, 1941, President Roosevelt went before Congress to ask for a declaration of war. Encouraged to use that time to develop a long discourse on the deterioration of Japanese-American relations, Roosevelt astutely said no. He would use his "fireside chat" on radio to the American people the next day to go into long details — but for his first dramatic message to Congress, as well as to the American people, he chose a six-minute address of remarkable power. He did not call on his favorite speech writers of that time, Sherwood and Rosenman, but instead drafted this brief message himself. Most of us recognize the famous line " . . . a date which will live in infamy." Before he fine-tuned his own speech, Roosevelt had written that phrase as "a date which will live in history." Roosevelt's choice of a little-used, obscure, but dynamic word made the message — as well as the word itself — memorable.[11]

Martin Luther King's famous "I have a dream . . . " speech also reflects the impact of well-chosen words which strike with power and leave lasting impressions on the listeners. Language from the minds and mouths of great leaders has moved nations and has caused changes of great importance in the world as far back as we have historical records.

How to Recognize Inappropriate Symbolic Behavior

When you seem to pay more attention to words than to the things the words represent, when you pay more attention to symbols than to what the symbols stand for, when you react solely to a person's clothes or personal appearance as a symbol of what he or she is and do not check any further in the territory to find out more about the person, you act symbolically.

Sometimes you react to words as if they were more than the things themselves. If someone says the word "snake," and you jump and

---

[11]For a discussion of rhetoric as poetry see Helmut Geissner, "On Rhetoricity and Literarity," *Communication Education,* vol. 32, July 1983. An interesting account of Roosevelt's writing his famous "day of infamy" speech is in William Safire's *The New Language of Politics,* New York, Random House, Inc., 1968.

scream although there is no snake nearby, you are behaving symbolically.

When you are exposed to a fact from the empirical world but refuse to abide by it and still cling to your verbal theory, you are behaving symbolically. Some people are very good at symbolic behavior. They much prefer to twist the facts to make them fit their theories and verbal maps than to change the theories to fit the territory.

No amount of saying that the world is flat is going to make it so. Some people still believe it is flat and will tell you that the pictures of the earth taken by satellites are fakes. To a lesser degree, students do the same thing when they receive a low grade on a paper and feel that it is not the paper which is mediocre, but the teacher who is unfair or biased against them, or the assignment which was lousy. At any rate, the problem lies outside of what they did.

It is often quite difficult to accept reality. It takes a very mature human being to cope with reality as it is and not as he or she wishes it to be. This ability is the essence of healthy and rewarding communication.

SUMMARY

In this chapter we have taken a close look at language and what language does to you — how it permits you to classify and put some order into the myriad stimuli of which you become aware; how it channels your perceptions and in a very unobtrusive way allows you to cut up the world into a certain shape; how the process of abstracting makes it impossible for the structure of language to be identical with the structure of the world it seeks to describe and give meaning to.

In our discussion of symbolic and empirical attitudes we have pointed to the need for checking the accuracy of the symbolic maps you use. In Chapter 6 we will describe the consequences of this noncorrespondence between language and reality and how to overcome common difficulties in meaning.

BIBLIOGRAPHY

Bavelas, J. B., and B. J. Smith: "A Method of Scaling Verbal Disqualification," *Human Communication Research,* Spring 1982, vol. 8, no. 3.

d'Anglejan, A.: "French in Quebec," *Journal of Communication,* Spring 1979, vol. 29, no. 2.

Fromm, E.: *Beyond the Chains of Illusion,* Pocket Books, Inc., New York, 1962.

Garner, T.: "Cooperative Communication Strategies," *Journal of Black Studies,* vol. 14, no. 2, December 1983.

————: "Playing the Dozens: Folklore as Strategies for Living," *Quarterly Journal of Speech,* vol. 69, February 1983.

Geissner, H.: "On Rhetoricity and Literarity," *Communication Education,* vol. 32, July 1982.

Kluckhohn, C.: *Mirror for Man,* Fawcett Publications, New York, 1963.

Korzybski, A.: *Science and Sanity,* International Non-Aristotelian Library Publishing Company, Lakeville, Conn., 1958.

Mackay, W.: "Language Policy and Language Planning," *Journal of Communication,* vol. 29, no. 2, Spring 1979.

Postman, N., and C. Weingartner: *Teaching as a Subversive Activity,* Delacorte Press, New York, 1969.

Pousada, A.: "Bilingual Education in the U.S.," *Journal of Communication,* Spring 1979, vol. 29, no. 2.

Safire, W.: *The New Language of Politics,* Random House, Inc., New York, 1968.

Sanders, J. S., and W. L. Robinson: "Talking and Not Talking About Sex: Male and Female Vocabularies," *Journal of Communication,* Spring 1979, vol. 29, no. 2.

Wood, R. E.: "Language Choice in Transnational Radio Broadcasting," *Journal of Communication,* Spring 1979, vol. 29, no. 2.

Chapter 6

MEANING:
IT'S IN YOU, NOT IN THE WORDS

In
a
Nutshell

Words don't mean; people mean. Meaning is the relationship you make between a word and what the word stands for. The relationship is created by people and is an arbitrary one, but it is usually agreed upon by members of a society. Meaning has two levels: "denotation," which refers to the agreed-upon relationship between a word and the critical characteristics people have agreed to have the word point to; and "connotation," which refers to the personal feelings associated with the experience you have had with the thing the word stands for.

Words have many usages which can be inferred from the contexts in which people use them.

Although each one of you can have your private meanings for words, it is only to the extent that your meanings are shared with others and thus are somewhat public that you can communicate at all.

Language pollution exists in our world of meanings to delude us, to distract us, to deliver us to sellers of goods and ideas. Confusion, ambiguity, and deception are three levels of meaning pollution most commonly found.

MEANING
Meaning and Communication

Language is your only map for charting the reality of what happens inside and outside your skin. It is the only tool you have for sharing and validating your images of these realities with other people. It is an enormously important tool which can be used for better or for worse, from which you can derive the greatest pleasures of shared intimacy, but which you can also use to promote and perpetuate the most insane delusions or fight the most vicious battles. The pains you experience from misunderstandings, as well as the joys you feel when someone truly understands you, give you an idea of the power of your linguistic tool.

A great deal of the misery you experience in your daily communication comes from common but irritating mix-ups with words.

> *"I know you believe you understand what you think I said, but I'm not sure that you realize that what you heard is not what I meant."*

In this statement is contained the core of the many communication mishaps that plague your personal and professional life. In this section we are going to take a closer look at the construct of meaning, so central to interpersonal communication theory.

Meaning is the key to interpersonal communication, and all the symbol-using you do is very simply meant to elicit a common meaning between you and others. The job of symbols is to make meanings appear in people's minds. If symbols elicit similar meanings in different people, then people "understand" the message.

Myths about Meaning

Meaning is often assumed to be a characteristic of words — something that is contained in words in a more or less permanent, natural, logical, and obvious way. Words not only are assumed to have meaning, but are assumed to have only *one* meaning.

The attitude which goes with these two myths is pretty smug. You feel that when you use a word with a certain meaning, then obviously everybody else will use it in the same way. You assume quite confidently that other people have the same meanings for words that you have — that is, if the other people are not idiotic, dishonest, or totally uneducated. The number of times you get into long arguments over the "real" and "proper" meaning of words still does not give you the clue that there is more to this business of meaning than meets the ear or the eye. Perhaps you know the story of the man who, when asked why a pig is called a "pig," replied, "Because it's so dirty."

In the next paragraphs we will take a close look at these two myths.

The first myth: Words have meaning

THE MEANING OF MEANING

"Meaning" is the relationship which you make between a symbol and what the symbol stands for. Meaning is *not* in words. Words are *not*

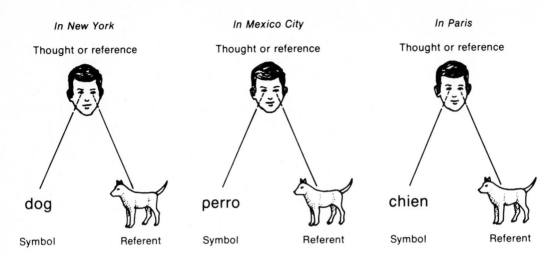

In New York	In Mexico City	In Paris
Thought or reference	Thought or reference	Thought or reference
dog	perro	chien
Symbol Referent	Symbol Referent	Symbol Referent

FIGURE 17. There is no direct relationship between the "referent" (the thing you are talking or writing about) and the "symbol" (the words you use). Only as these referents and symbols are related through the thoughts of a person (reference) do they have meaning. Meaning is not in the object or in the symbol but in the interaction of these through the human communicator.

containers. They are merely scratches of ink on paper or sound vibrations wiggling through the air. Meaning is not some sort of physical attachment traveling in the word, with the word, from one person's mouth to another person's ear. Meaning is in people. You use words to *elicit* meaning in people, that is, to call up a particular relationship between a symbol and what the symbol represents.

Caution: There is no necessary, logical, God-given, or correct relationship between any symbol and what the symbol represents. The relationship is made by people. It is arbitrary. It changes. Only to the extent that it is agreed upon by more than one person can it have communicative value. We will come back to this later in the discussion on connotations.

Ogden and Richards refer to the indirectness of the relation between words and things.[1] In Figure 17, we have adapted Ogden and Richards's original diagram so that we can compare meaning to a baseless triangle in which the three points are represented by an object, a symbol that stands for that object, and a human being. The relationship between the symbol and the object can be made only through the human being. The triangle has no base, because there is no necessary connection between the word "dog" and the animal running around. That you call the object by this particular name, this particular set of letters in that particular order, reflects only the fact that people at some time have agreed to do so. Thus the symbol came to *mean* the object. Actually, the word does not mean the object. It is you who mean the object whenever you use the word.

If you feel that this is linguistic nit-picking, bear with us some more.

[1]C. K. Ogden and I. A. Richards, *The Meaning of Meaning,* Harcourt, Brace & World, Inc., New York, 1959, pp. 10–11.

DICTIONARIES

Some of you might object to the statement that words do not mean anything at all. What about dictionaries, you say? Aren't they the supreme authority on matters of word meaning? Well, not really. Dictionaries do not set up authoritative statements about the "true" meaning of words but rather *record* what words have meant to certain authors, in certain contexts, at certain times. They also record the various *usages* of words at different times, in different parts of the country, in different contexts. Dictionaries provide us a historical record of how certain levels of society use words, but they can't predict how the next person you meet will use a word in a message to you. Dictionaries, then, might be useful to settle a bet on spelling, or on the origin of a word, or as a guide in playing Scrabble, but they will not provide you with the "true" or "correct" meaning of words.

MEANINGS ARE IN PEOPLE

Words don't mean, people mean. Meanings are in people. They are the internal reactions of the human organism to its environment. Meanings are personal—your own private property. You add to them, change them. But you cannot find meanings in unattached words. Meanings are in you, not in words. Words act as cues to elicit meanings in you and in others. To the extent that the meanings elicited in different people are similar, successful communication takes place. If there are no similarities of meaning, even if the words are identical, then communication goes awry. Meanings are not transmitted from person to person. They are elicited, called up, created internally. To use the word "dog" again: if we am thinking about a harmless little lapdog and say, "Dogs are good pets for little kids and are cheap to feed . . . ," what happens if *you* are thinking about a ferocious guard dog?

HOW DO YOU LEARN MEANING?[2]

Learning meanings is naturally associated with learning language, since meaning is the relationship you agree to make between words and what the words will stand for. The process starts very early, when human babies start imitating the sounds they hear around them. The sounds of 3- or 4-month-old babies are the same all over the world. A Chinese baby sounds very much like an American baby or a French baby. However, after not too many months, the sounds will become more and more like the sounds made by people the babies come into contact with, simply because when babies, for the first time, quite by accident, make a sound that vaguely resembles something parents can

[2]This discussion of the learning of meaning is based on David Berlo, *The Process of Communication,* Holt, Rinehart and Winston, Inc., New York, 1960, pp. 180–185.

recognize, they are rewarded. The parents are very likely to reinforce them by laughing, talking to them, and paying attention to them; and babies learn that this particular sound seems to go over big in their families. Therefore they do it over and over again. With practice and rewards, the sound gets to be more and more like the parents' sound.

But how do babies acquire meanings? How do they learn that this particular set of sounds refers to a particular object? Let's take the word "mother," or "mama," or "mommy" as an example. From the time babies are born they are fed, usually by their mothers. Food brings about a whole series of reactions in the babies. They drool, they make sucking motions with their mouths, they feel the milk in their mouths, they experience the warmth of another human being holding them while they are being fed, and they get full and contented after they have been fed. The babies' reactions to food are natural; they are not learned; and they are quite instinctive. What we have here so far are (1) babies, (2) food, and (3) the reactions babies experience in relation to the food.

Every time babies are in contact with food, however, they are also in contact with another human being, let us say the mother. Therefore we also have (4) a person. Every time babies experience food, they also experience the mother. The two are simultaneous, and babies learn that when there is food, there is mother. Because this happens over and over again, babies learn to associate the two stimuli (food and mother) and to them they are inseparable. Finally, babies learn to respond to the mother as they respond to the food. They drool when their mothers are around, even when there is no food. They start sucking motions with their mouths when the mother comes close, even when she brings no food. Babies learn to transfer their internal reactions from one stimulus to another. To them, food means mother. In addition, babies make another association. Mothers usually talk to their babies when they are fed, and mothers make sounds such as "mommy," "mama," etc. Now we have (5) a word. Babies learn that every time there is food, there is the person; and every time there is the person, there is this particular sound. Since they have already associated the food with the person, babies associate the person with the sound.

At this point, babies are ready for their third association: food and sound. The reactions they have to the food are now transferable to the person and to the sound that represents the person. To babies, the word "mommy" means food. Their internal meaning for the word "mommy" is thus associated with the experience they have had with their mothers. This experience starts with food, and of course, as babies grow up, becomes more diversified. As their experience with the person becomes more complex, so do their reactions to the person and thus to the word that represents that person. "Mommy" will come to mean other things besides food. It will come to mean love, play, cuddling, tickling, softness, warmth, spanking, etc.

The essential point here is that *the meanings you have for words grow out of the experiences you have had with whatever the words stand for.*

If your experiences with your mother have been generally pleasant, loving and warm, then your connotations, your meaning for the word "mother," will evoke something pleasant, warm, and loving. If they have been unpleasant, the word will, most of the time, evoke unpleasant reactions.

THE LEVELS OF MEANING: DENOTATION AND CONNOTATION
If indeed meaning is in you rather than in the words themselves, how can communication take place at all? How can you be sure that your words will be interpreted the way you meant them? Many times they are, and you probably don't run into a lot of semantic problems when you ask someone, "Please pass the salt."

Let us look at the concept of meaning a little more closely. If the things you talk about were always present to you and the people you speak to, you might not need a very extensive vocabulary to name these things, as you could simply point to them physically. When what you talk about, however, either is not physically present to you and your listeners, or has no physical referent, then you need symbols to perform the pointing function. This pointing function is called the "denotative" level of meaning. Words and other symbols vary a great deal in the number of details they point to, and they can in fact be differentiated into various denotative levels by looking at how many details they do point to. For example, the word "bookkeeping" points to more details than the word "dime." The word "business" points to more details than the word "inventory." The more abstract a word, the more details it is intended to point to, and the fewer the chances that you and your listeners will conjure up the same details when the word is used. Consequently, there are more chances for misunderstandings when highly abstract words are used. It is much easier to understand what is meant when someone says, "I want you to give me some salt" than if you hear, "I want you to give me some love." Many more characteristics or details are included in the word "love," and you may not be sure which of these characteristics was communicated. "Love" is a more abstract word than "salt." The more details involved in the denotative level of a word, the more chances there are that you and your listeners will pick your own special ones. Specific, less abstract words point to fewer details, and the risks of misinterpretations are decreased.

When you learned to talk, you basically proceeded through trial and error to figure out which detail was pointed to when a word was used around you. If you give an ice cube to a 1-year-old and say "cold," that sound could conceivably point to many sensations the child experiences, such as the shape of the ice cube, its color, the melting ice dripping on the elbow, the cold feeling, etc. Later the child might hear the word "cold" in relation to a drink of water. This time the child must remember which sensations from the first experience are similar to sensations from the second experience. The process of elimination is still not conclusive, however, because the two experiences have several characteristics in common and the child does not yet have enough data to decide which one to choose. Does "cold" refer to the watery sensation, or the color, or the actual cold feeling? Experiences will be necessary to isolate slowly the cold sensation as the one to which the word "cold" refers. In a sense, children are playing detective with language, and through a process of successive elimination they determine the common denominators between their experiences and thus the probability that certain words point to certain characteristics of these experiences.

This is basically how you learn the denotation of words. "Denotation" refers to the pointing process and reflects the agreed-upon relationship between a word and the critical details of its referent that people have agreed to emphasize. With very specific words which point to few details and have directly observable referents, the agreement on the denotative meaning of the word is generally widespread and there is little confusion about what is intended. This is why the "pass the salt" type of message does not usually get garbled and misunderstood.

Denotation is only one of the levels of meaning, however. The other level is called the "connotative" level and refers to the feelings you have developed in your experiences with whatever words point to. Connotations are private, personal, and never identical.

Because you are human, you have feelings in relation to every experience you go through. As you learn the denotations of words, you also learn to associate words with the feelings you experience. If the ice cube, the cold drink, and other cold-related experiences generated a pleasurable feeling, the word "cold" will elicit that pleasant association when you hear it used. The connotation of "cold" for you will be positive and pleasant. For someone else who experienced the bitter pains of cold winters without the comforts of a heating system, the word may always connote a negative experience. The important point here is that *the connotative meaning you have for words comes out of the experiences you have had with whatever the words stand for.*

Connotations are just about all you have when you deal with (1) words which do not have empirical referents and (2) words that are so abstract that they point to countless details. Words such as "justice," "truth," and "beauty" cannot be defined except by using more words, and their connotations are very likely to be quite different for different people.

IMPLICATIONS FOR COMMUNICATION

The fact that meaning is a multilevel concept has some extremely important implications for communication.

People have similar meanings only to the extent that they have similar experiences. Because connotations are private and are built on the feelings you develop throughout your life about things, people, and events, they can be shared only to the extent that other people develop similar kinds of feelings in relation to similar kinds of experiences. However, people never have identical experiences; therefore, they never have totally identical meanings at the connotative level. In other words, 100 percent successful communication is not possible. The Greek philosopher Heraclitus said that a person never steps in the same river twice. The person changes, and the river changes. Your experiences with your environment change constantly, if ever so slightly. As long as you live, you grow and change. If you do not remain the same, can you really expect other people to be like you? No two people are ever identical. No two people can ever live identical experiences. Even when facing the same circumstances, each person, because of his or her own set of filters, will experience the situation differently and develop a personal meaning for that experience.

As we mentioned earlier, some degree of understanding with others can be achieved because of the denotative level of meaning. Misunderstandings occur primarily in two ways: (1) with the use of those abstract and general terms which point to too many details, have no physical referent, or are likely to trigger many individual connotations; and (2) with the attitude that other people will automatically use words the same way you use them, that is, when you are not aware of the possible differences in meanings that people are likely to have.

That perfect communication cannot be achieved does not mean that you should not strive to improve your chances of understanding others and being understood by them. In interpersonal communications, much of your effectiveness will depend on how well you make yourself understood when you give others directions and how well you can interpret the information you receive from a multitude of different sources. Although it is unrealistic to expect communication to be perfect all the time, you can, if you want to, minimize the limitations that language places on your communication behaviors.

Having similar experiences facilitates communication. It is much easier to talk and achieve understanding with someone who has experienced things with you. A close friend will usually understand more easily what you are saying than a stranger.

Meanings are not fixed: They change as experiences change. Your experiences with things, people, events, situations, are never static. They change constantly, since your environment changes constantly. You change too. Even similar experiences are sometimes perceived differently at different times in your life. Your reactions and feelings about what is around you differ as you become different, as you see the world differently. Your meanings, thus, change.

The word "school" to 4-year-olds, who cannot wait to go to this mysterious and exciting place, means this anticipation, getting to be "big kids," all the nice stories their parents told them about what happens in school, etc. Two years later, after a year of kindergarten, the word "school" may call up the actual experience accumulated with their classmates, teachers, the building, and the activities. Still a few years later, the word may refer to homework, having to read books, learning, social activities, grades, failing or passing, being pushed by their parents to improve their grades, or not being able to watch a particular television program because they are told to go do their homework. When they are in high school, their meaning for the word "school" will have taken on still more connotations that will have grown out of their varied experiences in the course of their school career.

If they are popular leaders on campus, "school" may come to mean the place where they can exert some power and influence or a place to make friends. Or it may be a place to satisfy intellectual curiosity or a place to be totally bored. If our hypothetical students go on to college, here again, a whole new set of experiences, and thus meanings, will be added to their store of previously accumulated connotations. Graduate work will add still more; and if students become teachers, they will develop more experiences and more meanings. What the word "school" meant to you when you were 4 is different from what it means to you when you are 15, 18, 21, 25, and 50. The meanings you have for words really develop in a spiral fashion. You start with a very small association between a new sound and some kind of an experience; and each time you have the experience again, a new layer of meaning is added to the nucleus you started with.

You always respond to your environment in light of your own experiences. You often think that everybody reacts to things the way you do. It is difficult to think otherwise, because you feel that your own experiences must be somehow universal, but they are not. The ability (1) to recognize this fact, (2) to figure out what others' experiences are like, and (3) to try to see the environment as they do, through their eyes, is one key to effective communication. This ability is called by many names: "empathy," "sensitivity," "communication awareness," or "psychological adaptation." Whatever the name, it refers to a conscious awareness of human differences and a genuine attempt to see the world as another might see it—even temporarily—in order to understand why other persons feel the way they do about something and how they got to feel that way. This ability is premised on a great deal of curiosity about human behavior and a genuine interest in people. Communication often breaks down because of a lack of such efforts, because of the feeling that *my way* to see the world and understand it is the *only way* that makes sense—the right way.

The second myth: The fallacy of single usage

USAGE AND CONTEXT

To complicate things further, you often are under the delusion that one word equals one usage—one way of using it. Take the word "run" as an example. You can

Run a 50-yard sprint

Run a business

Run your hose

Have a *runny* nose

Have a *run* of cards

Run your household the way you like

Run out of time

Run out of cereal

Run out on somebody

Run over someone with your car

Communication would be rather simple if each symbol could refer to only one unique unit of experience. Of course, this is impossible, since (1) the world of experience is fantastically rich, complex, and infinite, and (2) different people cut up and perceive their world in somewhat different ways. By necessity our linguistic code is finite and limited (only about 500 words are commonly used in everyday communication), and each symbol in the linguistic code has to do double or triple (or even much more) duty. As a matter of fact, those 500 most commonly used words have over 14,000 different definitions listed in the dictionary, an average of 28 different meanings per word. Therefore, when words are used, you can never be entirely certain how they are meant to be interpreted unless you find out something about the person using them and the context of the situation in which they are used.

There is always an element of guesswork and approximation in the business of communicating.

We have tried to emphasize in this section that words have no meaning of their own. Meanings exist in people, and it is people who ascribe meanings to words by labeling a specific experience in a particular way (See Box 7.) If a given experience is labeled similarly by two different people, these people, then, are said to have communicated successfully, since the label will call up in their respective minds a similar experience. But remember: We are saying *similar*. Experiences are *never* identical. Meanings therefore can never be identical.

The clues for figuring out what is meant by a given word come generally from the context in which the word is used, that is, from the other words with which this particular word is used. A native of the United States will understand quickly the distinctions between the different

---

BOX 7. **Cocklebur and Lint Theory of Meaning**

As a humorous demonstration in a workshop, this "theory" was developed by the authors to show how we acquire different meanings for words based on our personal experiences. It is a way of describing the difference between denotative meaning (the cocklebur) and connotative meaning (the lint).

We found a collection of cockleburs, those seed pods which a number of different plants produce. They were about half an inch long, were shaped like a small football, and had a number of sticky, thorny bristles.

Each participant in the workshop was given a cocklebur to carry for a week — in a pocket, purse, jacket, trousers — wherever there was a place for this prickly little seed pod. At the end of the week all participants were supposed to check what had happened to their own cockleburs and compare them with those carried by others.

Cockleburs pick up lint from pockets the same way they attach themselves to the fur of animals, which is nature's way of distributing the seeds of the original plant. In a week's time the original cocklebur is nearly covered with bits of lint, threads, dust, and other collected debris, so that one can barely make out the original bur.

As the workshop participants learned, everybody had some of his or her own special lint on the spines of the bur, just as we all pick up our own connotations for words. The original burs were very much alike — the denotative meaning — compared with the differences added to the original meaning by our association (lint) — the connotative meaning. The analogy was clear.

usages of a word like "run" by looking at the rest of the sentence in which the word appears. Foreigners, however, get very distressed when they hear someone is going to "pull their leg," for they understand the words in their literal usage. And perhaps an older grandfather will be surprised to meet a long-haired, bearded, and disheveled-looking young man his granddaughter had previously described to him as "real neat."

PRIVATE USAGES

Language may act like a code. If you know the key to the code, you can decipher the secret messages you receive. If you know the people who send the messages, you can decipher even better the private meanings they intended to share with you.

A code is a powerful tool. It makes you belong to the group which shares it. It also excludes anyone who does not know it. In a given society we manage to have codes within the main code, languages within the language, that only a few privileged members of special groups understand. Do you use the same language — the same code — at home, with close friends, and in school?

Young people familiar with the latest slang can carry on a conversation which adults nearby might not understand. Most scientific desciplines develop their own language in an effort to be more precise and to narrow down the number of usages for a given word. To have gastroenteritis is more specific than to have a "tummy ache" or a "sore gut." However, the word "gastroenteritis" may be meaningful only to the medical specialist who has learned what it refers to.

The highly esoteric jargon of specialists can be an obstacle in communication when the specialists are not talking to other specialists but to laypeople. There is a story of a plumber of foreign extraction who wrote to the Bureau of Standards in Washington, D.C., that he had found hydrochloric acid good for cleaning drains, and was it harmless? The bureau replied: "The efficacy of hydrochloric acid is indisputable, but the corrosive residue is incompatible with metallic permanence." The plumber wrote back that he was mighty glad the bureau agreed with him. The bureau replied with a note of alarm: "We cannot assume responsibility for the production of toxic and noxious residues with hydrochloric acid and suggest you use an alternative procedure." The plumber wrote that he was happy to learn that the bureau still agreed with him. Whereupon Washington exploded: "Don't use hydrochloric acid. It eats hell out of pipes."

Can you make words mean what you want them to mean? After all, if the relationship between a symbol and what the symbol represents is an arbitrary one, if the fact that we call a chair a "chair" is just a convention agreed upon, then what prevents you from changing it and calling a chair a "stump"? Nothing prevents you from doing so, and much of the time you do call familiar objects by names known only to yourself or to the people in your close circle of friends.

However, the value of language or any symbolic system rests in the fact that it is a *shared* system, that is, a system known to more than one or a few individuals. You can make words mean what you want them to mean and play Humpty Dumpty (see Box 8), but then you sacrifice your chances of being understood by other members of the human race. Language with shared symbols is what binds us all together. If you choose to invent your own personal language, you are in a sense dropping out of human contact, for no one else will know what you mean. Unless you somehow have the power to impose your code (your language system) on other people and enforce it, you remain isolated. Schizophrenics may speak a language known only to themselves. Its form may sound grammatically like English, but the relation between its symbols and what they represent are known only to these lonely and isolated human beings.

BOX 8. **The Humpty Dumpty Attitude**

For those of you who use jargon, or have ties to dialects, there is a message in the speaking patterns invented by Lewis Carroll which can show you how your language can be turned into "jabberwocky." The story of Alice in Wonderland has some remarkable commentaries about the semantic world you may invent and how you may try to make sense out of word foolishness. The following selection underscores the importance of meaning and the effect it has on communication:

> "I don't know what you mean by 'glory,'" Alice said.
>
> Humpty Dumpty smiled contemptuously. "Of course you don't—till I tell you. I mean 'there is a nice knockdown argument for you.'"
>
> "But glory does not mean 'a nice knockdown argument,'" Alice objected.
>
> "When I use a word," Humpty Dumpty said in a rather scornful tone, "it means just what I choose it to mean—neither more nor less."
>
> "The question is," said Alice, "whether you can make words mean so many different things."
>
> "The question is," said Humpty Dumpty, "who is to be master, that's all." (Lewis Carroll, *Alice's Adventures in Wonderland, Through the Looking Glass,* and *The Hunting of the Snark,* Modern Library, Inc., New York, 1925, pp. 246–247.)

Yes, you can invent your own private language; but unless you can be "masters" — that is, unless you can make other people learn it and accept it and use it — you will not be able to communicate with anyone but yourself. The William Steig cartoon of the man huddled in a box saying, "People are no damn good" is perhaps the cry of bitterness of those who understand the imperfections and limitations inherent in all human systems. Yet communication, however imperfect as it may be, is your only thread of sanity and humaneness.

LANGUAGE POLLUTION

How Language Becomes Polluted

When language is used by people to say what in fact they do not believe, when words are used, sometimes unwittingly, sometimes deliberately, to cover up rather than to explain reality, our symbolic world becomes polluted. This means that language becomes an unreliable instrument for adapting to the environment and for communicating. It thus becomes unreliable for the solutions of human problems.

As with water and air pollution, too much garbage creates an ecological imbalance and survival is threatened. It seems that verbal garbage is piling up.

In his *1984,* George Orwell predicted that the official language "newspeak" would persuade the masses that "ignorance is strength" and "war is peace." Orwell wrote in 1949 that "the day to day falsification of the past carried out by the Ministry of Truth is as necessary to the stability of the regime as the work of repression and espionage carried out by the Ministry of Love."

A member of the editorial board of the *New York Times* thinks that we are well on our way to newspeak or, as he calls it, "doublespeak."[3] For example, the word "poverty" has been eliminated and replaced by "low income," a less alarming term. "Slums" and "ghettos" have long given way to the "inner city." "Prisons" are "correctional facilities."

The Nixon administration was noted for its word manipulation. Government officials were not "fired" but "selected out," and in some instances "terminated." Watergate doublespeak labeled "inoperative" a statement Richard Nixon had made earlier which later turned out not to have been true. The actions of a Watergate witness were labeled, not "wrong," but "inappropriate in the particular time frame."

In each case, the purpose of the euphemism, or pleasant substitute, was to make things appear better than they were or seem what they were not. This is not just a matter of semantics. In Hechinger's words, "Linguistic cosmetics are often used to create the impression that nasty problems have already been solved or were not really too nasty in the

[3]Fred M. Hechinger, "In the End Was the Euphemism," *Saturday Review World,* Sept. 3, 1974, pp. 50–52.

first place. The result: smug lack of concern. Inaction. A comfortable rest on political or even pedagogical laurels."[4]

When in the language of the bureaucrats[5]

"Doubtless"	means	"unverified"
"Interesting fact"	means	"drivel"
"Universally recognized principle	means	"a risky proposition"
"We are assigning major priority to the early completion of the preliminary stages of the program	means	"With any luck we can forget the matter completely"

or when the stationery of the Department of the Air Force in the Department of Defense carries the motto "Peace Is Our Profession," the index of language pollution has risen.

Some affectionate names have been given to the words which we use to obscure information. "Gobbledygook" is one such name, generally considered to be derived from the noise turkeys make when they are just sounding off and making no sense. Often gobbledygook will be used to confuse the reader or listener and to make that person feel "one down" for not understanding the jargon. A person originating such gobbledygook appears to be giving the message: "I know this stuff so well and you, stupid you, can't be expected to understand it anyway." Some conversations with computer owners fall into this category; they say such things as: "When I boot the machine, using 256K takes longer to get me a prompt, so maybe I'd better switch to a hard-disk system." Notice that there are not many long or difficult-to-pronounce words in that sentence, but you still can be made to feel left out or ignorant if you don't know the special jargon. Another term for such language is "bafflegab." Bafflegab is characterized by words providing more confusion than clarity. William Safire reports these examples of bafflegab about the economic status of the nation: "healthy slowdown," "rolling readjustment," "high-level stagnation," and "mini-slump," to refer to a recession.[6]

Writing for the Bureau of Land Management in Denver, Colorado,

---

[4]Ibid, p. 50.

[5]Examples taken from Henry A. Barnes, "The Language of Bureaucracy," in Neil Postman, Charles Weingartner, and Terrence Moran (eds.), *Language in America,* Pegasus, New York, 1969, pp. 46–53.

[6]William Safire, *The New Language of Politics,* Random House, Inc., New York, 1968, p. 26.

John O'Hayre, a federal employee, found this profoundly pumped-up paragraph:

A basic, although often ignored conservation principle in land treatment practices is the alignment of these practices to contour operations. Contour alignment, manifested in the direction of implement travel provides an effective and complementary attack on the forces of erosion. When soil surface disturbances run up and down hill, it is easily understood that artificial channels are formed in which run-off accumulates. As the slope of these channels increases, the velocity of the water movement accelerates, with resulting destructive energies." In the interest of training others to resist gobbledygook, O'Hayre rewrote the paragraph in direct terms as: *"In doing conservation work, always work on the contour if possible. That is the best way to control erosion.*[7]

Slogans are special cases of language pollution through distortion of meaning. The word "slogan" comes originally from the Gaelic *sluagh,* or "army," and *gairm,* or "a call," which gives us "a call to arms." For that reason slogans have always been short, uncomplicated, given to almost instant interpretation and action without a lot of confusing extra modifiers or disclaimers. "Yankee go home," a slogan, is more effective than saying: "Americans who don't appreciate us in this country ought to go back where they came from." In his book *Public Opinion,* Walter Lippman developed the argument that slogans are shortcuts to thinking and convenient ways to move a society through difficult and complex issues.[8] Slogans must be simple; they must be timely; they must have a rhythm to them; and above all they must appeal to a large number of people to be effective — that is, their meaning must have some importance to many people. Advertising slogans are very familiar to all of us. Effective ones fit the rules mentioned above, and advertisers spend millions to develop slogans which represent their products to a large group of people, are simple, offer a lot, and are timely and catchy. "Ford has a better idea"; "Things go better with Coke" (referring to a bottled soft drink); "Never had it, and never will" (referring to Coca Cola's competition, which is caffeine-free); "When you care enough to send the very best"; "Say it with flowers"; "Tonight make it Lowenbrau"; "Only your hairdresser knows"; "Diamonds are forever" — these are a few of the memorable slogans used by advertisers to impress a quick, unambiguous message on a busy public.

Embellishment is another form of word pollution. In this case, a simple statement is made ("No, you can't go to Suzie's house") and it gets

---

[7] *The Denver Post,* Nov. 7, 1965.
[8] Walter Lippmann, *Public Opinion,* The Free Press, New York, 1965, pp. 3–49.

blown out of proportion by a paraphrase of it ("Mom says that I have to stay home and that Suzie's house if off limits to me, probably forever.") The embellished form of "No comment" often appears in our news media as: "The official whose opinion was sought in an attempt to get the other side of the issue refused to be interviewed for this broadcast, and we were not able to secure any comment from him." Exaggeration of meaning is not always done deliberately, but it makes our reports more dramatic when we want to avoid being dull. During the term of Jimmy Carter's presidency, the press made bigger stories out of little ones in an attempt to dramatize his actions. When the President was paddling down a southern stream in a canoe, a rabbit swam by and Carter slapped at it, giving rise to news reports of the President being attacked by a mad, swimming bunny and having to defend himself with the only weapon at hand, a canoe paddle. Safire reports a similar anecdote, attributed to Henry Suydam, when Coolidge was president.[9] President Coolidge, known for his brevity of language, would say, "I'm not in favor of that legislation," and the next day the press would report: "President Coolidge, in a fighting mood, today served notice on Congress that he intended to combat with all the resources at his command . . . "

Three Levels of Polluted Meaning

When an intended meaning is successfully selected by someone else from among the many possible meanings, we feel good. "She really understood what I was trying to say . . . "; "I made it quite clear . . . "; "He got it . . . "; "They followed the instructions to the letter . . . "; and "We did exactly as we were told to do . . . " are all examples of satisfied, and maybe even surprised, comments on message-sent-was-message-received. Too often, something is missing from the meaning received as compared with the meaning intended. Or we intentionally mislead another. Let's look at three dimensions of meaning pollution, both unintentional and intentional. These categories may not be separate little boxes so much as overlapping positions on a scale, not discrete measures so much as general ranges of misleading construct of meaning. The categories are summarized in Table 3.

Confusion

Confusion is the first level. This occurs most frequently when language is unfamiliar and when ideas are complex. A person speaks a foreign language to you, and you are confused by the attempt at meaning. You don't get it. Or you are confused by an overload of information, or by words that are not familiar to you. You have no "referent" for the symbols. This leaves big blanks in your information. Confusion is disorder, chaos, being bewildered or perplexed. You really have no basis for

[9]William Safire, op. cit., p. 202.

TABLE 3. **Common Classes of Language Pollution**

Pollution type	Characteristics (how they show up in your communication)	Some communication correctives
Confusion (unknown meanings)	Foreign language Unfamiliar words Technical jargon Misused terminology	Ask for a translation. Ask for a definition of terms, or a restatement in other, more familiar terms, or a more direct statement.
Ambiguity (too many meanings)	Too many possible ways to define the words Vague references, hints Very general, imprecise statements or terms	Check to find out which meaning is really intended. Ask for more details. Seek examples, instances, clear cases.
Deception (obscured meanings)	Outright lies Distortions of data Incomplete data or careless reporting Nonanswers to direct questions	Confront with your own information. Seek some common or public data to check from. Ask for clarification, restatement. Rephrase questions if you don't get clear or adequate answers.

knowing. The best way out of this confusion is to start over — translate the language, develop a common referent, use words that apply to the person who is being addressed. Example: "As to the wiring for the interface, be sure to use twisted-pair cable for each signal and never fail to complete connection on the Return side" (instructions in a computer printer manual). The words may be familiar to you, but there is no referent for any of them; you end up being confused as to what to do.

Ambiguity   Ambiguity is the second level. This occurs most frequently when your choices of what to do are far greater than the "right" answer will tolerate. As compared with "confusion," which occurs when you don't know what to do or how to start, in ambiguous meanings there are too many possible ways to interpret the messages. Ambiguous messages are capable of being understood, but in more than one sense. They are often called "double meaning" messages. The words are equivocal, leaving you uncertain as to how to respond or act. Example: "When you go to the store, pick up something for supper." Does this mean the main dish, or just the meat, or a whole dinner's worth of groceries? "Something" is an ambiguous word, as are "sometime," "early," "easy," "often," etc. "Come over to see us some time . . ." is considered by many as so ambiguous as to be no invitation at all. Ambiguity may be created on purpose when you don't want to be pinned down, aren't certain of an answer, or don't know how to explain something. You can avoid being responsible for your statements if you put in sufficient ambiguity—nobody can pin you down to what you *really* said. Ambiguity can also be the result of careless use of words or of your assumption that your meanings are the same as the meanings in others. You may not actually intend to mislead another person, but because your words are not precise—not clear, not part of the other's referent system—some pollution of your meaning systems will occur.[10]

Deception   Deception is the third level. This occurs most frequently when you do not want another person to know something, or when you want him or her to behave in a certain way. You set out to trick that person, to delude or divert or defraud. Although there is an ethical consideration here, we are concerned also with the effects of this practice as a common device in our communication. Some deception may be harmless — a magician fooling an audience with sleight-of-hand, for example. Relatively harmless rhetoric goes into planning a surprise birthday party or responding to insistent questions like "How do you like my new hat?" Little white lies are often considered socially acceptable forms of deception if feelings or sensibilities are spared. Example: After the rather sudden death of his wife, a man we know approached the attending physician and in a tearful voice asked, "Doctor, was there anything I should have done that I didn't do?" The doctor proceeded to tell the bereaved husband that he should have brought his wife in for an examination many weeks earlier. Deception at that moment might have greatly relieved the guilt felt by the grieving widower. Much of the time we engage in deception because we want to protect ourselves or our self-image. We also find it useful to keep from getting into trouble. Example: "Did you do the dishes?" Answer: "I put them in the sink." Another example: "What time did you get in last night?" Answer: "I

---

[10]For two interesting articles related to unclear meanings, see Janet Beavin Bavelas, "Situations That Lead to Disqualification," in *Human Communication Research*, vol. 9, no. 2, Winter 1983, pp. 130–145, and Linda L. Putnam and Ritch L. Sorenson, "Equivocal Messages in Organizations," in *Human Communication Research*, vol. 8, no. 2, Winter 1982, pp. 114–132.

didn't look at the clock." Another example: "How much did that new sweater cost?" Answer: "I got it on sale." Too often we settle for the answer to some other question. ("Did you get the sweater on sale?" "Did you look at the clock when you came in last night?" "Did you just put the dishes in the sink, or did you wash them?") Deception does not have to be outright lies. It can be, and usually is, a more subtle pollution of the meaning experience by changing references or by answering questions others than those asked.

BIBLIOGRAPHY

Bavelas, J. B.: "Situations that Lead to Disqualification," *Human Communication Research,* vol. 9, no. 2., Winter 1983.

Berlo, D. K.: *The Process of Communication,* Holt, Rinehart and Winston, Inc., New York, 1960.

Cronen, V. E., W. B. Pearce, and L. Harris: "The Coordinated Management of Meaning: A Theory of Communication," in F. E. X. Dance (ed.), *Human Communication Theory,* Harper and Row, Inc., New York, 1982.

Hechinger, F. M.: "In the End Was the Euphemism," *Saturday Review World,* Sept. 3, 1974.

Lippmann, W.: *Public Opinion,* The Free Press, New York, 1965.

Ogden, C. K., and I. A. Richards: *The Meaning of Meaning,* Harcourt, Brace & World, Inc., New York, 1959.

Postman, N., C. Weingartner, and T. Moran (eds.): *Language in America,* Pegasus, New York, 1969.

Putnam, L. L., and R. L. Sorenson: "Equivocal Messages in Organizations," *Human Communication Research,* vol. 8, no. 2, Winter 1982.

Safire, W.: *The New Language of Politics,* Random House, Inc., New York, 1968.

Chapter 7

SEMANTIC TRAPS:
HOW TO AVOID THEM

In a Nutshell

The less-than-perfect fit between language and reality creates semantic traps which you need to avoid to enhance your interpersonal communication.

Stereotyping, labeling, polarizing, allness, frozen evaluations, and confusing observations and inferences are the most common semantic traps which affect interpersonal communication.

There are many ways to avoid these traps and help remove barriers to interpersonal communication.

You may adopt a scientific approach to language. You can describe rather than evaluate. You can quantify whenever possible rather than use ambiguous terms. You can personify by remembering the "to me" nature of your communication. You can clarify meanings.

You may choose a journalistic approach and ask factual questions such as: "Who?" "What?" "When?" "Where?" "How?"

You may rely on a general semantics approach and use extensional devices such as dating to remind you that people and things change, and indexing to remind you that members of a category are not all the same and that differences do exist among people and things.

THE INFLUENCE OF LANGUAGE ON YOUR COMMUNICATION

Discussion of the role language plays in how you see the world is not entirely academic. The lack of correspondence between language and reality and between language and your perceptions of reality has vital implications for your everyday communication. In this chapter, we will discuss the most common semantic traps and present some strategies which are useful for avoiding or overcoming them.

Language and Stereotyping

Language is a very powerful instrument which, quite literally, shapes the world that you know. The symbolic world does more than just describe the empirical world. It draws attention to certain aspects of the real world and thus influences your behavior. You behave on the basis of what you know. The classifying function of language is so pervasive in your lives that any time you are exposed to a new stimulus, to something or someone you are not familiar with, you ask, for example, "What is it?" or "Who is that woman?"

These questions beg for classification. You want to know what category this new thing or woman can be placed into so that you know how to deal with it or her. If the woman is a "lawyer," or a "radical," or a "college president," you then "know" what pigeonhole to put her in. If you know the attributes that people in that particular pigeonhole are supposed to possess, then you immediately "know" something about this new individual. If she belongs to the category, then she too should possess these attributes. This is the easy way for you to find out things about new people. It saves you the trouble of finding out what they are really like. You judge them on the similarities you infer they have with other members of the category. You tend to overlook what makes them different from everyone else. This is called "stereotyping."

Stereotyping is a direct consequence of classifying and categorizing. It means that you judge people on the basis not of what you know about them specifically and personally, but of what you know about the category they belong to. You stereotype people as students, teachers, blacks, whites, radicals, activists, Jews, Republicans, Democrats, communists, etc. The implication is that if they belong to the category, then they are all alike. You've seen one, you've seen them all. This blurring effect makes distinctions between members of a class or a category less visible. The problem with stereotyping is that it provides a shortcut for thinking and deters people from finding out for themselves what the person is really like and what makes that person unique and different from anyone else.

Stereotyping permits you to set up neat, well-ordered, oversimplified categories into which you can slip your evaluations of people, situations, and happenings.

Not only do you blur individual differences among the members of a category, but you often assign special characteristics to all the members of that class. The television character Archie Bunker epitomizes the man who operates his life on the basis of stereotypes and who never quite knows what to make of the "exceptions" he encounters.

Some years ago, in a classic study of stereotyping involving a deeply symbolic device, the automobile, three social psychologists asked people to characterize the owners of different makes of American cars.[1] Surely, since any make car is driven by millions of people, you would expect their owners to run the gamut. Yet the experiment showed that people had certain notions of Cadillac owners (rich, high-class, famous, fancy, important, proud, superior), Buick owners (middle-class, brave, masculine, strong, modern, pleasant), Chevrolet owners (poor, ordinary, low-class, simple, practical, cheap, thin, friendly), Ford owners, (masculine, strong, powerful, good-looking, rough, dangerous, single, loud, merry, active), and Plymouth owners (quiet, careful, slow, moral, fat, gentle, calm, sad, thinking, patient, honest). And these characteristics were not just inferred from socioeconomic status related to the price of the car. There were wide differences in stereotypes among the low-priced cars. Ford owners were youthful and adventurous, Plymouth owners were sensible and honest, and Chevrolet owners were just cheap. It is unlikely, of course, that all owners of these kinds of cars lived up to the stereotypes, although much advertising was affected by this research.

It is possible to attack stereotypes when you become sufficiently conscious of them. The civil rights movement and the women's movement have challenged ethnic and sexual stereotypes. Archie Bunker has changed over the years and may change still further.

The problem with stereotypes is not so much that they are generalizations about categories. Many generalizations are useful and valuable. In spite of the fact that no two events are identical, many things have differences which don't really make a difference. The red of traffic lights may be of different shades in different cities, but for the purposes of traffic control, a red light is a red light, and differences are slight and unimportant.

Of course, this kind of generalization is more dangerous when you deal with people. "A black is a black" and "A woman is a woman" are statements which will raise wide controversy and heated feelings, and might even stop further dialogue. Generalizations like these are dangerous for your communication, not so much because you imply that

---

[1]W. D. Wells, F. J. Goi, and S. A. Seader, "A Change in Product Image," *Journal of Applied Psychology,* vol. 42, 1958, pp. 120–121.

all members of the class are alike but because you imply that they are alike in possessing a particular characteristic. For one thing, it is almost impossible to determine scientifically whether the members of the category do possess that characteristic. (How would you gather data about Cadillac owners being "fancy," Buick owners being "modern," Chevrolet owners being "simple," and Plymouth owners being "thinking"?) For another thing, and this one is even more insidious, the characteristics assigned to the group are essentially *evaluative* rather than *descriptive*. Stereotypic generalizations (about ethnic, sexual, religious, and national groups in particular) are a way to evaluate people different from you with *reference to your own standards.* To think of your standards, your values, as right for everyone in the world and to judge others on the basis of those standards is called "ethnocentrism." This represents a frame of mind which, in essence, divides people into the "goodies" and the "baddies." Those people who you think have traits that you value positively are the "goodies," and those who you think don't are the "baddies." This is an extremely naive and dangerous frame of mind when your survival in this world may well depend on cooperation with people different from you. But stereotyping is the shortcut often used to bypass serious thinking and to avoid making thoughtful but time-consuming evaluations.

Labeling and Action   Language affects your behavior in other ways. You remember the old saying "Sticks and stones may break my bones, but names can never hurt me." If this were true, why would name-calling arouse so many violent feelings and reactions? You know that if someone calls you a name you don't like, it will provoke some kind of reaction in you, which you may not show but which nonetheless affects you. Few people like to be called "chicken," "dummy," "goody-goody," "moron," "cheater," or "phony." Most of you can add your favorite insults to the list. Names do hurt you; words do affect you.

Most of you react to labels. A college transcript is a record of the various labels you have accumulated during your academic career. The label A will bring you more positive responses from prospective employers or other schools' officials than the label D or F. Letters of recommendation are nothing but verbal labels. "Ms. Mary Smith is competent, responsible, and honest." Three labels right there, and they will elicit a particular reaction from anyone who reads the letter. The reaction would have been different had the letter read, "Ms. Mary Smith is incompetent, irresponsible, and dishonest."

Think of the language of advertising and its influence on your behavior. A department-store manager once tried the following experiment.[2] He had received a shipment of high-quality handkerchiefs and decided to place half of them on a counter bearing the sign "Fine Irish Linen — 50 cents each." The other half were placed on another counter and bore the sign "Nose Rags — 3 for 25 cents." The Irish linens outsold the nose rags five to one. To what were the customers reacting, do you suppose? The empirical world? The real handkerchiefs they could actually observe? No. They reacted to the labels and did not bother to check the territory to see if there were differences in quality between the "Irish linens" and the "nose rags." You react to the words which things are called, and it affects the way you react to the things themselves. You judge the book by the cover, in a way, when the name something is called affects how you react to it. Read the ads in a newspaper. People don't advertise "houses." They sell "cute," adorable," "exquisite," "elegant," "dandy," "glamorous" homes. Look at restaurant menus. What something is called may well determine how much you will pay for it!

Would you prefer to read "steak" or "piece of dead cow" on a menu? Words have a kind of power over you, and you react. Would many men buy an after-shave lotion called "Desertflower," or "Caprice," or "Golden Lace"? More likely they would prefer a product called "Brut," "Karate," "English Leather," "Jade East," or "Nine Flags." Derogatory ethnic and religious labels are deeply resented by most people. Police officers do not enjoy being called "pigs," and the very fact that this word is shouted by demonstrators in run-ins with the police is a good indication that name-calling is a powerful tool to vent anger and frustration and to hurt others. In other words, language does affect the "reality" of your world, particularly if you act as if there were more to words than just squiggles on paper or wiggles in the air waves.

Polarization: Real and False Opposites

You tend to think (and therefore to speak) in terms of opposites. Black is the opposite of white. Young is the opposite of old. Happy is the opposite of sad. Bad is the opposite of good. Our language is built on polar terms, which describe items on one side or another. You like to divide your world into competing opposites, into dichotomies. Language is not as differentiated as reality. However, you must talk about differences, and your tendency is to provide two (perhaps three, if you try hard) alternatives.

To give you an idea of how much polarities are expressed in our language, try this test. Fill in the middle point of this scale with *one word*

---

[2]William Haney, *Communication and Organizational Behavior,* rev. ed., Richard D. Irwin, Inc., Homewood, Ill., 1967, p. 379.

which fits a middle point between the opposite pairs, as in the first example:

black	gray	white
bad	_____	good
success	_____	failure
stingy	_____	generous
polite	_____	rude
honest	_____	dishonest

If you live in a world where in western movies the guys who smoke and drink and shoot somebody in the back wear black hats, then you expect those wearing white hats to be clean-living, fast-drawing, honest cowboys who win the girl in the last reel. One is all bad and the other all good. Few people have these pure qualities in real life, but these polarizing terms give you a shortcut in your thinking. You do not have to evaluate more than a few characteristics to determine who is good or bad, right or wrong. Our language supports dividing the world into these false opposites.

Polarization consists of evaluating what you perceive by placing it at one end of a two-pole continuum and making the two poles appear to be mutually exclusive. If you love, you cannot hate at the same time. If you are ugly, you cannot be beautiful. If you are honest, you cannot be dishonest.

There are, of course, some real opposites in your world, and you should not confuse them. A light switch can be on or off. A friend may be here or somewhere else, and that same friend may be tall or short in relation to some real standard of height.

Where you may have difficulties in your language adjustment is by treating false opposites as real ones—by having an either-or attitude about persons or events *when there are additional alternatives.* Most of you are good *and* bad, honest *and* dishonest, and much of the time you are neither and fall somewhere in between.

There are, therefore, more gradations in your empirical world than you may have language to talk about easily. It is important for you to recognize this limitation of your language system, because you have great difficulty in expressing gradations. Often it takes many words to do so, and rather than spending a long time explaining what you mean, you shortcut the process by choosing a polar term.

A Common Barrier to Communication: The Allness Attitude

Maps don't say all. A map of some territory is, by definition, only a partial representation of the territory. It would be silly to make a map in the same size and detail as the original area to be mapped.

In this respect, you are sometimes guilty of assuming that your words — as verbal maps — can do the impossible and say all there is to say about a topic. You have probably met people who act as though they know all about automobiles, or politics, or whatever. You may know that you don't say all about an event when you describe it, but you frequently act *as if* you had said all. This may be particularly true when you describe another person.

Two reasons why you cannot say all about something are: first, you cannot know all there is to know, and second, you don't have the time to tell all.

As you know from our previous discussions of perception and abstraction, whenever you observe, talk, listen, write, or read, you necessarily engage in abstracting. This means that you focus on only a portion of what is going on and neglect other facets of the event. It is impossible to know *everything* about even the smallest entity in our world. You certainly cannot say all if you don't know all. In addition, you cannot say all because our language stands twice removed from the event itself, and the symbols you use are *not* the event they represent.

In these days of expanding knowledge and fast-changing events, it is presumptuous to believe that anyone can know all there is to know about even the most simple matters. Yet you find commentators on politics or national policy sounding off as if they knew all. You tend to do the same thing when you talk about a friend — you mention how tall, how dark, how smart, how rich the person is, or what this person owns, such as a car, a stereo, a guitar, or some other item of interest. For cursory description, these items may serve to identify some features of your friend, but they do not tell all, and you may omit some items which to another person may be of considerable importance. Add to that the fact that your friend is known to you only partially no matter how much time you spend together or how much you feel you can predict about the friend's taste or behaviors.

Education is a process of finding out what you do not know and trying to fill in some of those gaps. The more you learn, the more you will tend to be tentative in asserting that you know all. The competent scientist is less sure of most things in his or her field of study than the person who is half informed. Alfred Korzybski (see the bibliography at the end of this chapter) coined the expression "allness" to refer to this attitude of pretending you can know all or say all.

An "allness" attitude can get in the way of learning. It can also mislead you into thinking that what you have heard or observed is all that you need to know. The danger of allness in your communication behaviors occurs when you treat people or events as if you know all, or can say all, as in statements like these: "All Texans are rich and loud," "All students avoid studying," "All Mexicans are lazy," "All blacks have a sense of rhythm," "All Chicagoans are gangsters," "All politicians are crooked," "All automobiles are unsafe," "Everybody cheats on income taxes," "Everybody knows beetles are harmless," and "Nobody wears hats any more."

One of the most difficult things to say is, "I don't know." When you sound dogmatically sure of something, can you for a moment entertain the possibility that you may be wrong, that you may not know a facet of the problem which could cause you to change your mind? Unless you are willing to leave that door open — unless you believe that there is more to know about it — you shut yourself off from learning and from satisfactory relationship with others.

An allness attitude is easily recognized when you hear statements such as the following:

"That's all there is to say about the matter. Period."

"Let me tell you all about . . . "

"That's not right at all."

"I know what I am talking about. I was there and I saw everything."

"You are absolutely wrong. The correct way to do this is . . . "

Such statements are often stated in a self-righteous tone and indicate much dogmatism, narrow-mindedness, and rigidity. Know-it-alls are seldom welcomed, except perhaps on quiz shows. The allness attitude may do much to prevent you from developing satisfying relationships with others and from communicating effectively with them. It implies a lack of awareness of the abstracting process. Such awareness is a first step toward improvement of your communication with others.

Frozen Evaluations and Change

Although you know that the world is in a process of constant flux, motion, and change, although you know that you are not the same person today as you were ten years ago, although you know that change is what best characterizes the reality you live in, you often act in your communication with yourselves and others *as if* you expected permanence. Language, of course, changes too. Words which were used in a certain way in the past are used differently now. Changes in slang are especially rapid. The special slang terms you use now in college are probably different from those you used in junior high school. Yet in relation to the constant changes of the empirical world, the pace of change of the symbolic world is much slower, and so your verbal classifications tend to be regarded as permanent, unchanging, stable. Although you may intellectually accept the fact that everything changes, it often comes to you as a surprise when you look at old photographs of yourself or of people you know, read old yearbooks, or meet old friends you have not seen in a long time. You are surprised because, although you know that you or they should have changed, you somehow do not expect the change itself or the extent of change.

In terms of your communication, your frozen evaluations may make you oblivious to the fact of change and may make you treat events or people as if they were static. "Once a thief, always a thief" implies that no change is possible. The reluctance of some employers to hire an ex-convict or a person coming out of a mental hospital attests to the pervasiveness of the no-change belief.

Confusion between Inference and Observation

Reports on what is going on around you are affected by what you see and what you think you see. You observe things and then begin making those observations fit what you know about your world. Inferences are what you add to your observations. They are the imagining and "certainties" you believe in.

If you saw a woman you know driving a new car, what would you think? She bought it? She borrowed it? She was trying it out? She was driving it somewhere for someone? You observed her driving a new car and began immediately to make inferences that would explain the situation.

You see two people standing in the hall arguing. You begin to make some inferences on what is happening and what is going to happen.

A teacher asks one of the students to stay after class. The first-level observation includes the student and teacher talking, whereas the many-leveled inferences can be the source of all kinds of stories about it.

An office worker shows up late. Can the employer infer that the worker missed the bus, overslept, doesn't care, has bad attitudes about being on time, or got trapped for fifteen minutes in the elevator?

You can mislead yourself when you let your inferences go far beyond what you can observe. You begin to mislead others when what you tell them is based on what you thought about it (inferred), rather than on what you actually saw (observed).

Statements of fact and statements of inference

In English two kinds of declarative statements are possible. You can look at a man and say, "He wears glasses." This is a *statement of fact* because it corresponds closely to what you observed, and it can be verified by others through observation. Or you can say, "He bought the glasses." This is a statement of inference which you make because the man is wearing the glasses, he looks honest, and few people would steal prescription glasses and wear them.

A statement of inference is a guess about the unknown based on the known. The "known" may be an observation or a series of observations (the man is wearing glasses). Or sometimes the "known" may

---

BOX 9. **The Kiss and the Slap**

In a railroad compartment, an American grandmother, her young and attractive granddaughter, a Romanian officer, and a Nazi officer were the only occupants. The train was passing through a dark tunnel, and what was heard was a loud kiss and a vigorous slap. After the train emerged from the tunnel nobody spoke, but the grandmother was saying to herself: "What a fine girl I have raised. She will take care of herself. I am proud of her." The granddaughter was saying to herself: "Well, grandmother is old enough not to mind a little kiss. Besides, the fellows are nice. I am surprised what a hard wallop grandmother has." The Nazi officer was meditating, "How clever those Romanians are! They steal a kiss and have the other fellow slapped." The Romanian officer was chuckling to himself: "How smart I am! I kissed my own hand and slapped the Nazi!" (Alfred Korzybski, "The Role of Language on Perceptual Processes," in Robert R. Blake and Glenn V. Ramsey, eds., *Perception — An Approach to Personality,* The Ronald Press Company, New York, 1951, pp. 170–171.)

---

be only an inference or a series of inferences (the man looks honest, etc.). (Box 9 gives an amusing example of inferences.)

Some guesses, of course, are more easily and quickly verifiable than others. Some are more probable than others. For example, if you go to the post office to mail a package at 10 A.M. on Tuesday, you are saying to yourself, "The post office is open." This is a statement of inference. You do not know for a fact that it is open. You have not observed it to be open. It is an inference which is (1) easily verifiable through observation (all you need to do is get there and observe whether it is open or not); (2) quickly verified (right away if you wish); and (3) highly probable (post offices are usually open on work days at 10 A.M., you have seen a sign telling what the post office hours are, you went there yesterday at 10 A.M. and it was open, and you went there last Tuesday and it was open).

Your decision to go and mail your package is thus based on a rather probable inference because the inference itself is based on past observation. Of course, something might have happened today that resulted in an unexpected closing. But that's a chance or a risk you have to take. In this case, however, because you were aware that you were making an inference, you assessed its probability, you figured out the odds, so to speak. You ran a risk, but this was a *calculated risk.* You based it on information and experience.

THE NEED TO DISTINGUISH BETWEEN STATEMENTS OF FACTS
AND STATEMENTS OF INFERENCES

If you look at statements of fact and statements of inference on the basis of how certain or probable they are, you can construct a chart such as Figure 18.

A fact or an observation belongs to the "high probability" end of the curve in Figure 18. Why not absolute certainty? Because even observations cannot be fully trusted. Remember our discussion of perceptional distortions? However, if you observe something time after time, and if other people agree that they observe it too, you can approach certainty. But you never quite reach absolute certainty. We hope this does not come as a shock to you, for many people feel very certain about many things. Your feelings of certainty, however, come partly from the validity you attach to your senses and partly from the validation you get from other people. If you see something green, and everyone around tells you it's red, and you know they are not joking, you begin to wonder. Inferences, on the other hand, never reach this "may approach certainty" level. Inferences are in the realm of lower probability. Some, of course, are more probable than others.

Why is it important to distinguish between statements of facts and statements of inferences? If you do not know that you are making an inference, then you do not know that you are operating in the realm of

FIGURE 18. Probability of statements of fact and inferences.

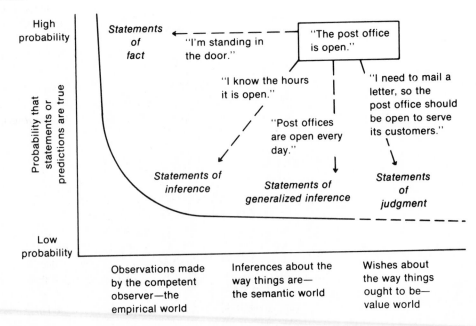

probability, in the realm of guesses. If you do not know it, then you are not likely to assess the probability of the inference. You are not likely to figure the odds. If you make an inference and treat it *as if it were* an observation, then you will feel that it is almost certain and that you don't need to do any checking. In this case you run an *uncalculated risk*.

Automobile accidents often happen because of this confusion. You drive 55 miles per hour on the highway and a car comes out on your right at an intersection. There is a stop sign on that entrance from the side road. You see the other car, you see the stop sign, you "know" it will stop, and so you proceed through the "protected" intersection at 55 miles per hour. As in too many cases on record, the other car does not stop at the stop sign (the driver does not see it, or does not see you, or is going too fast to stop in time, or guesses there will be time to go through). Both of you end up in the hospital, or perhaps in the grave. When you treat an inference as if it were an observation, then you feel quite secure instead of realizing that you should be dealing in terms of probability. If you think there is a probability that the other person may not stop, you will slow down.

William Haney gives the following suggestions to distinguish statements of facts from statements of inferences:[3]

Statements of facts	*Statements of inferences*
1. Can be made only *after* observation	Can be made *anytime*
2. Must stay *within* what one observes and not go beyond	*Can go beyond;* are limited only by one's imagination
3. Can be made only by an *observer*	Can be made by *anyone*
4. *Approach certainty*	Deal only with *probability*
5. Can be made only to the extent of the observer's capabilities and *competency*	Can be made by the *incompetent*

It seems necessary to add the fifth qualification (not from Haney) because some people are better-trained observers than others (and more honest) and therefore their statements about what they observe are more reliable. If a totally incompetent person looks at your car engine and makes a statement such as "Your carburetor is full of dirt" and gets agreement from several other mechanically incompetent people, you do not have a statement of observation, because these people may not even know what a carburetor looks like.

[3]Ibid., p. 195, Reprinted by permission of the author and the publisher.

HOW TO VERIFY AN INFERENCE

When you hear statements of inferences, you should assess their probability. How can you do this? How do you figure out the odds? How do you calculate the risk? The first thing to do is to check the source of the inference. Is the inference based on one observation or many observations, on observations made by one person or many people? What kind of people made the inference: competent, incompetent, trustworthy, biased, prejudiced, or deceitful?

You can make for yourself a scale of probability and place on the scale the different possible sources of your information. For example, when you want to determine whether the post office is open, and you are not in a position to find out for yourself through observation, you will have to take somebody's word for it. One person's word will be more reliable than another person's. If you call the post office and one of its employees tells you it's open, then your inference is pretty reliable (although it is conceivable that the person could lie, or that between the time of the phone call and the time you get there something could happen to make the office close). If you ask someone who just went to the post office, it is also quite probable the post office is open. If you ask someone who read the sign that indicates the hours the post office is open, it's a little less probable, unless you can be pretty sure this person has a good memory. If you ask a stranger in town, then that answer is not too reliable unless you have evidence to the contrary. The important thing to remember is that when you make inferences, you may or may not be accurate. You should be cautious in evaluating the source of your inferences before you act on them. You should try not to jump to conclusions until you can be reasonably sure that you are taking a calculated risk.

Statements of judgment Some statements are neither statements of facts nor statements of inferences. They are called ''statements of judgment'' because they reflect a value held by the person making the judgment.

''The food in the cafeteria is terrible.''

''The quarter system is better than the semester system.''

''She is beautiful.''

''He is really smart.''

These statements are a reflection of personal values. They say very little about what is being talked about and a great deal about the person who does the talking. The boy in love who says that his girl is the most beautiful girl in the world is talking not about the girl, not about the world, but about himself. When you say the food is bad, you are talking about *your* tastes in food. When you say someone is smart, you are talking about *your* criteria for smartness. Agreement among people on these statements proves very little about the validity of the statements. People are agreeing on values and not on observation.

You can operate better in life if you can distinguish between a statement about what's going on "out there" (statement of observation) and a statement about what's going on in somebody's head (inferences or statement of judgment). Your communication will be helped if you can determine where speakers or writers got their information: did they get it by observing and then state only what they observed? Or did they think they saw something which was colored by their assumptions, then make some inferences, and then report to you what they felt about the thing?

Example: The poet describes the beautiful sunset, and the scientist analyzes the wavelengths of the reds, yellows, and purples and gives you a report on the colors in angstrom units. Maybe you feel the sunset is beautiful too, but you are dealing in judgments. The young woman's hair may be "flowing silken tresses entrapping my soul" to the poet, but to the advertiser trying to sell with a pseudoscientific message the hair is a protein extension of the myriad head follicles.

Statements of judgments come from somebody's insides and appeal to your own insides. It helps when you find others whose internal reactions seem to agree with yours, but it makes the judgment no more reliable — only more widely expressed.

It is true that standards of judgment or values are similar within a particular culture. Standards of beauty, right, wrong, good, bad, fashion, and pleasure are learned in the same way language is learned. To agree that long hair looks bad on men does not make it a fact. It simply means that those who agree have the same taste and value about hair. Agreement based on inferences should not be confused with agreement based on observations. It is important to recognize the difference in order to be more tolerant of other peoples' judgments, particularly when they don't agree with yours. If you believe that simply because other people agree with your judgments you must be absolutely right, this will reduce your tolerance of those people who do not agree with you. It will also increase your need to convert anyone to your position, since it is so "true and right." Both results diminish the chances of successful communication.

Answerable and Unanswerable Questions

One of the differences between scientists and laypersons lies in the kind of questions they ask. Most of you make the assumption that simply because a question has been asked there must be an answer, somewhere, waiting to be found. Sometimes you are so convinced of the validity of this assumption that you keep looking for an answer that eludes you and you get ulcers in the process. Some questions are answerable, and some are not. Before you go frantically on the search for answers, you should know what was asked.

What is an "answerable question"? Essentially it is a question the answer to which can be found in the empirical world through observation. The answer is based on observations or on inferences that are capable of being verified by anyone in the position to make the observations. Scientists ask answerable questions, and then proceed to make observations in the empirical world to find answers. A question such as "How many pages are in this book?" is an answerable question. All you need do to answer it is count, and if you want to verify your answer, you may have someone else count also. If you both agree, your answer is very likely to be correct, because you found the answer by counting, in the empirical world, through personal observations. The question "Is this book your textbook for your speech course?" is an answerable question because the answer can be checked in the empirical world through observation. You can go to the instructor to verify the answer. You can go to the bookstore where you bought it and check its list of textbooks for courses.

Questions which do not have answers in the empirical world — answers that can be obtained through observations — are "unanswerable questions." This doesn't mean that they don't have any answers at all. Actually these questions usually have many different answers, but these answers are not based on observations. The answers to these questions come from the symbolic world. They are usually of two kinds: (1) questions of values or of judgments whose answers are found in people's minds, in people's values and beliefs; and (2) questions of definitions whose answers are found in the verbal classifications people arbitrarily agree upon.

Questions of values   For example, if someone asks you whether this book is good or not, no amount of observation of the book, no amount of looking at it, touching it, feeling it, or counting pages will give you the answer. Your answer will be based on your personal taste and values. The question "Does God exist?" is an unanswerable question. It cannot be answered through observation. It is answered in many ways, however, but the answers come from the symbolic world. They come from the particular religious values people have agreed to share. Different people will arrive at different answers — thus we have hundreds of religions. "Is premarital sex wrong?" is an unanswerable question. Different people give different answers to it. Total agreement is difficult because you are not dealing with an answerable question.

A great deal of controversy shook the Catholic church in the Middle Ages when theologians battled fiercely over the question "How many angels can stand on the head of a pin?'' Books were circulated. Doctoral theses were written. People called each other names, ''proved'' their viewpoints, and never did settle the question. A great deal of grief and energy could have been avoided had they realized that this was an unanswerable question. Speculations can be made, but the conclusion of these speculations should not be taken as Truth with a capital T, since the answers were found only in the minds or arguments of those writing them. This did not just happen in the Middle Ages. Think of all the controversies you are a part of today.

Some people are now arguing the existence of life on Mars. Until we have better data or observations than we have right now, the question as it is phrased is unanswerable. That does not mean you should stop asking it. It does not mean we should stop collecting data from space probes. It means that you should be very cautious in accepting the answers you get now, and you should not become angry at someone for arriving at an ''answer'' different from yours. It means that you should try to find out what accounts for the differences in ''answers.'' It means that in understanding what accounts for the differences, you can understand the phenomenon a little better and check the assumptions and inferences you have made that led you to believe in your answers. You should check what you mean by the word ''life'' as only one of the words that may need careful defining before you declare your views.

Questions of definition   Questions of definition have to do with the *meaning* you attach to words. They have to do with the arbitrary agreement of how you classify something. Take the questions: ''Is photography art?'' and ''Is bullfighting a sport?'' Whether photography and bullfighting fall into the categories provided by your definitions, the answers are essentially verbal, for the definitions are verbal. No amount of staring at a photograph will yield an answer. Those who reject the classifications or reject the values implied in your definition will probably disagree with your answer.

Louis Salomon gives some examples of classification questions in the legal world. The answers are important, although seemingly arbitrary, for the imposition of legal penalties or the granting of legal immunities hinge upon them.

1. Are peanuts nuts? (The Food and Drug Administration is responsible for enforcing accurate labeling of food products.)
2. Is an alligator farm a museum? (Liberal income tax deductions are allowed for contributions to museums.)
3. Is a coffeehouse a cabaret? (A cabaret license is expensive and often subject to special restrictions.)

4. Is a police slowdown in issuing parking summonses a strike? (There are laws penalizing public employees who strike.)

5. Is a ship that is registered in Panama but owned by a United States citizen or corporation an American vessel? (There is a legal minimum wage for crew members on American vessels.)

6. Is a man who has lost his job and refuses to take a new one that has been offered unemployed? (At issue is not only his unemployment compensation but the reliability of official statistics of "unemployment.")[4]

The process by which you arrive at these verbal definitions is relatively simple. Take a general category X. You say that to be classified as X, an object must have characteristics a, b, and c. Then you are confronted with the particular empirical object. You inspect it and find that it has characteristics a, b, and c. You say that the object is an X. But what if you had decided initially that to be an X, an object should have characteristics a, b, c, *and* d? In that case, the particular object you inspected a while ago would not be an X. The decision of what characteristics to include in the category is a verbal one, and the question of "what something is" is unanswerable in an absolute sense.

Your Hidden Assumptions   Whenever you do anything, your behavior is the product of a complicated system which includes personal observations, inferences based on personal observations, inferences based on other people's observations, and inferences based on generally accepted beliefs and values. Generally accepted beliefs and values are often called "assumptions." The term "assumptions" refers to things believed to be true or untrue. It is sometimes difficult to distinguish between inferences and assumptions because the words "infer" and "assume" are often used interchangeably. Yet assumptions are different from inferences in that an assumption is a generalized belief about something while an inference is taken from a specific statement about something. For example, you may *assume* that all lawyers are rich. If you know that Sally Jones is a lawyer, you may then *infer* that Sally is a rich woman. Your inference about Sally is based on an assumption about lawyers in general.

Assumptions generally come from the symbolic world. Why are you taking this course on interpersonal communication? You probably have several reasons for having enrolled. Perhaps the course is required, perhaps you were told it was a good course, perhaps you believe it will be an easy A, perhaps you think you need to improve

[4]Louis Salomon, *Semantics and Common Sense,* Holt, Rinehart and Winston, Inc., New York, 1966, p. 91. Reprinted by permission of the publisher.

your communication skills and you will have a chance to do this in the course, perhaps the instructor is popular because of his or her effectiveness in the classroom, etc. Your behavior — enrolling in the course — is the product of beliefs, assumptions, and guesses about the course and what it will do for you. How you came to hold these beliefs, assumptions, and guesses is largely the result of symbolic processes: listening to others and developing your value system.

Scientific American published an article some time ago about the black plague in Europe.[5] The article investigated the mass mood established by the plague. Of course, at the time (1348-1350) people did not know that the plague was caused by fleas on a particular type of rat. Because the cause of the disease was unknown and its effects were disastrous (hundreds of thousands of people died as a result of the disease), considerable fear accompanied the pandemic. And people acted according to certain assumptions: (1) The very religious considered it a trial sent by God, a punishment visited on the human race, and they sought out the Jonahs who they thought were responsible for this punishment. They found them, or so they thought, and massacred them — a consequence of assumptions. (2) Many others assumed that the plague was caused by the people living in the slums, and they reacted violently against them by burning down entire districts in some cities — a consequence of assumptions. (3) Others fled to presumably safe places and, relying on the belief that there would be no tomorrow, ate, drank, and were merry — a consequence of assumptions.

Now, why would anyone worry about how people acted way back during the years of the plague? The answer, of course, is to attempt to find some parallels to the kinds of assumptions which are *today* influencing our society, our culture. Implicit in this kind of study is an attempt to understand what kind of assumptions people operate under. *Understanding people's assumptions will help you understand their behavior.* Moreover, you need to know how to make intelligent assumptions if you want to behave intelligently.

For example, if you assume that you can fly, and, on the basis of this assumption, jump without a parachute from the tenth floor of a building, you will probably end up in the hospital, or worse, in the cemetery. The assumption was not very good. Therefore your behavior was damaging to yourself and other people. Before jumping, it would have been wise to check the validity of the assumption and then decide whether to jump or not. Checking the validity of any of your assumptions requires first that you be aware that you are indeed making an assumption.

[5]William L. Langer, "The Black Death," *Scientific American,* vol. 210, no. 2, 1964, pp. 114-121.

Belief and disbelief systems

According to the social psychologist Milton Rokeach, you all have inside you a system composed of all the things you "know" that you agree with — all the information, biases, prejudices, and beliefs that you have accumulated in yourself since the time you were born. This, Rokeach calls the "belief system." You also have inside of you a "disbelief system," composed of all the things you disagree with.[6]

On the basis of a whole complex system of assumptions, you go through life fortifying your belief system and attempting to cope with those things which fall into your disbelief system. For example, you may believe in God, you may belong to a specific church, and you may have a certain faith. This is your belief system in regard to religion. It is based on many assumptions about life, death, God, human relations, and organized religion, which have become often an *unstated, unarticulated* part of your symbolic world. Your disbelief system includes religions other than your own, atheism, etc. These beliefs and disbeliefs usually come from the symbolic world. You get them from your parents, your schools, your churches, your governments, your friends, the books you read, the movies you see, and the place of your birth. If you were born in the United States, you probably share many assumptions with other people born in this country — assumptions about freedom, civil rights, and democracy.

Rokeach further explains that you can be more or less "open-minded" or more or less "closed-minded." To be "open-minded," according to Rokeach, is simply to be open to information about one's disbelief system. In other words, if you believe that pot is good and disagree with the present narcotics laws, yet are willing to listen to information regarding the opposite position, you have begun to open your mind. If you can listen to those who have views different from yours, if you are willing to subject yourself to information contrary to what you believe in, then you have begun to open your mind. How many people regularly read the newspapers or magazines that reflect a political and social orientation drastically different from their own? How many Democrats will attend a Republican rally, not to heckle or boo, but to listen to what the other person has to say?

If you are able to admit that you *all* operate from a system of assumptions that you may not even be able to identify, and to admit further that someone else's assumptions may have a good deal of validity *for that person,* then you have begun to open your mind.

Bruno Bettelheim, the child psychiatrist, wrote an article for *Life*

[6]Milton Rokeach, *The Open and Closed Mind,* Basic Books, Inc., Publishers, New York, 1960.

magazine about the fearmongers and the hatemongers.[7] Read the following quotation, keeping in mind our discussion on assumptions and their influence on behavior.

> *They hate because they feel life has cheated them, has passed them by. Here in America, the assumption is that everybody, theoretically, can become president, or at least that everybody can make good in life. If we assume that we can all go to the top, it follows if we do not there must be something wrong with us.*
>
> *This is a painful conclusion. It attacks the very roots of our self-respect and leaves us open to the developing of some degree of self-hatred. And because all hate is basically retaliatory — a backlash at a seemingly hostile world — we grow to hate others. . . .*
>
> *But the prevalence of hate in America is essentially related to the tremendous demands individual Americans make on themselves that they cannot live up to.[8]*

Idealization, frustration, Very often the feelings you develop about yourself, other people, and
demoralization: the world around you stem from the assumptions you have about your-
The IFD disease[9] self, others, and the world. You plan a party, you plan a career, you plan to go see a movie, and in most cases you build up expectations about these events. You hope that the party will be successful and fun, and that you will have a ''good time,'' whatever your definition of ''good time'' may be. You expect to ''succeed'' in whatever career you choose. You go to the movies, expecting to be entertained and spend a pleasant evening. This is the stage of *idealization*. You dream because you are a human being and you can use language to talk to yourself and make all kinds of predictions. You can tell yourself that you will have a good time with the blind date you were just matched with. You can start making all kinds of dreams about what he or she looks like, how you are going to get along, and how successful you are going to be. You may even see a permanent relationship in the future. At the idealization stage, your imagination goes free, and you get involved in making maps about the territory to come. Then the time arrives when you do go out with the blind date, you do see the movie, you expect a promotion, or you are at the party you anticipated so much. And it just isn't what you expected. The party or movie is a real flop. The partner

---

[7]Bruno Bettelheim, ''Why Does a Man Become a Hater?'' *Life,* Feb. 7, 1964, p. 78. Reprinted by permission of the author.

[8]Italics ours.

[9]Wendell Johnson, *People in Quandaries,* International Society for General Semantics, San Francisco, 1980.

for the evening turns out to be an insensitive creep. You are not promoted in your job as you expected.

When this happens, you are usually ready for the *frustration* stage. You may get upset at whatever you perceive to be the cause of your frustration — the people who arranged the blind date or the unfeeling, insensitive employer who does not appreciate you. You may even feel that you have failed, that somehow you are not as good as you should be.

You are then ripe for the *demoralization* stage, in which you feel that there is just no hope and that you are definitely a failure. You can't ever get anybody interesting to go out with; everyone rejects you. You can even look around at the people in your world and find evidence that they really dislike you.

How many of you have never been depressed? Depression is a common feeling and usually stems from a conflict between your idealized assumptions about the future and about yourself and what you perceive really happens to you in a given situation. The larger the gap between your idealizations and what happens to you, the more depressed you tend to become.

Read the quotation from Bettelheim again. If you make demands on yourself that you cannot live up to, you are in for frustration, perhaps hate, and certainly demoralization. If you set unrealistic verbal goals for yourself, you are bound to be disappointed.

But where do you suppose these goals come from? Where do you get the idea that you will get A's or B's or C's in college? Where do you get the idea that your social life will be a roaring success? Here, again, from assumptions you make that come partly from your past experiences in the empirical world, but mostly from the symbolic world, from what you read and hear, from television shows and movies. Buy this brand of toothpaste and be a social success. Use this kind of mouthwash and get married the next day. Propaganda. Slogans. Words. You often believe them. You often act on claims without really inspecting them to find whether or not they have any validity.

The IFD — "idealization-frustration-demoralization" — disease is essentially a word disease — a disease that occurs because your symbolic world is often polluted by unrealistic promises and predictions. Claims are made by advertisers who ask you to buy a product which cannot provide you with what they implicitly or explicitly promise you. Propaganda is used by politicians and demagogues who are making promises they will not be able to fulfill — words and promises which have very little likelihood of ever representing an honest-to-goodness real world.

In relation to the IFD disease, if what you experience does not fit what you expect, you can do two things. You can change what you experience, or you can change your expectations. If you want to be the star of the basketball team and don't make the team, you can practice and practice and practice to improve your performance, or you can lower your expectations and decide you just want to play basketball for fun. If you are quite short, it might be better to lower your expectations, since your performance is not likely to improve to the point of making the team. The problem here is one of assessing the validity of your assumptions again. Where does the assumption that you can make the team come from? Is it just a totally unfounded dream, based merely on wishful thinking? Does it come from people in your environment who are able to assess your capabilities accurately and are encouraging you in this direction, or from people who are blind to the fact that you may not be good at playing basketball but who still encourage you to wish for it? Have people told you that it was "easy" to make the team? Do these people know what they are talking about?

What we are talking about here is the need to be aware that you do operate on the basis of assumptions. You need to uncover these assumptions and where they come from in order to assess their validity. Assumptions that once were valid may be useless now. Unless they are consciously reevaluated, you may keep doing things that are no longer useful to you and to others. Unless your idealizations are kept in check by your evaluation of the validity of the assumptions on which they are based, you run the risk of developing a full case of frustration and demoralization.

AVOIDING THE TRAPS

Before getting into the strategies you can use to avoid or overcome semantic traps, let us emphasize some basic points about interpersonal communication.

Point 1: You learn by discovering for yourself, not by being told. For that reason we have used a laboratory approach to provide you with data about communication, and exercises, games, and interactive activities to provide you with some opportunities to discover what happens to you in your communication contacts with others.

Point 2: Communication is not random. It is deliberate and can generally be predicted if you understand sufficiently the factors involved. Particularly, you can predict those times when communication will *not* bring you the desired results because all human beings pay attention to things in a pattern which is the product of their own uniqueness and their cultural environment. We will later go into the "whys" of your communication, but for the moment we will concentrate on the "whats" — that is, the use of symbols, perceptions, observations, inferences, meanings, and verbal habits.

Point 3: Your communication can stand improvement. You spend too much of your time in confusion and misunderstanding which might not be necessary if you applied some simple checks and balances. You are misled too often by propagandists, advertisers, friends, and enemies who may know more about communication than you do, and who may put their knowledge of human behavior to use, often to your disadvantage.

Point 4: Nobody can do anything about your communication behavior except you. Because communication begins inside you, you are the first organism affected by what is seen, heard, felt, smelled, or tasted. You must respond to whatever comes to you, and you do so by ignoring, attending to, rejecting, accepting, or somehow making use of the noises and sights and sensations around you. Understanding yourself and your relations to these stimuli is the starting place for understanding your own communication behaviors and those of others; how much you may be interested in changing your behaviors is up to you.

If for that reason it becomes important to make some adjustments in your behaviors, the guidelines and suggestions in this section may be useful. They have proved useful to many people in many workshop and laboratory situations. Not all the suggestions will work for everyone, because you may feel differently about your need to adjust your communication. You also respond differently to suggestions such as these, which will make sense to one person and seem silly to another. Some suggestions may excite you, and others may turn you off completely. There is no "royal road" to communication success, no magic key to open the door to communication effectiveness. You will notice that all the items which follow are based on point 4 above, because they all require *your* efforts. *No one can give you a "communication improvement pill"* or feed you better communication as a fortified ingredient in your breakfast cereal. It takes effort on your part; only a charlatan would sell you a program in which you would suddenly emerge as a great communicator without your own efforts and motivation.

A More Scientific Approach

Here are some ways you can inspect more critically your own communication and that of others. They are based on the idea that a more scientific approach to using symbols will bring you closer to the empirical world and help you avoid some of the traps of language which we have discussed in the preceding sections.

Describe

A statement such as "He drinks a lot" or "She is a lousy teacher" is not a description, but an evaluation. To make these same statements more descriptive, you can show what the person did — "He had six drinks at that party" or "She failed me in her course" — which developed your evaluation. In scientific terms, this may be called an "operational definition," as it describes what happened so that another observer can also see it happen. It leaves out the experimenter's value judgments. The evaluative statement tells more about the speaker than it does about the subject. "He drinks a lot" says that you have a value system about drinking and that his drinking exceeds your norms. Such a statement does not convey much information about the drinker but does say something about you.

To describe, try to stick to those data which can also be seen by someone else who may not share your value system. As the good experimenter knows, there is always danger of bias in an experiment simply because observations are being made. Werner K. Heisenberg, a renowned physicist, in 1925 articulated the principle that the results of any experiment can be distorted simply by the fact that observations are being made. Be aware of the Heisenberg principle of language. You tend to insert something of yourself in every observation you make and hence into the statements you make about your observations.

Quantify   Think and speak in terms of quantities instead of highly abstract and ambiguous words. How far is "far" when you tell a friend the car is parked not far away? How hot is "hot" when you get ready to eat spicy food? How expensive is "expensive"?

You cannot follow a cooking recipe with only vague terms in it, and an engineer does not build a bridge to support "lots of cars." Yet you often try to work together and understand each other with vague terms to describe your personal world—"many," "few," "some," "heavy," "tall," "fat," "soon." Or "I'll be home early." The vagueness of our language, in addition to the fact that each of you has a personal yardstick, scale, clock, or thermometer, tends to lead you unnecessarily into confusion.

Personify   There is a great "to me" factor in our communication. Your language is a personal expression of the minority report you make on the world around you and the people in it. "It was a good movie" is a statement of the effect of the film on you. Because you use some criteria which may not be shared by others, it is important to remember that this is a "to me" statement, and you should at least think that way whether or not you actually say the words "to me" or "in my opinion." If you announce that dogs are better pets than cats or goldfish, you can probably get an argument from someone around you. Can you also diminish the dogmatism of your comment by inserting the "to me" factor?

When you use value terms in your statements, it is appropriate to remember that these may be only "to you." Others may not agree with your evaluations of good, bad, hot, cold, sincere, smooth, fat, salty, honest, beautiful, or rich.

Clarify Don't be afraid to ask other people what they mean by a word they are using, and be prepared to clarify your own use of words to others. This does not mean only those polysyllabic words which you may never have heard before. This means those many, many words which have several kinds of meanings and may be as common as "tall," "short," "big," "little," "soon," "late," "honest," "help," "think," "see," or "hear." It is quite possible that the word being used by someone calls up an image in you which is far from that which the other person intended. If you will remember that words have many meanings depending on who is using them, you may find yourself seeking clarification or providing clear definitions to others.

A Journalistic Approach: Asking Questions Another way of more critically examining your communication is to ask the following questions, borrowing from the traditional technique of the journalist. Although these questions are phrased as if you were the receiver of communication, you should make these same tests when you send messages to others.

Who is speaking? Is the speaker someone who has had direct observation of the things he or she is talking about? Is there bias in the speaker's report to you? Does the speaker have the ability to make statements of fact or of judgment? How sound are the sources? In other words, who made the observations on which the information is based?

What is the speaker saying? Is the speaker using the words or symbols as you would use them, or do these words mean something else to him or her? What is the obvious content of the message? What else is not obvious? It is important to look critically at the substance of what is being said in terms of the language used and the meanings you may attach to the language.

When did the speaker observe the facts he or she is reporting? Were the speaker's observations made recently or a long time ago? Firsthand or by hearsay? When he or she is telling you about them, does the circumstance of that "when" have an important place in the communication?

Where was the speaker when the thing happened? Is the speaker's account a report of personal observations, or was the speaker not involved? (Where the speaker chooses to tell you may also be a significant factor in the total communication — in a group or alone, in a public statement or in private.)

Why is the speaker reporting this to you? What will be achieved by your receiving this message? Are there actions required or expected if you hear this message? Could this message have been left unsaid?

How is the speaker telling you? Is there more to the message than just the words being used? How does the speaker know about it? Was the information from a good source such as direct observation? How do you know the speaker is reporting accurately to you?

A General Semantics Approach

In the development of the language-adjustment system called "general semantics," Count Alfred Korzybski postulated an extensional-intensional continuum, which we have called the "symbolic-empirical continuum."[10] Korzybski developed five "extensional devices" together with the "is" of identity to assist people in making their language fit better the empirical world it describes. He recommended that these be used either aloud or silently as we communicate with others, and in our thinking about our communicating.

Dating Use dates mentally to indicate to yourself, and possibly to others, that you are aware that people and things change with time. If people and events are in process, then it is important to indicate your understanding of the changing nature of these supposedly static objects or occurrences. You are not the same *today* as you were in 1970, and a recognition of that difference is important to your understanding one another. You tend to react to someone you have not seen for a while as if that person had not changed, and as if you had not changed. An ex-convict knows well what it feels like to be haunted by people who react as if lives were not in process, constantly changing. You recognize the process nature of your world when you get an up-to-date road map. You would not think of planning a car trip with a twenty-five-year-old map.

Your verbal maps must likewise be kept current, so that you will not be misled into thinking that things are just the way they used to be, that your ways of dealing with your environment never need revising. Being aware of the "dating" device may help you adjust to a changing world and make your language reflect this adjustment.

Indexing Look for differences within supposed similarities. You can avoid stereotypes, you can help distinguish between things which may seem alike, and you can soften your attitudes and reduce your dogmatisms by a conscious effort at not lumping together what looks alike on the surface. This practice is called "indexing." You must remember that differences are closer to the empirical world in which no two things are ever identical — similarities appear to you as a result of the abstraction pro-

---

[10]Alfred Korzybski, *Science and Sanity,* 4th ed., The International Non-Aristotelian Library Publishing Company, Lakeville, Conn., 1958.

cess. You see similarities by disregarding differences. Your language should be similar in structure to your world of difference and uniqueness and should represent the similarities you abstract. An index subscript attached to a generic noun can help maintain a healthy balance between the two aspects of your world. If the generic noun emphasizes similarities, the index shows the difference. Professor$_1$ ("professor" is the generic noun; "1" is the index) is not the same as professor$_2$; and student$_1$, student$_2$, and student$_3$ may all have different qualities. You need to recognize these qualities, and not treat all professors and students alike in your thinking and action.

Etcetera "Etcetera" is a mental device to help you avoid the idea that you can say all. Although Tom Wolfe in his "new journalism" makes frequent use of "etc." and other ellipses,[11] use of "etc." in your English composition may be frowned on. Korzybski suggests that you recognize your own limitations of observation and reporting by using this device to indicate that there are things left out. "Education makes success" probably should have an "etc." after the word "education" and after the word "success" as well. Education, with some other factors, will produce success and some other things. Be wary of words like "always," "never," and "everybody."

Quotation marks Quotation marks are a device to remind you that words are used personally, and that not all possible meanings are covered. Highly abstract words are often put in quotation marks by an author when their meaning is specialized and the author wants to call attention to that fact. Use of quotation marks in your thinking and speaking helps remind you that your meaning may not be the same as someone else's. It is not unusual to see someone wiggle fingers in the air to indicate quotation marks when using a particular word, usually in satire. We often will say something like "She said she would be there (quote) early (unquote)" to indicate a special use of the word out of its context; placing a particular emphasis on a word with accompanying facial contortions may achieve the same goal.

"Truth" for you may not be "truth" for us. Words such as "reality," "fact," "crime," "God," "education," "freedom" certainly evoke different meanings in everyone. And the uses of these words may reflect different chronological meaning as well. "Truth" in science today is not the same as "truth" was for Newton.

---

[11]Richard A. Kallan, "Style and the New Journalism," *Communication Monographs*, vol. 46, no. 1, March 1979, p. 59.

Hyphens The hyphen device indicates that our words often divide the world into two competing opposites, and that often this is not appropriate. This device helps you avoid the either-or orientation of our language and the polarizing thinking of dividing things into opposites. "Good-bad," "mind-body," and "space-time" are ways of indicating a relationship between terms without making a dichotomy of them. Our language is burdened with outlooks from common dichotomies of competing and mutually exclusive categories. Your thinking tags along with your language, and you often fall into the semantic trap of dividing the world into either-or, into impossible blacks and whites without grays in between. If you want to indicate status or qualities of a person or group, it is not uncommon to use such terms as "socioeconomic" or "psychosocial." These alert a reader to recognize that the "social" qualities interact with the "economic" ones or "psychological" ones and are not considered competing opposites.

The "is" of identity One of our less useful language patterns is to talk as if things, people, or events had inherent qualities. The structure of language often compels you to identify, that is, to ascribe qualities to things and then react to those things on the basis of the labels. The verb "to be" in its various forms represents an easy temptation in that respect. When you say, "John is lazy," you imply that "John possesses a laziness quality" and hide the fact that the statement represents only your perception of John, one among the many other things about him you could select to talk about.

If you could not use the word "is" in that sentence, what would you substitute which would make it correspond more to the reality of the situation? Well, the statement represents your attempt to express your perception of someone. "John appears lazy to me" would be better because the statement would move from one of absolute certainty to one reflecting some tentativeness. It would also show that you, the observer, are aware that you are talking about *your perception* of John, not about him as he "really is." A more descriptive statement of what John did would provide more information, since it would give another person data about the behaviors you observed which led you to the evaluation you made. In other words, saying, "John did not take the trash out for two days and it bothers me," gives more data about John and about how his behavior affected you. It also implies that the not-taking-the-trash-out behavior is only one specific behavior which he may not exhibit again, and does not represent all of John's repertoire of behavior. The "lazy" label, on the other hand, implies that that's the way John is, that's all he is, and that's all he'll ever be.

Granted "John is lazy" is a lot quicker to say than "John did not take the trash out for two days and it bothers me." Human beings are more complex than an "is" can describe. Human transactions are far too complicated to be pinned down with the simple "is" equation. Identification statements, convenient shortcuts as they may be, appear to us to oversimplify what they represent and ultimately to mislead.

BIBLIOGRAPHY

Bettelheim, B.: "Why Does a Man Become a Hater?" *Life,* Feb. 7, 1964.

Blake, R. R., and G. V. Ramsey (eds.): *Perception — An Approach to Personality,* The Ronald Press Co., New York, 1951.

Haney, W.: *Communication and Organizational Behavior,* rev. ed., Richard D. Irwin, Inc., Homewood, Ill., 1967.

Johnson, W.: *People in Quandaries,* International Society for General Semantics, San Francisco, 1980.

Kallan, R. A.: "Style and the New Journalism: A Rhetorical Analysis of Tom Wolfe," *Communication Monographs,* vol. 46, no. 1, March 1979.

Korzybski, A.: *Science and Sanity,* 4th ed., The International Non-Aristotelian Library Publishing Company, Lakeville, Conn., 1958.

Langer, W. L.: "The Black Death," *Scientific American,* vol. 210, no. 2, 1964.

Rokeach, M.: *The Open and Closed Mind,* Basic Books, Inc., Publishers, New York, 1960.

Salomon, L.: *Semantics and Common Sense,* Holt, Rinehart and Winston, Inc., New York, 1966.

Wells, W. D., F. J. Goi, and S. A. Seader: "A Change in Product Image," *Journal of Applied Psychology,* vol. 42, 1958.

Chapter 8

LISTENING:
IS ANYONE THERE?

In
a
Nutshell

Listening is a vital factor in your interpersonal communication. You are constant consumers as well as originators of communication.

Listening is not the natural process that it is often believed to be. You have cognitive control over listening.

Improving your listening habits can be achieved by remembering these points:

1. Use time to think carefully about what is being said. The speaker speaks much more slowly than you can absorb ideas and think about them.
2. Think ahead of the speaker, and try to figure out what will be said next.
3. Make internal summaries of what is being said.
4. Identify the speaker's evidence and arguments.
5. Avoid getting stopped in your listening by letting your feelings interfere with paying attention. Let new and different ideas come in; don't close your mind.
6. See beyond distractions of the speaker's physical presence, language use, and speech habits, and beyond the physical distractions in your environment.

Active listening — that is, listening to the total message someone is sending — is based upon the internal attitude that the speaker is a worthwhile person and has worthwhile things to say. Active listening involves mirroring back to the speaker the feelings that came across through the message and developing a climate in which communicators can be noncritical, accepting, and nonmoralizing. Ask people to state one major problem in communication, and they are likely to include lack of listening. Supervisors complain that their subordinates don't listen; subordinates complain that their bosses don't listen; parents complain about children and children about parents; teachers complain about students and students about teachers.

INTRODUCTION   Listening is beginning to take its place as an important part of human communication. Corporations advertise in magazines and on television their programs to teach listening. Their concern is based on clear arguments that better listening can save many millions of dollars each year. How can listening make such dramatic savings? Estimates are that each error which needs correcting actually costs dearly in letter writing, phone calls, personnel time, machine time, materials, and lost orders or missed deadlines. Poor listening has begun to be identified as one of the primary causes of managerial and clerical error. As more and more business is conducted over the telephone or by other audio means, the costs of poor listening will undoubtedly increase. Teleconferencing, a newly adopted technology, depends on the listening skills of many people — one more example of how the speaking-listening relationship becomes a crucial factor in human communication. Another example: Waiting for an overdue delivery of dry cleaning, we learned from monitors in the central plant that the person writing down the delivery instructions had heard ``six'' instead of ``three'' as the route designator. It cost the cleaning company time to find the order, time and money to make the special trip to deliver, and extra time to fill out the report of the incident — all because one person did not listen well.

How often do you make small errors in listening when you arrange to meet a friend, to pick up an order, or to buy an item at a store for someone else? According to Rebecca B. Rubin: ``Too often students do not listen well enough to identify the main ideas in a class lecture or to understand the material presented in class. Too often students do not understand the directions for assignments given orally, let alone the expected performance standards.''[1]

Because so much education depends on a teacher talking and students listening, it seems necessary to devote considerable attention to listening as a help to learning. We may be too late. Business organizations, industrial and public agencies, and many corporate groups are now emphasizing the need for listening skills in their employees. As they bemoan the fact that people cannot listen well, they also place part of the blame on educational institutions where the skill and art of listening has historically been ignored.

At least part of the problem comes from a very narrow definition of listening, in which people concern themselves with getting only data or content. Speakers assume that ``anyone with two good ears can listen'' and that the listener will then know all they hoped to convey with their words and inflections.

---

[1]Rebecca B. Rubin, ``Assessing Speaking and Listening Competence at the College Level,'' *Communication Education,* vol. 31, no. 1, January 1982, p. 19.

KINDS OF LISTENING   It is rather obvious that unless someone listens, any effort to communicate will be lost. After all, communication, as a transactional process, involves the negotiation of mutual meanings, and how can that be accomplished if interaction remains one-sided?

Listening is crucial, therefore, not only in terms of getting the content of a message, which is called "deliberative listening" by Charles Kelly,[2] but also in term of understanding the feeling context in which the communication is taking place — "empathic listening," or "active listening" as Carl Rogers calls it.[3]

How do you feel when you are not listened to? Have you ever been in a situation where it became apparent that the person you were talking to was, in fact, mentally miles away from you and had not paid the least attention to your fascinating story? Pretty unpleasant, isn't it?

We can say quite safely without qualifications that people in general do not know how to listen. You all have ears, and most of you have no fundamental physical deficiency in your hearing mechanism. Yet you do not listen well. Many of your interpersonal communication problems can be traced to just this: You do not know how to listen effectively.

Daniel Katz, a communication scholar, wrote some years ago that the physical barriers to communication had all but disappeared, but that the psychological barriers remained.[4] Mission Control can send astronauts to the moon and back. The world was able to watch live on television the first men landing on the moon and hear the President talk to the two astronauts standing at attention hundreds of thousands of miles away. Soon, telephone companies tell us, you will be able to talk to people on the telephone and *see* them on a private television screen hooked up to the receiver. The technological "miracles" surprise hardly anyone. Actually, they have become such a part of American life that most people were quite bored with the third moon mission up until the time a crisis developed and it looked as though the astronauts were in danger and might not come back.

However, if the physical barriers of communication have disappeared, the psychological barriers still remain. We still do not understand our children, our students, our teachers, or our friends. We still have difficulty making sense to one another, and about one marriage in three ends up in divorce or separation.

---

[2]Charles M. Kelly, "Empathic Listening," in R. Cathcart and L. Samovar, (eds.), *Small Group Communication*, Wm. C. Brown, Dubuque, Iowa, 1979, pp. 340–348.

[3]Carl Rogers, "Communication: Its Blocking and Facilitating," *Northwestern University Information*, vol. 20, 1952, pp. 9–159.

[4]Daniel Katz, "Psychological Barriers to Communication," in Wilbur Schramm (ed.), *Mass Communication*, University of Illinois Press, Urbana, 1960, p. 316. (Originally published in *Annals of the American Academy of Political and Social Sciences*, March 1947.)

Listening is a major ingredient of the communication process, and the tremendous lack of skill in that area is primarily responsible for many of the problems you experience with other people.

Norbert Wiener, the mathematician, wrote, ''Speech is a joint game between the talker and the listener against the forces of confusion.''[5] Unless both make the effort, interpersonal communication is quite hopeless.

THE PROBLEM
Poor Listening

A few statistics will give you an idea of the extent of our problem. For years Ralph Nichols and his associates[6] conducted many intensive studies at the University of Minnesota to test the ability of people to understand and remember what they hear. The listening ability of thousands of students and hundreds of business and professional people was examined. In each case the subjects listened to a short talk and were later tested on their grasp of the content. These studies led to the following conclusions:

1. Immediately after people have listened to someone talk, they remember only about half of what they heard — no matter how hard they thought they were listening.
2. The University of Minnesota studies, confirmed by studies at Florida State and Michigan State,[7] showed that two months later people will only remember 25 percent of what was said. In fact, people tend to forget one-third to one-half of what they hear *within eight hours.*

To summarize these statistics simply, we can say that whenever you listen to someone talk, *you miss about half of what a person tells you,* and two months later you will remember only one-fourth of what was said. When you think of all the time you spend being talked to, and all the energy you expend trying to remember the things you are told, it seems as though the whole thing is a pathetic waste of time. Think of all the hours you spend sitting in a lecture hall listening to your professors, or all the time you spend in an office listening to someone tell you what to do and how to do it. Think of all the hours spent telling things to your friends, colleagues, and parents. Perhaps not even one-fourth of what you tell them will register and stick. What is the use of hearing lectures if you neither understand nor remember what is being said?

[5]Norbert Weiner, *The Human Use of Human Beings,* Avon Books, New York, 1967.

[6]Ralph Nichols and Leonard Stevens, ''Listening to People,'' *Harvard Business Review,* vol. 35, no. 5, 1957.

[7]J. J. Kramar and T. R. Lewis, ''Comparison of Visual and Non-Visual Listening,'' *Journal of Communication,* 1951, p. 16.

Some Causes of Poor Listening

There are many complex reasons for poor listening. Often you deliberately tune someone out because you don't like that person, or because you are bored or simply tired. However, many times your poor performance in listening is involuntary. To gain insight into the reasons for poor listening, we must dispel three myths which are quite pervasive and have obscured an understanding of the process.

Myth 1: Listening is a natural process

If you believe that listening is natural, then it follows you never need to learn it. Breathing is a natural process. No one had to teach you how to breathe. This was the very first thing you did, all on your own, the minute you were born. The myth that listening is something natural that you do normally, unconsciously, and automatically is most detrimental to your improvement in that area. You will never learn what you believe you already know. If something is natural, inborn, automatic, then there is not much *you* can do about it. You have it, or you don't. You are good at it, or you are not.

A pioneering study by Rankin gave us some statistics which have been quoted and retested for many years.[8] He reported that about 70 percent of our waking day is spend in communication; of that amount about 45 percent is spent listening. We spend about 30 percent of our time speaking, about 16 percent of our time reading, and only about 9 percent of our time writing. (Other studies report that you learn about 85 percent of all you know by listening.) As more and more audio techniques are perfected and used — telephones, walkie-talkies, tape cassettes, etc. — you may be constantly decreasing the amount of time you spend in writing or reading. Other compilations by Sam Duker, Paul Keller, and others (see the bibliography at the end of this chapter) indicate that although the amount of listening research has increased since the 1950s, it in no way represents the amount of communication investigation which listening behaviors deserve.

Think of a normal day and how you spend your communicative time. You spend many hours listening to people talk to you. If you logged your communication in its four forms, you might not be far off the 45 percent for the listening part. Yet, when you look at what you are taught from the time you are small children, you can see that learning to write and read takes up many of your school years. Twelve years of English is not unusual, and when you go to college you still have to take English composition. All these years are spent mastering the difficult skill of writing, a skill you will probably use only 9 percent of the time. Think how difficult it was to learn to read and how slowly many of you still read. Perhaps you are now taking a speed-reading course to

[8]Paul T. Rankin, ``Measurement of the Ability to Understand the Spoken Language,'' unpublished Ph.D. dissertation, The University of Michigan, 1926.

improve your skill, a skill you use only 16 percent of the time. Speaking was also a skill you had to learn. Your parents or teachers may have spent years trying to get you to say, "I am not" instead of "I ain't."

But who taught you how to listen? Did you ever have a course in grade school, high school, or college to teach you how to listen more effectively? The answer is probably no. There are unfortunately too few of these courses available in the formal education system. Why? Because for too long people have assumed that listening is natural and need not be learned. This is sheer nonsense. Listening is a skill just as writing, reading, or speaking is. It needs to be learned. It certainly can be improved. Most of you learn how to listen on your own, picking up the habits of those around you. Unfortunately, those around you are not much better off than you are, for they picked it up on their own, too. You do not know many people of whom you can say, "He really is a good listener," and so most of the time you pick up bad habits that will hinder your interpersonal communication for years.

Myth 2:
Hearing and listening
are the same

Although, as Clevenger points out,[9] the relationship between hearing and listening is a complex one, and despite the fact that in some cases it is difficult to distinguish between them, hearing and listening are generally two distinct processes. Most of you, unfortunately, treat them as one and the same. You do this when you assume that just because you have uttered some words in front of someone else, that person will know and remember what you said. The fact that the someone else was awake and not deaf is no guarantee that he or she listened to what you said. The fact that we "expose" students to some facts and ideas about a particular discipline in a lecture is absolutely no guarantee that they learned anything at all. They may have heard the noises made by the professor talking, but that is no assurance that they listened and retained.

Hearing is a natural process. Provided your ear is not damaged and your brain is functioning normally, you cannot help hearing sounds of a certain intensity. Hearing is essentially a process of energy transformation (the technical term is "transduction" and refers to a process whereby energy in one form is transformed into another form). What happens during the hearing process is the transformation of acoustic energy into electrochemical energy. It happens like this: A sound wave hits your eardrum, a thin but tough membrane stretched across the auditory canal. The eardrum, as a result of being hit, vibrates. The vibration is transmitted next to three little bones (ossicles), the anvil, hammer, and stirrup. The bone vibration is then transmitted to a fluid in the coch-

[9]Theodore Clevenger and Jack Matthews, *The Speech Communication Process,* Scott, Foresman and Company, Glenview, Ill., 1971, pp. 65–80.

lea, the endolymph. These vibrations are still acoustic waves. As the waves move through the fluid, they disturb tiny hair cells. Depending on the amplitude and frequency of the waves, some hair cells are stimulated more than others. If a given hair cell is stimulated above its threshold, it emits electrochemical impulses which activate the eighth cranial nerve. From then on the nervous system takes over, and the brain then reconstructs a representation of the initial sound. At that point, you hear. Naturally, there is more to hearing than just the process of energy transformation through the ear mechanism. The nervous system in involved, too. You have little or no control of the process of hearing. If your hearing mechanism and your brain is normal, you cannot help hearing.

But you can help listening whenever you want to. You can tune out any speaker, any time, at will. Listening is a higher cognitive process which is under your control. Why, then, do you decide to tune out? Basically, the problem is caused by the fact that you think much faster than you talk. The average rate of speech for an American is about 125 words per minute. This is slow going for the human brain, which can process, with its 13 billion cells, about 800 words per minute. In listening, the difference between the speaking rate and the thinking rate means that your brain works with hundreds of words *in addition* to those you hear. It means that your brain will continue to think at high speed while the spoken words arrive at low speed. You can listen and still have some spare time for your own thinking. The use or misuse of this spare time holds the key to how well a person can listen to the spoken word.

Most of you misuse the spare time by going on private sidetracks. You daydream while you are "listening" to a friend or to a lecture. At first, this presents no problems, for you are able to catch every word the friend or the professor is saying and still think of what you are going to say next, what you are going to do tonight, etc. There is plenty of time to do all this extra thinking. Actually, you can hardly avoid doing this, since it has become a strong habit over the years. You go back and forth between what the speaker is saying and your private world. But sooner or later you stay a little too long on one of these mental sidetracks, and when you focus your attention back, the speaker is ahead of you. You have lost something that was said. If it is something important, you may not understand the rest of the conversation, and therefore you find it easier and easier to slide off on your sidetracks for longer and longer periods of time. When the speaker is finished, it is not surprising if you actually heard only half of what was told you.

Myth 3:
You are speaking to a
mass audience

Myths 1 and 2 centered on the listener and explained what makes it difficult to listen well. Myth 3 is oriented toward the speaker and what makes it difficult for him or her to be listened to well.

When you find yourself talking to several people, you often assume that you are being heard in the same manner by every one of your listeners. This assumption is implicitly based on the premise that you are talking to a mass audience, that every individual member of that audience is identical and therefore will respond in like manner to what is heard. First of all, the individual members composing any audience are not identical. They are quite different people with different interests, different needs, and different motives for being there and listening to you. Some are friends, some are enemies, some are smart, and some are dull. Some are happy to be there, some can't wait until they can get away. Some have pressing problems at the time, some are relatively free from strong anxieties. These individual differences account for the fact that these people may or may not go on private sidetracks, may or may not stay very long on their sidetracks if they do tune out once in a while. It also explains the fact that they may all tune out at different times and literally hear different parts of the conversation. No wonder you often come out of a conversation asserting very dogmatically that "The speaker said such and such" and find that another person who was also there affirms emphatically that the speaker certainly did not. You almost feel as though you had been listening to two different speakers. Perhaps the half you missed was the half the other person heard.

MORE EFFECTIVE LISTENING

If listening is essentially up to you, how can you become better at it? How can you acquire better habits? No amount of reading and hearing about it will ever make you better. Listening is a skill, and as for any skill, practice is essential. What we can do in a brief section here is to draw your attention to some things to watch for, but you will have to do the watching. You will have to try it for yourself over and over again. As you incorporate some of these suggestions in your behavior, you may find that listening comes a little easier, but progress will be slow and hardly noticeable at first. Listening is hard work. Unless you are willing to accept the difficulty and make the effort, your habits will not change.

For convenience, we have grouped our suggestions into three main categories. The first category deals with the differential time between the speed of the spoken word and thinking. The second category involves the content of what is being said. The third category considers the psychological factors in our listening.

Use Your Time More Effectively

Instead of going on private sidetracks which have nothing to do with the topic being discussed, think about what the speaker is saying.

Think Ahead of the Speaker

Try to figure where the speaker is going and what the next point will be. This may be easy with some speakers who are well organized and who present their points clearly. However, most of us are not very clear and organized, and that may make the work of the listener hard. However, if you are interested in getting what the speaker has to say, you may have to do much of the organizing for yourself.

Summarize What the Speaker Is Saying

Break what is being said into the main points and the supporting points. Most speakers tend to repeat themselves and often go on tangents that may or may not be related to the topic. As a listener, your task is to sift what is important from what is only supporting material. The speaker sometimes helps you make the distinction by emphasizing a point with voice cues or repeating it several times, or telling you that this is a key point to be remembered. Teachers will often use the blackboard to write what they consider their main points and key words.

Identify the Speaker's Evidence

Ask yourself questions about the speaker's sources and their validity. Do you find the evidence convincing, complete, valid?

Listen between the Lines

Listen for the *two broadcasts.* To listen effectively one has to listen to two broadcasts at the same time. The first broadcast is the content of the discussion, the words the speaker is saying, the topic itself. The other broadcast comes from all the nonverbal signals the speaker is sending while talking: the tone of voice, gestures, and facial expressions. The second broadcast tells you about the speaker's feelings and gives you a great deal of information on how to interpret what the speaker is saying.

You will remember that in our discussion of meaning we emphasized that you must understand both the nonverbal and the verbal aspects of a message if you wish to understand fully what another person is trying to communicate. Listen for the feelings the speaker is putting across. Don't be misled by the apparent triviality of some statements, or by what appears to be only "small talk." Oftentimes you do not know of any other way to make contact with others, and what you are truly saying to another person goes beyond the words you use. A little girl coming home from school in tears saying she hates school and does not want to go back may really be saying that someone made fun of her at recess and she was hurt. Unless the parents listen for the little girl's feelings and try to make it easy for her to tell the story, they may brush her aside by saying, "This is ridiculous; of course you want to go back to school." They will thus miss the point entirely.

Listening between the lines is very difficult. It takes a great deal of sensitivity and patience, for people have innumerable ways of erecting defenses and hiding behind them. Only patience and a willingness to spend the time deciphering the subtle dimensions of a person's communication will make you successful in your attempts to understand others.

Be Aware That Listening Is Affected by Emotions

Human beings are not machines. They have feelings, emotions, which play a fundamental part in their interpersonal communication. There are things you like and things you do not like, things you are afraid of or ashamed of, things you like to hear and things that are so threatening you would rather not hear them at all. As a result, quite unconsciously, you have a tendency to tune out what you do not want to hear and to listen better to what you agree with. If something is said which might cause you to change one of your perceptions, the threat of dissonance has been introduced. Any potential change in your perceptions involves strong feelings, and the first of these feelings is usually confusion and frustration. To reduce the frustration, you often flee mentally from the situation by tuning out what the speaker is saying, or by distorting it so that you won't have to alter your perceptions. This is not done deliberately by any of you. Actually, if and when you are told that you are doing this, you very righteously deny it. Your emotions often blind you to what is actually happening in you.

When you do not agree with a speaker, you have a great tendency to prepare a rebuttal while the other person is still talking. You hear the first few words or sentences, get an idea of what the speaker is saying, decide you don't agree, and here you go preparing your answer and waiting impatiently for your turn to speak. Sometimes, you don't even wait, and you interrupt the speaker, who never gets a chance to finish his or her thought. Unfortunately, when you do not hear a speaker out completely, you really do not know for sure what is being said. You may think you do, but incomplete statements may not represent a fair sample of the speaker's thoughts. People you do not agree with are often the most difficult people to listen to. Usually you have little difficulty listening to someone telling you how great you are or how smart you are, but listening to a professor who tells you your paper certainly did not deserve any better than a D is a lot more difficult.

We again arrive at the concept of the open mind. You must be willing to listen to information which goes contrary to your belief system. And even though you think that your paper deserved better than a D, you should be willing to hear the other side. The professor may happen to have some good reasons that will make sense, even to you, *if you are able to let them come in,* rather than shutting them off on the basis that the professor obviously dislikes you and that's why you got a D.

Try to Avoid Being Distracted

We know that children's spans of attention are very short. The younger the child, the shorter the span. In fact, most adults also have a short span of attention and have difficulty concentrating on the same thing for a long period of time. Naturally this varies with each individual, but think of the difficulty you have as a student litening to a fifty-minute lecture, even when the lecturer is an outstanding professor. Because it is hard to sustain attention for very long, you get distracted very easily. The sources of distractions come from (1) within you, when you day-dream, (2) the outside environment (outside noise, people passing by, someone waving, the temperature of the room, etc.), and (3) the speaker. This last category merits some discussion.

You often get distracted by a speaker's accent, mannerisms, style of dress, language, delivery, etc. Some people simply won't listen to a man who wears long hair or a woman who is dressed too flashily. Or if they are willing to listen, their listening will be affected by the precon-ceived ideas they have formed from the speaker's dress or appearance. This of course is hardly conducive to effective listening. It is difficult to fight off these distractions. Yet as you become aware of all the little things that can get in the way of good listening, you may be in a better position to train yourself to overcome them. In addition to the physical distractions created by the appearance of the speaker, the use of lan-guage may turn you off. Most of you react very strongly to certain emo-tionally loaded words, trigger words. Whenever these words are pro-nounced by someone, it's as though a red flag had been waved in front of your nose, and you react, usually emotionally and strongly. These words, of course, are different to each of us. If you can identify these words, they somehow lose some of their impact on you when you hear them, and at least you may not block out what a speaker has to say simply because one of your own loaded words was uttered.

Ralph Nichols and Leonard Stevens in their book *Are You Listening?* make some suggestions about listening habits which we have summa-rized below:[10]

Ten worst listening habits	*Ten best listening habits*
1. Calling the subject ''uninteresting.''	Tuning in to see if there is anything you can use.
2. Criticizing the speaker's delivery, personal appearance, necktie, etc.	Getting the message, which is ten times as important as the speaker's appearance, etc.
3. Getting overstimulated and preparing a rebuttal.	Hearing the speaker out before you judge him or her.

[10]Ralph G. Nichols and Leonard A. Stevens, *Are You Listening?* McGraw-Hill Book Com-pany, New York, 1957.

Ten worst listening habits	*Ten best listening habits*
4. Listening only for facts.	Listening for main ideas, principles, and concepts.
5. Trying to make an outline of everything you hear.	Listening two or three minutes before taking notes.
6. Faking attention to the speaker.	Not relaxing while listening; in good listening there is a collection of tensions inside.
7. Tolerating distractions in meeting.	Getting up and doing something about distractions — by shutting a window, closing a door, requesting the person talking to speak louder, etc.
8. Avoiding difficult material.	Learning to listen to difficult material.
9. Letting motion-laden words affect you.	Identifying your own greatest word barriers.
10. Wasting the differential between speech speed (100 to 300 words per minute) and thought speed (cruising 800 words per minute).	Making thought speed an asset instead of a liability by: **a.** Anticipating the next point to be made. **b.** Making contrast and comparison. **c.** Identifying the speaker's evidence. **d.** Practicing mental recapitulation.

ATTENTIVENESS It is not enough just to listen. You must be *perceived* as listening. In other words, the speaker needs some indications from you that you are actually listening. This quality, or factor, is referred to as "attentiveness."[11]

An attentive communication style generally adds to the effective-

[11]Robert W. Norton and Loyd S. Pettegrew, "Attentiveness as a Style of Communication," *Communication Monographs*, vol. 46, no. 1, March 1979. p. 13, et seq.

ness of a person as a communicator, or at least improves how you may be seen as a communicator. One possible exception is that if you work so hard at being attentive that you talk little in social situations, you may be seen as low in leadership and power. In general, however, the practice of "appearing to listen" may be as important as listening itself. Norton and Pettegrew conclude from their research that an attentive style of communicating involves both sending and receiving messages — you must let the other person know, usually by talking and adding data or your own examples, that you are following actively. (See the section on feedback later in this chapter.) In that way, attentiveness is not just listening behavior in the most strict sense; it may involve actions and speaking as well.

The same authors point out that attentiveness need not always be positive or supportive. You can listen critically, suspiciously, negatively, unfeelingly, or judgmentally and still exhibit the qualities of attentiveness. During a bitter argument or a serious debate you may be paying very close attention to the other's points. This issue becomes important when attentive listening gets mistaken for agreement. Consider the following account by one of the present authors:

> A student came to my office with a long list of reasons why he should not take the final exam. At the end of the discussion, I refused the request, although I made notes and could recite back each argument and his reasons. He later reported to a friend that I didn't listen to him. On the other side, I went to the office of a dean and asked for support for a project. In detail I described the advantages and the minimal costs involved. The dean, after going carefully over my proposal and spending an hour asking clear questions, said no. Later I caught myself in a conversation with another faculty member saying that I had an excellent proposal but the dean didn't listen.

In both cases the fact that a "no" answer was given was not honestly related to attentive listening. But your expectations are for only positive outcomes of attentive listening. Habits of working with other people clearly have led most of us to believe, even if it isn't always true, that if the other person is really paying attention, you will get agreement. When you don't get agreement, you may want to blame it on listening rather than on differences of opinion, bad arguments, competing resources, or other factors.

ACTIVE LISTENING   There is another dimension to listening which the psychotherapist Carl Rogers and his associates have pointed out.[12] This dimension goes

---

[12]Carl Rogers, "Communication: Its Blocking and Facilitating," *Northwestern University Information*, 1952, vol. 20, pp. 9–15.

beyond the psychiatrist's field to permeate all areas of interpersonal interaction. Listening is more than a skill to improve communication. Listening, or "active listening," as Rogers calls it, reflects a whole orientation to life and to people. This orientation implies that *to listen is to have the creative power to imagine how it would make sense to say what the other person is saying*. It implies that the other person is fundamentally important and worth listening to, worth giving some of your attention, energy, and time.

In a sense, you cannot fake active listening, because paying attention to the suggestions we listed in the preceding paragraphs is not enough. You must *feel* deep inside of you that people are important in their own right, and you must feel that by listening to them you are sharing with them your feelings of respect. Active listening, Rogers points out, must be firmly based on the basic attitudes of the listener. You cannot use it as a technique if your fundamental attitudes about people are in conflict with its basic concepts. If you try, your behavior will be empty, and everyone will recognize it. Unless you have a spirit which genuinely respects the potential worth of an individual and trust that person's capacity for self-direction, you cannot begin to be effective listeners.

What does active listening consist of? Very simply, *it is listening to a person without passing judgment on what is being said, and mirroring back what has been said to indicate that you understood what feelings the speaker was putting across*. It seems simple enough. However, the implications of this procedure are tremendous. By withholding judgment and by showing that you understand the feelings of another person, you tell that other person to be free to say more, you tell that other person there is no risk of being judged and found stupid or silly. You remove the threat that another person always presents to the personal defenses. Effective communication is free to happen once that threat has been removed. By mirroring what another person says, you help build a climate in which you can be accepting, noncritical, and nonmoralizing. People then feel safer.

Remember the example we gave earlier of the little girl coming home very disturbed over her day in school and crying that she did not want to go to school ever again. As a parent and as an active listener, what can you do to find out what is bothering the child? Her statement that she does not want to go back to school may be only her awkward way of indicating to you that she has a problem, and she may not even know herself exactly what the problem is. Asking her why she does not want to go back to school may not get you anywhere because chances are she will tell you that she hates it, and she won't know specifically why. If you tell her that this is a stupid thing to say and that of course she does not mean it and she likes school and wants to go back, you are passing judgment and telling the child she does not know what she's talking about (no one, not even a 7-year-old, likes to be told that), that you know better what's good, and that you know better than she does what she is really feeling. That's precisely the one thing no one knows better than this little girl. She knows better than anyone else what she is experiencing inside of her at that moment, even if she is not articulate enough to tell you. The result of your response will probably be more tears, and the child will clam up. You will still not know what really is bothering the girl.

As an active listener, you would simply mirror to the child what she just told you. "So you feel bad about school today." This simple sentence tells the girl you have been listening to her, that she communicated her feeling to you adequately, and that you are not passing any judgment. She is free to say more and probably will. "Yeah, I don't want to go back, I hate recess." If the mirroring process continues, you will probably get the whole story from the child very easily. (She hates recess because today everyone teased her, and no one wanted to play with her. She felt awkward and left out — feelings no one really likes to experience. Her way out was to decide not to go back to school, so that she would not have to experience this again.) Once she has communicated her feelings and feels that she was understood, it will matter a lot less, and chances are she will be able to cope better with the problem.

All of you want to be listened to and understood. Otherwise, you feel you are not worth much, since people won't even think enough of you to take the time to listen to you. What do you hear most people complain about? Not being listened to. "I can't talk to my parents; they never listen." Or, "I can't talk to my son; he just won't listen." Or, "I am quitting this job. My boss never listens to anything I say. It's as if I did not exist."

To listen actively to another human being may be the greatest gift you can give. The power to listen is a remarkably sensitive skill, perhaps the greatest talent of the human race. It is certainly the skill that makes interpersonal communication truly effective and rewarding for all concerned.

The ways you choose to listen can influence others. How *you* listen may well determine how others will listen to you. Listening is truly a transactional process.

LISTENING AS A COMPLEX PROCESS

You should by now have the impression that listening as a part of our communication is a complex as well as an important factor in interacting with others. It is likely that the future will see more and more listening courses in our schools at all levels. We will also see more and more emphasis placed on finding out how well people listen, or assessment of listening skills as well as skills of reading, writing, and speaking.[13]

Listening is generally considered to consist of not only hearing, but the added dimensions of understanding, paying overt attention (attentiveness), analyzing what is heard, and then acting on the basis of what has been heard. Critical evaluation is also an important component — you should be able to spot the reasons one speaker is understandable and another is not. In understanding, you are expected to get main points, details, and something about the purpose of the speaker and a relation between the purpose, points, and details. Understanding also includes an ability to summarize or report back basic data. A little-emphasized part of listening consists of spotting the reasons a person is speaking, the persuasive devices used, and the relation between the speaker's motives and methods.

In addition to these complex skills, there is the dimension of feedback. Feedback is a specific response to the transaction of speaking-listening. Following directions is one very clear way of giving feedback to a speaker that you actually listened to and understood. Giving and receiving feedback is an integral part of our communication. It becomes the action phase of our listening; it operationalizes the transactions of speaking-listening behaviors. We devote the remainder of this chapter to a discussion of feedback.

LEARNING TO GIVE AND RECEIVE FEEDBACK

An integral part of reducing barriers in communication is making optimum use of feedback, both in giving and receiving it. You need to practice giving clear indication of how much a message sent to you is actually received and also train your senses to observe clearly how your messages are responded to by others.

To start, let us say that all human beings need the contact of relationships and that organizations and the people in them do not operate in a vacuum. Even a hermit, living in a cave in a mountainside, has contacts with the environment which make it essential to respond. When hermits are hungry, they must find food, responding to the message from their stomachs. When they feel the cold wind blow, they respond by seeking shelter or putting on protective clothing. Although hermits may have little verbal communication, they still must be involved in

---

[13]A summary of recommendations made recently to the Massachusetts Department of Education is typical of assessment moves and is contained in "Recommendations for Assessing Speaking and Listening Skills" by Philip M. Backlund, Kenneth L. Brown, Joanne Gurry, and Fred Jandt, in *Communication Monographs,* vol. 31, no. 1, January 1982, pp. 9–17.

sensing feedback and adjusting their moves to what happens to them in their surroundings.

Because few of you are hermits, you need to adjust not just to the cold or to hunger, but to the constant stream of messages you get from others in the course of a day. The number of messages you send or receive may vary, just as your ability to react appropriately may vary from one person to another. In this way you begin to identify those who can give clear instructions, those who can do what they are asked, those who can understand complex information, those who have difficulty in grasping new ideas. Much of the ability to perform well in assignments is related to the ability to give and receive feedback. The sensitive person can pick up the cues offered by another who does not understand instructions — maybe it is the professor responding to a quizzical look on the face of a student by asking "What is not clear in what I have been saying?" The sensitive person also can predict what parts of a message may be subject to confusion, and restate or clarify those parts without even being asked, simply because he or she has anticipated the hearer's confusion.

In communication, people need to share meanings of words and messages. It is important for them to know that communication is transactional — that is, it takes place between people under rules which they agree to follow. One of the rules is that if someone looks angrily at you after you have made a remark, you need to figure out what it was you said to make that person angry. Another rule is that if the listener smiles and nods, you are thereby permitted to continue with that kind of message. So your transactions are affected by the kinds of feedback you receive — whether negative, which pulls you up short, or positive, which encourages you to go ahead. In Chapter 6 we discussed meanings of words. If the meanings for words vary from person to person, so do your emotions vary. It is important in your communication transactions to be aware of both content and emotion.

There is a tendency in all of you to sometimes pretend you understand when you really do not. It is not considered intelligent to ask, "What do you mean by . . . ?" and you may try to avoid looking stupid. As a result, you may miss some important messages by pretending and may give the other person feedback which is false. Two factors are important here: first, that you try to give more honest feedback about your depth of understanding, and second, that you make it easy for the other person to say he or she does not understand. If you can reduce the other person's anxiety about asking questions by suggesting in advance that you may not be making your message clear, you may receive more honest feedback. On the other hand, you may have to swallow your pride and admit that you do not understand, and thus provide more honest feedback to the other person's message.

Preparing the way for a message has been called "feedforward" for an obvious reason—it sets up the possibility of getting feedback. Making use of appropriate feedforward, as in the example above, should assist the feedback process. You may also precede a statement you make with a feedforward phrase such as, "If you have no plans for tonight . . ." or "Let's talk about next week's assignment . . . ," which gives the cues to your listener that you expect a response and the direction you want the discussion to take.

The concept of feedforward should not be described apart from feedback; rather, it should be considered as a specialized activity within a total feedback system. Feedforward will help anticipate actions. It may be an intrapersonal plan for "What will I do if . . . ?" or "If the chair is empty, I will sit by Sally because there is something I want to tell her," or "If Dad says no when I ask for the car, my following argument will be . . ." When communication actually begins is difficult to pin down. Two people riding together on a bus as strangers will make a number of moves to test whether or not the other is ready to talk, and to find out what they will talk about. Feeding forward in your communication will usually result in more appropriate responses in one another as you begin to operate the give-and-take of communication.

We mentioned above that not only content but also emotion is involved in the feedback process. Your attention to feedback will help you verify *who you are* in relation to others, as well as *what is said.* In Chapter 4 you read about interpersonal "needs." Keep in mind that you discover who you are by watching the reactions of others. By developing the ability to give and receive feedback, you also may better meet your interpersonal needs. Some of these needs are implied in the following suggestions based on workshop experiences.

In workshops where training has been conducted on giving and receiving feedback, it has been shown that your "guesses" about how others see you have been significantly improved when you are given feedback.[14] Just having feedback available, however, is not enough. You need to know how to handle it—that is, how to give it appropriately and how to receive it intelligently. Some suggestions for giving and receiving feedback follow.

---

[14]Gail E. Myers, Michele T. Myers, Alvin Goldberg, and Charles E. Welch, "Effects of Feedback on Interpersonal Sensitivity in Laboratory Training Groups," *Journal of Applied Behavioral Science,* vol. 5, no. 2, 1969, pp. 175–185. See also: Charles A. O'Reilly and John C. Anderson, "Trust and Communication of Performance Appraisal Information: The Effect of Feedback on Performance and Job Satisfaction," in *Human Communication Research,* vol. 6, no. 4, Summer 1980, pp. 290–298.

Focus Feedback on Behaviors Rather Than the Person

You generally can look more objectively on what you do than on what somebody says you are. Your behaviors, or actions, are only a momentary part of you, and therefore you feel more comfortable about being challenged to change them. If someone calls you ''dishonest,'' it sounds quite different from saying that you acted ''dishonestly'' in a given situation. You cannot tolerate very well an attack on ''you,'' which is what much criticism sounds like. If someone is critical of your *behavior,* you can more easily accept responsibility for that action, rather than tell yourself you are a product of your genetic inheritance and for that reason cannot possibly be blamed nor think of changing.

1. To describe behaviors you use adverbs — e.g., ''loudly,'' ''kindly,'' ''happily,'' ''grumpily,'' or ''sincerely.''
2. Avoid the use of adjectives relating to the qualities of the person, to personality — e.g., ''bigmouth,'' ''kind,'' ''happy,'' ''sorehead,'' or ''sincere.''
3. Behaviors include those things a person does well as much as the things done badly. In describing behaviors you tend to concentrate on those which need improvement, but a person can often learn much from feedback about those actions which facilitate, support, or improve communication. Descriptions of behaviors should not be evaluative or selective, but should comment on what went on.

Focus Feedback on Observations Rather Than Inferences

1. Observations are those things which could be seen or heard by anyone, but inferences are your own interpretations or conclusions about what went on. If you spice your observations with inferences, you tend to obscure feedback, and so you must be careful to differentiate when you are making inferences, or extensions of your observations.
2. Observations involve what is going on, not what happened at some previous time or some persistent characteristic you have noticed over a long period. In training groups, the term ''here and now'' is used to keep participants involved in what is happening and hence more concentrated on observations public to everyone. Research has shown that feedback given as soon as appropriate after observation will be more specific, more concrete, and generally more accurately reported.
3. Observations should be reported in terms of degrees of more or less, not as black-and-white, either-or dichotomies. This helps you keep in mind the ''quantity'' of the behavior rather than a category which is too frequently judgmental and subjective. Behaviors are very active, alive, and related to other behaviors in a more-or-less continuum rather than in a static good-or-bad polarization.

Focus Feedback on Description Rather Than Judgment

1. As in the case of focusing on behaviors, to use description is to avoid evaluation of the other person or of his or her actions. Description attempts to remain neutral, but judgment takes sides.
2. Concentrate on the "what" rather than the "why." Again, the "what" of the behavior is observable by others and therefore can be checked for accuracy. The "why" of a person's behavior is inferred and leads you into the dangerous area of "intentions" and "motives" and the emotionalism which goes with it. It may be useful at times to explore the "why" of behaviors, but this should be done with the help and consent of the person being discussed.
3. Most of you enjoy playing "shrink" to all your friends, but you should realize that your analysis of the other person's behaviors may be more subject to your own aberrations than to theirs. If you concentrate on the "why," you may miss much of the very useful "what" of feedback.

Focus Feedback on Sharing of Ideas and Information Rather Than Giving Advice

1. You need to feel a joint responsibility for the outcome of the feedback encounter and be ready to assist others rather than direct their responses.
2. Telling others what to do with the information you give does not leave them free to determine the appropriate course of action *for them.* Giving advice is a poor attempt at problem solving which does not give other people leeway to make their own choices.
3. Explore alternatives rather than provide solutions. If you concentrate on a variety of available responses, you can help move toward a more satisfactory answer. Too often you have ready at hand a list of solutions waiting for the problems to come along which might fit. When you offer a solution, ready-made from your own experience, it may not be useful to others, because their experiences are different or because the problem may not be exactly as you saw it.

Focus Feedback on What It May Do to the Person Who Receives It

1. If giving feedback is only making *you* feel good, you may not be helping as much as you are imposing.
2. Be aware of how much feedback another person can handle at one time. Avoid the long recitation "and then you did . . ." after the recipient has given you some feedback that he or she is full to the brim. After that time you are only satisfying your own need, and not the other person's need.
3. Emotional reactions may result when feedback is given at the wrong time or place. This is particularly true in the more sensitive and personal areas of human behavior. Even if you have some worthwhile points to make, they should be presented with the recipient in mind.

BIBLIOGRAPHY   Backlund, P. M., K. L. Brown, J. Gurry, and F. Jandt: "Recommendations for Assessing Speaking and Listening Skills," *Communication Education,* vol. 31, no. 1, January 1982.

Cathcart, R., and L. Samovar (eds.): *Small Group Communication,* Wm. C. Brown, Dubuque, Iowa, 1979.

Clevenger, T., and J. Matthews: *The Speech Communication Process,* Scott, Foresman and Company, Glenview, Ill., 1971.

Duker, Sam: *Listening Bibliography,* New York, Scarecrow Press, 1964.

———— (ed.): *Listening: Readings,* New York, Scarecrow Press, 1966.

————: "Doctoral Dissertations on Listening," *Journal of Communication,* vol. 13, no. 3, June 1963.

Keller, Paul W.: "Major Findings in Listening in the Past Ten Years," *Journal of Communication,* vol. 10, no. 1, March 1960.

Kramer, J. J., and T. R. Lewis: "Comparison of Visual and Non-Visual Listening," *Journal of Communication,* 1951.

Myers, G. E., M. T. Myers, A. Goldberg, and C. E. Welch: "Effects of Feedback on Interpersonal Sensitivity in Laboratory Training Groups," *Journal of Applied Behavioral Science,* vol. 5, no. 2, 1969.

Nichols, R. G., and L. Stevens: *Are You Listening?* McGraw-Hill Book Company, New York, 1957.

————, "Listening to People," *Harvard Business Review,* vol. 35, no. 5, 1957.

Norton, R. W., and L. S. Pettegrew: "Attentiveness as a Style of Communication," *Communication Monographs,* vol. 46, no. 1, March 1979.

O'Reilly, C. A. and J. C. Anderson: "Trust and Communication of Performance Appraisal Information: The Effect of Feedback on Performance and Job Satisfaction," *Human Communication Research,* vol. 6, no. 4, Summer 1980.

Rankin, P. T.: "Measurement of the Ability to Understand the Spoken Language," unpublished Ph.D. dissertation, University of Michigan, 1926.

Rogers, C.: "Communication: Its Blocking and Facilitating," *Northwestern University Information,* vol. 20, 1952.

Rubin, R. B.: "Assessing Speaking and Listening Competence at the College Level," *Communication Education,* vol. 31, no. 1, January 1982.

Schramm, W. (ed.): *Mass Communication,* University of Illinois Press, Urbana, 1960.

Weiner, N.: *The Human Use of Human Beings,* Avon Books, New York, 1967.

Chapter 9

NONVERBAL COMMUNICATION: COMMUNICATING WITHOUT WORDS

In a Nutshell

Your silences are as much a part of your interpersonal communication as your words. Silences are not random; they may be appropriate or inappropriate, which is also true of your verbal communication.

You communicate nonverbally through the inflections of your voice, your tone, your pitch; you use gestures, body postures, and facial expressions to communicate a whole range of meanings to the people you interact with. You also communicate nonverbally through your clothes and the objects with which you surround yourself.

Touching is a very significant part of your communication repertoire, and the rules you follow about whom to touch, where to touch, how frequently to touch, and in which situations to touch are heavily based on cultural factors.

Time and space are important features of the communication system you use with others. Proxemics, or the study of distance, can be useful in helping you understand the relational dimension of your interpersonal communication.

Nonverbal communication is often used to express feelings and emotions. If the messages you receive through the verbal system do not seem to fit other messages you receive through the nonverbal system, you usually rely on the nonverbal dimension of communication to interpret what was really meant. Nonverbal messages help you verify the intentions of other speakers and also reinforce their verbal messages.

INTRODUCTION

In Chapter 5 we contended that to be communicated at all, an experience has to be translated into some symbolic code. As far as we know now, what goes on in a person's brain does not get transmitted to another person's brain directly without the mediation of a symbolic system. So far in this book, we have concentrated mostly on verbal systems — that is, communication through the use of words — and have neglected a fundamental aspect of everyday communication: nonverbal communication, or communication without words.

The study of nonverbal communication is relatively recent. For a long time people felt that unless words were involved, communication did not take place. This attitude was, and still is, reinforced by the fact that our culture places a strong emphasis on the virtues of speech. In spite of a few wise sayings ("Silence is golden," "One picture is worth a thousand words") you value glibness, praise a "gift of gab," and consider silence in many social situations a weakness. In groups, silent members are more often than not perceived as the least influential members of the group.

This common attitude about silence, or the absence of verbalized noise, is rooted in a misconception about the nature of communication: that communication can be turned on and off — on when you talk, off when you do not. Nothing could be more misleading. There is no opposite to communication. As you saw in Chapter 1 and as we will discuss in this chapter, one cannot *not* communicate. Your silences and other nonverbal aspects of communication are no more random than your words. They, too, are systematic expressions of meanings which you use, often quite unconsciously, in your interpersonal contacts.

The range of nonverbal communication is impressive. In this chapter we will deal with four aspects of nonverbal communication: (1) silences, (2) how you send and receive nonverbal messages, (3) the contextual patterns of nonverbal communication, and (4) some characteristics of nonverbal communication.

SILENCES

Silences Occur in Interpersonal Communication

You and your new date are driving on your way to a movie. After some time of idle chatting about the weather, where you go to school, where your date goes to school, what courses you are taking, and the kind of movies you like, you run out of things to say, and silence sets in — long, heavy, embarrassing silence. Your date just sits there, and you can't think of another thing to say. In desperation you turn on the radio.

You have just been introduced to a person sitting next to you at a dinner, and after the usual small talk neither of you finds a thing to say; the best you can do is to stare at your napkin or appear very busy fiddling with the silverware.

These two examples are not unusual. They illustrate two principles about silence: (1) Silences are an integral part of interpersonal communication. They occur more often than you think. (2) Silences in many cases are perceived as embarrassing. You somehow feel they should not happen; and when they occur, you try desperately to fill the gaps they create. Silences, however, are not to be equated with the absence of communication. Silences are a natural and fundamental aspect of communication, often ignored because misunderstood.

> As most students of social interaction are aware, lapses in conversation are so potentially embarrassing that participants will often resort to noisy "masking" behaviors to fill in the silence — coughing, clearing the throat, sighing, whistling, yawning, drumming the fingertips; or they may utter meaningless "sociocentric sequences" such as "but ah," "so," and "anyway" in the hope of nudging a partner into taking a turn.[1]

Most studies of lapses (or "latencies," as they are sometimes called) in speaking exchanges have concluded that the person who cannot handle such gaps easily is considered a less competent communicator. The person who manages better the periodic silences which normally occur in much of our communication is thought to be more effective. Think about the people you know with whom it is "easy to talk." How do they handle the little lags in your speaking flow? How do you share the responsibility with them for "keeping the conversation going"? When lapses occur among your peers, or with your very close friends, do you react the same way as you do when lapses occur when you are in the presence of people you want desperately to impress?[2]

Effective communication between people depends heavily on silences because people take turns at talking and at being silent when listening. Unless one is silent, one cannot fully listen. Unless you know that silences are a part of the gamut of communication, you will continue to be afraid of them and avoid them instead of making full use of them.

Silences Are Not Random

Perhaps you have noted that we use the word "silences" in its plural form. This is deliberate. We want to stress over again that there are many different types of silences, each with a meaning of its own and different implications and consequences for communication. When you

---

[1]Margaret L. McLaughlin and Michael J. Cody: "Awkward Silences: Behavioral Antecedents and Consequences of the Conversational Lapse," *Human Communication Research,* vol. 8, no. 4, Summer 1982, p. 299.

[2]Ibid., p. 314. See also: J. Cappella and S. Planalp, "Talk and Silence Sequences in Informal Conversation," in *Human Communication Research,* vol. 7, no. 3, Spring 1981, pp. 117–132; and W. B. Stiles, "Verbal Response Modes and Dimensions of Interpersonal Roles," in *Journal of Personality and Social Psychology,* vol. 36, 1978, pp. 693–703.

say you like silence or are afraid of it, you really fail to acknowledge the many differences between types of silences. If one is to understand communication, one must differentiate between the many types of silences and meet them with an appropriate behavior.

For example: (1) Silence when you are terribly angry, frustrated, gritting your teeth, ready to blow up, yet tensing up so as to not let the steam out, is different from (2) silence which occurs when you are attentively listening to an important broadcast or a fascinating lecture or story. In both cases no word may be spoken, but what goes on inside you in terms of feelings, reactions, emotions, and thoughts is quite different. Not only does your silence stem from a different cause, but your actions, expressions, and movements reflect that difference. (3) Silence when you listen but are bored is different from the preceding two silences. The silence of boredom expresses a withdrawal from the situation, a negative evaluation of what is going on; it implies an attitude of superiority which often offends those toward whom it is directed if they perceive it. The bored student listlessly looking out of the window indicates through facial expressions that the teacher is not worth listening to, a reaction the teacher will probably resent if he or she "reads" the student's silence. Earlier in this chapter we mentioned (4) the silence which occurs when you cannot think of a thing to say (on a date, at a dinner, or in any situation involving people you do not know well). During these social encounters, talk is expected. Silence represents what is feared the most, and when it occurs, makes you feel terribly inadequate and self-conscious. (5) Silence when you are thinking about a point made by a speaker is different from (6) silence which occurs when you do not understand what the speaker said. In the latter you may be so confused that you do not even know what to ask in order to get some clarification. (7) Silence can be reverent, meditative, or contemplative. Perhaps you silently pray; or perhaps you take a walk and encounter something so beautiful that you are speechless and the sight stirs deep emotions in you. (8) The silence of allness, the dogmatic "There is no more to be said on the matter, that's all there is to it" is quite different from (9) the silence of lovers or friends who may simply hold each other's hands and do not need to say anything at all to communicate their feelings. The latter is a comfortable silence, a silence you do not need to break, a silence you treasure because it reflects the depth of a relationship. People who know each other well often do not need to talk to communicate well. A glance, an understanding smile, or a look is all that is necessary. Words are not needed. (10) The silence of grief is another type of silence. "So they sat down with him upon the ground seven days and seven nights and no one spoke a word unto him. For they saw his grief was very great" (Book of Job). This is a difficult silence. You know intuitively that words don't begin to express the sympathy or the concern you want to share with a person who grieves. Sometimes, just being there is enough. (11) Silence can be a challenge, like the silence of the pouting child or the stubborn and angry friend, or the silence in a classroom toward the very last minutes of a period when the teacher asks, "Do you have any questions?" and students almost dare each other to say one word which might trigger the teacher to continue talking after the bell.

This list of silences is not exhaustive. There are many, many different types of silences which mean a lot of different things. What we are trying to establish here is an awareness that silences cannot be lumped all together. Each must be interpreted on its own. The reactions to each of these silences should be different because each means something different. You do not respond the same way to someone who is silent because of grief as you do to someone who is silent because of anger. Oftentimes, though, you misunderstand a person's silence. You frequently think that silence is a sign of anger, hostility, or withdrawal, not realizing that it may mean other things. Typical communication breakdowns between roommates often start this way. Mary does not speak to Sally one morning, because she is thinking about an important assignment due that day which she must finish. Sally, who does not recall the assignment, thinks that Mary is angry with her. Without checking any further, Sally starts pouting because she is upset to think Mary is angry with her. Mary, noticing Sally's silence, may decide not to speak to her until she is in a better mood, thus confirming Sally's conviction that Mary is angry with her. A whole chain of negative reactions can be easily set off, each woman's silence reinforcing her belief that the other must be angry at her. They are both on their way to a classic case of communication breakdown.

A sensitivity to silences is imperative to two-way communication. This means sensitivity to your own silences and to the silences of others to whom you would speak. If you are silent because you are thinking about a point the speaker made, or if you are puzzled by what the speaker said, you should let him or her know. If people are silent when you speak, you must be able to read the cues that will tell you the reasons for their particular silence. Do they misunderstand you? Do they clam up because they are resisting what you are saying? Are they bored? Did you lose them? Unless you know (1) that silences can be interpreted in many different ways and (2) that you can learn to read the cues which will tell you what they mean, your interpersonal communication may not be as effective as it could be.

There are many cues available which help you to understand people's silences. The way they move, their gestures, and their facial expressions will tell you a great deal about the reasons for the silence. We will analyze these in detail in another section of this chapter.

Silence May Be Appropriate or Inappropriate

Just as you may say the wrong thing at the wrong time, you may respond silently to a situation requiring talk, and not be silent when you should. A person who is engaged in serious thinking will probably not welcome the friend who comes barging in and talks a mile a minute about trivial things. When people are worshiping in church, they usually resent a loud intrusion by tourists exclaiming about the beauty of the ceiling or the woodwork.

On the other hand, in some social situations, you may be called a snob or someone may clap you on the shoulder and say, "Whassamatter? You're being awful quiet," when others think you should be talking. The conversation need not be significant, but silence may be perceived as an indicator that you do not approve of what's going on or that you would rather be someplace else. Even if this is true, you know that it is not polite to give that impression. So, usually, you chat away at the same level as the rest of the crowd. You talk about the weather, the decor of the room, or what you do for a living, and these simple exchanges set up avenues for further communication. Being silent in such situations seems to have very little virtue, as your social acceptability depends on your saying something, however inane it may be. Silence when the situation requires some form of verbal exchange makes you appear antisocial and drives people away from you. Another person's silence is not a reassuring factor. It is often perceived as something threatening. So when your neighbor hollers at you, "Nice day," you usually come back with an equally profound, "It sure is." Both of you have made contact and feel reassured that you are not isolated.

HOW YOU SEND AND RECEIVE NONVERBAL COMMUNICATION

We said earlier that to understand another person's silence one should be sensitive to the nonverbal cues that are being sent out constantly. You send and receive a complex system of nonverbal signals consisting of tone of voice, body movements, gestures, things people surround themselves with, and a whole range of messages conveyed by touch. Actually you often interpret these nonverbal signals without quite realizing it when you form impressions of people, when you decide whether you like someone or not. In your interpersonal communication you make many decisions based on an intuitive interpretation of the nonverbal code, such as when to laugh, when to move, when to relax or tense up, and when to continue or to end a conversation.

In this section we will examine the various ways by which people send and receive these nonverbal signals.

The study of nonverbal communication not only has been associated with research in many fields, but has been popularized by recent writers who cater to a very widespread interest in these so-called "hidden systems of communicating." In a brief essay on "body lanugage," Judith Hall Koivumaki mentions popularized versions of this study and also points out, "The topic is relevant in sociology, psychology, psychiatry, ethnology, and anthropology. There is no single, correct methodology for studying nonverbal communication."[3] In recent research, the concepts of "life space," "personal bubble," and other influences of *proxemics* (or the study of how close people can operate to one another) are diligently studied in relation to other aspects of human communication.

The many influences of nonverbal patterns on our communication have only begun to be studied. Curiosity about how people influence each other has a great deal to do with the sudden wave of interest in "body language," or nonverbal systems, and the popularity of writings on the subject — especially the how-to-do-it kind of books. These books seem to promise you an easy way (1) to check up on the other person by watching nonverbal behaviors and (2) to learn how to manipulate or control others by practiced nonverbal cues almost guaranteed to get the "correct" response. Before you develop illusions that these techniques of reading and using nonverbal clues will help you control the world, let us make three disclaimers.

First, just as words are spoken in context and mean something only in relation to what is going on before and after, so do nonverbal symbols mean something only in relation to a context. To pick out one gesture, or one eye movement, or one body posture, and say that it tells you exactly what is going on in the other person is like saying that you can tell what that person means if you hear only one or two spoken words. Nonverbal behaviors are part of a dynamic, flowing, ongoing process of communication and must be related to other cues and behaviors if you are going to "translate" accurately or completely.

Second, the gesture you see or the wink you catch or the nod you detect *may* all be part of an ongoing communicative "sentence" or paragraph; but on the other hand, they may be symbolic of nothing more than the other person's discomfort. A hand gesture may be nothing more than moving to a more comfortable position; a wink occurs when an eye gets dry or an eyelash gets misplaced, and a nod may be an unconscious nervous twitch or an attempt to adjust the "transmitter's" hair or collar. In other words, be careful not to place too much emphasis on the psychological meaning of a nonverbal act unless you can eliminate the possibility that it is simply a natural, physical reaction. And remember that the other person may not read your messages at all.

[3]Judith Hall Koivumaki, "Body Language Taught Here," *Journal of Communication*, vol. 25, no. 1, Winter 1975, pp. 26–80.

Our third disclaimer relates in some ways to the first two. It is that nonverbal messages are different for different people. Gestures which fit one culture may be neither appropriate nor understood in another. Since you learn your gestures from the people around you, you are likely to repeat those which are known and not as likely to make up a whole system of nonverbal communication that is not useful to you with the people around you. In addition, studies on lying, studies on male-female abilities, studies on nonverbal messages in the classroom, etc., all point to differences which occur quite normally. For example, research on male-female sensitivity to nonverbal cues generally reports either that females are more cued to the nonverbal, or that there are no differences; but no research shows that males excel in reading the nonverbal.[4] Different cues which may be ''leaked'' or given away during lying have been studied; and differences seem to occur in the way a person expresses tension or relaxation in social settings as single behaviors or as patterns.[5] Other research indicates that nonverbal expressiveness in the classroom has some potential for affecting learning.[6] All these ideas point to the concept of individual-situational differences which will have an affect on both the kind of nonverbal cues you may send, and who will be reading them. Nonverbal messages, both sent and received, depend on many factors.

With these disclaimers comes an ethical consideration. If you become an expert in ''reading'' others' nonverbal messages — especially those nonverbal messages they are not aware of — what is to keep you from manipulating others for your own gain? It seems to be done all the time. In sales, negotiating, courtship, classrooms, and in many other common settings, the people with greater sensitivity to the nonverbal seem to have an advantage. In his popular book *Manwatching*, Desmond Morris makes these interesting comments:

> *Frequently the human animal is unaware of his actions — which makes them all the more revealing. He concentrates so hard on his words that he seems*

[4]Myra W. Isenhart, ''An Investigation of the Relationship of Sex and Sex Role to the Ability to Decode Nonverbal Cues,'' *Human Communication Research,* vol. 6, no. 4, Summer 1980, pp. 309–318; Ross Buck, ''A Test of Nonverbal Receiving Ability: Preliminary Studies,'' *Human Communication Research,* vol. 2, no. 2, Winter 1976, pp. 162–171.

[5]Henry D. O'Hair, Michael J. Cody, and Margaret L. McLaughlin, ''Prepared Lies, Spontaneous Lies, Machiavellianism, and Nonverbal Communication,'' *Human Communication Research,* vol. 7, no. 4, Summer 1981, pp. 325–339; George J. Keiser and Irwin Altman, ''Relationship of Nonverbal Behavior to the Social Penetration Process,'' *Human Communication Research,* vol. 2, no. 2, Winter 1976, pp. 147–161.

[6]Janis F. Anderson and Julie Gardner Withrow, ''The Impact of Lecturer Nonverbal Expressiveness on Improving Mediated Instruction,'' *Communication Education,* vol. 30, no. 4, October 1981, pp. 342–353.

to forget that his movements, postures, and expressions are telling their own story. It should be added, though, that this book is not intended as an aid to dominating one's companions by reading their secret thoughts. A bird-watcher does not study birds in order to shoot them down. In the same way, a man-watcher does not take unfair advantage of his special understanding of human behaviour.[7]

All these disclaimers point up an important lesson. Before you try to play shrink with your friends as you analyze their nonverbal behaviors, get to know the context of their moves and make sure that the moves have a purpose within the dimensions you are interpreting. Even then, remember that the same gestures do not always mean the same things when used by different people. Although there tend to be general kinds of nonverbal messages that you can expect to ''mean'' consistent things in your environment, there are many special and unique uses of moves, inflections, facial expressions, body postures, and gestures which could mislead even the experts.

There is always a ''what'' and a ''how'' dimension to your communication transactions. You not only say something to someone, but you say it in a particular way. You are familiar with the cliché ''It's not what she said; it's how she said it.'' The ''how'' of your communication gives clues about (1) interpreting what you say and (2) the kind of relationship you have with the person with whom you are communicating.

Much of the ''how'' of communication is carried out through nonverbal communication. In this section, we want to describe some of the nonverbal clues which permit you and others to understand better what is communicated in a given transaction. These clues include paralanguage, gestures, facial expressions, body movements, object language, and touching.

Paralanguage   The spoken word is never neutral. It is always affected by the tone of voice, the emphasis or inflections given, the breaks in the sentence, the speed of delivery, the degree of loudness or softness, and the pitch of the voice. These nonverbal factors are called ''paralanguage.'' As you know, a simple ''yes'' can express a lot of different feelings, such as anger, frustration, resignation, lack of interest, agreement, or challenge. A short sentence such as ''I'll do it'' may ''mean'' any of the following:

''I'll be really happy to do it.''

''I'll do it, but it's the last time.''

''You always make me do what you want.''

[7]Desmond Morris, *Manwatching,* Harry N. Abrams, Inc., New York, 1979, p. 8.

"All right, you win."

"Don't worry, I'll take care of it."

"You're so dumb I'd better take care of it myself."

Which of the meanings is implied can usually be determined by the tone of voice, the inflection of the voice, or the stress placed on each separate word. The meaning of the sentence lies not in the words alone but also in the vocal expressions, or paralanguage, always associated with the words.

Some years ago a record came out in which two renowned actors carried on a seven-minute dialogue using only two words: "John" and "Marsha." The two talented artists managed to express so many different feelings and emotions that the story they were telling came through loud and clear. Meaning was exclusively carried in the paralanguage.

In everyday life you naturally rely on words themselves *plus* their paralanguage features to develop your meanings about what people are telling you. There are times, however, when you get distracted and miss the words themselves. If you have to respond and do not wish to admit you have not been paying close attention, you will rely on the paralanguage features alone to interpret what was said. This happens often at cocktail parties where people involved in small talk do not pay full attention to what is said and respond almost automatically. It may be pouring rain, but if someone says in a convincing tone, "It is really nice out, isn't it?" chances are the response will be an equally convincing "It sure is."

You often get upset not so much at *what* people say, as at *how* they say it. "He sounds so sure of himself that I always feel like contradicting him." You tend to respond to people in relation to these paralanguage features without quite realizing what exactly you react to. If you can learn to pay attention to how you respond to people's tone of voice or intonations, you will understand better why you may be attracted to some people and turned off by others.

Gestures Gestures were probably one of the first means of communication human beings developed, long before oral language appeared. All cultures have a system of meaningful gestures which either accompany spoken language or stand alone in conveying a particular message. You nod your head to say "yes" (but in some cultures, nodding means "no") and shake your head sideways to say "no." The hitchhiker's hand gesture is recognizable in most automobile-using cultures. You extend your hand to shake someone else's as a greeting and not as a hostile gesture. The language of the deaf is probably one of the most sophisticated systems of sign language.

You usually accompany your speech with a considerable number of hand gestures. If you've ever tried to give directions to someone over the telephone, you probably have caught yourself uselessly waving a hand in the air. Some cultures are known to be more expressive with the hands than others. The French, Spanish, and Italian, and other Mediterranean cultures, for instance, are quite effusive with their hand gestures. Sometimes certain gestures become automatic. Students are usually quick to recognize the familiar gestures of their professors. Impersonators of famous people rely on pose and gestures, in addition to their voice imitations, to create their characters. Gestures are often used to give emphasis to words. Sometimes, the emphasis may be placed on the wrong word if the speaker's timing is bad, and you may get the impression that the message is not sincere.

Gestures are culture-bound. That is, they are learned within the society and culture in which you belong. Just as you learned to speak your native tongue, you learned a pattern of gestures to accompany your verbal language, and you learned how to interpret this pattern of gestures.

Here again, let us emphasize that no behavior, no gesture, has meaning of and by itself. Gestures contribute to the creation of meaning in interpersonal communication and point to certain attitudes or emotions. But gestures and their potential meanings seldom have a one-to-one correspondence. With the exception of *emblems* and *signs,* which are denotative gestures pointing to one commonly shared referent (the thumb of the hitchhiker, for example), gestures, like words, do not contain meaning but help create meaning.

Gestures help in many ways to interpret the content of communication. They *help define roles*. The way you greet others tells them whether the occasion is formal or social, friendly or distant. Large gestures are often attributed to authority and dominant figures while small gestures are often associated with meekness, discomfort, and lack of an authoritative stance. Gestures also *monitor* the flow of interaction. Scheflen defines monitors as actions which regulate or maintain order in interpersonal communication.[8] Shaking the index finger is a gesture frequently used by parents to tell a child that he or she is not behaving according to their expectations. A hand movement may indicate a desire to stop someone's flow of conversation, or a wish to have the other person slow down and give you a turn. Gestures are also used to establish the context of a relationship; some gestures are associated with courtship behavior and some with authoritative behavior, for example.

---

[8]Albert E. Scheflen, *Body Language and Social Order: Communication as Behavioral Control,* Prentice-Hall, Inc., Englewood Cliffs, N.J., 1972.

Facial Expressions and Body Movements

You are seldom immobile or expressionless. Your face moves and your body moves, and these movements communicate a great deal about your feelings, emotions, reactions, etc. Some of the time these movements are conscious and intentional, as when you deliberately smile at a friend, frown to express dissatisfaction, or raise an eyebrow to show surprise. Much of the time, however, these movements are so much a part of you that they appear unintentional and unconscious. When you attempt to hide a feeling, you often give yourself away without realizing it; the way you move toward or away from a person, the way you sit — tense, relaxed, on the edge of the chair, slouched, etc. You tend to lean forward when you feel involved and interested, and to lean back when you are not. The way you walk often indicates to others if you feel good, happy, and cheerful or sad, gloomy, tired, and dejected. You indicate your perception of status by your postures. You tend to relax around people of equal or lower status and tense up around people whom you perceive as having higher status. You sometimes feel that someone is disrespectful simply because he or she talks in a more relaxed manner than you think is appropriate.

Watching another person's face for cues is a common experience for all of you. When you hear a friend say something which can be taken several ways do you quickly look at the friend's face to see how he or she "meant" it? Even at a public lecture when you are in the back row, you concentrate on the lecturer's nonverbal messages and usually wish you could see the speaker's face as well as the broad gestures. Television has given us the advantage of close-up shots of a speaker or a narrator whose facial expressions then become a significant part of the total message. Researchers in media have studied the effects of non-verbal signals from commentators and reporters. One such study of potential bias by television news broadcasters, although inconclusive in its findings, did point out that news broadcasters showed different facial expressions when talking about different political candidates, and that even untrained observers (you and I) can detect those different expressions. The study also mentioned that because many such broadcasters are professional performers, they have more control over their facial expressions than most people do.[9] Of course, tone of voice is very important in the television medium, but the fact is that facial expressions and other subtle gestures can add much to what the announcer says. Much more needs to be learned about how facial expressions affect others, not only in interpersonal relations, but also in public appearances where important social and political issues may be decided.

[9]Howard S. Friedman, Timothy I. Mertz, and M. Robin DiMatteo, "Perceived Bias in the Facial Expressions of Television News Broadcasters," *Journal of Communication*, vol. 30, no. 4, Autumn 1980, pp. 103–111.

How you look at a person communicates a great deal. A teacher sensitive to nonverbal movements and expressions can tell a resistive, belligerent, challenging student before that student ever says a word. There is no magic—or, as we often call it for lack of a better word, "intuition"—involved. It is a simple interpretation of subtle yet visible cues which are sent or given away by the student's posture and the way he or she looks at the teacher. Whether you look at a person for too long or too short a time will also communicate something.

You may stare to express disapproval, or indicate by prolonged eye contact with your spouse or friend that it is time to leave the party. Intense gazing into someone else's eyes connotes intimacy, usually of a sexual nature, or may be a way to establish superiority and command.

Object Language   As most people do, you probably spend some time worrying and thinking about your physical appearance. Our culture places a lot of emphasis on physical attractiveness, however that may be defined from year to year and from fashion style to fashion style. Physical appearance is one of the major determinants in first impressions. What you look like and what you wear communicate something to others. As Dale Leathers notes, "You communicate your own identity by means of your visible self."[10] For most of you, the major medium of communication by appearance is clothing.

Clothes do serve many functions from a communication point of view. They can express emotions and feelings. Bright colors suggest youthful vitality, while grays and dark colors reflect a more sedate and subdued mood. Suggestive clothes, such as low-cut dresses, slit skirts, and tight slacks, carry sexual messages. Recently, books on "how to dress for success" have become popular and are used as a guide by both men and women to help them achieve the appropriate appearance. Your clothes have a great impact on your behavior as well as the behavior of the other people you associate with. Uniforms, for example, are rich in communicative value. Clothes also help differentiate among people. Young people do not dress the same way older people do. Clothes reflect socioeconomic differences as well as cultural and ethnic ones. In fact, a study by Gibbins revealed that people do make judgments about each other on the basis of the clothes they wear and that there is a good deal of agreement about the meaning conveyed by certain types of clothes.[11] Most of you choose the clothes you wear on the basis of how well you think other people will like them, not just for

[10]Dale G. Leathers, *Nonverbal Communication Systems,* Allyn and Bacon, Boston, 1976.
[11]K. Gibbins, "Communication Aspects of Women's Clothes and their Relation to Fashionability," *British Journal of Social and Clinical Psychology,* vol. 8, 1969, pp. 306–307.

comfort or durability. "Object language," then, refers to the meanings you attribute to objects with which you surround yourself. The clothes and jewelry you wear, your hairstyle, and the decorative objects in your house are all part of object language. They say something about you because they represent to some extent deliberate choices you make. Clothing and jewelry are particularly revealing. You usually dress differently for different occasions; and if you don't, you are still communicating something about yourself, about your attitudes toward others, your sense of appropriateness, your upbringing, your values. Clothing is symbolic. Some young people's attire is rich in colorful symbols of their choice. Some people are so concerned about what they communicate with their clothes that they will buy them only in certain stores which guarantee the particular kind of status they seek, whether they be secondhand stores, army surplus stores, or fashionable boutiques. A wedding band or an engagement ring communicates something quite specific about a person.

You often react to others in terms of what they wear and what this means to you. A woman wearing a police uniform has told us nonverbally a great deal, if not about herself personally, at least about the role she can be expected to play in certain situations. Studies have been conducted for many years on the general subject of how people respond to uniforms (as a result, some police forces have adopted different types of "uniforms" for their officers) and on such socially oriented subjects as responses of people to the clothes worn by petition circulators, or beggars, or salespersons, or candidates for office. Hairstyles, beards, and ornamentation (jewelry, headbands, etc.) have all been used in informal and formal investigations to test reactions of respondents to such varieties of object language.

All material objects help you in making inferences about the person who displays them. You cannot ignore these objects and decide they do not count, just as you cannot decide that a person's words do not count. It occurs too often, unfortunately, that the inferences you make may be wrong or the objects' meaning misinterpreted. So it happens in verbal communication. You must be cautious in interpreting the nonverbal messages communicated through dress and other material objects, just as you must be careful in interpreting a person's words. You must remember that the choice of what to wear and what to say is still yours, and you have to take the responsibility for, and sometimes the consequences of, the misunderstandings they might generate. If you truly wish to communicate effectively with others, you cannot operate on the assumption that it's their responsibility to understand you. You have some responsibility to help them understand you. Just as you do not speak Chinese to an Italian and expect him or her to understand, you perhaps should not be surprised that certain clothes or hairstyles may be misunderstood in some situations. If you think that you should not be judged for what you wear, remember that, whether you like it or not, clothes are a part of communication, and therefore say something about you.

Communication by Touch

Touch is one of the first modes of communication of the human being. Infants learn much about their environment by touching, feeling, cuddling, and tasting. Linus's security blanket in Charles Schultz's cartoons is a symbol of all the objects children become attached to which they particularly like to touch, feel, or keep. We communicate a great deal by touching. A pat on the back, shaking a hand, or holding a hand can express more than a lengthy speech. Lovers know this. Mothers do too. In their book *Speech and Man*, Brown and Van Riper recall an incident told by one of their students which dramatically illustrates the power of a touch.

> A student was presenting to a class the view that verbal language, in the main, disguises the speaker, and that the real burden of a communication is sent in the nonverbal broadcast. This he illustrated with a story not to be forgotten. He said he was driving on a superhighway one morning at dawn, and an automobile approaching at a high speed began to sway crazily from one side of the road to the other. It eventually plunged off the road, crashed into a concrete pole which broke off and fell over the automobile, bringing it to a halt. The student stopped and ran to the man's aid. The victim was hanging out of his automobile, apparently dead, his face covered with broken windshield glass. The student began to lift the glass from the man's face and the man shook his head slowly. Without opening his eyes, he mumbled, "Give me your hand." The student took the man's hand and in a few minutes the man died. The student said, "In those moments I was told about death as no words will ever tell me."[12]

In American culture, except in a few well-defined situations, touching is linked with intimate interpersonal relationships, and is thus taboo for most other types of relationships. Many people thus refrain from touching others in more casual encounters for fear their behavior might be misconstrued or simply because they are afraid of or do not like physical contacts. When they must stand in line, Americans will usually form an orderly single line in which everyone waits patiently for a turn. In Arab countries, on the other hand, lines are almost unheard of; con-

[12]Charles T. Brown and Charles Van Riper, *Speech and Man*, Prentice-Hall, Inc., Englewood Cliffs, N.J., 1966, pp. 54–55. Reprinted by permission of the authors and the publisher.

siderable pushing, shoving, and touching are involved in most gatherings, and such behavior is not considered distasteful. American children learn relatively young to kiss their relatives hello and good-bye. Spanish children frequently kiss not only their relatives but adult friends and acquaintances as well when they encounter them and depart from them.

Touching is a powerful communicative tool and serves to express a tremendous range of feelings, such as fear, love, anxiety, warmth, coldness. The importance of touch in your communication is evidenced by the number of common expressions in the English language which somehow connote touching. Ashley Montagu lists a few of these figures of speech: rubbing people the wrong way, stroking, describing someone as a soft touch or as thick-skinned or thin-skinned, getting in touch, making contact, handling people carefully, getting under someone's skin, being skin-deep, being touchy.[13]

Touching is so important in the healthy development of human life that infants who are not handled, cuddled, stroked, caressed, and touched get sick and sometimes die.[14] The touching dimension of interpersonal communication is a transactional process by which the self develops. By being handled and touched, a baby becomes aware of his or her body. Lack of adequate touching in early childhood can leave serious emotional scars which often affect the development of healthy intimate adult relationships.

Touch is indeed a mode of communication. Those you love and feel close to you will touch more often than you would casual acquaintances or strangers. The relational dimension of interpersonal transactions is often displayed through touch. While everyone can touch a baby or a young child, few people find it comfortable to touch a person of high status or in authority.

How you touch also communicates something about your relationship with another person. A tender and gentle touch does convey positive feelings. A hard push or abrupt shove usually communicates negative feelings, unless, of course, some other nonverbal signal indicates that rough play is acceptable.

Where you touch has high communicative value. Areas of the body which can be touched are usually culturally prescribed, and most of the time quite carefully so, because of the potential sexual meaning which touch connotes.

---

[13]Ashley Montagu, *Touching: The Human Significance of the Skin,* Harper & Row, Publishers, Inc., New York, 1978.
[14]Ibid, p. 35.

CONTEXTUAL PATTERNS FOR NONVERBAL MESSAGES

The anthropologist Edward T. Hall in his fascinating book *The Silent Language*[15] was one of the first scholars to probe into the contextual dimensions of interpersonal communication. Interpersonal communication does not occur in a vacuum. It takes place in a cultural context — that is, a system of norms and rules — which determines to a large degree the variables of the communication process. You are usually unaware of the cultural context which influences your communicative behavior because it is so familiar and "normal" to you. You sometimes see it when you contrast your cultural context with that of a foreign culture. The two most powerful factors which affect your interpersonal communication are time and space.

Time

Time is a form of interpersonal communication. In our culture, time is almost treated as a thing; you gain time, waste it, give it, and take it. Time is precious, a rare commodity in your rushed lives. Time speaks.

In American urban white culture, punctuality is valued, and tardiness is considered insulting. Being late for an appointment or in turning in an assignment may lead to unpleasant consequences. However, what is considered "late" varies not only with each individual and his or her personal sense of time but also with the situation, the other people involved, and the geographic area. For example, you may have a very important appointment with a person of higher status than yours — perhaps a job interview. Usually, you will try to be "on time," and this may mean about five minutes before the appointed time to five minutes after. If you arrive fifteen minutes after the appointed time, you will probably apologize and offer some explanation for your delay. The kind and extent of your apologies and explanations will vary according to how late you are. If you are only five minutes late, you may not have to say anything. If you are ten minutes late, you may feel that you have to apologize briefly but need not give any reason for the delay. If you are half an hour late, you will probably apologize profusely and need to explain thoroughly what kept you. If you are an hour late, you will not expect the other person to be still waiting for you. If the other person is still there, as when you meet your date at home and show up an hour late, you expect him or her to be very upset.

With a close friend the extent of tardiness may be increased without drastic consequences; but here too, a scale will be established to determine whether you owe an apology or not, and, if so, the extent of that apology. Apologies are needed at some point, however, because extreme tardiness may be taken as an insult or a sign of irresponsibility.

---

[15]Edward T. Hall, *The Silent Language,* Doubleday & Company, Inc., Garden City, N.Y., 1966.

In some cultures, tardiness may not be perceived as insulting, and one can go to a meeting hours after the appointed time without upsetting anyone. In Mexico, for example, it is not uncommon to arrive an hour and a half after the appointed time and still be considered on time. In the United States this would, of course, be considered very late and very rude. An American meeting a Mexican would feel insulted to have to wait so long and would probably expect a good story to account for such a delay. The American would be quite upset at hearing no story, for the Mexican would, in his or her eyes, be on time and thus would not feel the need to explain anything. Unless you know and understand another culture's sense of time, you may get very frustrated, and this naturally affects the way you communicate with members of that culture.

Arriving early at an appointment communicates as much as arriving late. In some circles where it is fashionable to be late to parties, the early arrival of a guest may throw the host and hostess into a panic, and they may be quite upset that their guest was not polite enough to arrive later.

Time communicates in other ways. A telephone call at 3 A.M. somehow communicates a feeling of urgency and importance. People don't usually call you at that time of the night just to ask how you are and to say, "Gee, it's been a while since we've seen each other."

If you are two hours late coming home during the day, your family or friends may be quite worried and upset, but their fears will be less intense than what they would be if you were two hours late after midnight.

Space The space in which your interpersonal communication takes place affects you in many subtle ways that you are not always aware of. Each of you has a "personal space," a sort of invisible bubble around you, which you feel is yours and which you do not like to see intruded upon without express permission. Although each of you sets his or her own personal boundaries, there are recognizable cultural patterns which regulate the handling of personal space and interpersonal distance.

Edward T. Hall has identified three major interpersonal distances he calls "intimate," "social," and "public," which govern most of your interpersonal relationships.[16] The "intimate" distance ranges from very close (3 to 6 inches; soft whispers, secret or intimate communication) to close (8 to 12 inches; confidential information) to near (12 to 20 inches; soft voice). The "social" distance ranges from 20 inches to 5 feet, and the "public" distance from 6 feet to about 100 feet.

When people violate the unspoken rules of interpersonal distance (get too close when they should be at a social distance or stand too far

[16]Ibid., pp. 163–164.

away when they are expected to be more intimate), you generally feel uncomfortable. When someone you did not invite comes too close to you, you tend to move away. Your territory is marked, and you may let others approach, but not too closely unless you specifically decide to let them. The uncomfortable feeling one gets in a crowded room often comes from the fact that too many people are too close to one another. If someone crowds you at the library or at the cafeteria by sitting too close to you, you unconsciously move away by moving your books, tray, or chair away from the intruder. If for some reason the intruder moves closer, you try other avoidance behaviors. However, you rarely ask people in words to move away from you. If they do not respond appropriately by understanding your nonverbal avoidance moves, you usually change places in the library, or leave the cafeteria as soon as you can, feeling that your lunch was spoiled.

Appropriate interpersonal distances vary from culture to culture. As Hall points out, the comfortable distance for most Americans to stand for social conversation is about 2 to 3 feet. In France, Mexico, Brazil, or the Arab countries, however, the comfortable distance is somewhat shorter than 2 feet. Should two men, an American and an Arab, engage in conversation, a subtle ballet is likely to follow: the Arab moves close to the American and looks intently into his eyes. The American, uncomfortable because the other one is too close, tries to reestablish a distance he finds less disturbing by moving back. The Arab, feeling that the American is too far from him for social conversation, moves in closer, and the American moves back farther. Each feels somewhat upset about what is perceived as "pushy" (the Arab moving in too close) or "unfriendly" (the American moving away).

Interpersonal distance is one of the ways you have to express feelings. You tend to move closer to people you like and away from people you do not, if you have a choice. You sometimes take great precautions to avoid walking near someone you do not like.

Proxemics, the study of spatial relationships, reveals that your perception of space or of the territory people occupy is more a function of cultural and social conditioning than of biological or genetic factors. With people, territory is culturally defined. The space you occupy has boundaries which are determined mostly by cultural conventions and are learned so early that strong feelings are associated with the internal "intuitive" reactions to territorial violations. Somehow you "just know" when someone is "too close" or "too far," and you may not really be sure how you came to know it. Yet the distance "feels" right, or it does not.

Space communicates, or rather, you use space to communicate. The story is told of a wife sitting close to her window in the car while her husband was driving. She commented regretfully that they used to sit much closer together during their courting days a few years ago. The husband replied, "I haven't moved!"

Some general comments about our "life space," proxemics, or how close we tolerate others can be made based on the twin assumptions that (1) people have carefully drawn distances, based on many factors which they use when dealing with others, and (2) those distances are not always honored by other people. Burgoon and others developed a number of hypotheses based on previous research studies, and additional studies are being conducted on these and other hypotheses.[17] Attractive people are more liked, more persuasive, and better understood if they come closer than the normal distance than if they are either at the expected distance or farther away. High-status people also are better liked, more persuasive, and better understood if they come in closer than expected. If you are a person of high credibility, then you will be more liked if you stand close while low-credibility persons will not. Distance will also make a difference in how to punish someone: while giving negative feedback you will be better liked if you stay farther away than expected, and people feel threatened at a greater distance by a punishing source than by a rewarding source.[18]

People, like animals, have the tendency to own space, a tendency which is called "territoriality." Territoriality acts as a sort of extension of personal space. Cars are very much an extension of the self; your house, your desk, and sometimes your chair become extensions of yourself. You may get irritated if someone else enters your territory uninvited.

Territoriality is usually defined culturally. Territoriality most of the time provides an advantage to the owner of the territory. Playing a home game is somehow easier than playing in the competing team's home field. You may feel more at ease and comfortable on your own grounds, and the other person is at a slight disadvantage. The question "My place or yours?" is a loaded one. If a supervisor calls you to his or her office to discuss some business matters, there is a certain advantage for the supervisor associated with that territory. If, on the other hand, your supervisor meets you in your office, on your turf, then you have a subtle but real psychological advantage. Some territories are considered neutral. For examples, hallways, lobbies, public places, cafeterias, etc., belong to everyone. Communication which takes place in such

---

[17]Judee K. Burgoon and Stephen B. Jones, "Toward a Theory of Personal Space Expectation and Their Violations," *Human Communication Research,* vol. 2, no. 2, Winter 1976, pp. 131–146; Judee Burgoon and Lynn Aho, "Field Experiments on the Effects of Violations of Conversational Distance," *Communication Monographs,* vol. 49, no. 2, June 1982, pp. 71–88.

[18]Ibid., pp. 142–143.

neutral places takes on certain characteristics. Observe, for example, your communicative behavior with one of your teachers. You may meet him or her in a hallway and exchange some pleasant small talk, an appropriate "hallway conversation." However, should you switch the topic and mention that you would like to discuss an upcoming assignment, chances are your teacher will suggest that you both meet in his or her office — no longer neutral territory. The teacher, deliberately or not, reestablishes authority in the relationship (becomes one-up) by getting back into the superior position, one which will give greater control of the situation. The advantage may be a subtle one, yet it matters. It matters a great deal in diplomatic relations, where the location of peace talks or negotiations is indeed crucial. Such negotiations are invariably held in neutral territory where neither party has an undue psychological or logistical advantage over the other. If you are in a dominant position with someone and wish to change to a more equal relationship, then you may choose to communicate on grounds other than your own to compensate for your superior position. You may hold the conversation in the other person's territory or in a neutral place.

Special elements other than interpersonal distances also affect you. The arrangement of a room, the shape of a meeting table, or the size of a classroom in relation to the number of students occupying it all influence the development of interpersonal communication. Researchers have found, for example, that communication is distributed more evenly among people sitting at a *round* table than among people sitting at a *rectangular* table. At a rectangular table, people sitting at the ends are more likely to be talked to and to talk than the other group members. Robert Sommer has made extensive studies of seating arrangements and their influence on people's perceptions of competition, cooperation, and togetherness.[19] Figure 19 describes three basic arrangements. Sitting face to face across a table, for example, is likely to be perceived as competition. Most competitive games, in fact, are played face to face. When you sit face to face on the other side of someone's desk, you may tend to perceive the situation in competitive or adversary terms. A cooperative seating arrangement is more likely to be diagonal or side by side. In fact, we talk about being "on the same side" in arguments or discussions. In diagonal seating, close contact can be maintained, although the corner of the table or desk provides some safety from unwanted intrusions into your personal space. Working together on the same project, particularly if you must manipulate objects together, is enhanced by side-by-side seating. Observe desk

[19]Robert Sommer, *Personal Space,* Prentice-Hall, Inc., Englewood Cliffs, N.J., 1969, pp. 58–75.

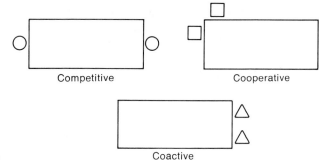

FIGURE 19.
Seating arrangements.

and chair arrangements in your teacher's office, for example. Does the teacher move out from behind the desk to talk with you? Is there a chair available at a diagonal angle? Are the chairs set on the other side of the desk, inviting a face-to-face seating? Do you ever sit side by side when you and the teacher work on your schedule or when you discuss a grade you received on a term paper? Although the seating arrangement is not the only factor involved in maintaining control or producing competition or cooperation, these nonverbal factors do not happen randomly, by accident. People do choose how they arrange their offices, at least within the structural limitations imposed by the shape and size of the room and the organizational constraints of how many chairs they get to work with. People do choose, to some extent, how they position themselves in relation to others. These moves have great communicative value.

CHARACTERISTICS OF NONVERBAL COMMUNICATION

The Impossibility of Not Communicating

You cannot not communicate. The nature of human communication is such that it is unavoidable. As we pointed out earlier, you can refrain from communication with words but you cannot escape nonverbal communication. To say nothing and remain silent is in itself a form of communication. You cannot stop from moving and expressing yourself with your gestures and facial expressions. Whatever you do or do not do communicates something about yourself. Interpersonal communication is inevitable when two people are together because all behavior has some message value.

Interpersonal communication may not be conscious or intentional, or successful, but it takes place. Unless you know this principle and try to understand the communicative value of other people's behavior and your own, the potential for interpersonal breakdown looms large.

The Expression of Feelings and Emotions

Nonverbal communication is your primary mode of communicating feelings and emotions. You usually communicate about content and tasks through verbal communication. Verbal language is your primary mode of communicating cognitive information and dealing with the business at hand. Nonverbal communication, however, is your mode of sharing feelings with one another and dealing with the process of human relationships. Words usually carry *content information;* nonverbal communication expresses *affective information.* From the way you look at someone you may communicate love, hate, dislike, interest, trust, sexual desire, admiration, acceptance, scorn, etc. — a full range of human emotions which you do not always express verbally. Gestures such as tapping your fingers or your foot can communicate impatience, boredom, or nervousness. Your face has innumerable ways of expressing likes and dislikes, approval and disapproval.

Information about Content and Relationship

Nonverbal communication usually includes information about the content of a verbal message. Nonverbal communication gives you the clues that you need to interpret the verbal messages you hear. The same words (same content) said in different tones of voice should probably be interpreted differently. The tone of voice, among other nonverbal messages, is a clue as to which interpretation to make. Unless you are sensitive to the interpretive dimension of interpersonal communication, you may not interpret the words you hear adequately and thus may increase the likelihood of having communication difficulties with those around you.

Nonverbal communication also gives you information about the nature of the relationship between you and those with whom you communicate.

Reliability of Nonverbal Messages

Nonverbal messages are usually more reliable than verbal messages. In some interpersonal situations, the context of a message does not fit the affective information about that message. The man says, "I love you," but somehow his tone of voice and other nonverbal signals he sends deny the very words he just spoke. He says one thing at the content level, but the opposite thing gets communicated nonverbally. What *is* the woman to believe? The words or the nonverbal signals?

A woman assures you that she trusts you, but her behavior toward you consistently denies her words. What are you to believe? The words or the behavior?

You know intuitively that words alone are not enough to establish the authenticity of a message. You know this because all of you know how easy it is to lie with words. You do it in many social situations when you assure a hostess you had a wonderful time, and she replies that she was delighted you could come, and neither of you really means the words spoken out of social courtesy. It is, however, much more difficult to "lie" nonverbally and express feelings you do not really feel. Talented professional actors and actresses are few. Most of you have difficulty faking over a long period of time the feelings you do not experience. Students may fake interest in the classroom for perhaps ten minutes, but to sustain the fake interest for the whole class period without giving themselves away is extremely difficult. Nonverbal expressions are thus considered more believable than words. If a verbal message conflicts with what is expressed nonverbally, you thus tend to believe the nonverbal message. You rely essentially on nonverbal cues to get your impressions of how honest other people are in their interpersonal relationships, rather than on what they tell you about themselves.

The people you trust are usually those people whose nonverbal behavior confirms and reinforces the content of their verbal communication. You know that they speak their true feelings, and that they do as well as they say.

Lewis and Page suggest that there is a definite relationship between the nonverbal messages in a classroom and the kind of learning which takes place.[20] Having studied the writings of commentators on nonverbal messages and applied those principles to the classroom setting, they report that students develop confidence in teachers' honesty and authenticity by watching for nonverbal cues. They also conclude that "the student who possesses less verbal facility, who has learning disabilities, and who is culturally disadvantaged relies even more heavily on nonverbal communication in the classroom." They go on to say that this student not only checks on the reliability of the communicator, but also expects to get clarification of verbal material by watching the nonverbal system. Such an exchange places great responsibility on a teacher to be aware of and honest in nonverbal communication.

BIBLIOGRAPHY

Anderson, J. F., and J. G. Withrow: "The Impact of Lecturer Nonverbal Expressiveness on Improving Mediated Instruction," *Communication Education,* vol. 30, no. 4, October 1981.

Brown, C. T., and C. Van Riper: *Speech and Man,* Prentice-Hall, Inc., Englewood Cliffs, N.J., 1966.

Buck, R.: "A Test of Nonverbal Receiving Ability: Preliminary Studies," *Human Communication Research,* vol. 2, no. 2, Winter 1976.

[20]Phillip V. Lewis and Zollie Page, "Educational Implications of Nonverbal Communication," *ETC.,* vol. 31, no. 4, December 1974, pp. 371–375.

Burgoon, J. K., and L. Aho: "Field Experiments on the Effects of Violations of Conversational Distance," *Communication Monographs,* vol. 49, no. 2, June 1982.

————, and S. B. Jones: "Toward a Theory of Personal Space Expectation and Their Violations," *Human Communication Research,* vol. 2, no. 2, Winter 1976.

Cappella, J. N., and S. Planalp: "Talk and Silence Sequences in Informal Conversation," *Human Communication Research,* vol. 7, no. 3, Spring 1981.

Fast, J.: *Body Language,* Pocket Books, Inc., New York, 1981.

Friedman, H. S., T. I. Mertz, and M. R. DiMatteo: "Perceived Bias in the Facial Expressions of Television News Broadcasters," *Journal of Communication,* vol. 30, no. 4, Autumn 1980.

Gibbins, K.: "Communication Aspects of Women's Clothes and Their Relation to Fashionability," *British Journal of Social and Clinical Psychology,* vol. 8, 1969.

Hall, E. T.: *The Silent Language,* Doubleday & Company, Inc., Garden City, N.Y., 1973.

————: *The Hidden Dimension,* Doubleday & Company, Inc., Garden City, N.Y., 1966.

Hocking, J. E., and D. Leathers: "Nonverbal Indicators of Deception: A New Theoretical Perspective," *Communication Monographs,* vol. 47, no. 2, June 1980.

Isenhart, M. W.: "An Investigation of the Relationship of Sex and Sex Role to the Ability to Decode Nonverbal Cues," *Human Communication Research,* vol. 6, no. 4, Summer 1980.

Keiser, G. J., and I. Altman: "Relationship of Nonverbal Behavior to the Social Penetration Process," *Human Communication Research,* vol. 2, no. 2, Winter 1976.

Koivumaki, J. H.: "Body Language Taught Here," *Journal of Communication,* vol. 25, no. 1, Winter 1975.

Leathers, D. G.: *Nonverbal Communication Systems,* Allyn and Bacon, Boston, 1976.

Lewis, P. V., and Z. Page: "Educational Implications of Nonverbal Communication," *ETC.,* vol. 31, no. 4, 1974.

McLaughlin, M. L., and M. J. Cody: "Awkward Silences: Behavioral Antecedents and the Consequences of the Conversational Lapse," *Human Communication Research,* vol. 8, no. 4, Summer 1982.

Molloy, J. T.: *Dress for Success,* Warner Books, New York, 1976.

————: *The Woman's Dress for Success Book,* Warner Books, New York, 1978.

Montagu, A.: *Touching: The Human Significance of Skin,* Harper & Row, Publishers, Inc., New York, 1978.

Morris, D.: *Manwatching,* Harry N. Abrams, Inc., New York, 1977.

O'Hair, H. D., M. J. Cody, and M. L. McLaughlin: "Prepared Lies, Spontaneous Lies, Machiavellianism, and Nonverbal Communication," *Human Communication Research,* vol. 7, no. 4, Summer 1981.

Scheflen, A. E.: *Body Language and Social Order: Communication As Behavioral Control,* Prentice-Hall, Inc., Englewood Cliffs, N.J., 1972.

Sommer, R.: *Personal Space,* Prentice-Hall, Inc., Englewood Cliffs, N.J., 1969.

Stiles, W. B.: "Verbal Response Modes and Dimensions of Interpersonal Roles," *Journal of Personality and Social Psychology,* vol. 36, 1978.

INTERPERSONAL STRATEGIES

Chapter 10

INTERPERSONAL TRANSACTIONS: THE RULES OF THE GAME

In a Nutshell

You are involved in a transactional communication with another person (1) when you take each other into account, (2) when you differentiate your role relationships, and (3) when you conduct your interaction by a set of agreed-upon rules.

Interpersonal transactions operate at two distinct levels: the denotative or content level and the relationship level. The relationship level of interpersonal transactions performs two functions: (1) an interpretive function, in which verbal and nonverbal cues tell you how to interpret the messages you receive; and (2) a relational function, which serves to tell you and others how you see yourself, how you see others, and how you see the relationship between you and them.

Communication among nonequals is based on differences among people, usually an authority dimension; communication among equals is based on similarities among people who treat each other as peers.

Role conflict and differences in determining the beginning of a communication event are at the root of many communication difficulties. Other communication problems, such as double messages, are also the source of typical communication breakdowns. When you send one message through your words but at the same time send the opposite message through your facial expressions and tone of voice, you may throw your listener for a loop, since he or she won't know which of the messages you really meant to send.

INTRODUCTION

As we discussed in Chapter 6, the process of constructing meaning is at the core of communication. When you exchange messages with other people, the symbols you trade back and forth do not in themselves constitute communication. Meaning must be created, and it is the process of creating meaning which is called "communication." In Chapter 6, we stressed that meanings are highly personal and based on reactions to your life experiences. However, in some way you learn to construct meanings in social contexts, and this means that you tend to construct meanings like those of the people you live with and interact with.

It is because you collaborate with others in learning to construct meanings that you can engage in coordinated activities with other people, and it is because you are able to take other people into account that you can develop expectations of what others will do or what you think they expect of you. Sharing meanings and sharing expectations, as Bonnie Johnson explains it, are the prerequisites for organized action.[1]

THE STRUCTURE OF COMMUNICATION TRANSACTIONS

Because communication is transactional, you can learn to construct meanings with others and learn to develop mutual expectations. A transaction is the basic unit of study in communication, and it can be quite simply defined as *two or more people who mutually and simultaneously (1) take one another into account, (2) figure out their roles, and (3) conduct their interaction by a set of rules.*

We are now going to explore further what the three components of a transaction are.

Taking One Another into Account

A transaction takes place when one or more people are mutually and simultaneously taking one another into account. As an outsider observing other people, you may not always be able to tell whether other people are taking each other into account. When you are a participant, however, you are quite aware of the process. Say, for example, you stop at a red light and casually look at the man driving the car stopped next to you. For a moment, perhaps, the other driver is not aware that you are looking in his direction. All of a sudden, however, he turns around and *sees you seeing him.* If you are still looking, you *will see him seeing you seeing him.* This is now a communication transaction. It frequently happens that you are aware of someone else's presence while that person is not aware of you at all. The little boy who waits until his mother has turned her back to stick his tongue out is well aware of his

---

[1]Bonnie McDaniel Johnson, *Communication, the Process of Organizing,* American Press, Boston, 1981.

mother's presence and acts on the basis of her momentary unaware-
ness of his behavior. This is communication if the child or some third-
person observer *constructs meaning out of the situation* and behaves
on the basis of that meaning. But it is not a transaction. A communication transaction takes *mutual* awareness and is the prerequisite for organized behavior, because when mutual awareness exists there is the possibility of mutual influence on one another. The actions of one person
may affect the actions of the other, and vice versa. A transaction occurs
only when there is the perception of being perceived by another person. You must see yourself being seen.

Transactions are more than just physical interdependence. For one
thing, communication transactions can be carried on over the telephone. For another, what matters is the perception of the other person's perception. You stand in a roomful of strangers at a party, and
your eyes meet someone else's. Perhaps you acknowledge the mutual
look by a smile or a nod of the head. Contact is established. You perceive the other person and are aware of his or her perception of you.
The process is mutual. A transaction is taking place, and meaning is constructed which potentially can lead to organized activity.

The concept of transaction as mutual perceptions is rich in implications. Your own behavior is fair game for the other person to construct meaning which then shapes his or her own behavior. As you
observe the other person's behavior, you too construct meaning which
subsequently shapes your behavior. Because construction of meaning
and mutual perceptions are practically simultaneous, it is very difficult
to untangle the process. To assess another person's behavior, you must
always assess the part you may have played in shaping that behavior.
What you perceive in another person may depend in part on what that
other person perceives in you.

Back to our example of the party where your eyes meet those of a
stranger. Perhaps the stranger looked at you, perceived you as a
friendly type, and because you were smiling, smiled. Simultaneously,
you looked at the stranger, you perceived him or her as a friendly sort
because you saw a smile, and so you smiled too. Who smiled first? The
"chicken-and-egg" question again. As far as you are concerned, you
smiled because the other person smiled. But your smile may have been
the trigger for the other person's smile. As far as the other person is
concerned, he or she smiled because of your smile. The important thing
here is that what you perceive in others may well depend in part on
what they perceive in you.

To summarize this discussion, let us emphasize that a transaction
takes place when (1) you are doing something, (2) another person is
doing something, (3) you are aware of the other's behavior, (4) the
other person is aware of your behavior, and as a result (5) you are

aware that the other person is aware of you, and (6) the other person is aware that you are aware of him or her.[2]

Mutual Role Definitions

Transactions are characterized by the fact that people assume roles in relation to one another. These roles play a significant part in shaping people's behaviors. Roles not only limit the range of behaviors you can expect from an interpersonal encounter, but permit you to develop expectations about other people's behaviors and serve as a guide to interpreting these behaviors and constructing meaning.

Roles are patterns of behaviors felt to be appropriate for specific situations. They are expected behaviors of people who are in certain positions. For example, you are in the role of a student part of the time, and as a student you are expected to do certain things in relation to other people. You are expected to go to classes, listen to your professors, take examinations, read books, write papers, and so forth. Your role as a student is defined in relation to the roles played by other people such as professors, school administrators, and fellow students. Your behavior as a student is different from your behavior as a mother or as a supervisor. Certain behaviors are expected of mothers, students, and supervisors, and these behaviors are defined not in isolation but in relation to other complementary sets of behaviors, other roles. You are not a mother without a child to mother, you are not a student without a teacher to learn from, and you are not a supervisor without someone to supervise.

Types of behaviors that are expected in a given role relationship are usually the product of the value system of a society, a group, or an individual. (As Box 10 suggests, in our society today, television may be a factor in shaping roles.) You learn to act out these behaviors as you grow up in your society and begin imitating people around you. Roles that people play reflect what society agrees is appropriate for the situation.

In any transaction with another person, you are faced with a decision about what role you need to take in relation to the role you think the other person will take and the role you think the other person expects you to take. All transactions reflect negotiated role relationships. In your communication transaction with others, you must always face the issue of role relationship negotiations. Because everyone can be cast in many different roles, you need to determine which role is appropriate for you, considering your evaluations of (1) the situation, (2) the other person, and (3) yourself.

---

[2]William W. Wilmot, *Dyadic Communication: A Transactional Perspective,* Addison-Wesley, Reading, Mass., 1979, p. 81.

BOX 10. **Television and Role Development**

Much criticism has been leveled at television for its part in developing roles for people. Learning our social roles from the shows on television can be both a good and a bad experience. Some television characters may not be the best role models for us to follow — such as the aggressive bully who gets away with intimidating others, or the dishonest person who is not caught in the act or punished, or the generally disagreeable character whose language and behaviors are not socially acceptable. Television may portray to young children (as well as to adults, who also may be affected by role models on televison) family behaviors which vary from their own experience. Research has shown that shows about family life depict the least amount of violence and aggression and the most amount of cooperative and affiliative behaviors. Children may actually see a better form of family life on television than they see in their own experience. If children believe that family life should be "like that" in real life, then the influence of television, in this instance, may be helpful in developing healthy family roles. Learning consumer behavior is also related to media viewing habits and family communication patterns. The process of learning from television is itself less significant than the influence parents exert over their children to watch programs that ensure healthy role development. (Nancy L. Buerkel-Rothfuss, Bradley S. Greenberg, Charles K. Atkin, and Kimberly Nuendorf, "Learning about the Family from Television," *Journal of Communication,* vol. 32, no. 3, Summer 1982, pp. 191–201. See also Roy L. Moore and George P. Moschis, "The Role of Family Communication in Consumer Learning," in *Journal of Communication,* vol. 31, no. 4, Autumn 1981, pp. 42–51.)

In other kinds of activities, role development may be just as strongly influenced by television. A study of the driving habits of television characters shows a relationship to attitudes of viewers about their own driving. The conclusions suggest that some driving-age viewers accept irregular driving behavior (such as "burning rubber" and screeching brakes) as "normal." They believe that speeding is all right and that most speeders don't get caught, that seat belts are unnecessary, and that dangerous driving will not have serious consequences. They also believe that the proper roles are for males to drive and females to be passengers; that young people (in their twenties) do more irregular driving than others; and that vans, trucks, and sports cars are the most likely vehicles to drive in a dangerous or irregular way. (Bradley S. Greenberg and Charles K. Atkin, "The Portrayal of Driving on Television, 1975–1980," *Journal of Communication,* Spring 1983, vol. 33, no. 2, pp. 44–55.)

Television may deserve its reputation as a generator of roles for regular viewers. With so many types of programs available, there is no shortage of models, or examples, for us to pattern our lives after.

The situation   Where and when communication occurs are powerful guides in determining which role is appropriate. You would not behave the same way at a funeral and in a bar. You are expected to behave differently when you study and when you play, when you go to a football game and when you attend a performance of the local symphony, when you go to a formal dinner party and when you go to a picnic, when you work at the office and when you return home. The professor who always lectures, whether in class, at the coffee shop, at home, or at parties, exhibits role rigidity and is unable to determine that professorial behavior is inappropriate in situations other than the classroom. Because you can assume a large number of possible roles with others, the situation or the context of the transaction is crucial in helping you determine what role to choose at a given time. The example of Greg is not uncommon. Greg is a graduate student at a state university where he teaches an introductory management course. He also works three afternoons a week in a local retail store. Bob, the store's assistant manager, is a few years older than Greg, and they are very good friends. They go out frequently together. Bob is also picking up a few courses at the university, and happens to be in the class Greg teaches this semester. Possible role relationships between the two men are numerous. They can relate as supervisor-employee in the store, friends and peers when they go out, and teacher-student when they are at the university. It is important, of course, that both define the situation in the same way. Both, in a sense, must agree that these three situations call for different behaviors. But suppose they don't agree. If Greg defines the store situation as a friendship situation, and consequently talks to Bob in a very informal fashion, while Bob feels that at the store he is boss and expects to be treated with some deference, their relationship is likely to experience a good deal of stress.

The other person   Whenever you communicate with another person, you have some idea of how that person is going to behave, based on (1) the professional role you expect that person to play, (2) the person's age, and (3) the person's sex. How you come to know what roles other people play is based partly on your previous personal experiences with them, and partly on what you know about how people in those roles generally behave. Different salesclerks may act differently, but you can at least expect to be waited on and helped when you want to buy something. You do not expect the clerk to invite you for coffee or deliver a lecture on nuclear energy.

PROFESSIONAL ROLES
Role expectations are often tied to professional labels, and you expect certain behaviors from a physician, a minister, a police officer, a social worker, etc. Once you know what role you expect a person to play, it

becomes easier to figure out that person's behavior. If you see an adult jerk a child by the arm and push the child forcefully into a parked car, you may understand the situation one way if you know that the adult is the parent of the child or another way if you think that the adult is not related to the child. In one case you may observe a frustrated parent dealing with a recalcitrant child while in the other you may witness a kidnapping.

AGE ROLES

Aside from professional expectations, you may have ideas about how people of a certain age are supposed to behave. A tantrum by a 3-year-old does not "mean" the same thing as a tantrum by a 50-year-old. The same behavior is interpreted differently depending on the age of the person.

SEX ROLES

Another important source of role expectations comes from sexual differences. Although sex role stereotyping is now being challenged seriously, you may still have learned to expect that boys don't cry, girls play with dolls, boys become engineers or doctors, and girls become housewives or secretaries. The same behavior in a man or a woman may be interpreted quite differently simply because of the sex difference. For some, a man who cries is weak while a woman who cries is just emotional. The same behavior which in a man can be seen as appropriately assertive, ambitious, and go-getting may be seen in a woman as pushy and aggressive.

Nowhere has this ambiguous role of women been displayed more clearly than in the "how to be successful" books for women. Not only do the authors disagree on how to measure success for a woman (and some don't even try, but leave that up to the individual woman to decide for herself); they give varying kinds of advice on how to reach this undefined "success".[3] What a woman does buy with one of the career books is a set of role assumptions about how the society will treat her — a clear indication of the impact of role differentiation by sex. According to Barbara Bate and Lois Self, "Assumptions and values about work and its economic and social dimensions affect not only individual readers, but also social perceptions of roles, power, satisfaction, and worth."[4] It should also be cautioned, however, that sex may not always be the most significant factor in human communication; gender may not

[3]Barbara Bate and Lois S. Self, "The Rhetoric of Career Success Books for Women," *Journal of Communication,* vol. 33, no. 2, Spring 1983, pp. 149–165.
[4]Ibid., p. 163.

always determine role relationships. A study by Fisher on the differential effects of sex composition of dyads found that the cooperative or competitive orientation of the people involved in the study had more influence than their gender.[5] Fisher was testing the idea of different communication patterns, styles, and roles in women and men. Other research supports the idea that situations, verbal devices, and a variety of little-known or untested factors may account for differences in role taking and in communicating behaviors.[6] There is also much evidence that the communication patterns of men and women may be more alike in most aspects than our folk wisdom or our superficial guesses may have led us to believe, even though males see themselves as ''more precise'' as communicators, and women see themselves as having a ''more animated style'' than men.[7]

Yourself We discussed in Chapter 3 the part which self-concept plays in your perception of the world around you. How you see yourself affects not only the roles you choose to play but also, and very importantly, how you will play them. You may decide to become a physician, and the professional role of a physician is in part set for you by the generations of doctors who have preceded you and by what society demands from its healers. But you can choose to be a distant, impersonal, disease-oriented doctor or a warm, compassionate, caring, people-oriented physician. You may decide to be a professor; and here again, there are many ways for you to enact that role, from the high-minded and scholarly researcher who lectures occasionally to hundreds of students, to the teacher who ''just loves to teach freshmen.''

Consequences of role *definitions* Role definitions are important to you because once you figure out what role you need to take and what role the other person is likely to take, you have a great deal of information about what behavior is expected of you and what you can expect of the other person.

Roles spell out how you will dress (you do not wear a swimsuit at the office), how you will speak or be spoken to (whether swearing is

[5]B. Aubrey Fisher, ''Differential Effects of Sexual Compositions and Interactional Context on Interaction Patterns in Dyads,'' *Human Communication Research,* vol. 9, no. 3, Spring, 1983, pp. 225–238.

[6]Ibid., p. 237. Also see Patricia Hayes Bradley, ''The Folk-Linguistics of Women's Speech: An Empirical Examination,'' in *Communication Monographs,* vol. 48, no. 4, March 1981, pp. 73–90.

[7]Barbara M. Montgomery and Robert W. Norton, ''Sex Differences and Similarities in Communicator Style,'' *Communication Monographs,* vol. 48, no. 2, June 1981, pp. 121–132.

permissible or not), what kinds of duties and privileges and rights you may be entitled to (whether you get the key to the executive washroom). Roles determine whom you communicate with. If you are a salesclerk, you have to wait on the customers. If you are a student, you talk to other students most of the time, to a professor fairly often, to a dean seldom, to a president rarely if ever, to a trustee probably never. As a new employee you will communicate with your fellow coworkers, supervisors, and perhaps your supervisor's supervisor, and rarely with the top-level executives of the organization, unless you meet them at a company function.

Roles also influence the content of your communication. As a student you may need to talk about the course with the professor. Should you meet the same professor on a bus or at the supermarket, you will probably talk about school-related topics. Roles limit conversational topics, and the professor is not obligated to talk about anything else. Some professors never feel quite comfortable stepping out of the professor-student relationship and prefer to maintain the distance they feel the role requires. Supervisors often believe rigid role boundaries are necessary to maintain their authority over their employees. Although they may act in a pleasant and friendly way with their employees at work, they maintain a professional distance outside the organization when they see their employees in other settings. "Not mixing business with pleasure" is a way to avoid complicated role relationships and the potential problems they may create.

When you first encounter someone, you experience a lot of ambiguity. This is because the role negotiation has to start from scratch. As we mentioned earlier, you determine what role to take on the basis of (1) how you define the situation and how you think the other person defines the situation, (2) how you define your role for that situation and how you think the other person defines your role, and (3) how you define the other person's role and how you think the other person defines his or her role. If you are meeting a new person about whom you know nothing, it is extremely difficult to determine how he or she will think. You rely on obvious behavioral cues such as physical appearance, dress, age, and sex to make some assumptions about "who the person is." You may engage in small talk and, through that cautious process of exchanging banalities, find out more about each other. This is how you jointly build and define roles which will bring some element of predictability and comfort to the relationship.

An example of roles: The man in the middle
This is the story of Jackson, as told in workshops and seminars to illustrate the complexities of role taking. It is only partial, because it focuses on Jackson himself and does not complicate itself by placing all other participants in a similar central spot. (If you want the challenge of addi-

tional discovery, you may want to imagine what happens when each of the "others" in Jackson's world takes the role in the center focal point.)

JACKSON

At stage 1 (see Figure 20), Jackson is a real live human being, who breathes, eats, goes to work, helps raise the family, and plays golf at the club. He is a physical entity almost 6 feet tall, with a weight, hair color, and characteristic walk which his friends can recognize. When the people in his life meet him on the street, they know that this is their acquaintance named Jackson. He occupies space and has a perceivable identity which changes only gradually, except when he buys new clothes, cuts his hair differently, or grows a moustache. He is, therefore, a collection of sufficiently identifiable features that many people would notice his picture in the newspaper or pick him out of a crowd.

FIGURE 20. Stage 1:Jackson and a few of the people in his world. Stage 2: Jackson has a mental picture of himself, and the others have their mental pictures of Jackson (the boxes). Stage 3: Jackson has an ideal version of what he would like to be like, and those around him also have their idealized Jackson (the little clouds).

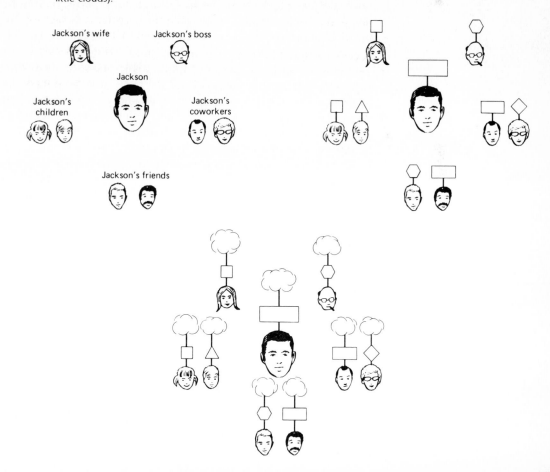

At stage 2, with the addition of some boxes over his head and the heads of others, we begin to develop Jackson beyond the physical attributes we all can agree on. Jackson has a picture of himself in relation to what he believes, whom he likes, what he knows about his job, how he brings up his children, and how he can cure his golf slice. In the course of his day he talks to many people, only a few of whom are represented in this illustration. Each of those he talks with has a picture of Jackson: how honest, how smart, how important he is. It is at this stage that Jackson's pictures are talking to the pictures others have of him. When Jackson talks to the men and women working for him, he has his own picture of himself, and the employees have theirs of him (plus, of course, their own pictures of themselves, but we said that we were not going to complicate this illustration in that way).

What these people hear from Jackson will depend on how they see him. How effective Jackson is in communicating with them depends on how well he understands the kinds of pictures these people have of him. If the boss calls him in, it would be important for Jackson to know the kind of picture the boss has of him so that he can understand what is being said. Does the boss trust him to carry out a job? Does the boss overexplain an assignment because he thinks Jackson is less smart than Jackson thinks he is? Going around the circle, we have many pictures of Jackson in the heads of the people he knows, and it is not likely that the pictures are identical. His wife and his children may see him differently, and his friends at the club probably have another picture of him. Jackson very probably adjusts his role from boss to employee to husband to father to golfer as the demands of his associates come into play.

Who is Jackson? Is he the pictures in his own head — or those in the heads of his friends? More likely, he is none of these for very long, and all of them in part, and he changes as his role changes. There may be no "real" Jackson except as he is seen by others. Jackson's communication will be affected not only by the pictures he has of himself in relation to others but also by the pictures they have of him. He finds out about these pictures by getting feedback from others and trying out new guesses about the pictures.

(The first thing is to know that these pictures exist, and the second is that how others see us affects our communication. When we seek and receive feedback, we may accept, reject, puzzle over, or misunderstand the feedback, depending, first, on how well it is given in terms of honesty, clarity, and consistency and, second, on how well we are prepared to receive it.)

If Jackson enjoys playing golf with his friends, he seeks some assurances that it is all right to do so. His friends will give him feedback by inviting him to join a foursome, by being pleasant when they are together, by making frequent dates for golf, by telling him they enjoyed it and telling others who in turn may report it to him. If they don't want him to play in their group, they will send signals to him, such as filling up the group without him, playing at times not convenient to Jackson, exhibiting rude behaviors during the play or afterwards, or suggesting to him (very unusual) or to others (more usual) that he is a bore on the golf course and they wish he would leave them alone.

Jackson has a choice: he may accept what he sees and hears as a disapproval of his presence and seek another group, or he may ignore the messages of disapproval and continue to play with the group. If the information that he is not wanted is too hard to take, he may rationalize that they are not good enough to play with, or too good, or they want to bet too heavily, or that they always play at some time which doesn't fit his schedule. If he ignores the feedback he receives, the others will ask, "Why doesn't he understand that we don't want him?"

This brings us to stage 3, a further complication of the process of roles and behaviors. Above the picture Jackson has of himself is a cloudy, ethereal, kind of ideal self — what Jackson would really like to be. This is a part of his self-perception — a wish he makes about himself.

In the same way, above the pictures of his associates is a cloudy idealization of what they would like Jackson to be. If he is pictured by his assistants as grouchy and mean, their cloud would probably be a wish that he were friendly and kind. If the boss expects Jackson to be punctual and alert, that will be part of the boss's cloud. If the boss also pictures him as punctual and alert, the picture and the cloud will have a lot in common, and the boss will react in a predictable way toward Jackson. If, on the other hand, Jackson shows up late for work, the boss has a picture of him as being tardy, although his ideal for Jackson is punctuality. This conflict will be reflected in the messages the boss sends Jackson; and unless Jackson has some idea of what is wrong, he may be confused and disappointed by some of the boss's reactions. (We should remind you again that we are focusing only on Jackson, and that each individual in this drama also has an "idealized self" to consider besides the "idealized Jackson.")

Jackson's wife married an ideal man according to the idealizations which were developed during their courtship, and so she has idealizations of what he should be like — often she wishes he would help with the laundry or be more attentive to the children or somehow give her an identity she seeks. When Jackson tells his wife that he is going off to play golf, her response may have no direct relation to his playing golf, and he may have a hard time figuring out why she said she had to do the laundry.

Some of the idealizations may be more predictable than others. If Jackson is conscious of the value systems of his associates, he may come closer to understanding their ideals for him. In many of his activities there are rules to be followed: a boss should praise good work as well as criticize errors; husbands should share in household tasks, golfers do not talk while a player is putting; fathers give their children allowances; workers don't lose their temper in the office, etc. In many of these instances, Jackson can guess pretty well how his "others" would like him to behave. He may choose, then, whether or not to live up to those expectations. At least he is aware of how his behaviors may be viewed if he knows some of the values these people expect him to live up to.

PRINCIPLES BEHIND ROLES
Before we leave the Jackson story, let's suggest some principles you may draw from this example:

1. The greater the discrepancy between the pictures you have of yourself and the pictures others have of you, the greater the chance for misunderstanding and ambiguous feedback.
2. The greater the discrepancy between your picture of yourself and your ideal self, the greater will be your dissatisfaction with your communicative behaviors.
3. The greater the discrepancy between the pictures others have of you and their idealizations of what you should be like, the less chance there is for satisfactory relationships to develop.
4. Your pictures of yourself and the pictures others have of you are the result of behaviors toward each other.
   a. You find out what you are like by having people respond to you; that is, from the feedback you get from them.
   b. Others find out what you are like by collecting their reactions to your behaviors toward them.
5. Your idealization of yourself is related to your value system, and the expectations of others toward you are likewise related to theirs.
   a. The role you play has much to do with your idealization of how a person in that role should act.
   b. You depend on feedback from others to tell you not only how they perceive you (their pictures) but also how they would like you to behave (idealization).

Rules for Communicating   As we mentioned earlier, your communication transactions are characterized by a mutual negotiation of the relationship with the other person or persons involved. You define not only the situation but also the nature of the relationship by determining the roles that you will play in the particular circumstance. Similarly, the other person is involved in the same process and offers his or her definition of the situation and of the nature of the relationship. In doing so, the other person confirms, rejects, or modifies your definition.[8]

Rules of disclosing are being studied not only to determine what factors are involved, but also to find out how much of the disclosing is a personal matter (a developed habit, or trait, of the individual) and how much is related to interaction: as one person discloses, the other is expected to reciprocate.[9] The twin problems of how much to risk (expressed as vulnerability) and how much candid expression to expect from others have been studied, raising some question about the real value of "open communication" between people. Explicit disclosure may not always be a positive factor in your conversational relations, especially when your information puts a burden on the other person.[10] (See Chapter 3 for more discussion of disclosure.)

Role negotiation is particularly clear in new relationships, where much energy is spent mutually figuring out what roles are appropriate and comfortable. New dating couples, for example, spend much effort on figuring out how their relationship is to be defined. How much intimacy, how much sexual involvement, how soon, initiated by whom, are questions which are not always explored directly and out loud, but are often dealt with through a subtle trial-and-error system where both partners decipher the little verbal and nonverbal clues which tell them how to proceed.

Although this process appears to be intuitive and solely based on the idiosyncracies of the particular situation, there are certain rules that govern the establishment of role relationships. Sometimes the rules are very explicit, as in the case of professional dyads like doctor and patient, doctor and nurse in a hospital, or supervisor and worker on an assembly line. In organizational settings job descriptions usually define what people are expected to do and how they are expected to relate to others. Status, authority, and lines of communication are spelled out to codify in some way the interpersonal relationships necessary for accomplishment of the work.

In social situations, books of etiquette and manners, commonly accepted social codes, and traditions define for people how they should communicate with others, what they should say, how they

[8]Paul Watzlawick, Janet H. Beavin, and Don D. Jackson, *Pragmatics of Human Communication,* W. W. Norton & Company, Inc., New York, 1967, p. 133.

[9]James J. Bradac, Charles H. Tardy, and Lawrence A. Hosman, "Disclosure Styles and a Hint at Their Genesis," *Human Communication Research,* vol. 6, no. 3, Spring 1980, pp. 228–238.

[10]William K. Rawlins, "Openness as Problematic in Ongoing Friendships: Two Conversational Dilemmas," *Communication Monographs,* vol. 50, no. 1, March 1983, pp. 1–13.

should say it, when they should say it, and what they are expected to do.

However, most of the time the rules for establishing social transactions are implicit, that is, not formally established in written form.

Many of the rules that govern your nonverbal communications with others fall into that category. For example, one of our cultural rules says that *when you talk to people, you must look at them and they must look at you,* preferably in the eyes or in the face. You will usually feel somewhat uncomfortable if your listeners look everywhere in the room but at you when you are talking to them. Students who look out the window or at the ceiling or who concentrate on what is happening in the back of the room irritate teachers because they violate the rule. Teachers who lecture without ever looking up from their notes annoy students, because they, too, violate the rule. You tend to distrust and not like people who will not look at you when you talk to them. Shifty eyes appear to mean insincerity.

Another rule about looking has to do with how long you look at someone you are talking to. If you maintain eye contact for a very long period without averting your eyes, you communicate more than just passing interest. In a totally new relationship, sustained eye contact usually communicates an intensity and a level of intimacy not usually expected of passing and fleeting encounters. If someone you do not know well maintains eye contact with you, you have the choice of either deciding that the person is violating the implicit social norm that governs length of eye contact, or you may redefine the situation as a potential sexual advance.

Another implicit rule states that *if you do not talk to people, you should not look at them.* It is considered impolite to stare at someone you are not actively communicating with. When you are not talking to someone, you usually avoid looking at him or her. If you do look and then get caught at it by the person you were looking at, you will usually feel embarassed and will quickly shift your eyes away — or start talking. Observe what happens in schools, public hallways, streets, and offices. Two people are walking toward each other. Most of the time they have noticed each other from a distance but need not acknowledge each other yet (it is safe to look at another from far enough away). However, as they get closer, they must do one or two things if they are to follow the rules that govern interpersonal nonverbal communication: (1) They can act as if they do not see each other and thus not have to say anything to each other; if you don't look at someone, you don't have to talk. In this case, they may look at their feet, at the ceiling, or straight ahead in order to avoid the other person's eyes. (2) They can look at each other. If they choose this course of action, they must acknowledge each other by a few words or at least a nod of the head; if you look, you must talk. It is difficult to look and be looked at and not to talk. Elevators are another interesting place to study the looking and talking behavior of people. Close physical proximity makes it impossible to pretend not to see other people, yet you can stare intently at the floor numbers as the elevator moves and keep silent — or you can make profound statements about the speed or slowness of the elevator.

Other rules are also implicit. Appropriate times for you to disclose something personal to a friend, for example, cannot be looked up in Emily Post's book of etiquette or Ann Landers's column. It ultimately depends on you and your friend, how you have defined the relationship, what kinds of interpersonal risks you are willing to take, and a host of other factors.

In ongoing relationships, the rules that govern communication transactions come partly from the explicit cultural and social norms which broadly define the type of relationship you are involved in, but also from jointly developed rules that are implicitly agreed upon by the parties involved. Married couples, for example, over the years evolve a system for dealing with each other and with events that come up in their lives. What topics of conversation are taboo, who does the dishes, who picks up the kids at school, who initiates sex, who invites people over for dinner, who handles money matters, who makes decisions — all these and many other aspects of the relationship follow a pattern which, for better or for worse, gives the relationship some degree of stability, predictability, and meaning.

Families develop their own rules for their transactions, and children as well as spouses know that if these rules are broken, the result will be heated arguments, misunderstandings, hurt feelings, anger, and confusion. Besides television (discussed in Box 10 earlier in this chapter), family members look to other media to find out what they should do, how they should behave, what kinds of roles "those people out there" play with each other. If it is true that magazine advertising follows the norms of a society rather than sets the norms, then it is possible to tell something about how the society looks at families by watching the changes in advertising. Very potent information about how to act in a family comes to most of us (children and adults) from advertising, particularly magazine advertising. Studies of the portrayal of family intimacy in ads over more than fifty years report that the roles shown have changed. Although in the ads most women continue to clean house, launder, and cook meals, the number of ads portraying women as sex objects has declined.[11] One of the few historical studies on portrayal of men in

[11]Bruce W. Brown, "Family Intimacy in Magazine Advertising, 1920–1977," *Journal of Communication*, vol. 32, no. 3, Summer 1982, pp. 173–183.

advertising indicates some slight change in the roles shown.[12] "In general, men have increasingly been portrayed in stereotyped roles, but in women's magazines the 'manly' activities were replaced by more decorative roles."[13]

As a newcomer in an organization, you have to learn not only the formal rules or policies which regulate your work, but also the implicit rules which regulate people's interpersonal communication and which give the organization its personality. You may learn that there is no use speaking to Helen until she's had her first cup of coffee, that shop talk is a no-no during breaks, that if you want to get something done Mike is the one to talk to, etc.

An interesting feature of organizational communication involves what has come to be known as the "Pelz effect" after its originator, D. Pelz.[14] Briefly, the "effect" is that if you are a subordinate working for a supervisor, your satisfaction with how the supervisor appears to you to do the job is directly related to how you see that supervisor getting along with his or her superiors up the line. Called "upward influence," the ability of your supervisor to get along with superiors will have a direct effect on your morale and your productivity. There is also a difference in your attitude about your superior if you see that person as supportive or nonsupportive of you.[15] The Pelz effect clearly relates to our argument that the *content* of our rules and of our roles, or how people actually behave toward each other, is very directly related to the relationships we believe have been established.

THE RELATIONSHIP LEVEL OF COMMUNICATION

Communication transactions are not simple phenomena. To understand them fully you must realize first that they operate at two distinct but simultaneous levels. This was discussed in Chapter 1, but we will deal with it more fully here.

As we mentioned in Chapter 1, the content level of communication deals with what a message literally refers to. This level has to do with what you normally consider the information of the message. A statement like "Get out of here" gives information about a possible course of action, a move someone must make from here to somewhere else.

[12]Gerald U. Skelly and William J. Lundstrom, "Male Sex Roles in Magazine Advertising, 1959–1979," *Journal of Communication,* vol. 31, no. 4, Autumn 1981, pp. 52–57.

[13]Ibid., p. 52.

[14]D. Pelz, "Influence: A Key to Effective Leadership in the First Line Supervisor," *Personnel,* vol. 29, 1952, pp. 209–217.

[15]Frederic M. Jablin, "Superior's Upward Influence, Satisfaction, and Openness in Superior-Subordinate Communication: A Reexamination of the 'Pelz Effect'," *Human Communication Research,* vol. 6, no. 3, Spring 1980, pp. 210–220.

Words in the sentence help you call up the denotative meaning implied. However, should you read the statement out of context, not knowing who said it to whom, with what tone of voice, facial expressions, and gestures, you would have a difficult time interpreting what was really meant. Was the person angry or joking? Was the person in a proper authority position to give such an order? These questions uncover the fact that some information is missing and that there is more to the statement than the simple content level. What is missing in this example is the *relationship level,* which performs two basic functions: interpreting content and defining the relationship.

Interpreting Content All communication transactions, unless they are purposely taken out of context or stripped of all inflections, contain information which tells you how to interpret the content or information of the transaction. Interpretation comes from (1) nonverbal cues, generated along with the verbal messages, which qualify the message; and (2) verbal cues, which specifically give information about the interpretation to be made. "Get out of here" takes on a different meaning if it is said with a smile than if it is said with shouts and frowns. If the nonverbal cues are not enough to help the other person figure out what was meant, the addition of "I am only joking" or "I mean it, damn it!" can provide additional data for the interpretation of the message. Every gesture, every expression, how you handle physical distance and time, how you dress, how you choose to organize the words of your message, how you stress specific words — all this convey information which is crucial in helping others understand your intentions and what you are trying to say.

Much of the information you need to interpret messages you receive comes from nonverbal communication. We described these nonverbal factors more thoroughly in Chapter 9.

Defining the Relationship Defining the relationship between you and others is a part of every communication transaction. A statement such as "Please, Jill, have this letter typed and make three copies" conveys the expectation that Jill will carry out the order and indicates that the relationship between the two people is such that the speaker can legitimately make the request and expect it to be fulfilled. If the answer to the request is "Yes, right away, Mrs. Jones," Jill confirms that she, too, sees the relationship as one where Mrs. Jones can expect to make requests. Compliance with the request is in itself a confirmation of the definition of the relationship, and the use of the first and last names shows that both agree to define the relationship as a superior-subordinate one in which Mrs. Jones has some degree of authority over Jill. In some cases, the definition of the relationship may be challenged, directly or indirectly. The challenge is direct and clear when the other person indicates in some way that he or she does not intend to comply. There are many ways to refuse compliance, and each way will communicate something about the nature of the relationship. If Jill says, for example, "Gee, I am sorry, but I just don't have the time right now — ask Susan," she implies that Mrs. Jones had a right to ask but no real authority to enforce her request. Relationship in this case is redefined as one of superior and subordinate who treat each other almost on an equal basis. If the answer is "I don't work for you!" the statement is a clear rejection of Mrs. Jones's attempted authority, and Jill indicates that she clearly rejects Mrs. Jones's right to make requests of her. Sometimes the noncompliance and the redefinition of the relationship are quite indirect and more subtle. For example, Jill might not overtly challenge the authority implied in Mrs. Jones's request but might simply not do what was asked, or she might do it sloppily or late.

Nonverbal cues such as voice inflections, tone of voice, facial expressions, and gestures are particularly rich in telling you how relationships are defined. Distance, how far from people you stand or how close to them you stand, also indicates much about the nature of your relationship with them. In watching others interact you need not hear the words exchanged between people to interpret what kind of relationship they have.

Relationships are defined in two basic dimensions (see also the discussion of rule 4, Chapter 1): *authority* and *intimacy*.

Authority   Some relationships are based on differences between the people involved, and these differences are often expressed in terms of dominance or submission. Teacher-student, mother-child, doctor-patient, and boss-subordinate are relationships which imply that communication will take place along dominant-submissive lines. Someone is up, dominant, and has the authority; the other person is down, submissive, and has less or no authority. Some relationships are culturally and socially defined that way, as in the case of mother-child, doctor-patient, and teacher-student. But the dominant-submissive roles may also develop in any relationship where tacit agreement exists about who has authority and who makes decisions. Husbands and wives typically develop such understanding of who is boss in the couple. Usually the more dominant one partner is, the more submissive the other becomes. More submissive behavior invariably elicits more dominant behavior. Both partners often tacitly agree to maintain the relationship on clearly defined authority lines. When the lines are challenged or questioned, the whole relationship changes, and sometimes the couple disintegrates.

Some relationships are based on equality. Friends tend to operate as equals, and so do professional colleagues. Recall our earlier example of Greg and Bob, who were not only friends but also boss and employee, student and teacher. You can see that the same two people can engage in communication as equals some of the time and as non-equals at other times. The ability to switch back and forth is a sign that they are not rigid and that they are sensitive to the communication styles appropriate for certain situations.

Intimacy Relationships are also defined in terms of the degree of intimacy present. ``Jill, please type this letter,'' ``Jill, honey, type this letter,'' and ``Miss Smith, type this letter'' imply different degrees of closeness and informality between the two people bound by the statement. Here again, information about the level of closeness and intimacy between people is revealed through the nonverbal cues people constantly give each other. When you touch people, stand close to them, look at their eyes as you talk to them, smile in certain ways, you communicate that you define the situation as one which permits a certain amount of closeness and intimacy. You all know people who clearly communicate by their demeanor, tone of voice, or attitudes that the relationship is formal and demands distance and no intimacy.

TRANSACTIONAL INCONGRUENCIES AND COMMUNICATION PROBLEMS Because of the nature of communication transactions and the fact that they evolve as people simultaneously negotiate roles and meanings with one another, numerous potential problems can seriously influence the effectiveness of communication and may jeopardize your ability to organize activities, to get things done, and to evolve meaningful relationships with others. In this section, we will review the possible problems that you may encounter in your transactions with other people. There are basically four types of issues which can influence the effectiveness of your communication: (1) role conflict and ambiguity, (2) misperceptions of cause and effect, (3) disconfirmation, and (4) double messages.

Role Conflict and Role Ambiguity[16] One of the difficulties with roles is that you fill many of them, and often several at the same time. The woman who gets promoted to a supervisory position and now must be boss to those who were formerly her peers may be confused about which role she should play when she deals with her employees. Is she still a friend or is she a superior? In addition, while she is a supervisor, she is also subordinate to her own boss.

[16]This section is based on a discussion about roles by Frederick E. Finch, Halsey R. Jones, and Joseph Litterer, *Managing Organizational Effectiveness: An Experiential Approach*, McGraw-Hill Book Company, New York, 1975, pp. 49–52.

In filling any role there are difficulties which stem from the fact that the various expectations you have about how to fill the role may not be consistent with one another. This is called "role conflict."

Role conflict   You experience role conflict when one set of expectations about how you should play a role conflicts with another set of expectations. The conflicts may have several sources.

INTRASENDER CONFLICT
Intrasender conflict arises when you receive inconsistent directives from the same person on how to do something. For example, you may be told by your teacher that you must do a complete review of the whole course content for a test and that you must be ready for it in a couple of hours. A huge amount of work is expected, and you must do it quickly.

INTERSENDER CONFLICT
Intersender conflict occurs when different people send expectations which conflict with one another. For example, a nurse may be told by the supervisor not to perform certain routine tasks which must be done by physicians. Yet the nurse may be expected to go ahead with these tasks by a rushed physician who demands their completion. Secretaries who work in a typing pool and report to a pool supervisor often find themselves in this kind of role conflict when they are asked by an executive to perform certain duties which may not be part of the job description given to them by their supervisor. For example, a secretary may be asked by an executive to run an errand which results in getting back to the typing pool late, thus earning a reprimand from the supervisor of the typing pool.

ROLE OVERLOAD
Role overload is present when the expectations others have of you are far superior to the amount of energy, time, and skills you have to fill them. You may have different midterm exams coming up the same week; your boss may expect you to work overtime on a special project to meet a crucial deadline; your husband may expect you home early to go with him to a dinner party to which both of you were just invited; your daughter may insist that you keep your promise to attend her last baseball game of the season and cheer her as-yet-undefeated team; your neighbor may be depending on you to keep her children while she attends a very special event because she could not find anyone else to baby-sit; your instructor may have assigned several articles to be read and reported on at the next class meeting in a night course you are taking. The conflict here is in terms of the sheer quantity of what is expected of you in the various roles you perform.

PERSON-ROLE CONFLICT

Person-role conflict occurs when somebody expects you to do things which are quite out of character for you. There are times when you may be expected to do certain things which do not fit your self-concept. If you see yourself as a compassionate person, it will be difficult for you to fire someone, particularly when the person to be fired may have great difficulty in finding another job, has five children to feed, has no spouse, etc. Yet your supervisory position may require that you let that person go. Some teachers find it difficult to give an F to a student they have come to like and whom they consider a friend.

Role ambiguity

Role ambiguity occurs when nobody tells you clearly how you are expected to act. You may have had the experience of starting a new job and being told very little about exactly what you are accountable for. For example, you may not have been told whether starting and quitting times are rigidly enforced, when you should take breaks, or whom specifically you should report to. Sometimes expectations about what you are to do are expressed in very general terms, such as "About half of your grade in this course will depend on your participation in class." What exactly is meant by "participation in class" often remains unclear throughout the semester.

Confusing Cause and Effect

Bateson and Jackson facetiously wrote that the rat who said "I have got my experimenter trained: each time I press the lever he gives me food" was refusing to accept the cause-and-effect sequence the experimenter wanted to impose.[17] As you recall, transactions are characterized by the fact that one person's behavior may be both cause and effect of another person's behavior. Disagreements about how to determine the cause of events account for many communication difficulties.

Here is a familiar communication problem between boss and subordinate which could just as easily be between teacher and student, or parent and child. The boss, a woman, constantly rides herd on the subordinate, a man, checks and double-checks everything, leaves no room for initiative and responsibility, and generally feels that the subordinate is, if not totally incompetent, in need of constant guidance. The supervisor explains her behavior toward the subordinate by stating that the reason for her close supervision is the inability of the subordinate to think for himself and to take initiative. If the subordinate did not make so many mistakes, she, the supervisor, would not have to check and double-check everything. In other words, the supervisor labels her

[17]Gregory Bateson and Don D. Jackson, "Some Varieties of Pathogenic Organization," in David McK. Rioch (ed.), *Disorders of Communication*, vol. 42, 1964, pp. 270–283.

behavior in a response to the subordinate's actions. "I have to decide everything *because* he can't take initiative."

The subordinate, however, perceives the situation quite differently. For him, there is no way he can take initiative, since the supervisor won't ever let him. He feels that there is absolutely no room for making even small decisions, and so he has given up trying. He also feels that because the supervisor constantly breathes down his neck and makes him nervous, it is hard not to make mistakes — and that there is no need to be accurate anyway, because the supervisor will check and recheck everything. He feels that no matter how well he does, she will always find something to correct. In other words, the subordinate labels his behavior a response to the supervisor's behavior: "I don't take initiative *because* she makes all the decisions."

The issue is not whether one is more accurate than the other. Each action is *both* cause and effect of the other, and in a sense, both boss and subordinate are right in their perceptions of the events. Yet because they perceive the same events from different perspectives, each gets caught up in a vicious circle which will lead invariably to more and more controlling on the part of the boss and less and less initiative on the part of the subordinate. Each will feel absolutely justified in responding the way he or she does, and *each will find justification for his or her actions in the actions of the other.* What is typical about this type of problem is that the individuals involved see themselves only as reacting to but not provoking others' attitudes and actions. Another way of asking about mutual cause and effect is the question "Which came first, the chicken or the egg?"

Self-fulfilling prophecies stem from such misperceptions. Say, for example, you believe that people in general do not like you. You will tend to act defensively, distrustfully, and sometimes aggressively. This kind of behavior is likely to generate unsympathetic reactions from people, thus confirming your original idea that they do not like you — a typical case of self-fulfilling prophecy. Sometimes misperceptions occur because people involved in communicative transactions do not have the same amount of information about a given situation *but do not know this.* For example, if you make a friendly gesture toward a woman you know, but for some reason the other person does not notice it and does not respond to you and you do not realize that she has not noticed, you may be puzzled by the lack of friendly response to your overture and wonder why you are getting the cold treatment. While you would not get distrubed if you knew that she was preoccupied and did not see you — giving a different meaning to the lack of response — you do get annoyed when you interpret the situation as a deliberate brush-off. Let's pursue this further. If you interpret the situation as a brush-off from your friend and get angry, you may behave somewhat coolly toward that friend the next time you meet. Your friend, of course, does not know that she gave you a brush-off on the initial encounter, since she was preoccupied and did not even notice you. She is now confused about *your* cold treatment and wonders why in the world you are not speaking. It is easy to imagine how the situation can, and often does, spiral in the worst way, as each of you continues to react more and more coldly toward the other. The only way to break the vicious circle is to communicate openly with the other person and ask why she is not speaking. Only then may you have a chance to untangle the snowballing process of cumulative, but wrong, interpretations each of you has made throughout the situation.

Disconfirmation   Frequent problems in communication can be traced to the lack of agreement, spoken or unspoken, about how roles should be defined. In the earlier example of Greg and Bob, it is possible for Greg to relate to Bob at the store not as an employee to a boss but as a friend to a friend. If Bob also defines the role relationship as friend to friend, no problem arises. However, if Bob wants to define the store situation as one where he is the boss and Greg the employee, communication between the two will quickly become strained and frustrating, and it may even stop altogether.

You may have experienced the frustration that comes from discovering that someone whom you perceived as relating to you with the casualness and friendliness you associate with social situations turns out to be a high-powered salesperson making a pitch. In this case, of course, the manipulation of the role definition is deliberate on the part of the salesperson, and your frustration comes from your being taken in, if only momentarily.

When one person insists on labeling a situation or a role in a particular way, it is annoying if the other refuses to label it the same way. You may define a situation as purely social while the other person keeps talking business. You may wish to define a relationship as only friendship while the other person keeps trying to make sexual advances.

Relationships among nonequals, when one of the people is in a legitimately dominant position (the parent with a very young child, for example), may need to evolve into a relationship of equals as the submissive person gains more information and is progressively more able to make his or her own decisions. Typical communication problems occur between parents and their children when the parents do not realize that normal dependency needs in children are replaced by the need to be on their own. Adolescents try hard to become equals with their parents, while parents often cling to the old unequal relationship. When you are elected chairman or chairwoman of the club, or you are promoted to a higher job, you may experience a problem. It is indeed difficult to change role definitions, because not only a redefinition of the other is required but also a redefinition of yourself in relation to the other person.

Double Messages   There are many ways in which problems arise in interpersonal transactions. A rather common type of problem is exemplified when the content level of your communication does not fit the relationship level. Your words say one thing and your tone of voice, for example, says another. An aggressively yelled "I am not angry" is really a *double message*. Your words say one thing (you are not angry), but your voice indicates another (you are angry). Which is to be believed? Which is to be reacted to?

The boss who says that employees are welcome to come to the office whenever they have a problem, but who consistently keeps busy in meetings outside the office or looks rushed when employees do come around, is sending a double message. The words say one thing, the actions another. Soon employees catch on, and few will make any attempt to talk about their problems with the boss. A teacher who says "My door is always open" and then is never in the office is giving a double message.

Double messages are not to be confused with the kinds of nonanswers to questions which pass for answers. Our discourse, or our conversation, is full of partial or even very indirect replies to questions or statements from others.

Example: "Shall we go to the movie tonight?" Reply: "I've got fifty pages of history to read before tomorrow." (This reply says something about a history assignment but only implies a response to the question about going to the movie.) One of our teaching colleagues suggests a proper follow-up. You: "Then let me ask you — How much history do you have to read?" Reply: "I already told you — fifty pages." You: "Okay, then answer the question about going to the movie."

Other examples of nonanswers which may sometimes be considered flippant, smarty, insulting, or snobbish are these from an interesting study on indirect answers.

Person A: "Are notebooks allowed during the final exam?"
Person B: "Are porcupines allowed in balloon factories?"[18]

Person A: "Going to be working at the office?"
Person B: "Do I dress up like this to mow the lawn?"[19]

---

[18]Robert F. Nofsinger, Jr., "On Answering Questions Indirectly: Some Rules in the Grammar of Doing Conversation," *Human Communication Research,* vol. 2, no. 2, Winter 1976, pp. 172–181.
[19]Ibid., p. 178.

Factors which effect how "flippant" answers are received by another person seem to be how close the relationship is, whether you are giving a "yes" or a "no" answer, and the relative status or power between you. Close friends are more often able to use such messages than mere acquaintances are; but you still might be considered hostile or smarty if you used flip responses to what your friend considers a very important or serious question.[20]

In dealing with others, you frequently depend on their knowledge and experience of you to prevent confusion. What is important here is that others must not only know how people in general communicate, but also have a special bit of information about you. As you deviate from what others know about "people in general," you become more special, perhaps even more difficult to understand. It is important, therefore, to give those around you all the unambiguous and clear messages you possibly can if they are to interpret your intentions adequately.

BIBLIOGRAPHY

Bate, B., and Lois S. Self: "The Rhetoric of Career Success Books for Women." *Journal of Communication,* vol. 33, no. 2, Spring 1983.

Bateson, G., and D. D. Jackson: "Some Varieties of Pathogenic Organization," in D. M. Rioch (ed.), *Disorders of Communication,* vol. 42, 1964.

Bauchner, J. E., E. A. Kaplan, and G. R. Miller: "Detecting Deception: The Relationship of Available Information to Judgmental Accuracy in Initial Encounters," *Human Communication Research,* vol. 6, no. 3, Spring 1980.

Bavelas, J. B., and B. J. Smith: "A Method of Scaling Verbal Disqualification," *Human Communication Research,* vol. 8, no. 3, Spring 1982.

Book, C., and K. W. Simmons: "Dimensions and Perceived Helpfulness of Student Speech Criticism," *Communication Education,* vol. 29, no. 2, May 1980.

Bowers, J. Waite: "Does a Duck have Antlers? Some Pragmatics of 'Transparent Questions,'" *Communication Monographs,* vol. 49, no. 1, March 1982.

Bradac, J. J., C. H. Tardy, and L. A. Hosman: "Disclosure Styles and a Hint at Their Genesis," *Human Communication Research,* vol. 6, no. 3, Spring 1980.

---

[20]John Waite Bowers, "Does A Duck Have Antlers? Some Pragmatics of 'Transparent Questions'," *Communication Monographs,* vol. 49, no. 1, March 1982, pp. 63–69.

Bradley, P. H.: "The Folk-Linguistics of Women's Speech: An Empirical Examination," *Communication Monographs,* vol. 48, no. 4, March 1981.

Brown, Bruce W.: "Family Intimacy in Magazine Advertising, 1920–1977," *Journal of Communication,* vol. 32, no. 3, Summer 1982.

Buerkel-Rothfuss, N. L., B. S. Greenberg, C. K. Akin, and K. Neuendorf: "Learning About the Family From Television," *Journal of Communication,* vol. 32, no. 3, Summer 1982.

Finch, F. E., H. R. Jones, and J. Litterer: *Managing for Organizational Effectiveness,* McGraw-Hill Book Company, New York, 1975.

Fisher, B. A.: "Differential Effects of Sexual Compositions and Interactional Context on Interaction Patterns in Dyads," *Human Communication Research,* vol. 9, no. 3, Spring 1983.

Greenberg, B. S., and C. K. Atkin: "The Portrayal of Driving on Television," *Journal of Communication,* vol. 33, no. 2, Spring 1983.

Hanser, L. M., and P. M. Muchinsky: "Performance Feedback Information and Organizational Communication," *Human Communication Research,* vol. 7, no. 1, Fall 1980.

Hocking, J. E., and Dale Leathers: "Nonverbal Indicators of Deception: A New Theoretical Perspective," *Communication Monographs,* vol. 47, no. 2, June 1980.

Jablin, F. M.: "Superior's Upward Influence, Satisfaction, and Openness in Superior-Subordinate Communication: A Reexamination of the 'Pelz Effect,'" *Human Communication Research,* vol. 6, no. 3, Spring 1980.

Johnson, B. M.: *Communication, the Process of Organizing,* American Press, Boston, 1981.

Mickiewicz, E.: "Feedback, Surveys, and Soviet Communication Theory," *Journal of Communication,* vol. 33, no. 2, Spring 1983.

Montgomery, B. M., and R. W. Norton: "Sex Differences and Similarities in Communicator Style," *Communication Monographs,* vol. 48, no. 2, June 1981.

Moore, R. L., and G. P. Moschis: "The Role of Family Communication in Consumer Learning," *Journal of Communication,* vol. 31, no. 4, Autumn 1981.

Nofsinger, R. F., Jr.: "On Answering Questions Indirectly: Some Rules in the Grammar of Doing Conversation," *Human Communication Research,* vol. 2, no. 2, Winter 1976.

O'Hair, H. D., M. J. Cody, and M. L. McLaughlin: "Prepared Lies, Spontaneous Lies, Machiavellianism, and Nonverbal Communication," *Human Communication Research,* vol. 7, no. 4, Summer 1981.

Pelz, D.: "Influence: A Key to Effective Leadership in the First Line Supervisor," *Personnel,* vol. 29, no. 3, 1952.

Rawlins, W. K.: "Openness as Problematic in Ongoing Friendships: Two Conversational Dilemmas," *Communication Monographs,* vol. 50, no. 1, March 1983.

Sigman, S. J.: "On Communication Rules from a Social Perspective," *Human Communication Research,* vol. 7, no. 1, Fall 1980.

Skelly, G. U., and W. J. Lundstrom: "Male Sex Roles in Magazine Advertising, 1959–1979," *Journal of Communication,* vol. 31, no. 4, Autumn 1981.

van Dijk, T. A.: "Discourse Analysis: Its Development and Application to the Structure of News," *Journal of Communication,* vol. 33, no. 2, spring 1983.

Watzlawick, P. J. Beavin, and D. Jackson: *Pragmatics of Human Communication,* W. W. Norton & Company, Inc., New York, 1967.

Wilmot, W. W.: *Dyadic Communication: A Transactional Perspective,* Addison-Wesley, Reading Mass., 1979.

Chapter 11

INTERPERSONAL CONFLICT: HOW THE GAME IS PLAYED

In a Nutshell

Communication as a transactional process strongly suggests that there are individual differences among people — differences which must be negotiated so that people can develop common meanings and can accomplish common goals. There are no differences without conflict.

Traditionally conflict was viewed as bad and avoidable. People who caused conflict were considered deviants, troublemakers, and a problem for those in authority, whether parents, teachers, or managers. More recently we have come to view conflict as both inevitable and potentially good. Some conflict can be functional and helpful, and may spur growth and positive change.

What is important is not so much that conflict is inevitable in our interpersonal relationships as how conflict is handled — how we respond to conflicts that are sure to arise.

People tend to use different strategies to deal with conflict. They are accustomed to certain kinds of negotiation or to other ways of handling expected conflicts. One response to conflict is to *avoid* the conflict altogether in the hope that somehow if you don't look, it will go away. Another response is to *defuse* the conflict by buying time — by seeking agreement on minor points until tempers have cooled or you get more information or you have a chance to see things in a different perspective. (Much international negotiation is built on that system of dealing with conflict.) Another response is to *confront* the conflict. Confrontation strategies fall into three categories based on the outcomes of negotiation: (1) Win-lose strategies are based on power and are very common ways for people to attempt to resolve conflicts. The conflicts seem to be solved by pulling rank, by using authority or force. Although appearing effective in the short run, win-lose strategies may not be effective in the long run if power shifts and the losers take the upper hand, generating even more fierce confrontations. (2) Lose-lose strategies are employed when both parties prefer to lose rather than see the other get any assumed advantage. Compromise is often a form of lose-lose — a middle-ground position is adopted which pleases no one, but does not give total victory or defeat to either party. (3) Win-win, or integration, strategies rest on the assumption that conflict is a symptom of a problem to be solved rather than a battle to be won and that with some time, some creativity, and some goodwill a negotiated solution may be found to permit integration of apparently opposite views. Creative exploration of potential solutions to problems through brainstorming or other problem-solving techniques can be highly rewarding as well as effective. Inexperienced negotiators approach conflict management tasks in a rather disorganized way, while experienced negotiators manage conflict with understanding and with deliberate attention to rules and processes.

CONFLICT AND NEGOTIATION

The dynamics of communication transactions directly involve the twin notions of conflict and negotiation. People are different, and their individual differences must be negotiated to develop common meanings of their intentions, their hopes, their behaviors, their interests, their values, and all significant issues. From such common meanings arise common actions and accomplishments. If everyone automatically and intentionally thought alike and wished alike, there would be no conflict. As you know, however, people are often different in so many ways that it is surprising when any common goals can be reached.

The Traditional View of Conflict

The notion that conflict is inevitable in interpersonal communication is relatively new. Most people have viewed conflict quite differently — they believe conflict to be evil, to be avoided, or to be hidden. Often you will hear people boast about how well everyone gets along in their family, office, plant, business, institution, etc. Some people will even tell you that their group never argues and never has any conflict, and that everyone gets along perfectly. In response to that kind of boast, you may be inclined to doubt the speaker's honesty or the speaker's sensitivity to what is going on in the world. A trouble-free, conflictless group would be hard to find among people who have normal human instincts of self-interest and commitment and a reasonable level of alertness and vitality.

Traditional assumptions about conflict implied that conflict was bad, avoidable, and the product of the behavior of a few undesirable individuals. Conflict was associated with anger, aggressiveness, physical and verbal fights, and violence — all basically negative feelings and behaviors. "Nice people don't fight," "It's better to get along," "Don't argue in front of the children," and "If you loved me, you would not argue" are all familiar messages which teach that conflict is basically a bad thing or that only a bad person would disagree, feel angry, or fight. Of course, the potential negative effects of conflicts are very real. On a grand scale, wars among nations are expressions of conflicts at their worst. On a small but no less painful scale, divorces, separations, resignations, psychological withdrawals, and embattled relationships are also examples of interpersonal conflicts and strife.

Although the assumption that conflict is bad is still with us in many ways, a new view about conflict has emerged, and communication analysts agree that the negative view of conflict is often inaccurate and, at best, limited.

A Contemporary View of Conflict

More and more writers are describing a new set of assumptions about conflict — and hence about negotiation — which reflect how people in many areas of endeavor, from business to education to personal life, view conflict today.[1] These newer approaches are based on the notion that conflict is inevitable, that it is usually determined by structural factors in an organization or group, that it is often predictable, and that it is an integral part of the process of change. Some degree of conflict, according to this view, is not only helpful but necessary for the stimulation of creative and energetic people.

Conflict is a natural part of any communication relationship. It is also transactional, by the definition we have used earlier. In other words, an interpersonal conflict cannot occur unless both parties perceive it. To express it still another way, you are as likely to have a one-person interpersonal conflict as you are to have a one-handed hand clap. Unless a conflict situation is seen and identified as conflict by all persons directly involved, there is no conflict and of course no cause for or potential for negotiation. You can express conflict in many verbal or nonverbal ways. You can clearly confront the other so that there is no chance to misunderstand your intention. Or you can get a conflict over misunderstanding. But however you develop an interpersonal conflict, it takes more than one; and as in any transactional communication, you must be mutually aware that conflict exists.

However close you may be to another person, however you make like or love the other, however compatible you may feel with that person or with a group, there will come a time when your respective needs, thoughts, feelings, actions, motives, values, or belongings will not match exactly. Result: conflict. No two people, no two groups, can ever be so alike as to always think, feel, and behave identically. Only by remaining out of touch with one another could you totally and permanently avoid at least a strong potential for conflict. Living happily ever after is the stuff of fairy tales. Living happily with conflict is the stuff of a mature, interpersonally sophisticated, realistic, and skillfully managed communication relationship. What matters is not whether conflict exists — and we claim that it always will exist in any relationship — but rather *how the conflict is dealt with.* Here is where you assume a responsibility for your communication. Even though you may not be able to do anything about the actual existence of conflict, you may be able to alter your approach to conflict situations and to the negotiations which may arise from them.

---

[1]Joe Kelly, *Organizational Behavior,* 3d ed., Richard D. Irwin, Inc., Homewood, Ill., 1980; Joyce Hocker Frost and William L. Wilmot, *Interpersonal Conflict,* Wm. C. Brown, Dubuque, Iowa, 1978; Deborah Weider-Hatfield, "A Unit in Conflict Management Skills," *Communication Education,* vol. 30, no. 3, 1981; Michele T. Myers and Gail E. Myers, *Managing by Communication,* McGraw-Hill Book Company, New York, 1981.

Possible consequences
of conflict

It would be nice if all our problems could be solved as easily as they are in television situation comedies; usually within an hour (sometimes in as little as a half hour) the people in our favorite shows get into trouble, conflict ensues, and by the time the program is coming to an end everything has worked out just fine. Solutions to conflict come even more quickly in the television commercials than in the programs themselves. As the commercial starts, a person has dingy teeth, "ring around the collar," water spots on the dishes, or a pet who will not eat what is offered. One quick application of the advertiser's product and the conflict is removed — a successful love affair with pearly white teeth, a husband's admiration instead of disdain, a successful dinner party with sparkling dishes, and a pet greedily consuming the advertised pet food and loving you instead of hating you. Your worst fears in facing conflict are that you may lose either the material goods you prize or the friends you may prize even more. For that reason, you have learned from an early age that conflict has only bad outcomes, that it can result only in ill will from others or a loss of goods, power, position, or friends.

Outcomes of conflict may be either constructive or destructive. Not all conflicts will have the same outcomes. Conflict is potentially destructive when it consumes so much of people's energies or resources that there is little left for anything else. Constant bickering and frequent disagreements tend to wear people out and to decrease motivation to commit themselves to a relationship. Embittered and conflict-weary people may ask plaintively, "Why spend effort to do anything if all we do is argue over it?" Conflicts, unmanaged, can interfere with work and with interpersonal relations, creating so much hostility and antagonism that people may refuse to have anything to do with one another. This damages a work crew, an office shift, a family, or any other signifiicant grouping of people.

Conflict, and especially fear or anxiety about having conflict, can lead to conservatism and conformity. The "groupthink" phenomenon[2] is based on the fear that conflict will result in severe negative consequences for a participant in a decision. You go along with the group because you fear public ridicule for being different, or you are pressured into following the "party line" or the official position. As a superficial consensus develops, you become less afraid as you see that no one is rocking the boat and that a happy, friendly, cohesive group remains. You are lulled into a feeling that everybody can't be wrong, and you are validated by the agreement of others — just as you fear

---

[2]Irving L. Janis, "Groupthink," *Psychology Today,* May 1971, pp. 5, 6, 43–46, 74–76.

being left out or put down if you create any conflict. The consequence of "groupthink" is a decrease in the effectiveness of decisions because no checks and balances are permitted in the process of solving problems, and no creative or unpopular new ideas can be brought in. In such cases, great leaders have made serious errors because they listened to the "yes men" around them — because they weren't challenged by their well-informed but conflict-shy subordinates. In most such cases it is not the conflict itself which is destructive so much as it is the fear people have of not agreeing.

Still another possible consequence of conflict is a destruction or neutralization of opponents. This usually occurs when the conflict situation is seen in terms of competing, mutually exclusive, and polar opposite goals — when one person has to lose if the other wins. If the goals are very important for both parties, an all-out war of wills can occur with potentially destructive outcomes. This happens in organizations when two people compete viciously for the same job, the same resources, the same title, the same sphere of influence, or attention from the same superior. Tasks cannot get done in that atmosphere. Coordination is not possible for the antagonists, and they frequently involve others in their conflict, making it necessary for everyone to take sides. Competition which is *open* is difficult enough to deal with. Secret or hidden competition may be so subtle that the people involved may not be able to figure out why a job is not getting done or why there seems to be low morale in the group. Part of the problem may come from the tendency so many people have to deny conflict or to try to pretend it is not there. In such a case, friends may become angry with each other for no apparent (or obviously talked about) reason; or they may be willing to lose advantages or even friendships just to make sure the other person doesn't get an advantage. "If I can't have it, you can't either" appears to be the hidden argument.

A final potential negative outcome of conflict relates to the withholding of information. In an extremely competitive atmosphere people become very cautious; if others are perceived as "enemies," each will attempt to keep the others from gaining an advantage. Information is a form of power, and those who have information or data have a kind of power over those who do not. We have known graduate students who refused to share lecture notes with fellow students. We have seen married couples not tell each other about impending financial crises in an attempt to be "one up." We have seen professional colleagues give one another false information about bidding procedures, about production quotas, about litigation processes, and about many other essential items. Unchecked and unmanaged conflict can lead to accidents of judgment from which it may be difficult to emerge successfully.

Positive outcomes of conflict

Conflict does have many potentially negative outcomes. It is easy to understand why people try hard to avoid or suppress it. Yet conflict has many benefits.

Tension and conflict often give people more energy or motivation. Some people thrive on competition. Conflict is a strong mobilizer of energies which otherwise might not be tapped or available. If a person feels that he or she has much to gain from successfully competing with others and winning, a tremendous amount of effort will be spent in order to win. "Winning is not the most important thing; it is the only thing" was the favorite saying of a very successful football coach. The super-salesperson who wants to be number one and will work day and night to increase sales volume ultimately benefits the company. Conflict leads to innovation, creativity, and change. If conflict is suppressed for the sake of conformity and security, few creative ideas are likely to emerge. Without new ideas for doing things, a group will stagnate and not move ahead. New ideas often come out of conflicting viewpoints which are openly shared and discussed. Better decisions and greater commitment result from individual self-expression. Open disagreement may lead to useful exploration of feelings, values, and attitudes, and thus cement a relationship through the sharing of intimate or personal information.

TYPES OF CONFLICT

While conflict used to be seen as resulting from personal quirks or the tricks of troublemakers, recent studies of conflict attribute it to other factors. There are three types of conflict, and in this section we discuss what they are: personal, interpersonal, and organizational. The three are summarized in Table 4.

Personal Conflicts

Personal conflicts occur within an individual whenever he or she experiences (1) conflicting needs, desires, or values; (2) competing ways of satisfying a given need or want; (3) frustration from blocks which get in the way of satisfying a need; and (4) roles which do not match.

Conflicting needs

It is quite common to experience conflicting needs or desires. Our discussion of motivation in Chapter 4 pointed out that at a given time you may need to fulfill competing desires, and sometimes these may appear to be mutually exclusive. There are three different types of conflict of needs which you can experience. In the *approach-approach conflict,* you may be motivated by attractive but mutually exclusive needs. In the *approach-avoidance conflict,* you may be motivated by wanting something and at the same time not wanting it. In the *avoidance-avoidance conflict*, you may be motivated to avoid two negative but mutually exclusive goals.

TABLE 4. **Types of Conflict**

Type	Common sources	Examples
Personal	Conflicting needs	Study or go out on a date (Approach-approach: You need or want to do both but can't.) Dull job but it pays well (Approach-avoidance: Both a good and a bad consequence are available.) Cheat or flunk an exam (Avoidance-avoidance: Neither option is desirable.)
	Competing ways of satisfying a need or want	Different ways to arrive at a goal (To rise in management do you take on all jobs or select ones which will give you instant recognition?)
	Frustration from blocks in the way	A person or circumstance keeps you from getting a promotion.
	Roles which do not match	Your church expects you to believe one way, and your professional commitment demands another view.
Interpersonal	Individual differences	"Generation gap" problems, cultural patterns, gender distinctions
	Limited resources	How to slice the pie equally (Who gets the car tonight? Who does your best friend spend time with?)
	Role differentiation	Are you the boss or the subordinate? (Who waits on customers? Who can you give orders to or take orders from?)
Organizational	Structure and levels	Does management have views different from labor? Executive committee of your club versus the membership
	Functions and goals	Sales versus production; judging who has vacation priorities or shifts
	Resources (goods, funds, power, authority, responsibility)	Only a limited number of titles of "vice president"; who gets the office with a window? Who gets a big budget?

APPROACH-APPROACH CONFLICT

Should you study tonight or go out on a date? Should you spend a lot of time on project A to please your supervisor, or should you really concentrate on project B, which is a lot more fun to do? Conflict often appears to be of the you-can't-eat-your-cake-and-have-it-too variety. Your need to be home as the children grow up may conflict with your need to get an education or to have a career. Your need to be independent, control your own life, and make your own decisions may also conflict with a need to be taken care of and to be able to depend on someone. Some needs may truly be mutually exclusive, yet many apparently impossible contradictions can be resolved by defining the situation differently and by challenging the implicit assumptions which underlie the definition of the conflict itself. Even if you keep your value of being a good parent, does it necessarily mean that you have to stay home all the time while the children grow up? Is it possible to define a "good parent" in some other way which might not exclude the possibility of going to school or of working part-time or even full-time? Attitudes about such issues are complex and often deeply rooted; and when that is the case, resolving the conflict by finding alternative ways to define the variables involved in the situation may be very difficult. Yet a patient spouse, friend, or supervisor may often be of great help in assisting someone in resolving such crippling personal conflicts. Sometimes counseling can help a person to sort out complex feelings and conflicting needs, and to develop a satisfying course of action.

APPROACH-AVOIDANCE CONFLICT

An approach-avoidance conflict is frequently experienced when the accomplishment of a goal has both positive and negative consequences. An approach-avoidance personal conflict can become extremely crippling when the negative factors are just as strong as the positive ones, and the decision needed to solve the matter thus becomes very difficult to make. Examples of approach-avoidance conflicts are numerous. Do you take a job which is dull but pays well? Do you tell your teacher that she made a mistake and run the risk of making her angry? Do you finish the term paper tonight in order to turn it in on time and thus let your girl friend down for the evening? If the negative consequences clearly outweigh the positive ones, the choice may be easy. If there is a clear difference between positive and negative outcomes, the conflict can be fairly easily solved. When, however, the positive and negative outcomes (1) are hard to define or quantify or (2) clearly balance each other out, the choice is extremely difficult to make. The conflict can be, and often is, so paralyzing that people develop symptoms of illness. Some can only withdraw from the anxiety-provoking situation, physically or psychologically. Such conflicts are frequent among women who run a household, among hard-working students, and in modern business organizations. Stresses associated with situations which demand constant decisions are intense. Statistics on the mental and physical health of salespersons, students, teenagers, mothers, and executives indicate that such stresses do take their toll in physical and mental breakdown, alcoholism, drug addiction, and often just poor job performance.[3]

AVOIDANCE-AVOIDANCE CONFLICT

The avoidance conflict reflects apparently equally unattractive options, and the choice requires deciding which is actually least unattractive. In some cases there is no way to avoid the situation, as when not choosing one alternative automatically results in your having to face the other. If you absolutely cannot stand your boss or teacher but also cannot afford to be without a job or to drop the course, you are experiencing an avoidance-avoidance conflict. Staying in the company or class means unpleasant interpersonal day-to-day transactions; leaving means no job or course credit. Either choice is unsatisfying. About all you can hope for is an improved job market, or a change in college requirements.

Conflict may also exist between a value that you hold and a behavior that is required of you. Conflicts of loyalty are frequently experienced by adolescents who value their allegiances to several distinct groups (their parents, their friends, their teammates, etc.) or who experience a clash between what they value dearly and what they perceive as the demands of authority figures. If you are an avid environmentalist, should you work for an industry which contributes heavily to pollution? If you value honesty, should you take a job in which you would have to withhold information from consumers or from the public? If you are basically a cooperative person, do you stay in a company or go to a college which rewards spirited competition? Do you become a party to illegalities, white lies, and other practices which you consider shady? Do you turn in a friend whom you saw cheating on a test? Such dilemmas are not always easy to solve.

Competing ways to satisfy needs

As you set your goals, you often discover that there are many ways to achieve them. What courses will satisfy requirements and at the same time be useful to you? If you wish to perform a socially useful function, make money, and have prestige, which profession or career will you choose? If you want to be promoted quickly in the company, should

[3]Ernest Dole and Lyndall Urwick, *Staff in Organization,* McGraw-Hill Book Company, New York, 1960.

you look for the kind of position where you will get a chance to stay in the same job for a while so that you can become an expert in that job, or should you go for the kind of position which will allow you to shift around laterally in the company? Which of these positions will allow for faster upward movement in the hierarchy?

Frustration from blocks Personal conflict often occurs when something gets in the way of reaching your goal. For example, let's consider June, the assistant vice president at a bank. A block has gotten in the way of her promotion, and Alex, the new supervisor, represents that block.

Psychologists long believed aggression to be the only response to frustration. If you are frustrated, you may kick the dog. Yet frustration can lead to many other defensive mechanisms. In June's example, she might respond in a number of ways to Alex. She might first bend over backward to be fair and nice — what psychologists call "overcompensation." Then she might feel angry and simply not help Alex to learn what he needs to know, a covertly aggressive reaction. Then she might withdraw physically and emotionally from the situation by avoiding him, by developing headaches, and finally by contemplating resigning from the bank.

Other reactions to frustration are possible. They include *fixation* — stubbornly continuing to work toward an unattainable goal or doggedly pursuing a course of action which has proved to be doomed to failure. Another reaction to frustration can be to seek *creative compromises* by redefining the frustrating situation or finding alternative ways to reach the goal. This alternative will be discussed in a later section.

Role discrepancies As we mentioned in Chapter 10, role conflict is a common experience for people who relate to different groups and are expected to behave in ways appropriate to the values held by these different groups. When the different groups hold similar values, there is little conflict. When they do not, there is tremendous pressure for the individual to be all things to all people, an impossible task. Belonging to both a political party and a church may not be a difficult task until some issue comes up that creates a conflict between politics and religion.

Interpersonal Conflicts As Gibson and his associates pointed out, interpersonal conflict occurs basically because of (1) individual differences, (2) limited resources, and (3) role differentiation.[4]

---

[4]James L. Gibson, John M. Ivancevitch, and James H. Donneley, Jr., *Organizations: Behavior, Structure, Processes,* Business Publications Inc., Dallas, 1982.

Individual differences As mentioned earlier in this chapter when we discussed the inevitability of conflict, the fact of individual differences is the very reason for conflict. Differences in age, sex, attitudes, beliefs, values, experience, and training all contribute to the way people see situations and other people. A young, aggressive, formally educated manager may see a situation differently from older managers with more seniority who came up through the ranks. Parents and children see the world differently on many issues. Some men refuse to get along with or take orders from women managers. In social groups there may be some degree of choice about whom to associate with, but it is unlikely that the same flexibility exists in the work or college environment. You associate with certain people because they are there and because you were assigned to the job, or you signed up for the course. Although you may have the ultimate choice of leaving the company or the class, if you stay, you agree to be with the people in your group. If they are much different from you, then some degree of conflict is inevitable.

Limited resources No organization, no group, no family ever has all the resources it needs. Financial resources, human resources, technical resources, and time are always somewhat limited; and a complete definition of the term "resources" should include everything we must share with others, including material things and our feelings or attention. Choices have to be made, and allocating such valuable resources wisely is one of most people's critical tasks. Because of this fact of life, constant choices must be made about who gets an allowance, space, jobs to do, typewriters, equipment, budget allocations, information, power, the family car, etc.

Competition is, in essence, built in when a system has scarce resources. Each person, or each group, competes to get a share of the pie. The smaller the pie, the more intense the competition. Distribution of resources should permit the organization or group to reach its goals. However, what one group or one person defines as the most effective way to allocate resources is not always accepted unanimously. In fact, each person in the group may have a different idea of the "best way" to do just this. The person who feels that he or she is not getting a fair share often develops antagonism toward others who are perceived to get more, or toward those who are seen to be the cause of the unfair allocation. Such conflict can lead to a variety of damaging behaviors. Sibling rivalry is intensified when sister Sally perceives that brother Tim gets the car more often than she does.

Role differentiation Interpersonal conflict often results from the failure to agree on which person can give orders to another. In Chapter 10, we discussed at length what happens when one person refuses to accept the role definition implied in another person's behavior. If you make a request (implying that you have some authority over the other person), but the other person refuses to comply and in essence refuses to acknowledge or accept your authority, then a conflict about relational control exists. Who is in control of defining the mutual roles? This type of conflict often occurs when two people basically agree about a certain course of action, but one of them refuses to go ahead and do it because the other initiated the idea.

A supervisor and an employee may both agree that a project needs to be finished before a certain deadline; but if the supervisor mentions overtime, the employee may balk. The balking is not so much caused by the necessity to spend more time at work but by having to accept the supervisor's authority. Had the supervisor said nothing, the employee would have probably suggested that overtime was needed to complete the project and would have volunteered to stay at work longer. However, in that case, the decision would have been made by the employee, who thus would have kept control.

Conflict between people occurs frequently not because there is disagreement about what to do but because people don't agree about who should be in control or should receive credit or have some personal need satisfied.

Organizational Conflicts

In many cases the potential for conflict comes from the structure of the organization itself. As organizations get bigger and more complex, they inevitably develop functions and roles which simply build in the potential for conflict.

A member of the board of directors of a large corporation is unlikely to see things the way a worker does. The president of a college doesn't see things the way a student does. The more levels exist in an organization and the more insulated they are from one another, the less information they share with one another and the less they know and understand one another. The perspectives, values, and goals of the upper levels are not usually the same as those of the middle or lower levels of authority. In a small organization, as in a single classroom, where few people are represented at each of the levels and where a great deal of communication occurs across levels, potential conflict is minimized. In large organizations where the levels are numerous, communication is more limited, and people may seldom see — let alone talk with — other levels, the potential for conflict is greater. Perhaps it is easier to fight with people whom you do not know personally. If you perceive "the administration" or "management" as the "enemy," it is easier to fight if you do not know the real people filling those roles. The impersonal "they" of large corporations or bureaucracies do not have faces.

Functional conflict is also inevitable. Different parts of an organization have competing needs as a result of what they have to accomplish. Many college departments compete openly for budget allocations, library funds, student enrollments, and salary levels. In the same institution, the teaching staff may compete with the nonteaching staff for support.

If a sales department must increase volume, salespeople may make promises about delivery schedules, discounts, etc, which will have repercussions on production, accounting, and advertising. Production may not be able to meet the delivery schedule, because purchasing has not been able to get raw materials in on short notice. While salespeople might like to have large inventories available, production and finance people are likely to resist building up stocks because of the cost of storage and of carrying unsold merchandise. If production is right in the middle of union negotiations, it is likely to feel that this takes precedence over anything else. Sales, however, may feel under pressure from upper management to increase volume and may well feel that its concerns take precedence over everything else.

In a hospital we worked with, a great deal of conflict existed between the physical plant department and the nursing staff simply because a new safety regulation came from engineering which stated that no small appliances were allowed on the floors, since many of these would not fit new required safety standards. Nurses, particularly those from the night shifts, were angry with engineering for preventing them from having coffeepots at their stations and resented what they felt was an encroachment by the engineers on the nurses' working conditions.

Conflicts between functions and levels are perennial and take many forms in different settings. University adminstrators are often pitted against faculty members. Medical and other hospital professionals are typically at odds with the hospital administrative personnel. Family members compete for television programs, the family car, or the cookies in the cookie jar. Sales and production people frequently fight design engineers or research people. The uneven distribution of power, repsonsibility, and authority makes it almost impossible for conflict not to develop. All persons in the group have feelings about how fairly they are treated and are sensitive about how privileges and rewards are allocated. Whether differences in treatment are real or imagined doesn't matter much in how people react to other people. If teachers, parents, or supervisors play favorites, or are perceived to play favorites, there is a great chance for conflict.

Our main point throughout this discussion is that conflict is a reality of life. It can be of great value when it prevents stagnation and stimulates exploration of new ideas and procedures. Conflict and airing of differences permit problems to be revealed, discussed, and solved.

Although conflict may appear dangerous or disruptive, it does have useful consequences when it permits people to constantly adjust or change. Rigid behaviors or structures which suppress the "reality" of conflict by ignoring it often provoke more violent types of conflict. People who are more flexible and open and allow for expression of differences are not as likely to have to deal with such violence. If conflict is faced and handled appropriately, it can be quite beneficial. The questions become: How can conflict be handled? What are some of the available strategies for conflict management?

CONFLICT MANAGEMENT STRATEGIES

According to Blake, Shepard, and Mouton, conflict management strategies can be classified into three general categories: (1) avoidance, (2) defusion, and (3) confrontation.[5] The three types are summarized in Table 5.

Avoidance

People often avoid conflict or potential conflict. They hope that somehow, if they don't look, the unpleasant situation will go away and they won't have to deal with it. It is tempting to believe in magic or deliverance. Yet pretending not to see a problem seldom makes the problem disappear.

There are many different ways to avoid dealing with conflict, and they include withdrawal, denial, suppression, and smoothing over. Some people simply leave the situation by walking out of a room, cutting class, quitting a job, falling asleep at a meeting, running away from home, or pretending to be very engrossed in some other activity. Some apparently overworked people who have absolutely no time for interpersonal relationships may be using work as a strategy to avoid involvement in conflict-laden situations. "I've got so much studying to do that I can't see you . . ." is a possible sign. Some people appear to be very accommodating in order to avoid conflict. Although the accommodator is indeed obviously bothered by something, he or she keeps pretending that everything is just fine. Some people change the subject of a conversation any time it gets close to something that might generate disagreement. Some people constantly joke and distract others so that nothing can really be taken seriously.

Avoidance strategies are used whenever people feel threatened by potential conflict and are afraid they might not be able to handle it effectively. Avoiding the situation is unlikely to solve the problem. Conflict may simply recur in other forms.

---

[5]Robert Blake, H. Shepard, and Jane S. Mouton, *Managing Intergroup Conflict in Industry,* Gulf Publishing Co., Houston, 1964.

TABLE 5. **Conflict Management Strategies**

Type	How to recognize the strategies
Avoidance	Withdrawal, denial, suppression, smoothing over, not facing reality of conflict; walking out, quitting a job, making jokes, "let's not argue," "we want to run a happy ship," "busy people don't gripe," "can't we just have a good time and not fight . . ." *Consequence likely:* Conflict will reappear in some other form, possibly more violent or vicious; it is not likely to go away just by wishing.
Defusion	"Let's come back to this later . . ."; calling for a short recess in discussions; asking to have someone go after (1) more data, (2) more experts, (3) more coffee and sandwiches. *Consequence likely:* You may get some small agreements, but the big issues will remain unsolved; at best you can get angry participants to cool off or rigid debaters to reconsider their frozen positions; at worst it will be a form of avoidance — see above.
Confrontation Win-lose or power strategies	"I am the boss (or your parent) and I say so"; pulling rank; railroading a vote; intimidation; not to be confused with athletic competitions or poker games; imposing rules; going by the book; hiding behind regulations and policies to enforce your way. *Consequence likely:* Any creative problem solving is stifled; there is bitterness and resentment by losers, who wait their turn for vicious retaliation if power shifts.
Lose-lose or compromise strategies	Settling for a middle ground which neither party wants just to make sure the other doesn't get any advantage; doing anything to keep the other from winning; "If you won't let me bat, I won't play." *Consequence likely:* A short-run compromise may get to be a habit, so the two parties never take turns or negotiate their differences; both parties come up short of what they could have obtained together.
Win-win or integration strategies	Show up when negotiators indicate that (1) conflict is a symptom of a problem to be solved, not a fight to be won, and (2) nobody has to lose completely. Face-to-face open negotiation is possible if point is to solve a problem, not to determine who is right. Time is spent defining the specified and unspecified differences, working at alternatives which will meet common interests. You look for ways in which positions are alike, not just opposed. You work from a "we," not a "we-they" orientation.

TABLE 5. **Continued**

Type	How to recognize the strategies
Win-win or integration strategies (continued)	*Consequence likely:* This is not a cure-all, but it provides an interesting and little-used option to the power plays and compromise we are accustomed to. At worst you can develop more ways of looking at each others' positions without solving the problem or gaining more understanding of why the other parties believe as they do. At best you can come out with a better solution than either party started with, greater trust, understanding, and respect, and a commitment to live up to the agreement. It takes time, but it may be time well spent for all participants.

Defusion

Defusion strategies are used when a person involved in a conflict decides to stall until tempers have some time to cool off. In defusion strategies, people attempt to seek agreement on minor points of the issue and avoid the bigger problem until they gather more information, cool off, or have a chance to see things in a somewhat different perspective. Defusion strategies permit some small agreement, but the bigger issues remain unsettled—sometimes for a long period of time. When this is so, defusion tactics may be only a form of avoidance.

Confrontation

There are three kinds of confrontation strategies based on how the confrontations turn out. Alan Filley, Robert House, and Steven Kerr refer to these kinds of outcomes as "win-lose," "lose-lose," and "win-win."[6]

Win-lose or power strategies

Win-lose strategies of confrontation are based on power. They are common ways of managing conflict. They are based on the idea that for conflict to be solved, one person must win. Furthermore, winning is not possible unless somebody else loses.

There are many different types of win-lose strategies. The blatant use of authority to overrule another person is frequent among managers or people in authority who, by inclination or sheer power, operate in an autocratic fashion. A conflict between a manager and a subordinate is resolved by the use of authority on the part of the manager. The "I am the boss" attitude is a way, at least on a short-term basis, to be on the winning side of a conflict or an argument. However, in the long

[6]Alan C. Filley, Robert J. House, and Steven Kerr, *Managerial Process and Organizational Behavior,* 2d ed., Scott, Foresman and Company, Glenview, Ill., 1976, pp. 166–167.

run, the conflict may be simply postponed rather than solved; and while pulling rank does enable a person to win an argument or a battle, eventually a manager's position is weakened if employees feel that they are being overruled on the strength of authority only.

Sometimes the sheer show of authority represented by status and rank is not enough, and a person may resort to mental or physical *coercion*. A mother dragging her 3-year-old from the store to the car is using physical coercion; she is bigger and stronger than the child. Disagreement or conflict with employees is simply resolved by threatening them with dismissal, demotion, a difficult assignment, or a dead-end job. However, more and more managers are aware that they must not simply tell but also sell their ideas.

As a result they may resort to another win-lose strategy, *railroading*. Railroading can happen through majority votes when discussion is stopped quickly and a call for a vote is taken before the issues at hand are thoroughly understood or discussed. If this happens too often and if the same group of people always end up in the minority, the losses come to be viewed as personal defeats and the majority rule can be destructive. Sometimes a small group of people who represent a minority can railroad their ideas through a meeting and win.

Interpreting silence as consent is a strategy which permits a small group or sometimes even one person to assume that everyone else agrees, thus preempting the need for open discussion of an issue.

A small minority may also agree ahead of time to present a strong united front on a given issue, thus intimidating the group into thinking that the idea has more support than it really has. Again, discussion is short-circuited to the benefit of a small group which wins while the others lose.

Filley and his associates have summarized the characteristics of win-lose situations as follows:

1. There is a clear-cut we-they distinction between the parties involved in the conflict.
2. Each party directs its energy toward the other party in an atmosphere suggesting that there must be total victory or defeat.
3. Each party perceives issues from its own point of view.
4. The emphasis is on solutions rather than definition of goals, values, and objectives.
5. Conflicts are personalized and are perceived as personal attacks.
6. Conflict resolution processes are not differentiated from other group processes, nor are they planned.
7. The parties take a short-term view of the issues.[7]

---

[7]Ibid., p. 167.

Typical win-lose situations include conflicts between supervisor and subordinate, labor and management, and parent and child. Although competition can have useful consequences, win-lose strategies are often bad because they are based on the use of power and because someone always loses. In win-lose strategies, any settlements which consider the mutual needs of the two competing parties are ignored. Creative problem solving is stifled. Although people might agree that one person loses this time but will win the next time, the win-lose strategy creates bitterness and resentment which eventually surfaces in one way or another. People on the losing end may bite the bullet and wait for the balance of power to shift. Retaliation then can be vicious, and personal vendettas can drain people of energy to the extent that they can no longer communicate.

Imposing rules, citing policy, and "going by the book" to solve a conflict are other win-lose strategies. These strategies avoid direct confrontation by hiding behind regulations. A person who does not want to take the responsibility, and the heat, for refusing a particular request, may hide behind a rule or regulation and say that he or she is really not responsible for winning and making the other person lose: "A rule, is a rule, and I must enforce it." Naturally, there are times when enforcement of rules and regulations is called for. However, when people hide behind regulations as a pattern for dealing with unpleasant situations, conflicts are not resolved but simply avoided.

Lose-lose or compromise strategies

Strategies in which everyone loses don't seem to be particularly useful ways of resolving conflict. They are, nevertheless, frequently employed. The lose-lose approach to managing conflict can take several forms. Sometimes in an argument people agree to settle for a middle ground which may satisfy no one completely but which at least does not give total victory or total defeat to either side of the controversy. If you want to eat at a Chinese place and your friend wants to eat at a French restaurant, you may finally agree to go for Mexican food. In this way, you do not win but neither does the other person. You agree to compromise. Compromises may be useful in the short run. However, if they become the customary way to settle differences, you may begin to feel that other people are more anxious to prevent you from winning than to really settle the issue. Competing departments in an organization often negotiate allocation of scarce resources on the lose-lose principle. One department may agree to cut down on something if another department does, too. Bribery is another lose-lose strategy: one party may pay a great cost to get another party to do something very disagreeable. A manager may offer you an important raise to do a boring job, for example; and although on the surface it looks like a positive way to settle the issue, both of you may lose partially. Parents often engage in bribing tactics with children.

Win-win or integration strategies

Win-win strategies for managing conflict are based on the ideas (1) that conflict is the symptom of a problem to be solved rather than a fight to be won and (2) that conflict can be managed so that nobody has to lose completely. Managing conflict through problem solving permits opposite views to work together and is a highly effective way of resolving differences. Face-to-face confrontation is needed, but the emphasis is on solving a common problem rather than on determining who is right, who is wrong, and who is to blame. Information needs to be openly exchanged in order to settle facts which bear on the problem. Talk about potential solutions to the problem should not start until the parties have jointly defined the problem to be solved. Positions which appear to be absolutely opposite on the surface can often be redefined creatively as part of a bigger problem in which both sides have a stake. Exploring potential solutions to the problem through brainstorming techniques can be very useful. You can come up with ways of managing the problem so that everyone has at least some needs met. It is important that most people involved in the conflict have a voice in suggesting alternatives for solving the problem. Many times an alternative course of action is discovered which none of the parties to the conflict would have identified alone. Through communication and participation, creative solutions can be developed and then tested and evaluated.

The outcomes of a win-win strategy for resolving or managing conflict are frequently (1) a better solution than either of the parties would have come up with and (2) greater trust, understanding, and respect among those involved in the situation. This may sound Pollyannaish and unrealistic, but a good deal of research shows that such strategies are effective. Naturally, problem solving and negotiated conflict management take time. When many people are involved, or the issue to be solved is trivial or inconsequential, a win-win approach may not be worth the time it takes. However, the more you rely on a method, the more proficient you become; and once you begin to think in terms of finding solutions to problems which meet apparently opposite needs, you learn to think differently and probably can deal with conflict differently. Rather than battling an imagined enemy, you learn to solve a shared problem with an associate. Much creative energy is freed in the process.

In a win-win approach, the parties involved must define a common ground and their mutual interest. Unless the problem is perceived in terms of "we" rather than "we versus they," little effort will be made to negotiate differences for everybody's benefit. The people involved need to understand that they may not have all the information required to solve the problem and that through communication more information will be generated. Often, neither party in a conflict has erroneous data. The facts of the situation may be shared by all, and the process allows people to get to know how others look at the same facts. Each person's needs affect his or her perception of what constitutes a solution. In such problem-solving sessions it is important that communications be orderly, that frankness and openness be encouraged and rewarded, and that people be free to disagree without being attacked for doing so. Partial agreement may be necessary and should be acceptable as a realistic basis for decision making.

Brainstorming should be used for generating alternative ways to solve the conflict. Brainstorming techniques mean open and spontaneous communication between the people involved. The problem has to be defined before solutions can be generated. When people are generating solutions in a brainstorming sequence, emphasis is on supportive communication. Everyone should be free of critical judgments, and everyone should encourage originality and unusual ideas. Evaluation of the solutions occurs only *after* solutions have been generated.

The win-win approach to conflict management works toward a solution which can satisfy, at least to some extent, all the parties involved. With goodwill, a little creativity, a commitment to refrain from imposing a solution that does not meet everyone's needs, and the patience and time to keep working until a satisfactory solution is found, very creative answers to problems can usually be discovered.

CONFLICT MANAGEMENT AND NEGOTIATION

Conflict is a reality of both public and personal life. How you view conflict will determine how you negotiate the management of your conflicts, and how successful your negotiating outcomes will be. If you think conflict is always something bad and to be avoided at all costs, then you will respond by negotiating in a defensive or aggressive way. You may miss much of the richness of interpersonal problem solving if you believe that conflict does not or should not occur. Conflict and happiness are not necessarily polar opposites.

If you admit that conflict happens, but you don't want any part of it — defusion strategy — you may be simply unwilling or unable to negotiate effectively. You may have the hope that if you take on a few small issues related to the bigger conflict that maybe the big one will get better. It rarely does. You may settle for a partial or short-run solution which can develop into an even bigger problem in the longer run.

Our suggestion, therefore, is to make use of enlightened negotiation skills to confront conflict. Rather than burying your head in the sand to pretend conflict does not exist, or trying to nibble away at a big conflict in unsatisfying defusing attempts, you can learn how to manage conflict through some negotiation skills. You will not solve every conflict every time to everyone's total satisfaction, but you can successfully manage many more of your personal and professional conflicts than you ever imagined you could.

Negotiation and Communication

Conflict management skills and negotiation skills are basically communication skills, as we will point out in Chapter 12. They include (1) diagnosing the nature of the conflict, (2) initiating a confrontation, (3) listening, and (4) problem solving. A brief preview of how those skills are related to communication follows, with more details on problem solving and negotiating in Chapter 12.

In *diagnosing the nature of a conflict* you may want to consider this prayer, credited to Reinhold Niebuhr and adopted by Alcoholics Anonymous:

> *God grant me the strength to change the things I can, the patience to accept the things I cannot change, and the wisdom to know the difference.*

These words seem most appropriate for a discussion of conflict negotiation. When you encounter potential conflict, you should ask yourself whether (1) this issue is one which affects you and has enough significant consequences for you to be concerned about it, (2) this conflict is caused by personal or value differences for which some objective solutions can be found, and (3) the other parties are willing and able to enter into a negotiated agreement—that is, a win-win problem-solving sequence. Some problems may simply not affect you directly. If you dislike smoking and no one in your environment is a smoker, then you may not be particularly dedicated to carrying on a strong antismoking campaign. On the other hand, if your roommate or closest friend chainsmokes in your apartment or car and the lack of ventilation is a contributing factor, there may be both a *reason for* and a *possibility of* change. It is difficult to change another person's value system or deep-seated beliefs. It may also not be necessary for you to change another's values in order to settle disputes. Your friend is always late. You value punctuality. It may be as useless to try to change your friend's value about being on time as it would be for your friend to change yours. To confront such a conflict you should "operationalize" the conflict and spell out carefully what *behaviors* you would like to see changed on what occasions. "I know you are not as interested as I am in arriving on time; but they close the doors of the theater promptly at 8:15, and if you are not in the lobby with me before then, I will go in without you and meet you at the first intermission." Essentially you can do something only about *your own behavior,* not the behavior or values of others. The often-used expression "Behave yourself" is a redundancy—you cannot behave someone else.

In other words, look at the causes of the conflict and make sure there is some reason to take on a negotiation. Don't fight battles when there are no reasons to fight—if you are not involved directly or have no confidence that any change will result. Make sure the sources of conflict are identifiable, real, and negotiable.

Timing is of great importance in confrontations. If your boss or your teacher is swamped, obviously worried about a lot of problems, and in a big rush, that is not the time to expect a leisurely discussion of a less immediate problem. Also, when you negotiate, you must state clearly and specifically (1) what the other party does and how it affects you tangibly, and (2) what you would like to have happen at the end of the negotiation or what you would like the other person to do. If those items are not clear to either of you, then it is important to begin exploring the problem together. Don't command your smoking friend to stop. You may assert that the smoking bothers you and tell how. You may ask that both of you work out some way to minimize the difficulty to you and continue to permit your friend to maintain a habit which is evidently important. Taking time to talk about the problem even before you demand some solution is another way to be sensitive to timing.

Listening as a collaborative act is important. Truly effective communication, and therefore negotiation, does not take place without taking into account what another party has to say. In Chapter 8 we discussed how important it is to pay attention to the feelings expressed as well as the words. Empathic or active listening has an important place in negotiating conflict. You must understand the needs of another person if you are going to negotiate solutions which potentially will meet them. You have a difficult time listening when you are emotionally involved in an issue, and you will be tempted to argue your point of view rather than paying attention to the other person's arguments. Yet negotiation will depend on the airing of both points of view.

Problem solving is the win-win approach to negotiation. You can gain much if you can treat conflict as a problem to be solved rather than a fight to be won or lost. Negotiation can occur in an atmosphere of mutual concern for getting to the root of a problem and managing the differences. In Chapter 12 we will discuss problem solving, negotiation, and other skills of interpersonal communication.

Skills of Negotiation

Chapter 12 includes a series of suggestions for rational problem solving through the skills of systematic decision making. In many kinds of conflict situations, this calm, objective, intellectually oriented decision-making approach can replace bargaining, power plays, manipulating, deadlocks, emotional outbursts, and jockeying for position. Following the steps recommended by Dewey and others, all parties to a problem may be able to sit down and work things out. On the other hand, there may be factors of competition or conflict which need negotiating skills beyond those described in Chapter 12.

Many writers and researchers are at work on the subject of negotiation. Workshops are available, seminars are taught, short courses are provided to people in corporations and professions. The Harvard Negotiation Project has become known as a group which "deals continually with all levels of conflict from domestic to business to international disputes."[8] Two members of the project, Roger Fisher and William Ury, have written a best-selling paperback on the subject of negotiation.[9] Fred Jandt, Gerard I. Nierenberg, Robert J. Laser, and many other consultant-teachers provide courses in which the skills of negotiating are taught to managers, union leaders, teachers, lawyers, executives, and any persons who are interested in improving their negotiating skills.[10] All have their own systems for approaching negotiation and conflict management; much of this work is based on research and years of experience in the field by those authors and others.

**Negotiation:
Content and Process**

Most literature on negotiation refers to the "mixed-motive" nature of negotiation, whether in international relations or in domestic situations. By that it is meant that parties to a dispute must reach goals which benefit them all, but which seem to be inconsistent, even competing and opposite at times. What we know is that people enter negotiation with some goals and that they conduct their communication by a set of rules which will have some effect on the outcome. *Content* of negotiation is what parties talk about, what their respective ideas are, what their demands and issues are, what they stand to gain or lose in the interaction. Important as these content issues are, they are only part of the negotiation. *Process* is the relational dimension by which people negotiate, their styles, their procedures, their tendencies to attack or withdraw, the rules by which they exchange information about the content.[11]

The outcome of some negotiations can be predicted by looking at how the participants behave (their power strategies) in relation to their prenegotiation expectations. In a study by William A. Donahue, those factors appeared to have an important effect on successful negotiat-

---

[8]Roger Fisher and William Ury, *Getting to Yes:* Penguin Books, New York, 1983 (originally published by Houghton Mifflin Company, 1981). The quote is from the promotional backpage.

[9]Ibid.

[10]Fred E. Jandt, *Conflict Resolution Through Communication,* Harper & Row, Publishers, Inc., New York, 1973. (A forthcoming book by Jandt is on negotiation.) Gerard I. Nierenberg (senior ed.), "The Art of Negotiating Newsletter," Negotiation Institute, Inc., New York, published eight times a year; Robert J. Laser, "Practical Negotiating Skills," program developed and reported in Laser, *Build A Better You,* Showcase Publishing Co., San Mateo, Calif., 1980.

[11]William A. Donahue, "Development of a Model of Rule Use in Negotiation Interaction," *Communication Monographs,* vol. 48, June 1981, pp. 106–120.

ing.[12] The study also concludes that your success in negotiating gives you an attitude about succeeding in the next set of negotiations.

Reciprocity in negotiation is a typical concern of parties engaged in conflict which calls for resolution. Do you take a negative reciprocity attitude (``an eye for an eye and a tooth for a tooth'') or a positive one (``do unto others as you would have them do unto you'') in approaching negotiation? Both of these attitudes are found in human interaction — whether you are in a labor-managment bargaining situation or dividing up candy among children. Besides having an effect on how you approach a negotiation, your basic style or attitude can affect how you conduct yourself in relation to others during the negotiation sessions.

For example, the choices of attacking or defending as basic strategies were studied to find out if the actions of one side affected the actions of the other.[13] Not surprisingly, the researchers determined that there is a tendency to answer an attacking strategy with an attack of your own. They further discovered that the general tone for the negotiation (in this case a simulated labor-management bargaining session) was set by the management side — perhaps the more powerful of two antagonists will have a greater influence on how the negotiation proceeds. In addition, the findings on reciprocity indicate that both the labor and the managment side of this simulation had initial tendencies: labor was inclined to take an offensive or attacking position, probably because it had little to lose by being on the offensive; management appeared to take a defensive stand initially, evidently attempting to maintain the status quo. Therefore, we may be able to predict that in similar power situations, (1) if you have more to give away than the others, you will act in a defensive way; and (2) if you have less power and are bargaining for more service, more money, more favors, more time, or a higher grade, you will take the offensive. If you have favors to give, the negotiation will place you in a more defensive, or even passive, stance.

These are only a few of the dimensions of negotiation. We recommend for your study the well-written book by Fisher and Ury men-

---

[12]William A. Donahue, ``An Empirical Framework for Examining Negotiation Processes and Outcomes,'' *Communication Monographs,* vol. 45, August 1978, pp. 247–257. In this paper the author studied interaction of the components of situation, social power, expectation, and personality.

[13]Linda L. Putnam, and Tricia S. Jones, ``Reciprocity in Negotiations: An Analysis of Bargaining Interaction,'' *Communication Monographs,* vol. 49, September 1982, pp. 171–191. The authors also tested the differences between male and female bargainers to study the effect of gender on the outcomes of bargaining sessions and the results seemed to contradict the earlier ``claims that female bargainers were too cooperative for the art of confrontation.'' Ibid., p. 190.

tioned earlier.[14] Their message is that the old-fashioned, and often unsuccessful, negotiating system concentrated on bargaining over *position*. They claim that the more people argue over position, the more locked in they will get; the more they defend and get committed, the more impossible it is to ever reach a negotiated agreement. "As more attention is paid to positions, less attention is devoted to meeting the underlying concerns of the parties."[15] People negotiate *to obtain satisfaction* more than to obtain goods or services. Taking notice of the internal motivations of parties can be a most rewarding and successful method of reaching agreement.[16] Fisher and Ury have named their proposed system "principled negotiation" or "negotiation on the merits"[17] to distinguish it from what they have called the less effective "positional bargaining." They propose four parts to their method: (1) separate the people from the problem, (2) focus on interests, not on positions, (3) invent options for mutual gain, and (4) insist on using objective criteria.[18] Negotiators following this set of steps can see the similarity to problem solving as the basic approach to negotiation. We have come back to the advice given by most modern teachers of negotiation: treat the conflict as a problem to be solved by competing parties, not as a battle to be won at the expense of the losing side.

Advance thought and preparation can help negotiation. Plan for what you will do in a bargaining or conflict-managing situation. Consider both the content (issues, ideas, data, resources, arguments, etc.) to be covered by your side and theirs, and the intangibles which will probably play a large part in how you behave toward each other. Among the intangibles are, of course, the desire to get satisfaction, to save face, to look competent, not to feel defeated, and to stand up for your rights, as well as many other personal or psychological considerations. If you can anticipate both process and content items, you will be better able to make use of your most effective style and techniques once bargaining starts.

As in many life situations, you may not have the final say in what is decided. "I'll have to ask my parents if I can go." "I'll have to check with the home office." "The trustees will have to approve this action."

---

[14]Roger Fisher and William Ury, *Getting to Yes: Negotiating Agreement Without Giving In,* Penguin books, New York, 1983. Fisher is director of the Harvard Negotiation Project and teaches negotiation at the Harvard Law School; Ury is associate director of the project and a consultant-lecturer.

[15]Ibid., p. 5.

[16]Ibid., p. 20.

[17]Ibid., p. 11.

[18]Ibid., pp. 15–98.

To determine who has the power to decide, finally and irrevocably, is one very important aspect of negotiation. Some people we know of had a child who purchased a time-shared condominium over the telephone when called by an unscrupulous agent. Both the child and the agent discovered that a 10-year-old — even one who talks like an adult during the bargaining — does not have final say in such a purchase. Know how much authority you have and also learn how much your opponents have.

Among the items to consider in preparing for negotiation is an agenda. After you have planned your arguments and your techniques, assembled your data, and checked it with friends or trusted associates, then you should write out an agenda as a checklist for your behaviors. Maybe the other parties will also set up an agenda. In that case you will make your first item of business an agreement on the agenda — which should determine what will be negotiated, by whom, and under what conditions of time, place, and sequence. A written agenda is strongly advised by most negotiators.

Finally, you must plan for what happens when you reach agreement. Do a formal statement of who is expected to do what, who gets what, and by what time, and under what conditions. Of course, if you are negotiating with a friend about whether to see a movie or go bowling, a written contract or agreement is not needed. You will need, however, in even the most informal negotiations, some well-defined understanding of what was agreed to. "We decided to go to the movie, right? So let's agree on which one and when to meet." "If we are going bowling, I have to remember to bring shoes." In many day-to-day negotiations we may forget to check the understanding of the other party as to what was really decided. How many times have you heard the expression, "Oh, I thought we agreed to . . . ." which comes up after you both thought it was perfectly clear. In more formal and serious bargaining, therefore, a written memorandum of agreement or memorandum of understanding is imperative. It should spell out not only the objective conditions of the agreement, but also the processes by which any actions or services will be carried out. Who has authority to sign, and therefore what is binding on either party? If these points have not been covered earlier, they must be included in the final documentation of the completed negotiation.

Table 6 is a compilation of items to be considered before and during negotiation based on our experience and on accumulated research data. You will see from this chart that we consider preparation for negotiation a singularly important part of the system. The center column has examples of what you should consider doing, either before or during the negotiations.

TABLE 6. **Preparation and Process of Negotiation**

Preparation stage	Specifics	Negotiation stage
Determine specific needs: 1. Intangibles 2. Material or objective needs	*Intangibles* include saving face, appearing competent to constituents, obtaining satisfaction, etc. *Objective or material needs* include a salary, goods, privileges, services, the use of items, a grade, a contract.	Explore the specific needs of the opponents, expressed or hidden: 1. Intangibles 2. Material or objective needs
Establish your own limits of authority.	What can you agree to without checking, and with whom? Under what conditions can you commit your side? What limits can you set on what you will settle for or hold firm on, and at what stage?	Explore the limits of the other party's authority on the same bases.
Set the maximum- and minimum-range limits for settlement: 1. Develop support and justification 2. Review possible concessions by you	What is the highest settlement you can ask for without being ridiculous? What is the lowest you can legitimately accept? What arguments can you use, and how far can you give in?	Probe for the ranges of the other party; go beyond the stated opening issues or items. If they make concessions, what do you have to give up?
Determine arguments, counterarguments, style, and technique of approach; plan your sequence to release arguments and data; anticipate tempo and atmosphere as interaction dynamics; rehearse.	Plan how to present your data or to make best use of techniques (hardball, dirty tricks, nibbling, etc.) or oppose them if used against you. Gradient of power is important: who sees whom as in charge or powerful. Timing of data can be set by you, but you need to control the dynamic process to do that.	Be alert to techniques used on you; counter if appropriate or expose them as tricks; ask for negotiation of the rules or procedures as well as content items; pay attention to dynamics.
Test ranges, arguments, and techniques with trusted friends and colleagues. Don't be afraid to ask for advice before starting.	Find friends who have been in similar spots and ask them for help; check with people to be affected by the possible outcomes of the negotiation; set up a backup who is available for you to consult with if you have doubts about how things are going, or who can give you an excuse to recess or confer.	Caucus with your team if it appears that your data or techniques are not serving you well; ask for recess to confer; don't appear to retreat, but ask to recess (as in basketball time-outs) only when you "have the ball."

TABLE 6. **Continued**

Preparation stage	Specifics	Negotiation stage
Draw up an agenda; print and distribute it. Include rules on how discussion will go as well as what to discuss, in what sequence, who will do what, and when.	Work on a way the agenda can favor your data or style or time frame. Try to control the negotiation issues and techniques with the agenda and to have it reveal the opponents' positions or data or time limits.	Agree on the agenda, point by point. Take time to negotiate common features if both sides have prepared an agenda. New form of an agenda must be written and openly agreed to.
Develop an attitude for attaining positive and mutually rewarding outcomes; have high expectations for the value of negotiation and the potential for the two sides getting together.	Treat the negotiation as mutual problem solving rather than open warfare in which one side will win; use techniques appropriate for power relations, situation, structure, personalities; separate the persons from the issues; focus on interests and needs of both parties, not on their expressed positions; keep checking on agendas and goals to see if you stay within the agreed limits of issues and procedures; look for new options to creatively meet all needs and goals.	Problem solve whenever possible; reciprocal use of nonproductive games or ploys may not be the only way to proceed. You have the option of reacting to anger either with anger or with calm. Attack-defend are possible sequences to use with discretion. You can control your own responses but not those of opponents.
Plan what happens when agreement is reached: 1. How to determine that issues are resolved 2. What the content of the negotiated document will be 3. What procedures will be used for completing the agreement 4. Whether an oral agreement will suffice for less formal negotiation (if so, be sure to ask the party to repeat for you the conditions you both agreed to)	Write it out and discuss text rather than oral agreements; check it out with others if possible; determine who will sign, how binding it is, and on which parties. A memorandum of understanding or a memorandum agreement have different kinds of commitment. Define all terms to satisfaction of all; define next steps in writing; ask any conditions or contingencies to be written ("what if the car is out of gas . . . ?" "what if your boss says . . . ?" "what if the membership refuses . . . ?" etc.).	Get agreement that an agreement has been reached; produce a document in writing after agreeing; determine who will be parties to the final decision, who will sign, what other procedures need agreement (write them out with timetable), how both sides anticipate implementing the final agreement; anticipate problems of nonpresent parties.

BIBLIOGRAPHY   Blake, R., H. Shepard, and J. S. Mouton: *Managing Intergroup Conflict in Industry,* Gulf Publishing Co., Houston, 1964.

Dole, E. and L. Urwick: *Staff in Organization,* McGraw-Hill Book Company, New York, 1960.

Donahue, W. A.,: "An Empirical Framework for Examining Negotiation Process and Outcomes," *Communication Monographs,* vol. 45, August 1978.

————: "Development of a Model of Rule Use in Negotiation Interaction," *Communication Monographs,* vol. 48, June 1981.

Filley, A. C., R. J. House, and S. Kerr: *Managerial Process and Organizational Behavior,* 2d ed., Scott, Foresman and Co., Glenview, Ill., 1976.

Fisher, R. and W. Ury: *Getting to Yes: Negotiating Agreement without Giving In,* Penguin Books, New York, 1983 (originally published by Houghton Mifflin Company, 1981).

Frost, J. H., and W. Wilmot: *Interpersonal Conflict,* Wm. C. Brown, Dubuque, Iowa, 1978.

Gibson, J. L., J. M. Ivancevitch, and J. H. Donneley, Jr.,: *Organizations: Behavior, Structure, Processes,* rev. ed., Business Publications, Inc., Dallas, Tex., 1982.

Jandt, F. E.: *Conflict Resolution Through Communication,* Harper & Row, Publishers, New York, 1973.

Janis, I. "Groupthink," *Psychology Today,* May 1971.

Kelly, J.: *Organizational Behavior,* 3d ed., Richard D. Irwin, Inc., Homewood, Ill., 1980.

Laser, R. J.: *Build a Better You,* Showcase Publishing Co., San Mateo, Calif., 1980.

Myers, M. T., and G. E. Myers: *Managing by Communication,* McGraw-Hill Book Company, New York, 1981.

Nierenberg, G. I. (senior ed.): "The Art of Negotiating Newsletter," *Negotiation Institute,* New York, 1983.

Putnam, L. L., and T. S. Jones: "Reciprocity in Negotiations: An Analysis of Bargaining Interaction," *Communication Monographs,* vol. 49, September 1982.

Weider-Hatfield, D. "A Unit in Conflict Management Skills," *Communication Education,* vo. 30, no. 3, 1981.

Chapter 12

INTERPERSONAL SKILLS:
MAKING IT WORK

In a Nutshell

Making your interpersonal communication work is sometimes difficult, and it usually requires that you develop and sharpen a set of skills. Among those skills usually considered important are: (1) problem solving and negotiating, (2) trusting, (3) reducing defensiveness, (4) developing an appropriate communication style.

Problem solving and negotiation involve first of all an attitude and then a series of steps to be followed. Sequentially, these include clarifying the problem, generating solutions, weighing the solutions, selecting the best solution, implementing it, and then evaluating the outcomes. Although we focus on interpersonal, or dyadic, communication in this book and often write about these skills as if they were used chiefly between two people, it is clear that much of our communication is group-centered. Most principles we review here are equally applicable to groups of more than two people. In considering communication in groups it is also natural to consider leadership as an interpersonal function. Ways of looking at leaders and at leadership will affect the way we work with others.

Trusting makes you vulnerable, since you let the behaviors of other people affect you. In order to trust, you must believe that the other person will not harm you and is able to do what he or she promises to do.

Being trusted by others does not happen magically. Interpersonal trust is built through a mutual process of taking a series of small risks with another person and is often called an "incremental" process. For a trusting relationship to be established three factors must be present: (1) You must engage in trusting behavior, even if you aren't sure the other person will do the same to you. You must take a risk. (2) You and the other person must not follow the impulse to exploit or take advantage of each other; and you must also not think the other person's trusting behavior as foolish or naive, or as the act of a "sucker." (3) You must be willing to work on (negotiate) the trusting and risking process a little bit at a time.

To reduce defensiveness you should use descriptive communication rather than evaluation. Use spontaneity rather than strategems. Use a problem approach rather than control. Be involved rather than unconcerned. Try sharing and flexibility rather than showing superior, rigid, or dogmatic attitudes.

Four questionable communication styles will be described in this chapter as unhealthy or dysfunctional: (1) blaming aggressively and demanding, (2) placating nonassertively and deferring, (3) computing intellectually and responding unemotionally, (4) distracting and manipulating. We describe a fifth style, leveling or assertive, as both more healthy and more functional.

PROBLEM SOLVING

The Sequence of Problem Solving

Ever since John Dewey proposed a series of steps in reflective thinking,[1] theorists have been developing refinements of that sequence. The six-stage proposal recommended here has its roots in Dewey's description of how he believed most people confronted problems or questions of choice of solutions: (1) People begin by recognizing the factors which make up a problem. (2) They examine the problem to find out its nature and scope and implications. (3) They search for a possible solution or some potential ways out of the situation. (4) They compare the available solutions for best predicted outcomes. (5) They select that solution, decision, or action which they believe will be best. (6) They evaluate the solutions and the process.

The sequence recommended here should include a seventh step: looping back to revise *at any step* in the entire process. With that understood, let us examine the steps as (1) defining the problem, (2) generating possible solutions, (3) evaluating and testing solutions, (4) deciding on the best solution, (5) implementing it, and finally (6) evaluating the process and adjusting.

Step 1: Clarifying and defining the problem

Figure out where the problem came from and what makes it important to you or your organization. See if you can state the problem clearly in simple, concrete terms and get group members to agree to the statement. Some members may suggest solutions at this stage, but that is premature. However right the solution sounds, unless the group has agreed on the definition of the problem, it is not likely to be effective. When groups have trouble arriving at solutions in later stages, the best technique is to return to this defining stage because it was almost surely the weak spot, very likely because solutions came more quickly than clarification of the problem. Avoid absolutely leaping to solutions even if you have dozens of good ones. Some group members may accuse the leader of wasting time and may say, "We all know what the problem is . . . ," but may then have difficulty defining it. The person who speaks for others who may or may not "know" what the problem is is a ventriloquist. There are times when definition of the problem comes from outside the group; if that occurs (if, for example, there are orders from above, or requests from another group), be sure that all the members of the group have the same data, concur in the definition of the problem or request, and have no questions about it. If clarification is needed, take time. Time spent in this stage will be a good investment, even when members are anxious to get on with recommending solutions and actions.

---

[1]John Dewey, *How We Think,* Heath & Co., Washington, D.C., 1933.

Step 2:
Generating solutions

Find all the solutions you can. This is a time for brainstorming. Spend no time haggling over whether or not certain solutions can be accomplished; just get down on paper or a blackboard as many proposed solutions as the group can generate. Members should be free to suggest even "far-out" solutions without fear of ridicule or argument. No one needs to fight for his or her own pet solution at this stage. An effective group at this step is characterized by members who feel free to suggest, but not compelled to justify.

Step 3:
Weighing the solutions

At this stage, people can defend their pet solutions. It is also the time to let go of your own ideas if you believe that some other solution has more merit. Logic and data should be emphasized as the group considers, challenges, questions, probes, and tests. An effective group at this stage is one which can operate nondefensively, one in which there is a climate which permits people to support each other's ideas as well as their own. Support must be provided so that all members, however quiet, can have their say. Avoid early voting or balloting on solutions. Seek consensus rather than testing by show of hands. This is done by discussing any doubts which are expressed and by encouraging doubters to articulate their concerns — and ensuring that no one is railroaded or overwhelmed by advocates with big voices or high status. Avoid ballots, which may result in split votes and split allegiances; encourage understanding of the positive implications of preferred solutions as well as expression of any uncertainties about their value.

Step 4:
Selecting the best solution

Make sure the "best solution" is best in relation to the defined problem and the needs of the group and not simply the most popular or the easiest to agree on. The kind of issue you are dealing with and the norms of the group will determine whether you vote or arrive at a consensus. In arriving at the best solution, make sure that it is (1) understood by all the contesting members, (2) appropriate to the identified problem, (3) possible to implement, (4) within the authority and responsibility of the group, and (5) arrived at by an appropriate and satisfactory means.

Step 5:
Implementation

Decide with the group who is going to be responsible for carrying out the solution. Delegation of actions or duties at this stage is important. A group may, having agreed on a solution, simply make the assumption that "somebody will do it." That seldom happens without direct commitment. The same people who arrived at the solution should be involved in implementing it. Being aware of that responsibility in advance helps sharpen choices of solutions; and, after the choice is made, implementation will bring the group together as the members directly share the outcome of the decision-making process. Not only the "who" of implementation is essential; the "when" and "how" should also be settled. A timetable and a list of resources are required to complete the process of making and carrying out the decision.

Step 6:
Evaluating

There is a tendency at this point to simply evaluate the solutions. While they are important, it is also important to evaluate how well the group survived the other steps and how individuals participated. Some evaluation on improving group functioning is useful. If members have become discouraged or if they cannot pull together, look at the reasons. Your group must evaluate its own work through all the preliminary steps to see how the final solution worked. Modern systems for evaluating outcomes are available, and using a system like PERT (Program Evaluation and Review Technique) can be useful in setting up a sequence for implementation. Evaluation is an attitude as much as it is an activity. It requires a generous sense of openness to look at both the content of the group sessions and the socioemotional behaviors of the people who interacted, and especially the leadership functions.

Your Role in the
Problem-Solving
Sequence:
Leadership

As the catalyst, facilitator, director, or manager, you can help steer a group through these steps in a way which is consistent with your abilities and needs as well as those of the group. In the rough-and-tumble of group interactions, you may be responsible for both the task accomplishment and the maintenance, or socioemotional, functions of the group process. It is not likely that all the task functions and the maintenance functions can be accomplished by the same person, even a most skillful leader. But these functions must be taken care of, and you need to exert influence to make sure that they are. In this section we examine leadership.

Socioemotional leading

We have described the task-related steps with which a group may solve problems or make decisions. Most of the discussion of the six steps was in terms of tasks. As those assignments are being met, what is happening on the socioemotional level? Below, in the same order, are brief suggestions for some maintenance (socioemotional) functions which should be attended to as the task moves along.

STEP 1: TEST FOR GROUP COHESIVENESS
Involve all those who want to participate in talking about the problem: avoid blaming or finding scapegoats in defining how the problem came about. Guide the group gently away from proposing easy or too-quick answers and keep them discussing the problem without stifling participation. Seek *feelings* about the problem as well as facts: Are members interested? Does the problem affect them? Are there moral or value issues involved which are difficult to talk about? What level of confi-

dence do members have in each other and in their own ability to solve the problem once it is identified?

STEP 2: DRAW THE MEMBERS OUT ALL YOU CAN
Encourage a supportive climate to generate the greatest number of solutions. Reward creative suggestions. Do not support any negative reactions to suggestions. Have one or more persons write solutions on a blackboard as they come up. Encourage spontaneity. Move quickly from one suggestion to the next.

STEP 3: TEST FOR RESOURCES
Who knows what? Who can do what? Do the solutions fit personal value systems as well as the organization's purpose and structure? Encourage the group to look at the best possible fit of solution to problem rather than searching for the "only" one. Assure them they are looking not for the Holy Grail but for the most adequate response to a felt need. Are members open in their reactions to each other and the issue? At this step it is important that everyone be free to comment.

STEP 4: CHECK CONSENSUS
Direct attention away from voting. Discourage shows of hands or ballots. Draw out any quiet members (silence may not mean consent at this step), and encourage expression of feelings as well as intellectual positions. Encourage discussion of psychological and social consequences as well as those of an economic and physical nature.

STEP 5: ENCOURAGE COMMITMENT
Encourage the group members to make promises to each other, not just to the leader or some absent boss. Commitment must be made openly and before all other members (avoid the situation where members sidle up to the leader after the meeting and promise to help). Be specific about names and dates and responsibilities. Check with those named to see that they understand. Do not assign responsibilities to absent members. Silent members are potentially nonsupportive; draw them into the action and get their testimony as witnesses for the project.

STEP 6: EVALUATE
As recommended earlier, have members evaluate the task without accusing each other of base motives. Evaluate the socioemotional involvements as openly as the group norms will permit. Insist that the group acknowledge that both were going on at the same time: "We generated solutions and agreed on a best one, but we also generated a lot of feelings about each other and the task as it went along." Can the group talk about the meeting with the hope of doing a better job together the next time?

Groups and leadership   Most of the situations we discuss in the rest of this chapter on interpersonal skills involve more than two people. *Decisions* are made in groups. *Trust* can be assumed to be widespread over an organization. *Defensiveness* must be reduced among team members. The five *communication styles* are as applicable to committees, clubs, families, and other groups as to interaction between two persons. Groups are everywhere. Your communication will inevitably involve groups. Many of the exercises in the Laboratory Manual (Part 4 of this textbook) involve group work; some include analysis of group activities as in the Laboratory Manual for Chapter 6. The section just above ("Socioemotional Leading") referred to an important part of group life — socioemotional interaction, or "process." The other part of group life, "task" — getting the job done — was treated generally in the sections on decision making, negotiating, etc.

Closely associated with the study of groups is the function of leadership. Although it is one of the most complex and widely studied aspects of human communication, the concepts of "leaders" and "leadership" will be treated only briefly here. If you want to find more material on these ideas, or if you want to review their historical development, refer to the bibliography; there are many excellent books on the subject. But watch out for the semantic trap of referring to "leaders" as static performers who "lead" in all situations; it is our contention that using the term "leadership" can better describe what is actually going on. For that reason we will refer to "leadership" as a dynamic process as we briefly review some leadership styles and some approaches used by scholars and critics to study this very important function in communication.

LEADERSHIP STYLES

Just as your views about the words "leader" and "leadership" will condition how you work in groups, so will your attitudes about how people work together. The definition of leadership styles ordinarily includes three categories: autocratic, or strongly boss-oriented; laissez faire, or leave-them-alone; and democratic, or participative.

Autocratic styles. An autocratic style tends to produce results at the expense of harmony or personal commitment. Such a style creates hostility and aggression, discontent, loss of individuality, and dropouts — but the quantity of work produced may be greater than in other forms of leadership management.

Laissez faire styles. Not the same as democratic groups, laissez faire groups tend to be leaderless and sometimes directionless, characterized by lots of play and very little work — and poorer-quality work. A laissez faire style does not generally create a lasting commitment to a group or a task and may generate dissatisfaction with other group members and the level of accomplishment. There is a tendency to defer decisions and activities, to be distracted from purposeful play or work.

Democratic styles. With democratic styles, work motivation tends to be higher than in other groups, with more self-starting effort. There is more originality, more creativeness, more mutual praise and organized common efforts, as well as more tendency to share group property and develop spontaneous subgroups (rather than competitive cliques). There is greater satisfaction with the work attempted and accomplished and with involvement, although total productivity may not be as high as in the autocratic style.

Summary. These generalizations were developed by early studies of groups at work and play. For an excellent brief report on leadership styles, see Goldberg's summary of the research and the theoretical analyses.[2] You should not infer that all groups are always led by the same leadership styles — the ebb and flow of group behaviors gives rise to a variety of styles which spring from a variety of assumptions about how leadership works.

APPROACHES TO LEADERSHIP

While studying leadership as a social phenomenon, researchers also found it necessary to make assumptions about transferring their theoretical predictions into learning systems. In other words, as you find out more about leadership, do you also learn more about how to do it better? Is there any way to train better "leaders" based on the research findings of investigators? Historically there have been a number of different ideas about how leadership might be improved — and how people might be trained in that particular skill.

Trait approach. One of the most common and certainly historically most persistent approaches to studying leadership analyzes those traits, or personal qualities, which characterize leaders. The focus is on the leader and what his or her personality is like. You try to figure out what traits or characteristics the "leader" has which people who are not leaders lack.

This has given rise to ideas such as the belief that being tall is a sign of leadership — for studies have shown that bishops are taller than

[2]Alvin A. Goldberg and Carl E. Larson, *Group Communication*, Prentice-Hall, Inc., Englewood Cliffs, N.J., 1975, chap. 6.

priests, that railroad executives are taller than ticket agents, that university presidents are taller on the average than college presidents. Pointing to Charles de Gaulle as a naturally tall leader, however, presents some paradox if you try to account for such short leaders as Napoleon and Hitler.

We have trouble with the trait approach because (1) we cannot find much agreement on what traits seem to be exclusively and consistently the property of leaders; (2) personality traits are difficult to measure and equate with patterns of leadership; (3) many of the characteristics which leaders seem to have also appear in nonleaders; and (4) it is difficult to train for many of these traits if we want to improve our leadership abilities: that is, how can you teach a 5-foot-1 person to become 6-foot-4?

Situational approach. Early studies showed that some things could be taught to people to make better "leaders" out of them. These theories contended that a person rises to the occasion of leadership. If you are trained to be ready for a situation, and you wait for that situation to arise, then you can become the leader when it happens. Several problems are presented by this theory, not the least of which is figuring out what kind of situation you should train for. If you do train to be ready in case of an atomic attack, for instance, and one never comes, maybe you have wasted yourself in waiting for the right situation. But from this idea of situations grew some additional insights into leadership.

Functional approach. This view gets away from the trait idea, giving significance instead to the actions which take place in groups. Different members of a group may perform some of the functions necessary to keep the group working toward some goal and working together smoothly. An emphasis on "the leader" misses the point, because no one person is likely to be capable of performing all the functions needed by the group. If you roughly divide the group functions into "task" (getting the job done) and "process" (maintaining the climate within which the group can work together), research has shown that these functions are generally handled by different people in a group. In other words, there may be a task leader and a process leader, both influencing the productivity of the group in different ways at different times as they perform their own special functions. With many other activities needed in a group, you can easily see that leadership functions can be distributed widely among group members and not simply centered in a "leader."

Contingency approach. More recently, the work of Fiedler particularly has developed the idea that leadership is a combination of (1) the kind of situation and (2) the style of the person performing leadership functions.[3] In this approach, Fiedler questions the older belief that a leader's effectiveness will improve as that person's influence increases over others. Rather, says the contingency approach, control sometimes helps some leaders and sometimes hinders some leaders. Leadership depends on finding the proper match between a leader's style of interacting with subordinates and the degree to which the situation gives control and influence to the leader. Situations include such factors as the respect and trust of followers, the power of a position, and the structure of the task. A situation in which respect and trust and power are high or low and the task is highly structured or quite unstructured is especially good for the task-oriented leader. A situation in which these factors are moderate is better managed by a relationship (process-oriented) leader. Other studies[4] also confirm the idea that leadership is affected by subordinates' attitudes about the person making the leadership attempts.

In summary: Leadership   In attempts to study and train for leadership, several approaches have been tried. When it was discovered that traits could neither explain leadership nor provide a means for training leaders, some new approaches were developed. Situations were inspected in which leadership was demanded, and much scholarly attention was focused on the leadership functions performed in organizations and in groups. Researchers began to realize that people should be better trained for leadership roles, and a great attempt was made to prepare leaders. Most recently the simple system of functional leadership has been questioned by supporters of approaches which say that leadership is a combination of certain things a person habitually does and the kinds of situations in which those particular actions are most appropriate. Leadership training, therefore, has been presented as a selection of certain styles to be used in certain circumstances.

This, of course, is not the final word on leadership or leadership training; new research is going into many more facets of this important function of today's interdependent society. Whatever approach may be most current, or whatever theories may be emerging, there is only one certainty: human communication will inevitably be at the very center of it all.

[3]Fred Fiedler, "The Trouble With Leadership Training," *Psychology Today,* February 1973.

[4]Alvin A. Goldberg, L. Crisp, E. Seiburg, and M. Tolela, "Subordinate Ethos and Leadership Attitudes," *Quarterly Journal of Speech,* vol. 53, no. 4, December 1967, pp. 354-360.

BEYOND DECISIONS   Most people approach their communication with others with a hope of mutual understanding and with a great desire not to botch things up. Although people sometimes deliberately mislead others, we are convinced that most of you want to communicate effectively with others and are interested in developing mutually satisfying relationships.

Interpersonal communication is complex. You know from your experience as well as from reading this text how easy it is for communication to go awry. The next important questions are: How can you make it work? What skills are necessary to enhance your communication with others? How can the skills be sharpened or developed?

In Chapter 8 we discussed a fundamental communication skill: listening. In this chapter, we will provide additional answers to these crucial questions. We must warn you here, however, that there is no simple cookbook approach to improving interpersonal communication. This chapter will not provide you with ten-easy-steps-to-success-in-your-communication-life. Just as toothpaste and mouthwash are really not the key to social success, nobody can give you a communication pill which will automatically transform you into a communication star.

However, there are some basic factors which contribute to interpersonal effectiveness. We will discuss three of these factors in the remainder of this chapter: (1) the art of trusting, (2) the reduction of defensiveness, and (3) the use of appropriate communication styles.

THE ART OF TRUSTING   What does it mean to trust? How does trust relate to interpersonal communication? Whom and when do you trust? How do you demonstrate that you can be trusted? These are important questions, and they do not have simple answers. In this section we consider trust on the basis of a provocative and sensitive analysis by Rossiter and Pearce.[5]

The Situation Context of Trust   According to Rossiter and Pearce, you can experience trust only when your relationship with another person is characterized by *contingency, predicability,* and *alternative options.*

"Contingency" refers to a stiuation in which the outcomes of another person's actions significantly affect you. If what somebody does has no effect on you, there is no need for you to trust that person.

"Predictability" refers to the degree of confidence you have in what the other person will do. You guess about the other person's behavior or intentions. In situations where predictability is low, you cannot have much confidence that the other person will behave in a certain way. You may have hope but no trust.

[5]Charles M. Rossiter and W. Barnett Pearce, *Communicating Personally,* The Bobbs-Merrill Company, Indianapolis, Ind., 1975, pp. 119–145.

Finally, ``alternative options'' implies that you are free to do something else beside trust. Trust is present only by choice.

If any one of these three characteristics is missing, we cannot speak of trust. When the three characteristics are present, trust *may* develop. The word ``may'' is deliberately emphasized here because, as we will discuss, trust is an option and is never automatic. If what happens to you depends on another person's behavior, if you have some basis for predicting how the other person will behave, and if you have a choice about your own behavior, then you are in a situation in which trust *may occur*. This is usually the case in a manager-subordinate, husband-wife, or roommate relationship. The other person's behavior may affect you significantly, you have some basis for determining whether your predictions about the other person are accurate, and at least some of the time you have options about what to do. Table 7 gives examples of situations in which you must decide to trust or not to trust.

TABLE 7. **Situations for Trust**

Characteristic, and how to check on whether it is present	A clerk in a store is showing you a bicycle you want to buy.	A friend offers to meet you at 6:00 and give you a ride home.	Driving in traffic, you stop at a red light and wait for it to turn green.
Contingency — Does it make any difference to me what the other person does?	You want the bicycle to be as advertised; you will have to live with your own decision to get it or not.	Accepting the offer will save you both time and worry about how to get home; you will depend on the ride.	The effect of stopping is not getting into a collision. You have to trust that those behind you will stop as you do and that those in the cross lanes will only go when the light is green.
Predictability — Can I count on the other person?	Check out the reputation of the store; think about your own experiences with clerks; consider how bicycles generally hold up after you take them on the street.	Is your friend known to be punctual? Does the friend's car work all right? Are there other factors which could keep the friend away?	Most drivers obey the stop signals. Although the orange light is dangerous to run through, red and green are usually predictable.
Alternative options — Can I personally do anything about trusting or not?	Check out what you can see about the bicycle; get a guarantee on all parts. If you are not satisfied that a trust situation is possible, then don't buy the bike.	Walk; take a bus; ask another friend to back up the offer; phone the friend just before 6:00 to check.	Don't drive; take a bus. If you do drive you are very dependent on other drivers to obey the signals and not run into you, especially after the light turns green for your lane.

The Belief Basis for Trust

When you trust another person, you take a risk, or at least you increase your vulnerability to that other person. Trusting means that you will let the other person's behavior affect you. To do so you must believe that the other person is both willing and able to behave in ways that will not hurt you.

In other words, you trust another person when you believe that person won't hurt you. Intentions are not enough. Abilities are crucial. Is the other person able or competent to perform the action you predit will take place? After all, a friend who is not a qualified brain surgeon may be very well intentioned and may never wish to hurt you, and yet you may not "trust" him or her to perform brain surgery on you. The reverse is equally true. Although you may perceive somebody as quite competent, if you also perceive that person's intentions to be devious or self-serving, you are not likely to trust.

How Do You Develop Trusting Relationships?

Being trusted by others does not happen by magic or by mechanically following a technical manual which specifies the steps to be taken to "make others trust you." In fact there is no sure way to make other people trust you. While trusting other people only *sometimes* encourages them to trust you, distrusting them *almost always* will make them distrust you.

You cannot make someone trust you. If someone is bent on misunderstanding you and refuses to perceive you as either well intentioned or competent, there is very little you can do to change that person's interpretations of what you are like. Anything you do can always be misinterpreted, and everthing you say can always be held against you, and taken as further "proof" of that person's original conception of you.

Trust is built through risks mutually taken one by one in a given relationship. For example, if you make yourself vulnerable to another person — that is, accept the fact that his or her actions may affect you adversely — and if the other person accepts your initial move by not hurting you and by making himself or herself vulnerable to you, then mutual trust building is started. You may then make yourself a little more vulnerable, and so may the other person. And the process goes on as you work together, taking more risks.

Rossiter and Pearce contend that for a trusting relationship to be established, three factors must be present: (1) You must trust even though you are not sure that the other will reciprocate. (2) You and the other person must be willing to trust, that is, (a) not follow impulses to exploit the other and (b) interpret the other person's behavior as trustworthy rather than foolish. (3) You must both be willing to negotiate the process through incremental steps, a little trust at a time.

You cannot force trust on other people. If they are intent on distrusting you, they will always find something to support their belief that you are not trustworthy. Ultimately all that you can do is trust in the hope that the other can and will respond in kind. Of course there is no guarantee that this will happen; and as you take risks in making yourself vulnerable, there is always the possibility that the other person will see you as a fool and will take advantage of you. You must, therefore, always decide whether the risks are worth taking and whether you can afford to take them. In a sense, this implies that to have others trust you, you must actively take some initiative and not simply wait for others to make the first move. If you want to be trusted, you have to make the first gesture, and the opening gambit always involves some amount of risk.

Developing trust in others is not simple. It depends on both your behavior and the ability of the other person to trust and to take risks. You have little control over another person's ability to take risks. However, you do have some control sometimes over the degree of risk involved for the other person, should he or she trust you.

If you are reliable in the messages you send — if most of the time you do what you say, your actions match your words, and your nonverbal messages fit your verbal ones — others can develop the ability to predict your actions and thus minimize their chances of guessing wrong about what you will do.

You can sometimes have some degree of control over the outcomes of risk-taking behavior. How you respond to people who take risks and make a mistake may affect to a large extent their decision to take risks again. You may tell an employee, for example, to go ahead with a project on his or her own and that you will support whatever he or she comes up with. If you bawl out the employee when the product is not exactly as you would have wished, you make it unlikely that the person will believe that you meant what you said. Parents who encourage children to tell the truth about some matter may then punish them for the behavior they confess. It's likely that those children will learn to withhold the truth or tell lies because the risk of being truthful did not pay off.

How Do You Decide to Trust?

There are times when you know that you had better not trust another person. Get-rich-fast-without-doing-anything deals smack of deceit. If someone appears trusting toward you, there is no sure way to know whether the person is truly wishing to build a trusting relationship with you or is only giving you the opening lines for a con game. Thus you are faced with the decision whether to trust when you should not, or not trust when you should. If you prefer to err in the direction of trusting when you should not, you may be perceived by some people as warm, compassionate, and nice, and by others as gullible and stupid. If you choose to err in the direction of not trusting when you should, you may be perceived by some people as hard-nosed and shrewd, but by others as distant and not trustworthy. As a manager, as a teacher, as a parent, as a friend, you have to come to terms with this issue. Do you buy the sob stories some employees give you to get out of work and therefore run the risk of being perceived as a patsy, or do you act like a hard-nosed supervisor who is not easily conned? In either case your behavior will affect that of your employees.

The kind of cooperation you get from people who work with you and for you ultimately depends on whether or not trust exists in the relationship. Your friend's response to a request for a loan depends on whether or not your relationship is based on trust.

THE REDUCTION OF DEFENSIVE CLIMATES

Much of your interpersonal communication depends on how you define the situation in which you find yourself. You appraise the threatening or nonthreatening quality of your interactions with others in terms of your self-esteem. Much of your communication with others involves some kind of risk, since communication means presenting to others a definition of yourself, your role, and the situation — a definition they may reject. What the communication climate is like and how you can change it are an important part of your guesses about how much risk is involved for you in a given situation. You behave on the basis of how safe you think you are. If you do not feel safe, you are likely to use defensive strategies to protect yourself. Perhaps you have been in a classroom situation in which the teacher keeps insisting that students participate by discussing issues openly, only to shoot down their comments or ridicule them when they do. It does not take you long to figure out how stressful offering comments and being publicly cut down by sarcasm may be. You learn quickly that the climate is not safe, and your communication will probably be characterized by defensive strategies designed to protect yourself.

The professor-student relationship is not all that different from any other dyadic relationship. People always figure out whether they are safe or not, and their communication and behavior will rest on that assessment. Defensive strategies are simply an indication that a person does not feel secure in some way, at some level.

Why do you feel insulted or have your feelings hurt? "An insult is a valuation of the individual by others which does not agree with his valuation of himself," according to Lecky,[6] who goes on to discuss how people deal with such contradictions. Other writers have asserted that the basic reason for defending yourself in interpersonal situations is related to your unmet needs for reinforcement from others.[7] Both these ideas seem to say that when you think about yourself in one way, you would like others to agree with that opinion. If you see yourself as smart, you'd like others to see you that way too and not discover ways in which you are not smart. If you like to be considered a good musician, you are anxious to be supported in that evaluation by the things people see you do and what they say to you and about you. Each of you has a self-image to maintain. Each of you also values opinions and support from some persons more than others. Some of your friends are more important to impress than others; some of the people in the world are more significant than others in how you pay attention to what they think (or say) of you. The degree to which you need reinforcement (positive feedback) from others and the degree to which that need is not met will determine how defensively you may act in your communication. You also encounter social situations which are stressful in the sense that you are afraid a blow will be struck at your self-image if you do not behave as you think others expect you to behave. You can also damage your self-image if you do not live up to your own expectations just as much as you can by not living up to the expectations of others. For those situations you may employ defensive strategies designed to protect yourself from negative feedback, from embarrassment, from losing face. You look in each other's eyes to find yourselves, but sometimes you are afraid to look.[8]

Defensive Strategies

How then do you defend yourself? Your defensive strategies when you respond to an *actual* threat are somewhat different from your defensive strategies when you respond to a *potential* threat. In the first case, you adjust; in the second, you avoid.

---

[6]Prescott Lecky, *Self-Consistency: A Theory of Personality,* The Shoe String Press, New York, 1961, p. 136.

[7]Fritz Heider, *The Psychology of Interpersonal Relations,* John Wiley & Sons, Inc., New York, 1982. Kim Giffin and Bobby R. Patton, *Fundamentals of Interpersonal Communication,* Harper & Row, Publishers, Incorporated, New York, 1976.

[8]"It is not possible, of course, for us to be perfectly accurate in judging others' opinions of us, but the correlation is usually high enough to suggest that the self-concept is in large part controlled by what we see reflected in other people's eyes." Carl H. Weaver and Warren L. Strasbaugh, *Fundamentals of Speech Communication,* American Book Company, New York, 1964, p. 157. Other discussion of some defensive strategies is based on Weaver and Strasbaugh's chapter on motives.

Adjustment The best defense is a good offense, according to many coaches. In your verbal games, you tend to follow that advice when you verbally attack any persons who may be a threat to you. If it is too risky or too rude to attack directly — to tell your boss to go jump in the lake may cost you your job — you can attack indirectly by using sarcasm or ridicule, by questioning the other person's motives or competence (thereby becoming a threat to the other person), by putting the other person down , or by excluding others from your conversation through use of specially selected jargon words, the latest slang, private jokes, private references, or topics known to be of great discomfort to the other person.

Besides this *verbal aggression* some other common adjustment strategies are *rationalization, denial, fantasy,* and *projection.*

When you acknowledge that a threat is present, but tell yourself that you can handle it without loss of face or embarrassment, or that it is really not that important to begin with, then you engage in *rationalization.*

Saying that a threat does not exist, or, when another person has threatened your self-concept, telling yourself that it wasn't meant that way, that you misinterpreted, that "she would never do such a thing," is moving from rationalization to *denial.*

If you really want to make the situation appear brighter than it is, and believe the best, and overcome the threat by replacing it with a more pleasant situation, you can call up your imagination and convince yourself by *fantasy* that another thing is happening instead of the threatening one.

In *projection,* you make use of the technique of assuming that others are thinking, feeling, or saying things out of an anxiety which they are trying to cover up. You can say the other person is acting aggressively toward you only to cover up his or her own problems of anxiety or aggressiveness, a reflection of *your* feeling of anxiety in the face of the threat, which you project onto the other person.

Avoidance If you see a threat coming, you may use strategies which are different from those you use after you have experienced the distressing situation. One way to avoid threats to your self-image and communicative personality is simply to get out of the way, or not to put yourself into situations where you have to communicate with others in potentially embarrassing situations. If you want to sign up for a course in college and have no idea how to do it, you will delay until somehow the ambiguity of the situation is reduced so that you can safely risk making errors. The young man trying to get up enough nerve to ask a woman for a date is a classic example. He is afraid of being turned down, and so he solves the problem by not asking for the date. In her book *Report,*

Lillian Ross describes the behavior of a group of high school boys from a small Midwestern community on a senior trip to New York who refused to eat in restaurants.[9] They made up all kinds of excuses to avoid eating out, even were content to go hungry, and none of their excuses made sense. It turned out that they simply wanted to avoid the eating-out situation because they did not know how to order from a menu. When it was discovered that the restaurant placed them in a situation in which they might be found inadequate and which might prove embarrassing, their refusal to eat out made more sense and could be handled.

Besides the kind of *physical avoidance* we discussed above, another form is *retreat* as the threatening occasion comes closer. A child will have to go to the bathroom to get out of performing in front of the class. A person who has difficulty getting a vending machine to work may retreat quickly to get out of a public confrontation with a machine that is likely to win anyway.

Verbally you can avoid situations by two simple strategies, *invoking taboos* and *controlling information.* In the former, you avoid certain topics for fear that you might say or do things you will feel embarrassed about or hear things which might make you feel uncomfortable. Telling Polish jokes in front of your friend Kobos may embarrass both of you. Referring to the insensitivity of university administrators when talking to a dean may not be worthwhile conversation. If you are sensitive about one of your physical features (nose, hair, chin, ears, etc.), you will not usually steer the conversation to those topics. Talking about divorce in front of children whose parents are recently separated is sometimes considered taboo. In such situations as these you may invoke a strategy to change the subject — you interrupt by calling attention to an activity or person nearby, you distract a speaker by moving away, you verbally intrude when the talk approaches a dangerous area. You may also use very ambiguous remarks to get away from sensitive areas; or you can say directly that you do not want to talk about it. One such comment can be used in almost every conversational situation: "I'm not sure that would apply in all cases." A variation can be most useful in turning from a taboo topic: "You must need a lot of information (or experience or knowledge) to go into that subject. . . ."

Information is also power. People who control information often control their environment and how people can interact. The person who can strategically withhold or dispense information can tightly control interpersonal situations. In work situations, the person "in the know" is sought after and generally believed. Deciding how much is

[9]Lillian Ross, *Reporting,* Dodd Mead & Co., New York, 1981.

good for others to know is a significant power in a communicating relationship. Office traffic will flow around the person who receives the confidential memos on what is happening or who gets the telephone calls from supervisors outlining projects or programs. By controlling the information which others may need, you can operate your interpersonal relationships on your own terms; you can avoid threats by being in charge of the basic raw materials of interaction, the content of messages.

Some common elements of defensive strategies

Defensive strategies have several elements in common which have been identified by Bennis and others[10] and have been investigated by many researchers. One common element is that defensive strategies encourage a *ritualistic* approach to your interpersonal communication and thus discourage freedom and spontaneity. In that way you rely on "cookbook" techniques to get by in your world and try to force each situation into a "recipe" you have memorized rather than responding naturally or openly. Another element is your tendency to hide some facet of your behavior which you feel will not be accepted by others, to minimize some feature of yourself. An opposite of this is to exaggerate some feature when you pretend, unrealistically, that you can do no wrong; that nothing should be unacceptable to others in any situation. Either of these two reactions displays a rigidity to the situations which is not appropriate — you should recognize that different behaviors are useful in different situations and are never always right or always wrong.

If you value open, free, honest, direct and trusting communication, what can you do to help build a climate that will increase the likelihood of developing such communication transactions? Again, let us emphasize that whether someone feels safe ultimately depends on his or her perception of the situation. Although you cannot control how people perceive, you can sometimes control to some extent the stimulus for their perceptions. You may present yourself in a nonthreatening way. It is up to them to perceive you as nonthreatening.

Defenses Provoked and Reduced

Jack Gibb has isolated several categories of behavior which are likely to provoke defensiveness and other categories of behaviors which are likely to help reduce defensiveness.[11]

[10]Warren Bennis et al., *Interpersonal Dynamics: Essays and Readings in Human Interactions,* rev. ed., The Dorsay Press, Homewood, Ill., 1979, pp. 211-212.

[11]Refer to Jack Gibb, "Defensive Communication," *Journal of Communication,* vol. 11, September 1961, for a more complete discussion of provoked defensiveness and additional references to these categories and others.

Evaluation or description Communication which appears evaluative, judgmental, or blaming tends to increase defensiveness. If you feel that people are judging you, criticizing you, or even evaluating you positively, you are likely to feel threatened. Farson and Gordon, for example, have openly questioned use of praise, or positive evaluations, as supportive or helping communication. In his article ''Praise Reappraised,'' Farson contends that if you watch the way people respond to compliments or praise, you will note that they invariably seem to react with discomfort, uneasiness, and defensiveness.[12] Their response is often a vague denial of the compliment or even a self-derogration:

''I really can't take credit for it. . . .''

''Well, it's nothing, really. . . .''

''You look nice, too. . . .''

''You did well, too. . . .''

''Oh, you're just saying that. . . .''

''Uh, that's OK. . . .''

These statements are all defensive statements, indicating that the situation was perceived as a difficult one. Often people get so flustered when they receive compliments that their discomfort is apparent through their nonverbal behavior. They squirm, they look away, they become flushed, they make denial gestures. Part of the reason for the discomfort is that evaluation, positive or negative, is still evaluation. In Farson's words, ''If we are weighed, we might be found wanting.'' Unless you have built a relationship you trust with the person giving the compliment, you may suspect that person's motives. ''What does this person want from me?'' is often the nonexpressed thought of someone who is receiving a compliment. It is also possible to predict that a negative item will follow a positive one; when you hear a compliment, you wait for the other shoe to fall because you are used to the ''sandwich technique.'' Briefly, this technique consists of praising someone about something, then following up with a criticism, then returning to something nice. It goes something like this:

> *''Honey, this is a beautiful picture (praise), but you are so messy. You shouldn't smear paint all over the place (criticism). Well, go ahead, honey, and show your pretty picture to Daddy (praise).''*

[12]Richard E. Farson, ''Praise Reappraised,'' *Harvard Business Review*, September–October, 1963.

No wonder the child doesn't know what hit him or her. In this way, you get schooled in waiting for the reprimand when you hear the compliment.

To avoid as much as possible either making or reacting to evaluations, describe rather than evaluate, make unvalued statements rather than critical ones, ask questions which are relevant and information-seeking rather than rhetorically evaluative. Sometimes a certain question sounds as though it is information-seeking when in fact it is evaluative or accusative. You hear it between parents and children, teachers and students, husbands and wives. It is "Why did you do that?" when asked with a tone of voice which clearly reveals an accusatory reaction.

Control or problem approach

Communication used to control others is bound to be resisted. The degree of defensiveness aroused depends on the degree of suspicion you have about the controller's motives. If you suspect ulterior motives, you get defensive. You have grown suspicious in a culture where control is often sugarcoated, "You don't want to stay up late and get all tired, do you, honey?" is a devious way of saying, "I want you to go to bed now." "What do doctors recommend?" is a question which sets up the answer that you should buy a product recommended by doctors but sold by that advertiser. Whether the message is personal, political, or commercial, it carries an implicit attempt to control a person who needs to be changed and is inadequate — and that makes it a threatening message. A preventative against control strategy is to address our communication to problems rather than to people, to issues rather than to personalities.

Stratagems or spontaneity

When you would like your motive not to be known, you employ stratagems, or devious measures, tricks, devices, or games with each other. When you suspect that a stratagem is being used on you, you resent it and become defensive. Most people have an aversion to deceit in any form. You do not like to be manipulated. You especially resent the idea that others might think you are foolish enough to fall for their tricks. By developing spontaneity in your relations with others and by not developing certain devices (use a firm handclasp and look someone in the eye and they're sold) for all occasions, but staying flexible in your interactions, you can avoid triggering defensive behaviors induced by your obvious or obscure stratagems.

Lack of concern or involvement

Any behavior which openly conveys lack of feeling, caring, or warmth says to others that you are not concerned. A detached and aloof attitude often gives the impression of rejection. Even by appearing neutral you can make another person feel unwanted. Defensiveness based on rejection or even the possibility of rejection is common. Overcoming this tendency can be described as becoming involved with others, showing empathy, and finding a level of concern for the ideas, the issues, the constraints, the abilities, and the behaviors of another person. As we described it in Chapter 8, an attitude of caring and involvement can be communicated by actively listening to others.

Superior attitude or sharing

When a person conveys to you a feeling of superiority over you, it brings out your defenses. Arrogance, distance, aloofness, haughtiness, and condescension all send you a signal that the other person is not willing or ready to develop a shared or equal relationship. You have difficulty communicating in that situation. Equality is sharing of similarities and differences without having to rank each other on every item or idea, without having to compete for "first place" in every exchange of ideas or messages.

Dogmatic attitudes or flexibility

People who come on as all-knowing, who appear to need to be right and to win arguments rather than to solve problems, and who tend to impose their views as the only right ones, are classic generators of defensiveness in others. For one thing, it is hard to communicate with such people unless you happen to agree exactly with their ideas. So dogmatic are they that you must agree entirely or you will be put down and judged negatively for holding the "wrong" ideas. People who have a provisional idea of what is going on, who act as if there were some other ideas to be heard, and who believe that truth does not necessarily always reside in their own insides can reduce defensiveness in communication. Being right does not mean that every other idea is wrong and must be stomped on; there are provisions for some error even in the best answers.

In summary: Provoking or reducing defensiveness

It is crucial to recognize that behaviors which provoke defensiveness are serious obstacles to effective interpersonal communication. People who communicate judgmentally and dogmatically, who need to control and manipulate others, who appear unwilling to develop a shared relationship based on mutual trust, make interpersonal communication particularly difficult. Once defensiveness is aroused, people tend to resort to shallow rituals and protective behavior. Ritualistic behavior, in turn, is likely to strengthen the motivation of the initial communicator for behaving the way he or she started to behave. Both sender and receiver are caught in the web of self-fulfilling prophecies. Their behaviors feed each other, each person's behavior arousing additional defensiveness in the other. There is no way out of a contest of attack-defend-protect. It is unlikely that the encounter will prove satisfying for either person, because behaviors which provoke defensiveness in the first place are likely to be attacks on the self-esteem of others.

COMMUNICATION STYLES

No two people behave in exactly the same manner, and the same person does not act the same way all the time. However, there are regularities in human communication. Although most people are quite capable of communicating in a variety of ways, they often choose to fall back on familiar patterns of handling their communication with others. Such characteristic ways of dealing with interpersonal situations are called "styles." People develop their own styles for communicating; and while it is possible to use many diffferent styles each person tends to repeat a preferred style in certain situations.

Before we identify some common styles of communicating, let us emphasize three important points:

1. A range of styles is available to all of you. There are many different ways to respond to interpersonal situations, and you use them all, at one time or another.
2. Each style is effective in some specific situations.
3. It is the habitual use of one style, indiscriminately, for all situations, which creates interpersonal problems.

The following description of communication styles is based on Virginia Satir's discussion of patterns of communication.[13] The five basic communication styles she describes are (1) the blaming or aggressive style, (2) the placating or nonassertive style, (3) the computing or intellectual style, (4) the distracting or manipulative style, and (5) the leveling or assertive style.

The Blaming or Aggressive Style

The person using the blaming or aggressive style tends to act in a demanding fashion with others. Blamers are fault-finders and come on rather critically with others. Blamers often act in a superior fashion and are often described as very bossy people. Carried to extremes, blamers become tyrannical and loud and get their way at the expense of other people's rights and feelings. Blamers send messages which imply that everybody else is stupid for not believing as they do and that other people's wants and feelings simply do not count. The major goal for blamers in interpersonal relationships is to win and dominate, forcing the other person to lose. Winning is often ensured by humiliating, degrading, and overpowering other people so that they are too weak to express and defend their rights. Blaming and aggressive behavior, unfortunately, often works, and it provides emotional release and a sense of power for blamers. Blamers get what they want without direct negative reactions from others. A blaming boss, particularly one who

[13]Virginia Satir, *Peoplemaking,* Hazelden Foundation, Center City, Minn., 1976.

holds power over you, may be feared and may scare you into doing what he or she wants. If you are overpowered, you probably will not take on the boss directly or openly.

In the long run, however, the consequences of the blaming style can be quite negative. Blamers usually fail to establish close relationships, and they feel that they have to be constantly on guard against other people's attacks and possible retaliation. They feel alienated from other people, misunderstood, and unloved. Blamers are usually lonely people.

The blaming style is not always dysfunctional. There are times when legitimate criticism and evaluation must be offered, when orders and directions must be given, when responsibility must be taken to fire or flunk someone, or when limits for acceptable behavior must be imposed. As we will see later, however, criticism and evaluation are usually much more effective when they are given in a leveling or assertive style.

The Placating or Nonassertive Style

Placaters always try to please and often attempt to ingratiate themselves. They often apologize, seldom disagree, and talk as though they could do almost nothing for and by themselves. They must always have someone else's approval. Placaters violate or simply ignore their own rights, needs, and feelings, and they are unable to express what they want in a direct and forthright manner. When they do express their feelings or thoughts, they do it in a very apologetic and self-effacing way that usually makes others disregard them. Placating (using a nonassertive style) says that the placater does not really count and can be taken advantage of. And indeed, placaters often are taken advantage of. Placaters show so little respect for themselves that they teach others not to respect them. The basic goals of the placater are to avoid conflict at all costs and to appease. Nonassertive superiors, for example, have great difficulty saying ``no'' to their employees' requests and end up trying to please everyone, which in the long run pleases no one. They are afraid of hurting people's feelings. They are worried that saying ``no'' or standing up for their own needs will cause other people to dislike them or to think them foolish, stupid, or selfish.

The Computing or Intellectual Style

People who use the computing style rely on intellectualizations to deal with interpersonal situations. The style requires an outward appearance of being calm, cool, and collected. Feelings are not allowed to show. A person using this style believes that emotions are best kept hidden inside, since they basically distract from the work at hand. The intellectual style requires emphasis on logic and rationality. People relying on this style are very distrustful of feelings and personal emotions. ``If people were only reasonable and used their heads, there would not be so many problems around here'' is their motto. Intellectualizers often feel quite vulnerable and deal with their fears of inadequacy by presenting a distant and aloof front so that no one can really get too close to them. Because they consider people to be unpredictable and irrational, they may choose professions which do not put them much in contact with other people. They prefer professions in which their status and authority will keep them at a distance from others.

The Distracting or Manipulative Style

The distracting style is based on not being involved with interpersonal situations. ''Avoid threatening situations'' is the motto. People using this style have developed all kinds of strategies to manipulate themselves out of unpleasant communication encounters. When encounters cannot be avoided, their style for dealing with people is characterized by distracting maneuvers, or by manipulating other people's feelings. Anger, hurt, and guilt are often used as ways to get to others. A boss may get employees to work overtime by appealing to their potential guilt feelings by using verbal ploys like, ''How could you let me down after all I've done for you?'' A parent will use the same strategy by calling children ''ungrateful'' or ''mean to your mother.''

The Leveling or Assertive Style

Levelers are able to stand up for their rights and express feelings, thoughts, and needs in a direct, honest, straightforward manner. Tone of voice, gestures, eye contact, and stance all fit the words that are spoken. Actions also match words, and assertive people follow through on what they say they will do.

If you are being assertive, you never stand up for your rights at the expense of another person's rights. You have respect for yourself but also respect for others, and you are open to compromise or negotiation. The basic message of leveling is ''This is what I think about the situation'' and does not imply domination or humiliation of the other people who may not happen to think or see things the same way. Leveling involves respect, not blind deference. The goal of leveling is better communication and mutual problem solving. Whenever conflicts of rights or needs arise, the attempt is to solve them by working together with the other people involved.

Although leveling and communicating assertively do not guarantee that you will get your way, this style can have positive consequences. It usually increases your self-respect and helps you to develop greater self-confidence. You will feel good about being able to say what you believe without fear. Whether others agree with you or whether they do what you want almost becomes incidental. For example, you may not get a raise after asking for it. But if you ask your boss in a leveling way and explain honestly and directly the reasons you are entitled to a raise, you will feel good to have expressed yourself and to have stood up for what you believed. If the boss gives you the raise, so much the better. If not, at least you will have the satisfaction of going directly to the issue. You didn't act like the placator, who would never ask for a raise for fear of being turned down. You didn't play the role of the manipulator who constantly complains to others about the unfairness of management. You didn't copy the aggressive person who yells and screams in useless and heated loud arguments with the boss. In any of those styles, besides getting or not getting a raise, you may develop very strong feelings of resentment and anger.

Many books are now available for those of you who wish to read more on the assertive style of communication. A short bibliography on the subject is included at the end of this chapter.

The basic point about assertive communication is that it is the style most likely to foster trust, self-respect, and respect from others. Those are all vital ingredients for effective interpersonal communication.

Summary of Styles   Communication styles show up not only in such important actions as buying a car, selecting a college, and asking for a raise, but also in common, everyday communication. When you talk with friends about plans for meeting at a coffee break, you can see the styles used by different people: "The only place I will go is . . ." (aggressive statement; no compromise or discussion permitted). "I'll meet any place; my schedule is not very important, and I don't want to put anyone else out . . ." (placating statement; "I'm not worth worrying about, so I'll do whatever anyone else wants to"). "If we have five minutes for each of us to get to a central place, then we should . . ." (intellectual, logical, analyzing statement; any decision is based on factors or forces outside the people themselves). "It's going to be tough to find time to get together; I'm not sure coffee is worth the effort . . ." (manipulative statement; an attempt to get control by suggesting that the meeting is not worth much). "For my schedule, the snack bar works out fine, and I like the doughnuts there. What do the rest of you think?" (assertive statement; says how the speaker feels and still leaves the situation open for discussion).

For another example of these communication styles and what they might mean see Table 8, which deals with a similar question.

TABLE 8. **Communication Styles**

In this table, the question content could be almost anything. You could be working out how to ask for a raise, how to talk to another person about buying a car together, how to decide to go on a vacation or trip with another person, or any other small or large decision. Assume, for this example, that the question is: "What movie should we go to see?"

Style	Statement	Translation (What is really being said)
Aggressive	"Only one movie in town is any good; we'll go to that one."	"My way or nothing"
Placating	"Whatever movie you want to see is fine with me. I never know what's good or bad."	"Poor dumb me; I'm really helpless."
Intellectual	"Reviews say that the new French film is directed, acted, and filmed well, and is a 'must'."	"I have no feelings about it myself, only the intellectual advice from others."
Manipulative	"I'm not sure I want to go to a movie."	"Coax me; I want to be in a position of deciding by playing hard-to-get."
Assertive	"I'm most interested in the new Robert Redford movie. How about you?"	"Here's what I want. What do you want?"

BIBLIOGRAPHY   Bennis, W., et al.: *Interpersonal Dynamics: Essays and Readings in Human Interaction.* The Dorsay Press, Homewood, Ill., 1979.

Dewey, J.: *How We Think,* Heath & Co., Washington, D.C., 1933.

Farson, R. E.: "Praise Reappraised," *Harvard Business Review.* September–October 1963.

Fiedler, F.: "The Trouble With Leadership Training," *Psychology Today,* February 1973.

Gibb, J.: "Defensive Communication," *Journal of Communication,* vol. 11, September 1961.

Giffin, K., and B. R. Patton: *Fundamentals of Interpersonal Communication,* Harper & Row, Publishers, Inc., New York, 1976.

Goldberg, A. A., L. Crisp, E. Sieburg, and M. Tolela: "Subordinate Ethos and Leadership Attitudes," *Quarterly Journal of Speech,* vol. 53, no. 4, December 1967.

————, and C. E. Larson: *Group Communication,* Prentice-Hall, Inc., Englewood Cliffs, N.J., 1975.

Heider, F.: *The Psychology of Interpersonal Relations,* John Wiley & Sons, Inc., New York, 1982.

Lecky, P. *Self-Consistency: A Theory of Personality,* The Shoe String Press, New York. 1961.

Ross, L.: *Reporting,* Dodd Mead & Co., New York, 1981.

Rossiter, M., and W. B. Pearce: *Communicating Personally,* The Bobbs-Merrill Company, Indianapolis, Inc., 1975.

Satir, V.: *Peoplemaking,* Hazelden Foundation, Center City, Minn., 1976.

Weaver, C. H., and W. L. Strasbaugh: *Fundamentals of Speech Communication,* American Book Company, New York, 1964.

Part 4

LABORATORY MANUAL

Introduction to the Laboratory Manual

GENERAL COMMENTS

You will find this laboratory manual, as well as the accompanying text, somewhat different from others you may have been used to. Other books tend to be full of information for you to acquire. The accompanying text material in this book provides a *method* for you to practice, as well as some information for you to acquire. The method of the text and the course is based on the simple premise that *people tend to learn better by discovering for themselves than they do by just being told.*

In communication study, particularly, we feel that it is important for students to experience their own communication and the communication of others. We need to watch communication going on around us. A laboratory situation is a relatively safe place to experience human communication, and it can be an interesting place to observe the limitations of human communication.

Another reason we believe experiences with communication can be valuable is that there is only one person who can do anything about your communicating — you. No one can change your communication habits for you. In the laboratory situation you can try out new communication behaviors if you want to, or you can refine the behaviors you feel are your successful ones. Only you can make the exciting discoveries of your own communication strengths and weaknesses, and only you can decide to change if you like.

Laboratory learning is, of course, not new. Any biology or chemistry student has put in hours of work in a lab. Although laboratories are somewhat newer in the social sciences, the applications are growing for laboratory learning in our educational settings. In communication laboratories there are no test tubes or microscopes. The apparatus is our language and paralanguage, and the experimenters are you — the students — and your instructor. In the process of laboratory learning you will be both the observer and the observed. You will learn about communication by practicing it with others in a protected environment where you will be able to see and analyze the consequences of your behaviors. In the laboratory you will hear yourself and others talk. You will raise questions about identity, alienation, relating, and caring. You will discuss roles, norms, games, values, strategies we hide behind, and masks we wear to protect ourselves. You will have the opportunity to examine your communication value system and how it affects you.

Finally, we hope you will discover that your communication is so involved with your attitudes that communication is much more a state of mind than it is a garble of words.

CLASS ACTIVITIES AND EXERCISES

Only by getting together to talk about things or getting on your feet to report to others can you begin to feel the impact of oral communication. The dynamic quality of human communication cannot be felt by simply sitting and reading this book or any other book; nor can it be felt by writing reports in the solitude of your room to be read by a teacher in the solitude of an office. Interaction is important to demonstrate dynamic communication and to learn about it.

Emphasis in these laboratory exercises is, therefore, on an exchange of ideas and impressions between students or between the students and the instructor. Some time ago, many of these activities were given the label "GOYF" by some of our students. They coined the term as an abbreviation, an acronym, for "getting-on-your-feet" exercises. When we announced that the intention of this game or this activity was to get the class members on their feet to think and speak (in that order), the students responded by providing this label. Some attempt was made to establish the expression "TOYF," for "thinking on your feet," but it never gained the support it deserved.

Recommended activities are grouped according to the subject matter of the chapters of the text. Some exercises, naturally, will demonstrate several different principles of communication, and so it must be admitted that the arrangment of the exercises is somewhat arbitrary. In addition to the activities for which you have worksheets in this book, your instructor may add other projects or class exercises from time to time.

The thrust of activity groups, again, is to have students thinking and speaking at various levels of communication abstractness. Oral communication activity is always encouraged, so that students can learn how to think and speak by doing it.

Feedback Blanks

Feedback blanks are provided in each of the following chapters. This is designed to give students another means of interacting with one another and with the course. Honestly given, the laboratory feedback can reflect a growing awareness of communication maturity for the class.

A collation or a frequent report back to the class is important if the maximum effect is to be obtained from the feedback blanks. Although it is fun to be able to comment on the class anonymously—nobody knows who did it—we would urge you to resist the temptation to cut and slash your friends by verbal abuse in the feedbacks. A faithful, unedited version of the feedback blanks as they were turned in is important to the success of the project. If students take advantage of secrecy and lash out or become profane or otherwise act indiscriminately, then the feedbacks ought to be curtailed. Answer the questions thoughtfully, and the results will be surprising to you.

Cases for Discussion

In most chapters of the textbook, anecdotes were cited which serve the purpose of illustrating, by stories, the principles of communication. A case is an extended anecdote. Cases are designed to give you some experience in solving other peoples' communication problems so that you can perhaps do something about your own.

Cases can be discussed in small groups (this is usually recommended in the laboratory sections) or can be discussed by a forum in front of the class. Some instructions on how to conduct a forum discussion are included below. Also included are some reflections on how groups tend to solve problems which come to them as cases. One such examination involves the stages a group tends to go through in arriving at a solution. Another examination, "Notes on Discussing Cases," should be helpful as your group gets together to conduct a case discussion.

Forum Discussion

The forum discussion may be "leaderless," leader-oriented, or some combination of the two. Avoid having each member make a pleasant, pat little speech and then lapse into silence. Try for interaction of ideas; try involving the audience and other members of the forum. Do not discuss the topic so thoroughly in your planning session that you lose spontaneity in your performance. Planning time should concentrate on selecting the topic and getting some kind of agreement on the terms to be used in your discussion. One person may introduce the topic to the audience, explaining the limits your group has set on the key words used. You may want a moderator to open the speaking and review it at the end, making sure to stay within your time limit. The idea is to stimulate thought and discussion, not necessarily to reach conclusions or obtain group agreement. In fact, your discussion may have to end at the most heated moment or before all questions are answered. Good topics include personal experiences: "how we handled a communication difficulty in the office or classroom," "children should be taught honesty in the home" — something based on your own communication experience. The forum is not a UN committee; family, campus, civic, church, or classroom problems are much more real to most of us than international issues.

How Groups Solve Case Problems[1]

A group will generally tend to go through several stages to arrive at a satisfactory solution in discussing a case.

Stage 1: The stage of condemnation and aggressive evaluation
   Participants take sides; they tend to put the blame for the communication breakdowns on one person or another, usually reflecting their own biases about the kind of people involved in the case. The tendency at this stage is to oversimplify the situation by blaming.
Stage 2: The stage of frustration and rejection
   Participants complain that they do not have enough data to solve the problem. They do not feel that they are given enough information to come to a solution.

---

[1]Eugene Rebstock, "General Semantics Training through Case Analysis," *ETC,* vol. 20, no. 3, 1963.

The discovery that we all must make decisions most of our lives on the basis of fragmentary or incomplete evidence is an important experience.

Stage 3: The stage of widening perceptions

Participants will begin to ask more probing questions and try to discover how the people in the case view the situation.

Analysis is made of past history and of other pressures acting on the people in the case.

Stage 4: The stage of alternative solutions and resolutions

Participants come up with thoughtful considerations of possible solutions.

Solutions grow out of the complexities of the situation and are proposed with a feeling for the consequences of actions growing out of the case.

Notes on Discussing Cases

1. Case discussion begins with the following areas:
   a. Details of the case and their relationships
   b. Inferences that are drawn by the participants in the discussion concerning why the event occurred; also, inferences about the motivations of the people involved in the case itself
   c. Illustrations and examples from personal experiences, as brought up by participants in the discussion
   d. Expressions of feelings about the actions and assertions in the case
2. What can be analyzed in a case:
   a. *The content of the sender's message*
      What was said? Do we have all that was said?
   b. *The kind of message that was sent*
      Was it written, oral, or both? Was it simple, clear, or ambiguous? What made it simple, clear, or ambiguous? What does this have to do with the way the situation developed?
   c. *The setting of the communication situation*
      Where did the incident take place — office or home; over the telephone or face to face? What kind of situation was it? Were people tense or relaxed, formal or informal?
   d. *The sender*
      What status does the sender have, and does this affect the communication? If so, how? What assumptions does the sender have toward the situation? What attitudes, opinions, or feelings? What kind of person is the sender?
   e. *The receiver*
      Same questions as those asked about the sender. In addition, what is the receiver's response to the sender's message, and how does this affect the communication?
   f. *Outside pressures*
      Did the situation occur in an environment which provided certain rules and regulations that governed the sender and the receiver? Was the message sent directly, or was it received through intermediaries?

Role-Playing Cases or Incidents

Many of the cases in this laboratory section can be performed as skits or dramas, either in small groups by themselves or in front of the class. Often a point can be made more clearly by a dramatization of the incident than by simply talking about it. If the class has a number of members who enjoy "acting" or doing skits, these exercises will lend themselves to such role-playing activities. There need be no elaborate props or staging. Much of the success of this kind of role playing depends on its spontaneity rather than on its polish — and so no rehearsals are needed for most "shows." It helps to clarify who the actors are and what the situation is — then let the actors go. Both the instructor and the students may want to enter into the decision about which exercises should be role-played, how long the skits will last, and whether the role playing will take place in small groups (several groups doing the same skits at the same time is called "multiple role playing") or by one or more groups in front of the class. Some technical hints on conducting a role-playing exercise follow.

Warm-up (planning time) should concentrate on establishing a problem situation and assigning roles. Performance is more spontaneous if each actor understands the "character" and liberates his or her emotions through that character. A "stage manager" may set the scene and identify the characters for the audience. More than one act may show a problem, its developments, and possible solutions. Try using techniques such as these:

Alter ego (a person stands behind an actor, and speaks his or her thoughts, interrupting by placing a hand on the actor's shoulder).

Soliloquy (this time the actor speaks the thoughts in asides to the audience, by changing his or her voice, or by some other sign to indicate that silent thoughts are being expressed).

Extensions (as with alter egos, several players stand behind the actor to represent different times of life or different points of view: a woman as she is this year or last year; a man as a father, a boss, a lodge member, etc.).

Interaction Observers

To help foster class discussion, it is possible to assign observers to cover groups in their discussions or to watch other situations in the class. A great variety of observing techniques are available; many are listed in the laboratory section for Chapter 12, where group activities are emphasized. But there are some early hints on acting out the observer role. Observers are usually appointed by the instructor for a specific activity or group project. You may be asked to report to the whole class or to certain groups. But how you make and report your observations should help the learning of all participants.

Observers have an advantage in not being directly involved in the discussion preparation; they therefore have time to observe interactions and communication behaviors. It helps to compare functioning of groups with functioning during other meetings of the class. Improvements should be noted. The observer role is meant to provide the audience (the entire class or the small group) with information and insights not available to everyone. Interaction during the planning session is very important; but consider also the effect of the group's efforts on the audience, the appropriateness of the problem chosen to demonstrate a principle, the development of the problem, the solutions offered, the clarity of the views expressed, and the communication behaviors of the group members (loudness, language, flexibility of delivery during preparation time and performance, tension in voices, nonverbal cues fitting the verbal ones, and other emotional responses to audience or situation). Observe not only the oral output, but the "feeling level" communication as well. Your report to the class should be brief (avoid the dull and pointless repetition of "then he said to her" and "she said to him," etc.).

"Goldfish Bowl" Observing

One special kind of observing occurs when a group sits in a circle or around a table and is observed by another group arranged outside it in another circle. The name given to this arrangement is "goldfish bowl," to describe the visibility of the inner group's activities.

Some of the group discussions call for this arrangement so that the persons observed can get feedback on their behaviors. This is carried out in a "pairing" arrangement — each person in the inner group is observed by a partner in the outer group. The feedback is given in dyads, usually personal kinds of observations. By swapping locations, the inner group then becomes the observer or outer group, and the former observers become the actors to be observed.

Another arrangement is the general observation system, where the entire inner group is observed and commented on by the entire outer group. One of the disadvantages of this system is that only part of the interaction is concentrated on by all observers and many individual actions go by unnoticed in the attempt to follow the most exciting "action."

The goldfish-bowl system has great potential for developing understanding of behaviors as they are reported by observers in a relatively safe atmosphere. It has a disadvantage in that often the inner group engages in "role playing" for the observers rather than interacting normally. After a short while, participants tend to forget the observers, however, and usually carry on their discussion easily.

Television-Playback Observing

The cases and discussion situations here do not specifically refer to the use of television recording, but it is an exciting system of observation and feedback. If videotope recording equipment is available to record the actions of a group or of performers in discussion or role playing or in individual presentations to the class, this can result in a very dramatic view of behaviors.

One method we have used is to have the class discuss an interaction which had been taped — but to do so before the playback. Then the playback is used not only to bring the incident back to life, but also to help participants check their perceptions of what went on.

The cost of playback equipment is sufficiently low so that many institutions have equipment available in their audiovisual sections or within departments. At least occasional use of this equipment brings amazing insights which are only partially developed by human observers making their reports to the class.

ASSIGNMENTS AND PROJECTS

Besides the activities you will have during class time, there are many other opportunities to explore human communication through a variety of assignments and outside class projects. Your instructor will assign those which are most appropriate with respect to the time involved and the interests of the class. In addition to the assignments suggested in this manual, the instructor may add tests or other assignments which do not appear.

Journal

The instructor may assign you the project of maintaining a journal of communication happenings. These will become a collection of your own observations of communication around you. Although the assignments for journal entries do not appear in every chapter of the laboratory manual, it might be useful to continually keep a "communication diary" of the things you notice about the communicative behaviors of yourself and others.

Scrapbook

A collection of newspaper clippings, notes, letters, printed ads, and other published or written materials will help you analyze the communication habits of the people who make news and who suffer from the same communicative difficulties as the rest of us. (Whereas the journal makes a record of your own private life and observations, the scrapbook will tend to be more sweeping in its scope and more distant in its relation to your personal life.)

Although there may be many individual and different ways to make a scrapbook, we suggest that you use a loose-leaf notebook as the basic part of your scrapbook. Then you can add pages (punched to fit the rings) as you add clippings. Trimming the clippings neatly will make your book easier to compile and to read. Instead of just putting the clippings together, we suggest that you paste them on standard-size paper so that pages of your scrapbook will be the same size. This also provides you with space to write comments on the clippings. From time to time the instructor may ask you to turn in the scrapbook or to share your latest collection of clippings by discussing some of them in class.

Communication Case

Another kind of outside assignment is the case which you construct from your own experience or the experience of others. The purpose of this assignment is to have the student describe and analyze a communication breakdown. The case should present a relatively complex problem which is still largely unsolved. If the problem is too simple and uncomplicated, all we have is an illustration which can be read with interest but which leaves little room for creative analysis. For that reason, the case should contain a record of misevaluations and breakdowns amenable to analysis with the principles and concepts presented in this course.

It should consist of three distinct parts: (1) *The description of the problem.* This part should be sufficiently detailed that it can be role-played. The case does not have to be of monumental importance to the future of the world, but it can represent the tragedies which befall us in our relations with others through faulty communication — as observed over a period of time. Deal with something you know about firsthand — the everday kind of mess we often make of our interpersonal communication. This is an objective report. Treat it as a third-person story, even if it happened to you. Try to minimize personal judgments, slant, and inferences. This first section is only a description of events: what happened to whom, when, and where. It may be written as a narrative or a dialogue, or in any form you wish. (2) *The analysis.* In this part you will analyze communication difficulties from the point of view of the behaviors described in this course and text. Include if you like some recommendations about how the behaviors you report could have been improved by applying some of the principles discussed in class. If you want at this point to propose solutions and inject your personal feelings about the case, you may do so. (3) *Your reactions.* Report the reactions you noted in yourself in carrying this assignment through from its inception (perhaps when you first read these instructions) to the completion of your paper. You are asked for your reactions to the assignment at this point, not your reactions to the case itself or the people in it.

Personal Improvement Blanks

At the end of each set of assignments you will find a personal improvement blank (PIB) which asks you some questions about your communication behaviors and the behaviors of those around you. It is designed to have you look at your communication as everyday life and not just as what goes on in class. Over the years students have reported that these exercises have provided them with a way of watching their own communication development (hence, "improvement") in a realistic way. As we wrote earlier, you are the only one who can do anything about your communicating. If that is so, then you must have some means of monitoring your changing behaviors or your attempts to try out new behaviors and the results of those attempts.

Other Assignments

Each section has related assignments: writing, making lists, studying outside sources, etc. Some of these will be assigned by the instructor as a way of giving you outside contacts with the material from the text itself.

You will notice that the assignments focus on the application of the theories and writings in the text. They are an attempt to get you to think in terms of communication as the dynamic process it is — affecting all you do and all you are.

SELF-PACING LABORATORY EXERCISES

If you are taking this class with a group of students in an organized course, the instructor will assign exercises and assignments for you to complete and group actions for you to assist with. It is possible to experience many of the same insights if you are studying this text alone. Although the group activities are difficult for the solitary student to manage, there may be some groups available to you and willing to take part in the games and activities. Certainly most assignments are possible to work on by yourself, as they are primarily designed to be accomplished outside of class time anyway.

One of the advantages of this laboratory approach over most other texts we are familiar with is the set of questions related to the exercises. From these questions the student can develop, whether in a group discussion or alone, the major insights of the exercises.

DISCUSSION QUESTIONS

A unique feature of this laboratory manual is the elaborate set of questions for discussion and the probes designed to assist class discussion. They direct attention to the principles brought out by the exercises and help the student relate the experience to theories and to the student's own life outside the classroom.

One of the major problems we have found in experiential learning settings is that games are played, exercises worked out, activities performed, and puzzles solved, but the main purpose of these experiences is often neglected — the transfer of learning from the experience into the actual behaviors of the student. This part of the class takes time; discussion should be detailed, involving, and extended. It should bring out the reactions of the students to the exercise and not just the instructor's knowledge. After all, the instructor knows these things about communication and is helping you, the student, discover them. Such discovery takes time; it develops in the discussion periods following the games and exercises.

Other questions and comments will be generated besides those provided by the authors; certainly the curious students will ask their own questions. In processing the experience for the class, a great emphasis should be placed on the discussion questions.

Even if you do not use all the exercises (as is very likely, since many more are provided than there is class time for), you might be interested in reading the rules or procedures of the exercise and then going over the questions in the discussion section. There are many chances for clarifying your own relations to communication as you work on the exercises. They will be magnified in their value if you spend time on the discussion and not simply on the game.

Chapter 1

YOU AND YOUR COMMUNICATION

FEEDBACK BLANK

EXERCISES

1-1.	What is Communication?	Discussion
1-2.	Communication Strengths and Weaknesses	Discussion
1-3.	Getting-Acquainted Dyads	On Your Feet
1-4.	Who Knows What?	Group Project
1-5.	Acquaintance Questionnaire	Discussion
1-6.	Giving Instructions	Group Project

ASSIGNMENTS

1-1. Words to Live By
1-2. Resolutions for the New Year
1-3. Eavesdropping
1-4. Journal, Diary, Scrapbook
1-5. Interview
1-6. An Estimate of Myself as a Communicator

PERSONAL IMPROVEMENT BLANK

FEEDBACK BLANK (Chapter 1)   DO NOT SIGN
1. Rate the productivity of this week's (session's) work for you. (Circle one number.)
      1   2   3   4   5   6   7   8   9   10
Not productive   Highly Productive

2. Rate how you think the rest of the class felt about this week's (session's) productivity.
      1   2   3   4   5   6   7   8   9   10
Not productive   Highly productive

Comments:

3. Comment on your contribution in the small group or in the class exercises. Did you speak too much? Too little?

4. Comment on the class activities this week (session). What did you like, dislike? What was helpful to you and why?

5. Add other comments, criticisms, questions, suggestions, etc.

EXERCISE 1-1
WHAT IS COMMUNICATION? (Discussion)

List all the things you can think of which are communication. First do this by yourself and then get together with others in a group to compare lists and to draw up a composite list to read or present to the class. (Your list will include such items as "speaking," "waving," "touching," "clothing.")

Discussion

A. When the lists are compared, the groups or the class can discuss the common elements in the items which make them "communication."

B. Classify the items by writing them on the chalkboard or on a chart for the class to see in two categories: (1) content (2) process communication. Can some communication items be classified in both categories?

C. Discuss the axiom "You cannot *not* communicate" in relation to the list of items you consider communication.

EXERCISE 1-2
COMMUNICATION STRENGTHS AND WEAKNESSES (Discussion)

Write down a list of at least five behaviors, habits, or tendencies you have which are communication strengths. Then write down three or more of your communication weaknesses.

In a small group of four or five, share your lists of strengths. An effective way to do this is to take turns: each person lists one strength, and then a list representing the group is compiled. (Duplicates should be noted and reported because any group should recognize the strengths shared by several members.)

Follow the same procedure with the communication weaknesses — sharing the list, or as much of it as you feel comfortable about. A composite group list of weaknesses can be compiled.

Discussion

A. What similarities do you find among different groups' lists of strengths and weaknesses?

B. Can most of you identify those communication habits and behaviors which are helps or hindrances to you?

C. Did the items as they were listed come as a surprise to any members of the groups? Did anyone have difficulty listing strengths and talking about them with the rest of the group? Was there any disagreement about whether someone's listed weakness was actually a weakness?

D. How many of the listed strengths depend solely on the "owner"? Do many of them also depend on a relationship with others?

E. How many of the listed weaknesses are possible to change or alter in some way to either neutralize them or turn them into strengths?

EXERCISE 1-3
GETTING-ACQUAINTED DYADS (On Your Feet)
1. Form pairs in the class (two-person groups are called "dyads").
2. Tell the other person in your dyad those things about yourself which you would like to have used in an introduction to the class.
3. Get the same kind of information from the other member of your dyad.
4. Check the material with each other (you might perhaps make some notes) to make sure the important items have been mentioned.
5. Introduce your partner to the class using the data gathered in your dyad and taking no more than a few brief sentences to let the rest of the class know some important things about your partner.
6. Variation on this exercise:
   a. Instead of introducing your partner to the class, join another dyad whose members have exchanged data about each other. The four of you then introduce each other — you tell about your partner; your partner tells about you; the others do the same.
   b. Tell your partner something which you do not want used in the introduction and find out something about your partner which should not be used. This can be something you don't like, such as your middle name, a nickname you prefer to live down, where you were born, the grade you got in some course, etc.

Discussion
A. After the introductions are made by each person to the class, discuss the process by which you found out material about the other person — that is, how you conducted the interview.
B. Appointing one or more class observers can help develop discussion on the types of information which students selected to make the introductions.

EXERCISE 1-4
WHO KNOWS WHAT? (Group Project)
Form small groups of four to seven members. The purpose of this exercise is to find out which member of the group can be counted on to know certain things or to be able to do certain things — in other words, to locate the talents, abilities, and interests in the group. For each of the following situations, ask group members to volunteer information about their own abilities to take part in the activity suggested. How do group members feel about taking part in those activities?

1. A group to plan a party and a dance
2. A group to solve a complex mathematics problem
3. A group to write and perform a one-act play for the class
4. A group to make drawings or illustrations of this group's behaviors toward each other
5. A group to arrange for a lecturer to visit the campus and meet some classes

Discussion

A. The communication needs of each of the five groups are somewhat different. Which seem to require greater cognitive or content skills (digital communicative behaviors), and which seem to require more relational or interpersonal skills (analogic communication)?

B. How would you rank the five activities if you were given a choice of which to participate in? Pick the one you would like best; then the least; then second best; then next to last; and finally the middle one. How many of the class members selected each group activity as their first choices? As their last choices?

EXERCISE 1-5
ACQUAINTANCE QUESTIONNAIRE[1] (Discussion)

Your instructor will read aloud each of the following incomplete statements. You will be allowed a minute to complete each statement. Write spontaneously. Don't think about the statements too much.

1. I am a _____

2. I am happy when I _____

3. Ten years from now I want to _____

4. This school is a _____

5. Next Saturday night I want to _____

6. My three heroes or heroines are

(a) _____

(b) _____

(c) _____

Discussion

A. In a small group discuss how you answered the incomplete statements. Expand on your "first-impulse" completions by talking with others in the group about why you gave the answer you did.

---

[1]Adapted from *Speech: Science-Art,* by Elwood Murray et al., The Bobbs-Merrill Company, Inc., Indianapolis, 1969, p. 74. By permission of the authors and the publishers.

B. After fifteen minutes in the small groups, the entire class can discuss the kind of information which is exchanged by the responses you made. Did you learn more about the items (the future, the school, heroes, etc.), or did you learn more about the persons making the completed statements? Does this suggest that we always talk about ourselves even when we are talking about other things?

EXERCISE 1-6
GIVING INSTRUCTIONS (Group Project)

1. Break up into small groups of five or six students. For every group formed there is an assigned "order taker" who does not participate in the group planning but must be out of the room or segregated from the planning session.

2. You are to develop instructions for performing a very common task: you will instruct a person from outside your group, the order taker, on *how to put on his or her coat.* In the preparation time (ten minutes) your group should develop a series of instructions to be given orally to your order taker. You will assume that this order taker has never seen a coat, does not know anything about coats or what they are for, and will not understand any of the words used to name parts of the garment. The order taker will just rely on what you will tell him or her to do — nothing more, nothing less.

3. After your group feels that it knows just what to say to the order taker to make him or her complete the task successfully, you will call the order taker and begin the actual order giving. The order taker will stand beside a chair. A coat is hung over the back of the chair. Start telling him or her what to do. . . .

4. Variations on this exercise include the following:

a. Using a set of Tinker Toys, your group will instruct the order taker on how to assemble a relatively complex item that you have worked out and sketched so that you can give directions orally but without showing the drawing to your order taker.

b. Give the order taker a sheet of paper and have him or her draw a figure (preferably not a very simple one) just from your oral instructions; or have each member of your group give one part of the instructions and not repeat them.

c. Tell the order taker how to sit down in a chair. Again, this person must assume no knowledge of the words used or the actions to be performed, but must follow directions exactly.

d. Explain to the order taker how to print the word "cat" from the moment that person picks up the pencil, pen, or chalk; include instructions on how to hold the instrument.

Discussion

A. When you start to give orders or simple instructions to another person, what assumptions do you make about how much others already know? What assumptions do you make about how much of your language is easy to misinterpret? What assumptions do you make about how clearly you yourselves understand the process?

B. If a person deliberately wants *not* to understand, or wants to make errors, do the English language and ordinary social attitudes permit him or her great opportunities to miscommunicate?

C. Do you realize how much of your behaviors and your information have come to you by imitation of nonverbal as well as verbal instructions?

D. When things don't go right in giving or receiving instructions, what is a very predictable reaction in the people involved? What does that do to communication?

ASSIGNMENT 1-1
WORDS TO LIVE BY

In folklore and collections of "wise sayings" there are many maxims or epigrams about communication. "Silence is golden" is one such maxim. "Children should be seen and not heard" is another. Many of the most popular sayings have opposites. For example: "Speech is God's gift to humankind" opposes the idea that "Silence is golden," just as "Truth comes out of the mouths of babes" says something quite different from "Children should be seen and not heard."

1. From any sources available to you (collections, interviewing others, etc.), find a list of at least five maxims or wise sayings about communication.
2. Find out whether there are also *opposites* of those sayings in folk wisdom and submit the list along with the five maxims from item 1.
3. Continue to collect communication maxims—especially those which have popular opposites.
4. Write a brief essay on why you think these folk sayings or epigrams may have opposites.

ASSIGNMENT 1-2
RESOLUTIONS FOR THE NEW YEAR

Concerning your own communication—not that of others around you—make a list of the things you would like to do better or ways you would like to act more effectively in your communication.

Remember that you are the only one who can do something about your own communicating. Your list should be limited to those behaviors or activities over which you can exercise control.

After you make the list of things to do, make another list estimating how you might go about accomplishing the new behaviors or new activities. This list should give you an idea of the possibility of change: Is it worth your effort to make the changes you put on your first list?

ASSIGNMENT 1-3
EAVESDROPPING

Listen to some conversations between other people (family members at dinner, strangers on a bus, etc.). Without identifying the people whom you have listened to, give a brief summary of one conversation which did not directly include you and analyze it for the principle of chicken and egg. How did you become interested in the sequence of statements? What did you hear and what did you miss in the flow of the conversation? Speculate on what other items of information were exchanged and how they might have affected the outcome of the conversation.

As another part of the analysis of this overheard conversation, try to estimate the relationship of the communication pattern in relation to equals or nonequals.

ASSIGNMENT 1-4
JOURNAL, DIARY, SCRAPBOOK

This is an excellent project to carry out over the term. Now is a good time to begin collecting a written record of your thoughts and reactions, and those of relevant others or those of a public nature.

1. A *journal* (as described in the introduction to this laboratory manual) is a collection of your personal observations of communication about you. It may be about the class or your outside contacts. It consists of brief notes or even essays on your response to communication in your environment.

2. A *diary* may be different from a journal, listing more specifically daily communication encounters of any kind which made an impression on you for some reason. It may have a more factual approach than the journal and might well include your extensive recitation of reactions to communications and subjective analyses.

3. A *scrapbook* collects the impressions of others and the communication habits of others. Cartoons, newspaper clippings, posters, etc., all may be used to record the communication activities of famous people in the news, or of less famous people whose communication actions contribute to the news or to a record of human interaction.

ASSIGNMENT 1-5
INTERVIEW

Go to the health center on your campus and interview doctors, nurses, or both to discover their views on the communication problems they encounter in their work with students or other patients.

How does a doctor make sure that instructions are clearly understood by patients? Are there any special problems in relating information to very sick patients? How does the use of technical terms affect the doctor-patient communication? Is it better to use technical terms or not to use them? Does the medical staff rely on information given by patients or on observations and examinations? Why? How do staff members get information from their patients? Can most patients answer the doctor's questions adequately?

Ask the medical staff any or all these questions. Give an oral report to the class or write a one- or two-page paper to summarize your findings and conclusions after your interview.

The assignment to make the contacts and interviews should be given to a group of the class or to a few individuals. Unless there are many different people to be interviewed, a large number of students coming to engage the health center or a doctor could be annoying.

As another option, the same assignment can be given to interview people in other professions besides medicine. Find professionals who use technical language or terminology on campus — the registrar, architects, teachers in specialized areas of study. Of course, it is not necessary to restrict the assignment to on-campus persons, but many of you do not know what a great variety of language use is occurring all the time right next to you.

ASSIGNMENT 1-6
AN ESTIMATE OF MYSELF AS A COMMUNICATOR

Your own communication experiences have provided you with a wealth of information about yourself in your relationships with others. How you see yourself in your communication with others has a strong effect on what you do. For this assignment you are asked to answer there questions:

1. How effective am I as a communicator in a one-to-many situation (having to talk to fifteen or more people)?

2. How effective am I as a communicator in small groups (committees, work groups, buzz sessions, etc.)?

3. How effective am I as a communicator in a one-to-one situation (talking to one other person)?

Note. It is essential that you write from your own point of view how you see yourself and not how you think other people see you. You do not need to ask others for their estimates of your effectiveness. However, you should be prepared to have class members read your paper.

Allow yourself enough time to do some thinking about the three questions before you write anything down on paper.

You should be prepared to read some of what you wrote in a presentation to the class; or the instructor may ask you to make an oral summary of your answers to these three questions in a few minutes of speaking in front of the class.

PERSONAL IMPROVEMENT BLANK (Chapter 1)

1. Write a brief report about a time when you tried to communicate with someone. What was the result?

2. List two relationships you have developed with others which are

  a. Equal; describe how they are equal:

  b. Unequal; describe how they are unequal:

3. Are you aware of situations in which you have to start from somewhere in your communication relations (the chicken-and-egg question)? Give a brief example. (When you go to report a car accident, how far back in the history of the car and the drivers do you begin the story? In your relations with someone else, what was the latest communication behavior which had an influence on you? Etc.)

Your name _____

Chapter 2

PERCEPTION: THE EYE OF THE BEHOLDER

FEEDBACK BLANK

EXERCISES

ASSIGNMENTS

PERSONAL IMPROVEMENT BLANK

FEEDBACK BLANK (Chapter 2)   DO NOT SIGN

1. Rate the productivity of this week's work for you.

    1   2   3   4   5   6   7   8   9   10

Not productive   Highly productive

2. Rate how you think the rest of the class felt about this week's productivity.

    1   2   3   4   5   6   7   8   9   10

Not productive   Highly productive

Comments:

3. At this point, how comfortable or at ease do you feel in this class? Why?

4. If you do not feel comfortable, can you isolate the reasons why?

5. Did you feel left out in any of the activities this week, in your groups or during any of the exercises? If you did, do you think anyone noticed?

6. Add other comments, criticisms, suggestions, questions, etc.

EXERCISE 2-1
THE ACCIDENT CASE (Discussion)

John Howell had been waiting at the corner to catch the bus for work. As he was standing there, a light-blue car driven by a young man of 19 was involved in an accident with a white car driven by a 26-year-old mother of two. John arrived at work and described the accident to Harry, a fellow worker.

"I was standing there at the corner waiting for the bus when I saw a blue car coming down the street at a fairly fast rate. At least it looked as though the car was going fairly fast. The driver was a young fellow about 19 or so who attends the university. He was on his way to class. Anyway, he must not have been paying much attention to what he was doing because he hit a car in the intersection. He hit the car at the rear, and the rear door was dented pretty badly. The college fellow was not injured; but the woman was shaken up, and one of her children lost a tooth. It wasn't a bad accident, but it sure shows you can't be too careful."

Harry went home that night and told his wife that John had seen an accident.

"John saw a bad accident this morning. He was waiting for the bus when a crazy college kid came roaring down the street. John said he was doing 90 and nothing. He must have been late for class, and he was not paying attention to what he was doing. He was probably listening to the radio or something. A woman was waiting at the intersection, and this guy just plowed into her. He did not even hit his brakes. The woman was hysterical. One of her children was all bloody and lost one tooth. They should take the guy's license away from him. If anybody can't drive better than that, he doesn't deserve a license."

What will Harry's wife think when she reads about the accident in the paper saying that the woman was given a citation for making a dangerous turn and failing to yield the right of way?

Discuss the implications of the story.

Discussion

A. For the person who did not see the event (this accident) is it possible to make up, or to imagine, details which were not part of the event?

B. When you report incidents to others, do you have more purposes than simply exchanging information? Do you, for instance, want to make a point about the way others drive or what college kids are like, or do you want to shock others with bloody and gory details?

C. How would you characterize the objectivity of perceptions shown by: (1) how John told Harry about what he actually witnessed on the spot, (2) how Harry told his wife about what John had reported to him, and (3) what appeared in the newspaper long after the event had been evaluated and judged by officers of the law and witnesses and a reporter?

D. If you are an insurance investigator for either of the parties involved, what set of perceptions will you need to rely on?

EXERCISE 2-2
AGREE-DISAGREE LIST ON PERCEPTION (Group Project)

1. Indicate whether you agree or disagree with the statements in Table 9. Mark A if you agree, D if you disagree, on the left-hand side of the table.

TABLE 9. **Agree-Disagree List for Exercise 2-2**

Individual			Group consensus	
(A)	**(D)**		**(A)**	**(D)**
____	____	**1.** The perception of a physical object depends more upon the object than upon the mind of the observer.	____	____
____	____	**2.** Perception is primarily an interpersonal phenomenon.	____	____
____	____	**3.** The fact that hallucinations and dreams are as vivid as waking perceptions indicates that perception depends very little upon external reality.	____	____
____	____	**4.** The reaction we have to what we see generally depends on learning and culture.	____	____
____	____	**5.** We tend to see what we wish to see or are expecting to see regardless of reality.	____	____
____	____	**6.** Given the undependable nature of perception, we can never tell the "true" nature of reality.	____	____
____	____	**7.** Though there may be reality "out there," we can never really know it.	____	____
____	____	**8.** We may eliminate the undependable in our perception by careful, scientific observation.	____	____
____	____	**9.** Scientific instruments, though they extend the limits of human perception, do not make perception any more real.	____	____
____	____	**10.** What we perceive is no more than a metaphor of what is.	____	____
____	____	**11.** Perception is a physical response to a physical reality. It is only when we begin talking about our perceptions that we begin to distort them.	____	____
____	____	**12.** If we are careful, we can see the world as it really is.	____	____
____	____	**13.** We react to our environment on the basis of what we perceive that environment to be like and not what the environment is really like.	____	____

2. Form groups of six or seven students and reach a consensus for each of the statements in Table 9. Record the group consensus on the right-hand side of the table.

Discussion

A. If you do not agree on the items, what does that say about your ability to speak to each other about what you "see" or "hear" beyond the very obvious fact that you may stand in different places or communicate with different people? Do your basic attitudes about perception, then, have an effect on what and how you perceive?

B. Had you thought about all these ideas on perception before you began making out your "agrees" and "disagrees"? What new ideas came to you while you worked on the list?

C. Because you had written down your A or D before the group got together, did you find it difficult to give up your answer? Would it have been easier for you to discuss these items without bias and objectively if you had not first written down your own ideas? In other words, do you go into your real-life groups with some ideas already firmly established? What happens to objective discussion if many of the people in the group already have a firm commitment to some idea? When people enter groups with a preset or preconceived idea of what should be done, this is often referred to as their "hidden agenda."

D. How did the group arrange to come to agreement? Did you understand what is meant by "consensus"? What does it mean? How does a group approach it?

EXERCISE 2-3
FIRST IMPRESSIONS (Game)

Your instructor will distribute a description of an individual. Read it and then select from the following list those traits which are most in accordance with the picture of the individual you have formed in your mind. Underline one adjective in each pair.

1. Generous	Ungenerous	10. Ruthless	Humane
2. Shrewd	Gullible	11. Good-looking	Unattractive
3. Unhappy	Happy	12. Persistent	Unstable
4. Irritable	Good-natured	13. Frivolous	Serious
5. Humorous	Humorless	14. Restrained	Talkative
6. Sociable	Unsociable	15. Self-centered	Altruistic
7. Unreliable	Reliable	16. Imaginative	Hard-headed
8. Popular	Unpopular	17. Strong	Weak
9. Important	Unimportant	18. Dishonest	Honest

Discussion

A. What are the implications for evaluating your friends when you can find such evident differences in your reactions to the person described?

B. Do you tend to judge others on the basis of a few very significant characteristics, or do you take into consideration many or most of the available appearances?

C. Are some trigger words included in your descriptions of others for the purpose of prejudicing or biasing attitudes about the described person?

D. How would you describe your best friend to your parents? How does a person describe an enemy in a similar situation?

EXERCISE 2-4
HOW MANY SQUARES? (Group Project)

Working by yourself, count how many squares there are in Figure 21. After your estimate is recorded in the space at the left and below the diagram, get together with some other members of the class and compare the totals you came up with. After you have had time to discuss any differences, put in the space on the lower right the number you agree on with the others in your group.

FIGURE 21. Exercise 2–4:
How many squares?

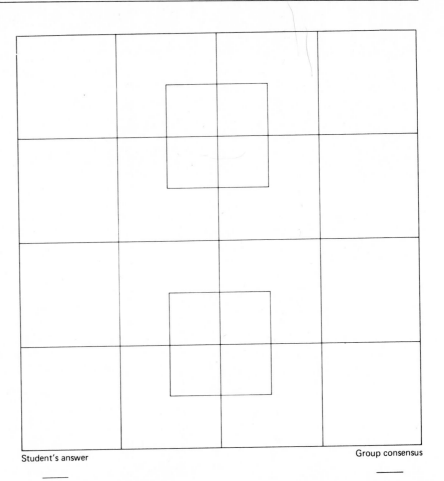

Student's answer   Group consensus

_____   _____

Discussion

A. If everyone did not come up with the same number, how do you account for the differences? Do people make different assumptions about squares, or do we simply see the same objects a little differently?

B. If you count the squares only once, do you come up with the same number as if you count them again? What happens when you take more time interacting with a problem, a puzzle, an event, an incident, or another person? Do you tend to see more completely, more deeply? What does this say about your first impressions of others or about your quick reactions to behaviors of others?

C. Is there some difference of opinion on how to define "squares"? Does that difference account for how many you can count? Do definitions affect your perceptions?

ASSIGNMENT 2-1
PERCEPTION IN THE ARTS

1. There are many films, novels, poems, and plays which take their dramatic strength from differences in perception. Some classic films of this kind include *Twelve Angry Men, Rashomon,* and *The Eye of the Beholder.* If possible, see one of these or read a synopsis of the story, and write a report on how perception was the pivot point of the action in the film.
2. Read the poem "Home Burial" by Robert Frost.
   a. Prepare a reader's theater presentation or an oral interpretation for the class. Lead a discussion on how the different perceptions of the same tragic incident are keeping the characters apart.
   b. Write a brief analysis of the interaction of the husband and wife based on assumptions about their perceptions. (This poem is in many collections of Robert Frost's work including *Poems,* published by Washington Square Press in New York in 1967.)
3. Read "The Blind Men and the Elephant," a poem by John Godfrey Saxe (in Chapter 2 of this textbook), and make a similar analysis of a group of blindfolded people asked to identify some common object. Write a dialog between these blindfolded persons as they argue which of their individual perceptions should be accepted as a generalized picture of the item or object.

ASSIGNMENT 2-2
NEWSPAPER CLIPPINGS

Examine the newspaper accounts of a recent controversial event. Examine also the various reports of the investigation commissions if any were formed and if those reports are available. From your investigation of these sources, identify the communication barriers and breakdowns which were involved in the situation.

Be prepared to discuss your clipping with the class. One variation of this assignment is to find clippings on lawsuits, investigations by Congress, contested elections, etc., and to take sides and explain how you gathered the information on which you are basing your arguments.

ASSIGNMENT 2-3
INTERVIEW

Do *either* 1 *or* 2 below:

1. Arrange an interview with a professional artist (painter, sculptor, musician, etc.) to discover his or her views on "art as communication." Report the results of your interview.
2. Talk to a public school teacher to find out how he or she views the communication role of the teacher in the classroom. Report the result of your interview.

Reports of these interviews may be written or oral. You may be asked to tell the class about the interview and to describe the setting in which you found the artist or teacher. Was the place where you interviewed the person a factor in the kinds of responses you received?

ASSIGNMENT 2-4
PERCEPTION INCIDENT

Think about what happened to you this past week — trivial and important things, happy and sad things. Were any of the unsatisfactory events of the week due to inadequate communication? If so, were any of the communication difficulties traceable to differences in perception between the people involved or to distortions in what was perceived which caused subsequent difficulties?

Write a brief summary of such an instance and analyze its consequences on you and the people around you.

Be prepared to talk about this instance in class. You may be asked to get together with another student and to work out a brief oral report on one of your "cases" or incidents, or to lead a class discussion about your case.

PERSONAL IMPROVEMENT BLANK (Chapter 2)

1. Recount briefly an event which occurred to you recently in which faulty perception caused a disagreement or misunderstanding. The event can be rather trivial. It is in trying to cope with disagreements at all levels of your life, not only the most important events, that you develop bad feelings.

2. If you recognize that a difference in perception is causing some problem between you and another person (or group), how can you go about trying to get others to understand that the problem may be one of *perceptions?* Be specific.

3. Cite a recent incident in which you were perceived unfairly. What was the result of the error in perception? Did it come out all right?

Your name _____

Chapter 3

SELF-CONCEPT: WHO AM I?

FEEDBACK BLANK

EXERCISES

3-1. "I Am"
3-2. What if You Were . . . ?
3-3. Johari Window
3-4. You're the Expert in Motivation

Group Project
Role Playing
Dyad; On Your Feet
Discussion

ASSIGNMENTS

3-1. Who Told You What?
   (Being Confirmed and
   Disconfirmed)
3-2. Roles You Take
3-3. Literary References
3-4. Changing Roles
3-5. Television Roles

PERSONAL IMPROVEMENT BLANK

FEEDBACK BLANK (Chapter 3) DO NOT SIGN

1. Rate the productivity of this session's work for you.

     1   2   3   4   5   6   7   8   9   10

Not productive   Very productive

2. Rate how you think the rest of the class felt about the productivity of this session's work.

     1   2   3   4   5   6   7   8   9   10

Not productive   Very productive

Comments:

3. In relation to this week's subject matter, were you assigned a role you did not like in any group activity? If people assign "identities" to you, what effect does this have on your reactions?

4. Did you enjoy working with your group? Why or why not?

5. Add other comments, criticisms, questions, suggestions, etc.

EXERCISE 3-1
"I AM" (Group Project)

This exercise responds to the question "Who am I?" in a positive way. It is designed to permit you to boast about yourself — something which society generally discourages. Most of you do not care much for braggarts or boastful people. Most of you are not accustomed to boasting about your own accomplishments or bragging about your good points. For a little while, then, you are asked to go against the norm that says nice people don't brag about themselves.

The class should divide up into groups of four to six members so that it will be easy for everyone to hear. The assignment is first to think about (and jot down on paper) five positive things about yourself — not what others think about you; *what you think about you.* What you're good at, why you are proud of something you know or can do, what you consider your outstanding or strong characteristics — all these are potential statements about who you are from a positive standpoint. After a few minutes to allow the group members to collect their thoughts about what they are going to boast about, some member of the group begins by giving one item about himself or herself. Following clockwise around the group, all members in turn make one statement about their good points. After the first round, you make the round again — each in turn making one statement. After all members have shared their five points, you should consult each other on which were the most interesting and then prepare to present them to the whole class in a general session, if there is time.

Discussion

A. Is it difficult to change an old habit of not boasting? How did you feel when you started to make up a list of items about yourself? Were you taught to be modest and self-effacing about what you know and what you can do?

B. Did hearing others make positive statements about themselves make it easier for you? Does this say something about how norms are changed in a society?

C. Why is bragging not approved of in our culture? Are all cultures like that? Are there some which you know about that prize the ability to boast of personal successes?

D. If you are not supposed to brag or boast about your achievements or your abilities, how do you expect others to know about them? Is there a communication channel or a practice that takes care of letting other people know about your successes? Would open bragging make a difference in how you develop a self-concept and reinforce positive self-feelings?

EXERCISE 3-2
WHAT IF YOU WERE . . . ? (Role Playing)

This is an exercise in assuming a role different from the ones you usually play. Here is a chance for you to act like some other person, and to demonstrate that people are really quite conscious of how roles are developed and what is expected of a person in any given situation or relationship. Pick one of these situations and role-play it (act out the dialog) for the class:

1. The President of the United States greets the prime minister of a foreign nation in the Rose Garden of the White House. (One person should be the President, and the visitor's role may be either imagined or played by another member of the class.)

2. You have been elected Miss Universe, and you step forward to the microphones to deliver your acceptance speech.

3. You are a famous novelist autographing your books at a local department store. You have been asked to talk to the store employees about how you came to write the best-selling book.

4. This is a role-playing situation for two or more persons. A parent has just discovered that his or her 12-year old child must undergo a very delicate and dangerous eye operation. The parent has elected to talk to the child about the impending operation, rather than having the doctor do it.

5. You have been selected to meet the governor of your state at the airport and act as official escort to the annual Chamber of Commerce dinner. (Select someone in the class to act as the governor you are escorting.)

6. You are to introduce the governor's speech at the dinner.

7. You are a famous baseball (or football) player and have returned to your old high school to talk to the graduating class.

8. This is a role-playing situation for two persons. You are the dean of students confronting a student leader in an attempt to get help in finding out who has been responsible for recent vandalism on the campus.

9. As a famous composer you have been invited to conduct the local symphony orchestra in one of your major works. Role-play your first session with the orchestra.

10. This is a role-playing situation for two persons. One student plays a local attorney who has decided to run for the office of city prosecutor, and the other plays a local news broadcaster who is doing an interview for the five-o'clock news.

Discussion

A. The class should decide how accurately the portrayal of any of these roles fits the expectations of most of the class members. Discuss your ideas of how you might have played a role differently from the person who did it. Why are there some similarities? Why are there some differences?

B. Where do you get your ideas of how that role should be played? Did you feel comfortable in trying out that role? In watching others?

C. Identify some roles you play every day and determine where you got practice in them. How do you know when to change your "act"?

EXERCISE 3-3
JOHARI WINDOW (Dyad; On Your Feet)
(See diagram and discussion in Chapter 3 in Part One.) Begin this exercise by yourself. Write down a list for each of the following:

"Five things I know about me that I'm sure others also know" *(Free area)*

"Five things I'd like others to know about me, but I'm pretty sure they don't"

"Five things I'd like to know about me which I suspect others may know but I don't"

After you have done that, find another person in the class and compare lists. Each of you should pick one item which is very important to you in each category. Ask (and answer) this question:

"What can I do to help others know about me and to learn about myself?"

Be specific in the reply to that question. Help each other develop ways in which an exchange of communication can be useful in getting others to know about you or helping you know more about yourself.

If there is time, it would be interesting for each pair of discussants to present *one of their items* to the entire class. First, list the kind of item (such as: something I want others to know about me) and then explain how you would go about letting it happen, or helping it to happen. Asking the class for their reactions to the information and how you can manage it is also a useful part of this exercise.

Discussion
A. In reviewing the quadrants of the Johari window, it should be emphasized that these vary with different relationships or situations. Your window is a different shape with different people depending on the maturity of your relationship.
B. Check the "free area" statements to find out *how* members of the class know whether or not others know those things about them. Then check with each other to see whether the "unknowns" are really unknown. How accurate are your pictures of how much others know about you?
C. In diagnosing the means of getting others to know about you, what communication systems or devices are available to you? How about when you want to know more about yourself and try to get others to tell you? Are there societal norms about giving honest feedback on *disagreeable* matters which may inhibit this exchange? Do you also have some difficulty *complimenting* one another?
D. If you poll the class on how much members know about each other, can you expect to get a wide variation of responses from your classmates? Do some know more things about you than others? Do some know more intimate things than others? Do some know almost nothing about you?
E. What relationships do you hope can be better developed by looking at how much is known between you and one other person? Is it easier to interact with your friends after you've shared many experiences? Explore reasons for different levels of interaction between you and specific others.

EXERCISE 3-4
YOU'RE THE EXPERT IN MOTIVATION (Discussion)
In the following cases, a need to motivate another person is evident. If you have some means available to you for motivating the individual, how can you go about it? Do you first decide what theory of motivation may be the most applicable (Maslow, etc.) and then proceed to solve the case? What does the person *need* in order to be motivated?

Case 1. Sally has been coming to work late mornings. Because other men and women in the office depend on her to assign their work, her lateness holds up the functioning of several people. You as her supervisor have found out that Sally received a good raise just six months ago in recognition of the fact that she had been a good worker for three years in the office. You want to have her become more punctual, to arrive at least on time with the others in her section. What do you say to her? (You may want to discuss this case in a small group session or plan to role-play it with others in the class.)

Case 2. Harry is clerking in the sports department of the store where you are a personnel counselor. You have received a complaint from the billing office that recently Harry's charge slips have been made out incorrectly, causing losses of money and time for the store. Harry also was accused by a customer of ''not paying any attention'' when asked questions about exercise bicycles, and the head of the sports department took over when Harry simply disappeared from the floor and ignored the customer. You are talking to Harry about his performance and hope to retain him, since he's been a very productive employee for six years.

Case 3. You are a news editor on a daily afternoon paper with six reporters assigned to you. They range in age from a person nearing retirement to a very new graduate of a journalism school. All six are bright and quick to locate news sources and to write their material when given assignments. In the past few weeks, however, the oldest member of your staff has failed to find time to cover the assignments and has not produced even reasonably good stories on his own. He is near retirement but would like to continue to free-lance for other publications after he retires in eighteen months. In the meantime, he has been most valuable to you and has been helpful in training the new people. You want to maintain his efforts both for his sake and for the sake of your successful news operation.

To make matters worse, the new reporter, a bright young woman named Jill, has also suddenly become uninterested in following up assignments and has turned in very sloppy copy. Although she fit in very well when she started with the paper just over a year ago, her production has decreased so much that you are left with only four of your six regular reporters to handle all the work.

Are these problems related? In order to motivate these two different individuals you must first determine what happened to their drive and interest. What approaches do you make to motivate their renewed efforts?

Discussion
A. If you discuss these cases in small groups in class, do all groups come up with the same solutions or recommendations? Are there different ways of motivating people? Are there different circumstances which require different treatments?
B. Compare the recommendations by class members to see if some general agreement can be reached on which approaches would be most effective.
C. As you discuss these cases and your recommendations, consider how much of what you propose is based on stereotypes of how workers ought to be treated and what people are really like in the jobs described. Lacking more specific data, for example, do you fall back on a stereotypical picture of the aging reporter as perhaps drinking too much, or the young woman reporter as being put down by her colleagues? Do you sometimes make motivational decisions in real life as much on the basis of stereotypes as on the basis of obtainable data? Do you tend to put people into ''typical'' roles and thus treat a person as a role and not as an individual?

ASSIGNMENT 3-1
WHO TOLD YOU WHAT? (Being Confirmed and Disconfirmed)
This assignment may be written out and handed in, or it may be used as a source for group discussion. After you have prepared your lists, the instructor may put you in groups to compare incidents with others. If you work with others on this assignment, it would be interesting to note that patterns of confirming and disconfirming behaviors seem to repeat themselves.

1. Recall an incident in your early life in which you received attention, good support, or compliments for something you did. As a result of that confirming action, what happened to your self-esteem? Has the incident had a lasting effect on how you feel about yourself in a similar situation now? Who was responsible for giving you the confirming response? How did you feel about that person?
2. Recall an incident in your early life in which you received disconfirming behaviors from someone you cared about. As a result, what happened to your self-esteem? Did that disconfirming behavior have any lasting effect on your own behaviors or what you think of how you are able to do something? Who was responsible for giving you the disconfirming response? How did you feel about that person?

ASSIGNMENT 3-2
ROLES YOU TAKE
List as many items as you can think of concerning what is expected of you in the role of a *student*. How did you find out what a student should be like — the role of a student? How do you find out, on the basis of the role you play, whether you are succeeding or not succeeding in that role? How do you feel about the kind of data you have to rely on to make your judgment on how you are doing?

Select another role you have (besides that of "student") and list as many items as you can which are expected of you in that role. If that role is a voluntary one, tell why you chose it. If it was thrust on you, analyze the forces which put you in that role.

ASSIGNMENT 3-3
LITERARY REFERENCES
Find the original story of Pygmalion and Galatea on which George Bernard Shaw based his play *Pygmalion*. Read excerpts from the Shaw play and compare them with similar parts of the successful musical *My Fair Lady*, which uses the same story. It is of particular importance to a class in communication to note that the character Professor Higgins was a teacher of phonetics who elevated a poor girl into high society primarily by making a change in linguistic patterns. "Language makes the person," this story seems to say. Does it also say that you can become what you believe you are? Discuss in class the meaning of the "Pygmalion effect" and how it relates to other behaviors you can anticipate.

ASSIGNMENT 3-4
CHANGING ROLES

Write a short essay on your own experience in trying to change a role you were cast in and decided not to follow. (A classic example with college-age people is the role in which parents tend to try to keep their "child," and the efforts a maturing student home from college is involved in to get the family to accept the new role.) Describe the role you intended to take, the former role, which may not have been as effective for you, and how you went about making the change. How successful were you in making the role change?

ASSIGNMENT 3-5
TELEVISION ROLES

Write a brief report on a television show you have seen recently, analyzing the following: (1) What behaviors did the characters show in order to make you like them, dislike them, believe in them, or oppose them? (2) Did the characters employ nonverbal as well as verbal behaviors to establish a role? (3) How do television writers help establish a character in a brief period of time?

PERSONAL IMPROVEMENT BLANK (Chapter 3)

1. Record briefly here something which you have found out about yourself in the very recent past and how it came to you. Was it as a result of getting feedback on some behavior of yours?

2. Is there something you would like to tell someone in this class about his or her behaviors which you are sure that person does not know? Without telling what it is, or telling who the person is, can you suggest some way of letting that person know this item?

3. Has your motivation in this class changed in the past few weeks since the term began? Has it become higher or lower? What could be done to improve a person's motivation to perform well in a class like this?

Your name_____

Chapter 4

ATTITUDES, BELIEFS, AND VALUES: WHO SHOULD I BE?

FEEDBACK BLANK

EXERCISES

ASSIGNMENTS

PERSONAL IMPROVEMENT BLANK

FEEDBACK BLANK (Chapter 4)   DO NOT SIGN

1. Rate the productivity of this session's work for you.

    1   2   3   4   5   6   7   8   9   10
Not productive   Very productive

2. Rate how you think the rest of the class felt about this session's productivity.

    1   2   3   4   5   6   7   8   9   10
Not productive   Very productive

Comments:

3. Did you observe people who were silent in your group? How many people? Was anything done to bring them out and encourage them to participate more?

4. How useful is this feedback for you? Can it be made more useful to you? How?

5. As you work in a group, do you become comfortable with others and not want to change? How would you feel about having the same people work together in the same small groups all the time in this course?

EXERCISE 4-1
VALUES; RHETORIC; BEHAVIOR (Role Playing)

In a small group (five or six people) make up a short skit or drama to perform for the class in which you demonstrate how someone's values, rhetoric, and behavior may not all be consistent. (For example, a father may tell his son never to cheat and also boast how much he beat the Internal Revenue Service out of on his latest income tax return.) You may want to make a drama in two acts, the first setting the stage for the inconsistent behavior or statements which show up in the second act. The drama may be taken from your own experience or from some public event.

Discussion

A. Is it hard to identify the actual values people hold when they talk and act as if the values were something else?

B. Even though you can see the inconsistencies of other people, is it easy to see your own? When you act differently from how you talk or believe, is it possible to reduce the dissonance of these inconsistencies for yourselves? Can you explain them to others? What does the term "rationalization" mean in this context?

C. In your drama did the class recognize the inconsistencies easily? Did they see things you missed as you prepared the skit? Are you sufficiently familiar with incongruencies among values, rhetoric, and behavior to see them before they become fully developed? Can you, in other words, anticipate situations in which they are likely to appear? Does that help your ability to predict what other people may do or say in relation to those events? Do others also predict your behaviors?

EXERCISE 4-2
INCONSISTENT BEHAVIOR (On Your Feet)

Each member of the class will write out for later presentation to the class an incident in which his or her behavior was not consistent with either the rhetoric or the value held. In individual presentations, each person will briefly describe the incident, avoiding analysis of the reasons for the actions. A simple statement of the event is enough. (Example: "After telling the rest of the student body to get out and vote in the campus elections, and handling the campaign for one of the candidates, I did not vote.")

Discussion

A. Are you able to identify those incidents in your life where you act in a way that is not consistent with what you say or believe? Each person has a chance to develop a brief statement about such an event.

B. Are there patterns to these events? Do many of you in the class seem to do the same kinds of inconsistent or incongruent things?

C. Speculate in open class discussion why these inconsistencies occurred. Is there a general pattern to the reasons behind them?

D. Are there more reports on inconsistent behaviors (in relation to rhetoric or values) or on inconsistent rhetoric? Or are there more on what you say about either your values or your behaviors? In other words, do people talk against their values as much as they may behave in a way inconsistent with their statements?

EXERCISE 4-3
WILL YOU FIGHT FOR IT? (Discussion)
To check the saliency of an attitude or a value (how important it is to you), work with a group of five or six people on this activity. Try to develop one or two issues which you agree would elicit each of the following reactions:

1. You would become curious about what was being said when you heard others talking about this particular topic or person or concept, and you would begin to listen more closely.
2. You would become mildly annoyed when someone spoke against this thing which you believe or hold as a value.
3. You would argue pretty strongly and might act rather upset when this topic was discussed.
4. You would become quite angry and either verbally attack the speaker or withdraw from argument when someone said something you did not like about this topic.
5. You would fight physically as well as verbally; you would come to blows over this issue or value.
6. You would risk your life, or be willing to die, for this cause.

Discussion
A. Since this was a group project, did you find difficulty agreeing on items which were equally important to all of you?
B. Which classes of items are you as a group inclined to agree on — those that elicit the most serious reactions or those that elicit the mildest reactions? Why?
C. Does this range of reactions describe most of your ways of reacting to attack on your beliefs or values? Do you hear comments about things in which you have no interest? How do you react then?
D. Are there values in society which have no interest at all for you? What would it take to get you interested?
E. How much of your reaction to these items is directly related to other people who would hold similar views? Were you affected in the group discussion by the weight of who else held those views?

EXERCISE 4-4
CONSULTANT ON RACE RELATIONS (Group Project)
You have been appointed to a national committee on race relations. Your assignment is to advise the President of the United States on how to go about reducing racial tension in all parts of the country — particularly that part closest to you and most affected by your potential influence. You

meet with four or five others of the committee and prepare a report for the President which you will give to the class in oral form. Considering that you are all involved citizens, interested in having your views heard, you should develop as broad a plan as possible. As your group develops the plan to present to the class, try to reach agreement on why you are recommending certain actions and what their consequences might be. When each group has made its recommendations to the class, you can analyze the various reports to see which values or behaviors are most commonly brought up by the different groups.

Discussion

A. What values of the society do your recommendations support or attack?

B. Is there some evidence that values are not entirely represented by the rhetoric (what many people say) or by the behaviors of those directly involved with the issue of race relations? Are there unpopular things to say? Are there unpopular and even illegal things to do? How much change in values has been represented by any changes in rhetoric or behaviors?

C. As you advise the President, are you realistic in how much influence he may have on the actual implementation of your ideas? What will the message (rhetoric) be from the President when he gets your plan? What will actually be done (behaviors)?

EXERCISE 4-5
SPEAKING UP FOR A COMMITMENT—A DIEHARD VALUE (On Your Feet)

In this exercise you can talk about that one value which is more important to you than any other. In a very brief statement to the class you should be able to identify — but not be called on to defend or explain — the value you really cherish. It is important for all the class to agree that holding a deep commitment to a value is a personal thing and should not be questioned or attacked by other class members. People's individual dignity is bound up in their deepest-seated beliefs. Each student in turn can stand up and make a brief statement, and then the class may discuss the general nature of these values.

Some values are more important (salient) to you than others. Some you are willing to change fairly easily, some less easily. There are some values you feel extremely committed to, either because of your upbringing or because of the various teachings (religious, social) you have been exposed to very early in your life.

If you were to identify the one value that holds the greatest importance in your life, the one value that you would not change under any circumstances, what would that value be? Can you explain why it is important to you?

Discussion

A. It is not always easy to tell others what you believe, even if it is clear to yourself. Did you have trouble putting your value or belief into words? Why?

B. If the class cannot agree to accept each person's statement as a part of that person, does it make a difference in how willing you are to speak up?

C. How did you feel when someone brought up a value which is not an important one to you? Did you think the other person's value was wrong? Did you give that person a ''right'' to hold that different value? Did you judge the person by what was said about that value?

D. Can you classify the values mentioned into a few categories? Where did class members get their values? Are there social institutions to help promote and maintain those values? Do they depend primarily on individual commitment?

EXERCISE 4-6
STEREOTYPING—DEVELOPMENT OF ATTITUDES (Forum)

Earlier the idea was developed that stereotypes are useful to you in your attempts to evaluate things on the basis of a few common characteristics which they share with a larger category. You react, not on the basis of what you know or feel about them individually, but mainly on the basis of what you know or feel about each category. In this way stereotypes become a shortcut to thinking, a way to react without having to work too hard to make decisions about people or events. Can you see the relationship between stereotypes and the development of attitudes? Do you depend on those basic attitudes to give you your ways of behaving? It has been said that a stereotype is a ''frozen attitude.''

For the class exercise, assign a group of four or six students one of the following topics to use as a basis for a panel presentation to the rest of the class. The format could be to seat the discussion group in front of the class and give each panel member a few minutes to make a statement about his or her ideas on the subject; then the discussion could be opened to the other panel members and eventually to questions from the class.

1. How is the grading system most widely used in today's schools related to stereotyping? How do you react to such statements as ''She is an A student'' and ''He is a D student''? What do they mean? What are the consequences of such statements?

2. Think of a specific stereotype that you may have about a particular group (e.g., religious, ethnic, or political). Try to explain how the stereotype developed and how it influences your behavior toward the members of the group. Be specific in describing the effects of the stereotype on your behavior.

3. Is it possible to treat an individual as an individual regardless of classification? Defend your answer. Use examples from your experience if possible.

4. List some attitudes you have held, or still hold, which you now consider to be stereotypes. How were they formed? Why? What has made you perceive them as stereotypes?

Discussion

A. Is it hard to admit to having stereotypes? Do you avoid talking about things in which you may be accused of having biases or prejudices based on stereotypes?

B. Is it easier for you to talk about grading systems than about religious issues? Why?

C. How did the presence of the class affect your participation in the discussion with others on the panel?

ASSIGNMENT 4-1
WISE SAYINGS AND FOLKLORE

Write down as long a list as you can of sayings which comment on inconsistent behaviors or differences between speaking and acting. Some examples are "Do as I say, not as I do" and "He always talks a good fight." Another example is characterization of the states where liquor has traditionally been prohibited as "voting dry and drinking wet."

Your list should be handed in to the instructor and should include an indication of what kind of inconsistency is represented—that is, rhetoric not representing values, etc.

ASSIGNMENT 4-2
SCALES OF ATTITUDE

Do *either* 1 *or* 2 *or* 3 below:

1. Go to the library and browse through the literature on attitude measurement. Select one attitude scale. Write a short paper in which you describe the scale and explain in what type of research it has been used. Tell what its advantages and disadvantages are, and explain how the authors of the scale made sure that it measures what it is supposed to measure.
2. Make notes on the research methods used, the conclusions reached, etc., and bring them to class for discussion in small groups or in general class discussion periods.
3. Find in a popular magazine some articles about attitudes and beliefs. Bring them to class to discuss. You may want to seek out persons who would help you make a presentation to class about some attitude or belief. If you can develop an idea of where your attitudes came from and ask others to inspect the origins of theirs, it provides an interesting discussion.

ASSIGNMENT 4-3
THEIR ATTITUDES AND OUR ATTITUDES

Write a description of the values and attitudes of a particular group of people you are familiar with which differs from a group you identify with.

Analyze the differences in attitudes and make some guesses about where they came from. If the other group (which believes a different way from the way you do) grew up in another part of the world or came from a different state, from a different size family, from a different ethnic background, etc., does that begin to explain something about the origins of your attitudes and beliefs? Be prepared to describe your own values and attitudes orally in comparison with another group you can identify.

PERSONAL IMPROVEMENT BLANK (Chapter 4)

1. Have you been confronted recently with any situation in which you altered your opinion of a friend or acquaintance on the basis of what that person said about one of your personal values or beliefs? Briefly recall that example.

2. If you had a question about whether or not a casual or distant friend believed as you do about something, how would you go about finding out an answer?

3. What does the term ''hypocrite'' mean to you?

Your name _____

Chapter 5

LANGUAGE: TRANSLATING PERCEPTIONS INTO COMMUNICATION

FEEDBACK BLANK

EXERCISES

ASSIGNMENTS

PERSONAL IMPROVEMENT BLANK

FEEDBACK BLANK (Chapter 5)   DO NOT SIGN

1. Rate the productivity of this session's work for you.

    1   2   3   4   5   6   7   8   9   10
Not productive   Very productive

2. Rate how you think the rest of the class felt about the productivity of this session's work.

    1   2   3   4   5   6   7   8   9   10
Not productive   Very productive

Comments:

3. Did anything you remember interfere with good communication in your group? Was there anything which held back understanding or prevented your working with each other effectively?

4. Did you observe anyone in your group who was silent (or nearly so)?

5. Can you give any examples of communication difficulties created by different use of the same words by different group members?

EXERCISE 5-1
WHAT DID YOU MEAN? (Group Project)

This is an exercise in defining terms. It works best with small groups of from six to eight persons. One person in the group makes a controversial statement about some current event or some philosophical or political stand. The rest of the group asks the speaker to define any terms which group members (1) are not sure they understand, (2) would not use the same way the speaker did, (3) are convinced the speaker has defined narrowly or think the speaker knows a common meaning for.

In order to continue to define words, the speaker must use additional words. They in turn are subject to question by group members under the same criteria. Whose definitions do you accept? At the point where the speaker runs out of either definitions or patience, the group may stop asking questions, and another group member may take on the role of ''definer.''

After a group has worked together for a specified time, the class will all get together to share experiences.

Discussion

A. What happened to the person trying to define the words? What feelings did that person have? Can the ''definer'' comment on what feelings arose in him or her as the group continued to question definitions? Did the definer run out of definitions? Are there certain words that we just ''know''?

B. Did the group itself become hostile or impatient toward the ''definer''? What makes feelings become involved? Is it that you simply expect others to use words the same way you do and therefore get impatient when they do not?

C. How do you know that you mean the same thing as others unless you give some time to ask about definitions? Is it more polite to simply go on listening when you do not understand? Do you think you agree many times when the definitions of words are not agreed on?

EXERCISE 5-2
WHAT'S IN A NAME? (Discussion)

The following quotation, taken from a play by Shakespeare, represents a common situation in literature. The names of families or of countries take on such a symbolic importance that enemies spend their lives in vengeful conflict. In a small group (five to seven members), analyze the dramatic impact of this situation. What happens later in the play as a result of the family names? Make a list of three or four such situations in literature. Then make a list of three or four such situations in real life which you know about. Select a few of the most dramatic ones to share with the class during a general discussion.

Juliet, of the Capulet family, addresses Romeo:

Tis but thy name that is my enemy;
Thou art thyself though, not a Montague.
What's Montague? It is not hand, not foot,
Nor arm, nor face, nor any other part
Belonging to a man. O! be some other name;

What's in a name? that which we call a rose
By any other name would smell as sweet;
So Romeo would, were he not Romeo call'd,
Retain that dear perfection which he owes
Without that title.

Discussion

A. Although many word-oriented prejudices may not result in death to the major characters, they make life miserable for those involved. Of the examples given by the groups, are any of life-and-death significance? Are any of the examples more subtle or more low-key?

B. Why does a story like the tragedy of Romeo and Juliet appeal to so many different periods of history and types of people? (Was *West Side Story* a simple remake of *Romeo and Juliet*?) Do you all understand how people can be so hooked on symbols that they do not act rationally?

EXERCISE 5-3
IRREGULAR CONJUGATION—THE CONJUGATION OF ADJECTIVES (Group Project)

Bertrand Russell, on a British Broadcasting Company radio program called *Brain Trust,* gave the following "conjugation of adjectives."

I am firm.

You are obstinate.

He is pig-headed.

The *New Stateman and Nation,* quoting the above as a model, offered prizes to readers who sent in the best conjugated adjectives of this kind. Here are some of the published entries:

I am sparkling. You are unusually attractive. He is drunk.

I am righteously indignant. You are annoyed. He is making a fuss about nothing.

I am fastidious. You are fussy. He is an old woman.

I am a creative writer. You have a journalistic flair. He is a prosperous hack.

I am beautiful. You have quite good features. She is not bad-looking, if you like that type.

I daydream. You are an escapist. He ought to see a psychiatrist.

I have about me something of the subtle, haunting, mysterious fragrance of the Orient. You rather overdo it, dear. She stinks.

In a small group complete the following statements, or make up some of your own to share with the rest of the class

I am stocky.

I am slender.

I love music.

I don't believe in excessive savings.

I believe in the new morality.

I live in a fantasy world.

I need plenty of sleep.

I believe that honesty is the best policy.

I am a casual housekeeper.

Discussion

A. What does this exercise reveal about the way you talk about yourselves as compared with how you talk about others? You would like your own behaviors and attitudes to be considered positive while those same characteristics in others might be questionable.

B. When speaking to another person, is it easier to be charitable than when you are speaking about a third party or an absent person? Face-to-face conversation is likely to make your evaluations less critical than if you are speaking about someone not present.

C. When you use the word "is" to describe someone, does that speak about behaviors or about some static condition or invariable quality? Does the static verb "to be" in all its forms limit your views of other people and their characters? Do you settle for one or a few characteristics when you use "is," and put blinders on your relationship by pretending you have adequately described another person?

D. Would a conjugation of verbs (describing actions rather than permanent and owned qualities) or even of adverbs be a more true-to-fact assessment of your friends and acquaintances?

EXERCISE 5-4
WHERE THE MONEY GOES (Discussion; Role Playing)

You are the chairperson for a committee to allocate funds among several agencies in the community. You have been given $10,000 to distribute among the organizations which community donors have given funds to support. Only a small amount of the money is specifically earmarked for an agency: Mr. Mintner gave $500 to the general fund with the clear commitment that it would all go to the Cancer Center; another anonymous donor gave a sum of $200 only if it would go to the Child Abuse Council. Other funds are not earmarked. You and your committee have only this one meeting to decide how to allocate the total amount. Agencies making their appeals, together with the amounts they are requesting, are listed below. Notice that they are asking for several thousand more than you have available to distribute.

Child abuse council. This council assists in the detection, prevention, and education of parents who abuse children, and provides medical aid for abused children. Asking for $6,000.

Cancer center. This center works with detection of cancer and referral to treatment centers, but does no treatment itself. Asking for $3,500.

Boy Scouts. Local chapters active in all city areas including the inner city. Asking for $2,500.

Girl Scouts. As with the Boy Scouts, all areas of the city appear to be served by this organization. Asking for $1,500.

Symphony society. Membership drives have recently not produced enough funds to keep its best musicians employed. Asking for $2,000.

Drug center. This agency is a center for advice and referral for addicts and for education of citizens of all ages and school centers. It distributes some medications but is primarily a referral center. Asking for $2,000.

Crisis center. This telephone system for advice and counseling for persons who are in trouble or are emotionally disturbed serves as suicide prevention and psychological referral center. Asking for $1,500.

Aid to the aged. This agency is an information center for elderly citizens, giving advice about their legal rights and pensions. It would like to expand its service to include recreation. Asking for $3,500.

1. First, working alone, make up a list of the amounts you would personally award to any of the agencies. Be ready to defend your allocations.
2. Working in a small group, try to reach a consensus on how much to allocate to the agencies. When you have reached a general conclusion, the class should meet so that individual groups can report on how they allocated the funds.
3. A role-playing situation can be developed from the different allocations by asking for a small panel of class members (four to six) to act as the allocating committee and hear the arguments from the appealing agencies. In turn, each pair of class members can approach the committee to ask why their request was not granted, or why their allocation was the size it was. By approaching the committee as a pair of pleaders for the agency, you will reinforce each other's arguments and resolve to get straight answers from the committee.
4. After the role playing is finished, ask the class to vote again on allocations. Determine whether the opinions of any class members were changed by the appeals of the agency representatives as they confronted the committee.

Discussion
A. How easy was it for you to make the allocations to these different agencies? Were there some which were your sentimental favorites? Did your social conscience dictate your choices? Could you defend your choices?
B. In the group discussion was it easy for you to stick up for your own allocations? Were there some agencies about which you knew so little that it didn't matter to you what they received? Would you have argued less if you had not written down your answers before joining the group discussion?
C. If there were several groups reporting, did they all come up with the same allocations? Why might there be differences? What does that say about committees or other groups who are given the responsibility of allocating scarce resources?
D. As the result of the role-playing part of the exercise, did any opinions change? Were you in favor of those changes? How were the changes brought about? By good argument? By majority impact? By logic? By emotional appeal?

EXERCISE 5-5
WHO SPEAKS ANOTHER LANGUAGE? (Goldfish Bowl; Forum)
Besides the variety of dialects in the United States, many people here are bilingual — that is, speak some foreign language as well as English. As your own experience will tell you if you have studied a foreign language, there are word traps which can catch you in some humorous, serious, or embarrassing incidents. Most travelers to a foreign country who have trouble with the native language will report such incidents.

In your class find out whether there are students whose native language is not English. If there are no naturally bilingual students, call on those students who are studying a foreign language or who have had a recent experience in a culture where a foreign language is spoken. Develop a "goldfish bowl" setting in which the bilingual students are in the center. They are to respond to questions from other students in a circle around them. Students in the center should be ready to compare experiences and reactions to reinforce the items of discussion.

Discussion
A. Begin the discussions by asking the foreign-speaking students to cite some example of language problems caused by mistaken meanings. (This may be especially true of slang or modernisms.)
B. Are there basic differences in cultures based on language use which can be identified by the foreign-language speakers? How does the native speaker of an Eastern language such as Chinese or Japanese address different members of the family? How does the speaker of French know when to use *tu* and when *vous* in addressing other people? Are there rules which you never break, or have you developed some exceptions to them? How does the speaker of Spanish explain to the English-speaking person that there are two forms of "to be" in Spanish whereas there is only one form in English? Can these two forms be explained in terms of different states of existence, permanent and temporary? Is that complicated for the English-speaking person to understand and difficult to adopt automatically? Do all these different ways of using language have an effect on how people think in those languages?
C. Do the students in the center of the "goldfish bowl" have any feelings about their language differences? Do students who speak only English have any feelings about speaking another language?
D. Is learning to speak another language simply a matter of finding a direct translation of one word for another? Are there different grammatical or logical constructions which must also be learned? What does this say about computer-generated translations?
E. Ask the bilingual students what their most difficult task was in learning English. What characteristics did they notice about those who speak English which may not be noticeable to those persons themselves? What was easiest about learning English? What characteristics of speakers of English made it rewarding to learn the language?

EXERCISE 5-6
MAP OF THE TERRITORY (Group Project)
On the basis of the material on map-territory relationships, the class will make an organization chart which represents the university or college. It is most useful to divide up into groups of four to six for this exercise so that each group can have someone to draw the chart as well as thinkers, organizers, and informed participants. Each group will come up with its own version of the organization

chart which represents the board of trustees (directors, etc.) all the way down to students — who are typically drawn at the bottom of such charts.

The individual group projects should be drawn on the chalkboard or on large sheets of paper and displayed in the classroom. The class can then discuss the reasons for differences or similarities among the "maps" of the college "territory."

Another version of this exercise is to give each group an assignment to construct its ideal college organization, rather than to describe what it may know about the existing structure. Follow the same procedures as above.

Discussion

A. Did the "maps" all represent the same kind of "territory"? That is, did some maps take into account the *offices* or *titles* in the organization rather than the *names* of people? Did some charts label *functions* rather than structure? Did some charts simply list all activities rather than the people who do them?

B. How much do students know about the workings of their institution? Once your group has agreed on which offices or persons to include, do you know how they relate to each other, and particularly how they relate to students?

C. Is there an official organization chart of the college with which a comparison could be made? Does it appear to be effective? Are some student maps better?

EXERCISE 5-7
WHO UNDERSTOOD YOU? (On Your Feet)

Think back over the last few years or so since you have been relatively mature and aware of your relationships with others. Try to determine which one person understood you better than anyone else did. It is not necessary that the person understood you for a very long period of time or that the person still understands you now. It is only necessary that you feel that for some period of time this individual understood you better than anyone else. Try to determine what it was about yourself, the other person, the situation, or any combination of these that made this understanding take place.

Jot down a few notes so that you will be prepared to speak during the class session. The discussion will be informal, and all students will be expected to take part for a few minutes.

Discussion

A. Was it the language you used with each other that made it possible for you to be understood?

B. What did you know about each other that may have helped understanding? Were you in a crisis together? Did you spend a special time with the other person? Were you "in tune" right away?

C. Generalize your reactions to the class members' reports on people who understood them. Are there some patterns you can identify? Age? Sex? Relationship? Factors of surroundings or situations?

D. What implications do those generalizations have for your communication with others? Can you make a theory from what students have reported? Are there suggestions for improving your communication with others?

ASSIGNMENT 5-1
WORDS AND WHAT THEY DO TO YOU

If a word were to be written on the chalkboard in your class, do you think you would have any reaction to it? Are words neutral? Are they without power to make us feel some kind of emotion? Write in the blanks below the words that would make you react in each way described, and turn your answers in to the instructor.

What is the most beautiful word you know? _____

What is the softest or gentlest word? _____

What is the ugliest word? _____

What is the most frightening? _____

What is the harshest or sharpest? _____

What word makes you feel lonely? _____

What word makes you feel angry? _____

What is the most overused or trite word? _____

What word makes you happiest? _____

ASSIGNMENT 5-2
DEFINITION

1. Scientists use the concept of "operational definitions" in their work. What is the difference between an operational definition and a dictionary definition?
2. Make up a list of words and see if you can find operational definitions and dictionary definitions for each. How do the definitions differ? What types of words have the greatest differences in definitions?
3. Try writing an operational definition for some nonsense word. Then, try to use the word in its various forms in sentences. Make a variety of sentences.
4. In class try out your different definitions orally on other students. Is it harder to define a word by writing it or by speaking the definition?

ASSIGNMENT 5-3
MINILANGUAGE

In many social groups, there is a standard miniature language that is different from the overall language. There are special meanings to common words, and there are new and invented words for special circumstances, events, or objects. On your own campus or in your own work group, there are probably several pet phrases and words in use. See if you can identify and define these phrases and terms. Are there some you don't understand? What do you think could cause this? Are there words you use with friends that perhaps others can't understand? What do you think causes this, and how does it affect communication between you and your friends? Between you and those who can't understand?

A variation on this is to divide into dyads and together work out some of the words or expressions which are unique to one group or another. What expressions do you use that some others do not understand — persons from another part of the country, from another part of town, from another generation?

In either situation, write a brief essay on minilanguage in which you answer the questions posed above. Describe how you discovered the language and what it sounded like at first. In conclusion you might speculate on how you related to those "others" who used the language.

You may prepare a brief oral report for the class in which you ask help in discovering meanings for some of the words which you have not understood, or which gave you some difficulty. Do members of the class already understand these words?

PERSONAL IMPROVEMENT BLANK (Chapter 5)
1. Can you think about things for which there are no words? Give examples of something you can think about for which there are no words.

2. Different words mean different things to different people. Give an example of a word which would have very different meaning to someone else from what it means to you.

3. Do you think you speak a dialect? Do you consider your speech ''standard'' or ''nonstandard''? Explain.

Your name _____

Chapter 6

MEANING:
IT'S IN YOU,
NOT IN THE WORDS

FEEDBACK BLANK

EXERCISES

ASSIGNMENTS

PERSONAL IMPROVEMENT BLANK

FEEDBACK BLANK (Chapter 6)   DO NOT SIGN

1. Rate on a ten-point scale how productive this session was for you.

  1   2   3   4   5   6   7   8   9   10

Unproductive   Productive

Comments:

2. What did you learn about your own use of language that will be helpful to you in communicating with others?

3. Did you learn anything about how people may abuse the language in ways they may not even be aware of? Examples?

4. How do you feel when others use polluted language on you?

	Column 1	Column 2	Column 3
0	integrated	management	options
1	total	organizational	flexibility
2	systematized	monitored	capability
3	parallel	reciprocal	mobility
4	functional	digital	programming
5	responsive	logistical	concept
6	optional	transitional	time-phase
7	synchronized	incremental	projection
8	compatible	third-generation	hardware
9	balanced	policy	contingency

Your instructor may ask you to get into small groups to devise a series of these meaningless phrases and to write sentences or paragraphs incorporating them. A variation on this exercise consists of the group members' getting together to plan a short speech in which they attempt to use as many of the expressions as possible. Suggested situations are a report by a member of the State Department to reporters on diplomatic relations in the middle east, a political candidate speaking to his or her constituents, and a lecturer on foreign policy.

Observers: A—Behaviors

Use the following checklist to record your observations of the group members' communicative behaviors.

1. *Group atmosphere.* How friendly, congenial, cooperative, and good-humored were group members toward one another?

2. *Conflict.* How much dissension or conflict (overt or covert) did you notice? Note the events that triggered the conflict, how members reacted to it (what they actually did in the face of conflict), and what effects it had on group members' communicative behaviors.

3. *Communication breakdowns.* Were there any instances when group members did not under-stand each other? Were there instances when group members tried to get their ideas across but could not? What prevented them from being understood? Was the breakdown mostly their own fault (were they inarticulate, off the subject, or confused?), or was it mostly the result of other members' failure to listen or lack of interest?

4. *Reducing barriers.* Did anyone make use of the barriers-reducing techniques mentioned in the text (Chapter 7)? What effects did these attempts have on the group's functioning?

5. *Feedback.* Did group members make good use of feedback? Were they able to give as well as to receive feedback from each other?

Observers: B—Amount of Interaction

There are many things one can observe when people communicate in a group situation. One, perhaps the easiest to observe, is the *amount* of communication taking place in a certain length of time — in other words, how much and how often, how little and how seldom people talk.

Another thing which can be observed is the direction of the communication flow, that is, to whom people talk.

A convenient way to record what is going on in the group, as far as amount and direction of communication are concerned, is to use a *flowchart* or a *sociogram* (see Figures 22 and 23).

In Figure 23, *Jo* talked eight times — four times to Mary, three to Sue, and one to Jim. Jo received eight communications.

Mary talked five times — three times to Jo, two to Sue. She received five communications.

Jim talked three times — two times to Jo, one to Sue. He received two communications.

Sue talked four times — two times to Jo, one to Mary, and one to Jim. She received six communications.

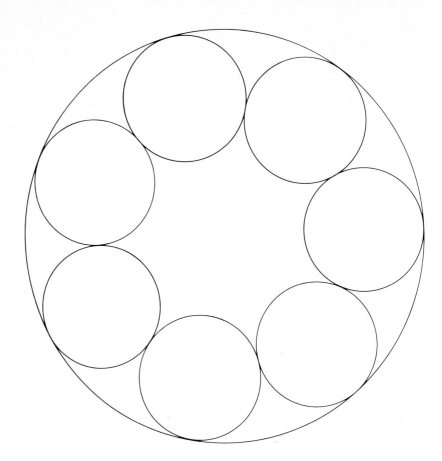

FIGURE 22.
Blank form for a sociogram.

The number of bars in the small circles indicate how many times this particular person spoke at the time of the recording. The arrows show who addressed speeches to whom. When a person talks to the whole group and it is difficult to tell to whom the remarks were directed, the arrows may point simply into the center of the circle.

If several observers are assigned to the same group, the observers can get together and decide to split their observations so that each observer will be assigned to watch only two or three group members and record on a flowchart the amount and direction of communication of these group members only. At the end of the observation session, the observers can get together again and make up a composite picture of all the group members by putting all the flowcharts together.

You will probably be asked to present your observations to the rest of the class. Use the blackboard to explain the flowcharts to the rest of the class. You will want to explain what a flowchart is.

Be sure to identify by name on your chart the group members you are assigned to observe. In your report to the class, the use of names is optional.

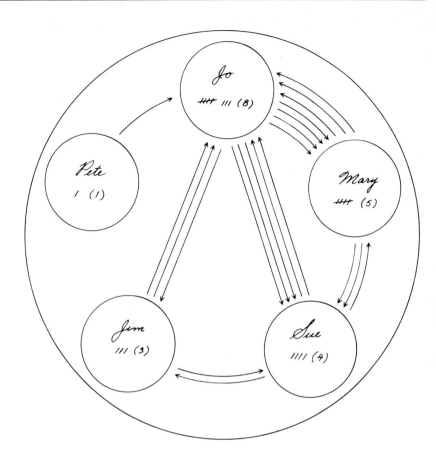

FIGURE 23. Sociogram.

Observers: C—Process Observations

There are many things that can be observed in a group. One way of examining a group is to look at the content the group has dealt with — *what* the group has talked about, its topic, its task. Another way is to look at *how* the group dealt with the content — what happened to its members as the group dealt with its content. The latter method is called "process" as opposed to "content," or "task."

Most communication problems in groups are not content problems but process problems or people problems. Problems are created less by what people talk about than by the way they talk about it and what they do to each other while they talk about it.

Here are some guidelines in the form of questions which should help you look at some of the things that pertain to the process of the group. We will concentrate in this section on (1) climate, (2) gatekeeping, (3) harmonizing, (4) aggressiveness, and (5) apathy.

1. Did anyone in the group attempt to develop and maintain a friendly and relaxed atmosphere? If so, what did the person(s) do?
   a. Told jokes.
   b. Was responsive to others when they made a comment.
   c. Praised others and their ideas.
   d. Agreed with and accepted others' ideas.
   e. Other — specify.
2. Did anyone attempt to keep the communication channels open by helping others to contribute to and particpate in the discussion? If so, what did the person(s) actually do?
   a. Directly asked someone who was silent his or her thoughts about the issue being discussed.
   b. Told the group that not everyone was participating and that perhaps the quieter members might want to.
   c. Helped a group member to "get into" the discussion by telling the rest of the group to pay attention.
   d. Other — specify.
3. Did anyone attempt to reduce disagreements and conflicts when and if they occurred? What did the person(s) actually do?
   a. Acted as a mediator between the opposite sides.
   b. Tried to reduce the tension by joking or by some other use of humor.
   c. Tried to provide an "objective" side to the issue.
   d. Other — specify.
4. Did you notice any aggressiveness or hostility in the group? If so, in what way did it manifest itself?
   a. Criticisms about the topic, the task, the class setup were voiced frequently.
   b. Criticisms about group members were expressed.
   c. Criticisms about ideas or suggestions presented were often expressed.
   d. Some group members were deliberately ignored, made fun of, etc.
   e. Other — specify.
5. Did you notice any apathy in the group? How did it manifest itself?
   a. Few people talked.
   b. Most group members looked bored.
   c. Some group members engaged in talking about things unrelated to the group task.
   d. Some group members removed themselves totally from the discussion by reading, doing homework, or writing letters.
   e. Suggestions or ideas "plopped" a great deal of the time. No one responded to them, and silence followed.
   f. There were long periods of uneasy silence.
   g. Other — specify.

Observers: D—Watching for Group Functions

At this stage of the class development, students should be able to make quite sophisticated observations on communication behavior in the small laboratory groups. As an aid in making and recording observations, a sample recording sheet (Table 10) is included.

Additional observations on the points covered in this unit can be made if students are assigned to observe the small groups during any of the activities chosen for this session.

TABLE 10. **Recording Sheet for Functions within a Group**

Roles or functions	Members' names
Group-task roles	
Initiator-contributor	
Information seeker	
Information giver	
Coordinator	
Evaluator	
Summarizer	
Group-maintenance roles	
Encourager	
Harmonizer	
Gatekeeper	
Standard setter	
Follower	
Self-oriented roles	
Blocker	
Recognition seeker	
Dominator	
Avoider	

How empirical are the members of the group you observed? When ideas are suggested, are they specific or at a high level of abstraction? Keep track of highly abstract terms exchanged. Do group members make an effort to clarify them or have them clarified?

Observe the nonverbal behavior of group members. Can you tell when someone gets ready to talk? How? What cues does the person give? Do other members get the cues? Are efforts made by group members to include the quiet members? What is actually done, and how do the quiet members respond to these attempts to include them in the conversation? Were there instances of categorizing or stereotyping in the group? How did it manifest itself? How did the members respond to it?

Group functions recording sheet. Directions: For each member place a check mark in Table 10 for each role that the person has played often in the group so far. Include yourself.

Observers: E—Functional and Dysfunctional Behaviors

1. What behaviors in the group seemed to be oriented more toward meeting individual members' needs than toward helping the group to accomplish the task at hand? (Examples of dysfunctional behaviors: dominating the discussion, cutting off others, horsing around, not listening, being overly aggressive, nitpicking, avoiding responsibility, smoothing over arguments, withdrawing, doing something unrelated to the task at hand, digressing excessively.)
   a. Who did it? What exactly did he or she do?

   b. What effects did this kind of behavior have on the group as a whole?

2. What behaviors in the group appeared to be aimed toward helping the group members to interact with one another effectively? (Examples: keeping members involved, harmonizing disagreements, reinforcing good contributions, relieving tension, encouraging cooperation, making friendly and supportive contributions.)
   a. Who did it? What exactly did he or she do?

   b. What effects did this type of behavior have on the group as a whole?

3. What behaviors in the group were focused on attempting to accomplish the group's task? (Examples: getting things started, sharing information, organizing, giving opinions, clarifying, summarizing, checking out consensus, keeping the group on the task.)

  a. Who did it? What did he or she do?

  b. What effects did these behaviors have on the group as a whole?

ASSIGNMENT 6-1
CREATING APHORISMS

Witty and quotable statements, called "aphorisms," are possible for anyone to create. At the University of Iowa, Professor David Hamilton has been, for the past several years, assigning the writing of aphorisms to his students. These make use of twists of meaning, language imagery, turns of definitions and meaning, vivid and brief statements, plays on words, and other games related to our language. See if you can create some aphorisms (or epigrams) of your own, being conscious of what linguistic tricks are being played in each and what purpose each is to serve — to amuse, inspire, instruct, etc. Below are some samples created by Professor Hamilton's students:

Taste makes waist. (*Play on words — pun*)

I think, therefore I must be around here somewhere. (*Satire*)

When you row the other fellow across the stream, you get there yourself. (*Inspiration*)

Put your money in taxes; they'll surely go up. (*Amusement*)

You've got to kiss a lot of frogs before you find your prince. (*Humorous advice*)

Nothing in the world is so powerful as a terrorism whose time has come; all ideas melt in its presence — even its own. (*Philosophical commentary*)

ASSIGNMENT 6-2
WORDS TO CONCEAL MORE THAN THEY TELL

In many of our interactions with others we use words as much to avoid giving information as to actually tell others something. Words which conceal more than they tell are used when we don't know how to answer, or when we actually intend to misinform, or when an answer at that moment would not be to our best advantage. Make a list of words which tend to be used by people who want to conceal something — find special words for each of the following situations (a few samples will help you develop your own list).

Family situations

"Soon" as an answer to "When can we go?"
"Early" as an answer to "When are you coming home?"
"We'll see . . ." as an answer to "Can we have a dog?"

Buying or selling

"To be perfectly honest . . ." — and you suspect that person is not.
"By the way . . ." — and you know here comes the hook. "Tell you what I'm going to do for you. . . ." Look out; here comes the hook again.

In the office

"Incidentally . . ." The request that follows will not be a very incidental one.
"Frankly . . ." Here comes bad news.
"It's up to you. . . ." Not really; it's more of a command.

In the classroom

"That's a good question. . . ." — And I haven't got a good answer ready just yet.
"Research has shown . . ." The items listed are all borrowed from . . .

PERSONAL IMPROVEMENT BLANK (Chapter 6)

1. In a recent news story about a political candidate or a member of the government, can you find any examples of language pollution which represent these levels of polluted meaning?

    a. Confusion

    b. Ambiguity

    c. Deception

2. As you observe the language of people around you, do you find that some of your friends are aware of the potential for confusion from polluted language, or do they seem to accept most statements at their face value? Give examples of polluted statements you heard used on you or your friends when you had a tendency to overlook the confusion they caused.

Your name _____

Chapter 7

SEMANTIC TRAPS:
HOW TO AVOID THEM

FEEDBACK BLANK (Chapter 7)   DO NOT SIGN

1. Rate the productivity of this session for you

    1   2   3   4   5   6   7   8   9   10

Not productive   Highly productive

2. Rate how you think the rest of the class felt about the productivity of this session.

    1   2   3   4   5   6   7   8   9   10

Not productive   Highly productive

Comments:

3. Did you notice anyone in class who depended on inferences when observations were available?

4. What kind of insights did you get from the exercises this week (session)?

5. Comment on your listening to the lectures so far.

6. Add other comments, questions, criticisms, suggestions, etc.

EXERCISE 7-1
THE UNCRITICAL INFERENCE TEST[1] (Game)

Instructions

This test is designed to determine your ability to think *accurately* and *carefully*. Since it is very probable that you have never taken *this type* of test before, failure to read the instructions *extremely carefully* may lower your score.

1. You will read a brief story. Assume that all the information presented in the story is definitely *accurate and true*. Read the story carefully. You may refer back to the story whenever you wish.
2. You will then read statements about the story. Answer them in numerical order. *Do not go back* to fill in answers or change answers. This will only distort your test score.
3. After you read each statement carefully, determine whether the statement is:
    a. T — On the basis of the information presented in the story, the statement is *definitely true*.
    b. F — On the basis of the information presented in the story. the statement is *definitely false*.
    c. ? — The statement may be true or false, but on the basis of the information presented in the story you cannot be certain. If any part of a statement is doubtful, mark the statement ''?''.
    d. Indicate your answer by circling either T, F, or ? opposite the statement

Sample Test—The Story

The only car parked in front of 619 Oak Street is a black one. The words ''James M. Curley, M.D.'' are spelled in small gold letters across the front left door of that car.

Sample Test—Statements about the Story

1. The color of the car in front of 619 Oak Street is black.	(T) F ?
2. There is no lettering on the left front door of the car parked in front of 619 Oak Street.	T (F) ?
3. Someone is ill at 619 Oak Street.	T F (?)
4. The black car parked in front of 619 Oak Street belongs to James M. Curley.	T F (?)

Remember. Answer *only* on the basis of the information presented in the story. Refrain from answering as you think it *might* have happened. Answer each statement in numerical order. Do not go back to fill in or change answers.

The Story

A businessman had just turned off the lights in the store when a man appeared and demanded money. The owner opened the cash register. The contents of the cash register were scooped up, and the man sped away. A member of the police force was notified promptly.

[1]Reproduced by permission from W. Haney, *Communication and Organizational Behavior,* rev. ed., Richard D. Irwin, Inc., Homewood, Ill., 1967, pp. 185-186.

Statements about the Story

1. A man appeared after the owner had turned off his store lights.   T F ?
2. The robber was a man.   T F ?
3. The man who appeared did not demand money.   T F ?
4. The man who opened the cash register was the owner.   T F ?
5. The store owner scooped up the contents of the cash register and ran away.   T F ?
6. Someone opened a cash register.   T F ?
7. After the man who demanded money scooped up the contents of the cash register,   T F ?
   he ran away.
8. While the cash register contained money, the story does not state how much.   T F ?
9. The robber demanded money of the owner.   T F ?
10. The robber opened the cash register.   T F ?
11. After the store lights were turned off, a man appeared.   T F ?
12. The robber did not take the money with him.   T F ?
13. The robber did not demand money of the owner.   T F ?
14. The owner opened the cash register.   T F ?
15. The age of the store owner was not revealed in the story.   T F ?
16. Taking the contents of the cash register with him, the man ran out of the store.   T F ?
17. The story concerns a series of events in which only three persons are referred to: T F ?
    the owner of the store, a man who demanded money, and a member of the police
    force.
18. The following events were included in the story: someone demanded money, a cash   T F ?
    register was opened, its contents were scooped up, and a man dashed out of the
    store.

Discussion

A. Be prepared to inspect your own stereotypes, assumptions, and inferences as they relate to the way you answered the questions.
B. Do you argue harder for your own answers when you have "declared" your stand?
C. Is this only a "tricky" kind of situation where you are asked to make definite statements about an event, or does something like this happen in your daily lives? Compare this example with the one in the text about whether or not the post office is open.

EXERCISE 7-2
WHAT'S HER NAME? (Game)

Try to untangle the following riddle:

A man went for a walk one day and met a friend whom he had not seen, heard from, or heard of in ten years. After an exchange of greetings, the man said, "Is this your little girl?" and the friend replied, "Yes, I got married about six years ago."

The man then asked the child, "What is your name?" and the little girl replied, "Same as my mommy's."

"Oh," said the man, "then it must be Margaret."

If the man did not know whom his friend had married, how could he know the child's name?

Discussion

A. There are many riddles like this one which are simply based on some assumption or inference which continually leads the respondent down blind alleys in an attempt to solve them. Do you have a favorite riddle which depends on inferences falsely applied for its success? [Example: the child's riddle "What's black and white and re(a)d all over?" depends on the hearer's mistaking the word "read," past tense of "read," for the word "red." Most riddles are better spoken than printed. The old answer to that riddle used to be "a newspaper" but the more sophisticated child now expects the answer "an embarrassed zebra."]

B. Are you more successful in solving this riddle by being able to talk with others — such as in a group project — than by working alone? Why?

C. Can you make a case for childhood riddles' being an effective force in helping the child become conscious of wrongly applied inferences, thus suggesting a survival value in developing linguistic acculturation? Or are riddles just so much childish fun?

EXERCISE 7-3
THE NINE DOTS (Game)

Objective. Draw a line through all nine dots below.

Restrictions

1. Start with your pencil on any one of the dots.
2. Draw four and only four straight lines without removing your pencil from the page.
3. You may cross lines, but you may not repeat them, i.e., trace back on them.

Discussion

A. This exercise is often used in training programs to demonstrate creative release and ways of looking imaginatively and freely at our world. Make some statements about the puzzle and its solution which would be appropriate for a workshop in (1) art, (2) sales, (3) assertiveness training, (4) music appreciation, or (5) photography.

B. For those in the class who may have known the answer to this puzzle, ask if they remembered more clearly and accurately (1) the exact means of reaching the solution (drawing the lines) or (2) the principle involved in solving the problem.

EXERCISE 7-4
NAME AND USE IT (Group Project)

A book is meant to be read. It also can be used for other things. Make a list of as many uses for this book as you can think of.

When you have just about exhausted the things you can write down about what the book can be used for, get together in a group of four to six others and compare your lists. Make a composite list of the best twenty-five uses for the book besides reading.

Discussion

A. Does the name you give to an object restrict your thinking about what it can be used for?

B. Is there a quality of "bookness" which restricts other uses? Can a book be adapted to do things which other items in our environment can also do?

C. Try the same exercise with the word "brick" instead of "book" and see if you find many of the same uses. Are there different uses suggested? Are there things which you can do with a book and not with a brick? (It doesn't take long to read a brick if all you are looking for is words.)

D. Did the *group* develop items different from those the *individuals* had developed before joining the group? What would happen if you all got together again with the assignment to develop another ten uses for a book besides those you already have?

ASSIGNMENT 7-1
ADAPTING AN OBJECT TO NEW USES

After looking at Exercise 7-4, about listing other uses for a "book" or a "brick," write a brief essay on an adaptation by someone you know of some simple object to a purpose for which it was not obviously intended. (For example, we know of a stranded motorist who used an old stethoscope as a siphon to transfer a small amount of gasoline from a friend's tank to his own.) Trace if you can the thinking process by which the participants arrived at the creative use of the object. Did they talk about other options first? At what stage in the event did they come up with the suggestion? Almost right away? After long hours of unsuccessful deliberation? If the adaptation was performed by one person, would it have been simpler or quicker if a group had been present?

ASSIGNMENT 7-2
NEWS CLIPPINGS

For this assignement you will compare a newspaper story about a current event and an editorial from the same newspaper in terms of the numbers of factual statements, inferences, and judgments found in the two clippings.

Step 1. Cut out a newspaper story on any current event (about 500 words). Underline in red all the reports of factual information (statements that are capable of verification through observations). Underline in blue all the statements of inferences (statements made about the unknown on the basis of the known). Underline in green all the statements of judgments (expressions of values).

Step 2. Cut out an editorial (about 500 words) and underline the statements of factual information in red, the statements of references in blue, and the statements of judgments in green.

Step 3. Write a brief paper to explain what you discovered when you compared the two clippings in terms of the *numbers* of facts, inferences, and judgments. What conclusions do you draw? Hand in your clippings with the completed assignment.

Step 4. Be prepared to read the two versions aloud. For the news story, attempt to keep your voice and inflections (paralanguage) as neutral as possible. When reading the editorial comments, put as much feeling into them as you believe the writer of the piece intended. A variation of this step would be to read only the factual material from the editorial, then read only the inferences and judgments.

ASSIGNMENT 7-3
SLANTING

"A youth and a man were killed and three teenagers were seriously injured today in two accidents."

1. Write a report of these accidents, inventing names and places.
2. Write a slanted report for a newspaper campaigning against juvenile delinquency. Be sure to

use only factual statements, as in the report above, letting your readers make their own inferences and judgments. The facts must be the same as in the first story.

3. Write a slanted report for a newspaper highly critical of the local city administration. Again, you are to use factual statements only, and the facts must be the same as those presented in the first story. Only the slant should differ.

4. In class, role-play this situation with you taking the part of a person who witnessed the accident about which you chose to talk. Make up the details as you go along. Does your oral report become more dramatic? Tell the class (or other actors in a role-playing situation) just what you saw. Another actor should tell you some other details as reported by other witnesses or by the news media. How do you suppose the reports could be made to agree with each other?

ASSIGNMENT 7-4
RECOMMENDATIONS

1. If your most disagreeable neighbor or acquaintance is offered a job in a distant city and you are asked to write a letter of recommendation, how do you do it? Write such a letter, using only factual data as you know it, helping this person to get the job. Then analyze your statements on the basis of what you chose to put in the letter and what to leave out. Also, what impression would the person receiving the letter have of your relation to the neighbor?

2. Imagine that the request for a recommendation about your disagreeable neighbor came by telephone. How do you respond to the questions asked by the caller in regard to the neighbor's character and integrity? Write a dialog as it might occur in a telephone discussion about the recommendation – the questions asked by the caller as prospective employer and the answers by you.

3. A club or fraternity you belong to has been asked to increase its membership by fifteen more members. Write a letter to a friend who is not a member and point out the advantages of joining this group (club or fraternity). After you have finished the letter, write an analysis of what inferences the recipient of the letter might make from the items you chose to report.

4. This same friend has been approved as a candidate for the club. Write a letter supporting this friend's candidacy. Then write an analysis of what inferences might be tapped by your letter when it arrives at the club executive committee.

PERSONAL IMPROVEMENT BLANK (Chapter 7)

1. Briefly describe a recent incident (which happened to you or to someone you know) in which statements of inference or statements of judgment were presented as statements of fact.

2. Briefly analyze a recent decision you had to make in terms of the use of assumptions or inferences in your making that decision. (The decision can be one of considerable importance such as buying a car, or of apparently more trivial nature, such as which items on a menu to order.)

Your name _____

Chapter 8

LISTENING: IS ANYONE THERE?

FEEDBACK BLANK (Chapter 8)   DO NOT SIGN
1. Rate the producitivity of this session for you.
      1   2   3   4   5   6   7   8   9   10
   Not productive   Highly productive

2. Rate how you think the rest of the class felt about the productivity of this session.
      1   2   3   4   5   6   7   8   9   10
   Not productive   Highly productive

   Comments:

3. Did you notice any listening behaviors which interfered with the conduct of the class or the group work?

4. Comment on your own listening during this class.

5. Add other comments or suggestions.

EXERCISE 8-1
LISTENING (Role Playing)
In a small group prepare a role-playing situation in which one actor is designated to listen to the following: (1) an elderly person, (2) a child, (3) a very attractive person of the opposite sex, and (4) a very important person.

Play the skit for the class. Use any topic of discussion for content. The content itself is less important than the interaction.

Discussion
A. Was there a distinct difference in listening with the different speakers? Were there similarities?

B. What generalization can you draw from the way most groups presented their actors in these settings?

C. How would you feel about the "listener" if you were each of the various persons doing the talking? Can you put yourself in the place of that speaker when you are such a listener?

D. What techniques did the listener use to indicate the degree of listening which was going on? Were the techniques discernible to the speaker? Did the speaker adjust to take those signals into account?

E. In the acts as presented, was there an emphasis on both verbal and nonverbal behaviors? Which seemed most effective in giving information to the other person? To the class? Are there nearly universal behaviors in listening?

EXERCISE 8-2
LISTENING BEHAVIORS (Discussion)
The exercise of repeating what the other person said before you can make your own statement (listening exercise) is a technique developed by Dr. Carl Rogers and has produced many an hour of frustration for the participants. It is not easy to repeat statements others make, even when you put them in your own words. When group members make long speeches, it becomes nearly impossible to synthesize the speech and its meaning. You are really not accustomed to repeating the statements of others, and for that reason a referee is suggested to help remind you that the rules of the game call for getting approval of a repeated statement before you can make your own contribution to the discussion.

Instructions to Participants
Your task consists of discussing any one of the topics for discussion listed below. However, you must follow these rules:

1. Each group member must first summarize, *in his or her own words* and without notes, what the member who spoke just previously has said and must do it to that member's satisfaction.

2. If the summary is felt to be incorrect or incomplete by anyone in the group, the referee will help clear up any misunderstanding.

3. When someone else summarizes what you have said, do not be too easily satisfied just for the sake of moving the discussion along.

Instructions to Referees

1. Read the instructions to participants and find out what topic your group will discuss.

2. Your job is to make sure that members stick to the rules throughout their discussion. They cannot speak unless they have summarized what the previous speaker has said to that speaker's satisfaction.

3. If you think that the summary is incorrect or incomplete, you must interrupt and help clear up the misunderstanding.

Topics for Discussion

Group A

Sports programs are of great value to a college.

Group B

Premarital sex relations — acceptable or not?

Group C

Grades should be totally eliminated in college. Why or why not? What other alternatives do we have to evaluate students' work?

Group D

Your task as a group is to rank the following statements that might describe the characteristics of an effective group. To do this, place a 1 in front of the statement that is the most important characteristic of an effective group, a 2 in front of the next most important characteristic, etc. Place a 12 in front of the statement least descriptive of an effective group.

You must work on this task as a group. You may organize for work in any way you wish, as long as you work as a group.

_____There is a healthy competitiveness among members.
_____Everyone sticks closely to the point.
_____Members perform leadership functions.
_____The group avoids conflict situations.
_____Each member gives and receives feedback.
_____The leader suggests a plan for each group meeting.
_____Aggression is openly expressed.
_____Informal subgroups develop spontaneously.
_____Members freely express negative feelings.
_____The goals of the group are explicitly formulated.
_____Information is freely shared among members.
_____Members' feelings are considered when tasks are performed.

Discussion

A. How easy was it to stick to the rules and repeat everything before starting your own statements? Did it get others upset? How did they show it?

B. Was there a tendency for participants to learn to make shorter speeches and to become more clear in their statements?

C. What other changes did you notice in the way people talked in this situation compared with the normal kind of give-and-take conversations? Does that say anything about whether or not we are really listening to each other in the "normal" situations?

D. Are there any features of this exercise which you might want to adopt for your own behaviors? Would you like to tell some special others about doing this exercise? Are you interested in reforming their listening habits? What about their wanting to reform yours?

EXERCISE 8-3
LISTENING FOR FEELINGS (Role Playing)

In Chapter 10, the topic of "confirming" behavior is related to what you do in your listening. When you do not listen to others, you do not hear their words; you also — and this is very important — tell them something of your attitude about them as persons. Role-play the following situations in which you make up dialog and action to suit what you think would happen. Concentrate as you do this on the effect your listening behavior would have on the feelings the other persons might have about themselves, about you, and about how you value each other as persons — not only on how you hear the words spoken.

Situation. Three people are discussing a movie. Select a movie which all members of the group have seen. One person should attempt to fill in the plot, cast of characters, etc., while another listens and helps. The third person should pay no attention to the "data" or information being presented but should only watch for errors in grammar, vocalized pauses, mispronunciations, or other personal slips by the speakers — including just plain ignoring the topic, mentioning people passing by, or relating other events outside the topic of the movie. (At the end of the role playing, ask the class and members of the group to react to how they feel about the "disconfirmer." What should have been done to make a more effective communication situation?)

Situation. A family is having dinner — two parents, three children. All the children attend school. The youngest wants to tell about something that happened today. None of the others pay attention but instead interrupt to have food passed or to laugh at a joke they heard on television, somehow managing to keep the speaker from ever getting reinforcement to tell the story.

Situation. A planning group in class is getting ready to speak on an assigned topic. One member continually makes suggestions which "plop" or never get acknowledged by the others. Later, when another member suggests the same thing, it may get picked up. Indicate in the role playing how silence toward a participant can make such a person give up membership in the group. Listening can be supportive activity on a personal level, or it can be a device to extinguish another person in a group.

Situation. A lecturer in front of an audience is met by a variety of listening behaviors. Role-play the kinds of listening which can take place and make use of "alter egos" (or persons speaking for the actors as if they were speaking their thoughts) to show what is happening in the listener and how that shows up in overt behavior.

Discussion
A. Use the situations above to develop some understanding of how listening behaviors affect others.
B. People too often think that the only time they are really letting others know much about them is when they talk. After these exercises, do you have a better understanding of how you affect people even when you are in the supposedly passive role of listener? Are you aware of the extent of this influence?

EXERCISE 8-4
THE CONSULTATION PROCESS[1] (Discussion)

Instructions to the Person (P) with the Problem
Choose a conflict situation on which you would like some help. It should be important to you and something you have thought a good deal about. It should be a situation you really want to do something about. In a group of three, you will have about ten minutes to tell about the conflict, about twenty minutes to discuss it, and about ten minutes with each of the other members of your triad to review feedback sheets.

Join freely and genuinely in the discussion — first with the person designated R, then with the person designated Q. Try to get help from them. Test their suggestions and explore their ideas. Try to give them a real understanding of your situation.

Note whether your feelings change. If they do, at what point during the discussion does the change occur? Try to see if there is any relationship between your changes of feelings and what Q or R does.

Instructions to the Recommender (R)
1. Listen thoughtfully to the conflict situation as presented.
2. Respond with any of the following attempts to help:
   a. *Recall* and describe a similar experience you or someone you know or read about has dealt with. Tell what was done to improve the situation. If P does not accept or seem to hear and you still see your description as a good solution, try to explain further.
   b. *Recommend,* in order, the steps you would take if you were in P's situation. If P does not accept some of these, make other proposals until you hit on something P finds helpful.

---

[1]Adapted from National Training Laboratories materials.

Instructions to the Questioner (Q)

1. Listen thoughtfully to the conflict situation as presented.

2. Your task is, by *raising questions,* to help P diagnose his or her own difficulty. Refrain from giving any advice or citing any experience of your own or of others. Keep probing to bring about new angles. Keep responsibility for the answers on P. You will have succeeded if you enable P to redefine the situation, seeing the difficulty as due to rather different factors from those P originally presented.

Consultation Process Feedback: Person with the Problem (P)

1. How did you feel during the consulting process?

2. What did R or Q do that helped?

    a. The recommender:

    b. The questioner:

3. What did R or Q do that did *not* help?

    a. The recommender:

    b. The questioner:

4. What did the consultants do that helped you define your problem?

5. Ideally, what would you have liked to happen?

Consultation Process Feedback: Recommender (R)

1. How did you feel during the consulting process?

2. What did you do that seemed helpful?

3. What did you do that seemed *not* helpful?

4. What did you do that helped the person describe and define the problem?

5. Ideally, what would you have liked to see happen?

Consultation Process Feedback: Questioner (Q)

1. How did you feel during the consulting process?

2. What did you do that seemed helpful?

3. What did you do that did *not* seem helpful?

4. What did you do that helped the person describe and define the problem?

5. Ideally, what would you have liked to see happen?

ASSIGNMENT 8-1
WHO LISTENED TO YOU?

A similar assignment was suggested earlier. With the information you now have about listening patterns and behaviors, write a brief essay about some person who you believe listened to you — not just in one instance, but over a period of time. Maybe it was a friend, a teacher, a parent, whoever. In your essay describe what listening patterns were obvious to you, and how you were sure that person listened. Then describe your feelings about being listened to, and how that made you feel about the person. Finally, generalize that experience in a summary of how people might use listening as a means of adjusting their behavior to others and the others' perceptions of them.

ASSIGNMENT 8-2
A LISTENING COURSE

As was pointed out in Chapter 8, few listening courses are part of the regular curriculum in elementary schools, high or middle schools, or colleges.

Assuming you believe that such a course could be offered, would it be beneficial to the students? In what ways? What should be in it? Who should take it?

Prepare the outline of a speech (or write an essay) addressed to the authorities of some educational institution you know in which you advocate the creation of listening courses.

ASSIGNMENT 8-3
INTERVIEW

Interview a member of a profession in which a great amount of time is spent talking and listening to people (doctor, lawyer, psychiatrist, social worker, teacher, executive, administrator, police officer, etc.). In the course of your interview, try to find out that person's view on the importance of listening on the job, the kinds of problems that result from poor listening, some of the ways of overcoming these problems, etc. Take notes and then report your findings to the class, or write them in a paper to be handed in.

ASSIGNMENT 8-4
OBSERVERS

Pay particular attention to how class members listen to one another. How can you tell when they are listening and when they are not? What do they do to reveal their listening or failure to listen? Who seems to be listened to most of the time? Are there any members of the group who are not listened to? How did you notice? How would you characterize the behavior of those members in the group who are not listened to? Were the group members sensitive to the way other members reacted to what they were saying? Did they make it easy for others to listen to them? From what you observed in this group, how would you describe the kind of behaviors which make it easy to listen to someone and the kind of behaviors which make it hard to listen to someone?

Write a report on what you have observed about the listening behaviors in this class either (1) generally, over the term; or (2) in a specific instance not related to this section or to the exercises on listening — take one session of the class or one incident.

PERSONAL IMPROVEMENT BLANK (Chapter 8)

1. What listening behaviors have you noticed in yourself in the past few weeks which might change? Was there a specific incident which made you think about your listening?

2. If you were to list the names of your three closest friends and put beside them the kind of listening they usually do, are they all alike? Different? What common features are there in their listening?

3. Which three people in your experience have demonstrated the best listening behaviors? How about the three worst?

Best	*Worst*
a. _____	**a.** _____
b. _____	**b.** _____
c. _____	**c.** _____

Your name _____

Chapter 9

NONVERBAL COMMUNICATION: COMMUNICATING WITHOUT WORDS

FEEDBACK BLANK

PERSONAL IMPROVEMENT BLANK

FEEDBACK BLANK (Chapter 9)   DO NOT SIGN

This feedback blank is somewhat different from the previous ones. Please read the directions before filling the form out.

Directions

Below are two sets of statements. You are to rank and order the times in each set from 1 (most like the meeting) to 10 (least like the meeting). Use this procedure: rank 1 first, then 10, then 2, then 9, alternating toward the middle.

The session was like this

_____There was much warmth and friendliness.

_____There was a lot of aggressive behavior.

_____People were uninterested and uninvolved.

_____People tried to dominate and take over.

_____We were in need of help.

_____Much of the conversation was irrelevant.

_____We were strictly task-oriented.

_____The members of the group were very polite.

_____There was a lot of underlying irritation.

_____We worked on our process problems.

My behavior was like this

_____I was warm and friendly to some.

_____I did not participate much.

_____I concentrated on the job.

_____I tried to get everyone involved.

_____I took over the leadership.

_____I was polite to all group members.

_____My suggestions were frequently off the point.

_____I was a follower.

_____I was irritated.

_____I was eager and aggressive.

EXERCISE 9-1
PARALANGUAGE—MEANINGS IN CONTEXT (On Your Feet)

The class should study the list of phrases or sentences below and imagine how they can be said differently to mean different things. Ask for two volunteers who want to say these lines to each other. When the two are on their feet in front of the class, they can take turns reading lines. After each reading, the class should guess (1) what the character of the message was intended to be (being playful or joking, being authoritarian, giving orders, asking help, etc.) and (2) what the implied relationship is between the two people — the one who speaks and the one spoken to.

After two people have finished their dialog and the class has guessed about the relationships and the "meanings," ask for two other students to read the lines and repeat the experience in a different way. A third pair of students could probably invent another set of relationships to demonstrate with tones and inflections which indicate what is being asked or ordered.

Sample statements follow (or you can make up some of your own):

"Get out of here."

"Come back."

"Are you busy?"

"What's that for?"

"Read it to me."

Discussion

A. Do you use a different tone of voice with people above you in status and those below you? Do you use a different tone of voice in relation to what you want to have done — like asking a favor, or giving an order to be carried out?
B. Not only does your tone of voice tell what you intend to have happen, but it tells the relationship between you and others. Was it hard to identify the roles being taken by the speakers? Where did you learn those specific ways of speaking to other people? If you listen to little children playing, are they imitating their parents' ways of speaking to each other?
C. If some of the relationships were difficult to guess, was it possibly because they were not very well defined? If two people are very much on the same level of authority, do they give orders to each other in a severe way?

EXERCISE 9-2
FIRST MEETING (Role Playing)

Role-play a first meeting between two people. Ask for pairs of students from the class to act out a situation in which two people are encountering one another for the first time. Ask the class to observe carefully the nonverbal as well as the verbal exchanges. Ask the actors to pay particular attention to their nonverbal behavior, so that they can discuss it later with the class.

Some sample situations: (1) Two students are assigned to be roommates in the residence hall. (2) Two parents of students who share a dormitory room meet in the room on the school visiting night. The roommates have described each other to their parents, but the parents have never met before. (3) A boy and a girl sit next to each other on a cross-country bus; or two men sit together on a cross-country bus; or two women sit together on an airplane. (4) You and another person are the only ones in a doctor's waiting room. (5) You are in the market for a new car. You enter the showroom of a local car dealer and are met by a salesperson.

Discussion

A. How much of the information about each other was exchanged by verbal as compared with nonverbal channels? What information was available to each person about the other? Did the performers seem to pay attention to the nonverbal cues?

B. When the encounter is over, what does each person report about the other? Does it take more than a few minutes to begin to draw conclusions about another person? How accurate are the first impressions? Are they more accurate if you draw your impressions from what you see as well as what you hear? Is the balance of verbal and nonverbal information more important than either by itself?

C. If you receive contradictory nonverbal and verbal information about the other person, do you tend to believe the nonverbal rather than the verbal information? Which channel (verbal or nonverbal) seems to you to be more reliable? Is that always true? Are there situations in which the opposite may be true?

EXERCISE 9-3
HOW DO WE MAKE OUR POINTS? (Goldfish Bowl)

The class is divided into groups of four to six students. One group sits in a face-to-face situation to carry on a discussion, and another similarly sized group sits in a circle around the first group to observe. As the inner group discusses some topic, it is observed as a whole by the outer group, with particular attention paid to nonverbal behaviors. After about ten minutes of discussion, the groups change places and the inner group moves out to observe the behaviors of the other group. (The same topic may be used for each group.) For the third discussion, all members of both groups get together to discuss their observations.

Variation. Instead of the inner group's being observed in general by the outer group, each member of the outer group is assigned one person in the inner group to observe for nonverbal behaviors (pairing up). Groups switch positions after about ten minutes, and for the next ten minutes each person observes his or her previous observer. The pairs then have a discussion in dyads to talk about what they observed each other doing during the first two discussions. If there is an uneven number of members, two "outer" members can observe one "inner" member, and then the outer person can observe two in the inner group after the groups switch places. The third discussion then takes place in a triad.

Discussion

A. In a general discussion following the group or individual discussions of the behaviors observed, the group can develop some general rules about nonverbal discussion behaviors. For example, when a person wants to get the attention of the group and have a turn at talking, what moves, gestures, or expressions are used? Are the same nonverbal signals used whether that person has talked before or not? Whether the person is a man or woman? Whether the person wants to agree or disagree? In other words, do "entering the conversation" signals vary according to content, place in the group, sex, age, or other factors?

B. Are there ways the group members can stop a person from talking without simply telling that person to "shut up"? What devices were available in the nonverbal channels to do this? Are there nonverbal ways to encourage someone to continue talking?

C. What other nonverbal signals are used? Emphasis? Questions? Disagreement? Supporting others' ideas? Did most of the members observed seem to use the same signals? Did the members seem to understand each other when such signals were used?

D. Since the group did not make up a special set of nonverbal system signals or messages, how did the members manage to get so much information to each other? Do we have a generalized system of handling each other nonverbally which we rely on in groups? Where did we learn to do those things? Did you ever have a class in nonverbal communication?

E. Did group members become self-conscious about their nonverbal behaviors because they knew they were being observed? Were any actions inhibited? Did there seem to be more reliance on paralanguage when the gestures, expressions, and moves were being observed closely? How do people respond when they know their actions are being evaluated? How did you feel?

EXERCISE 9-4
SHAKING HANDS (Game)

Each member of the class is asked to shake hands with another person, demonstrating the following:

1. A firm, confident handshake
2. A limp "dead-fish" handshake
3. A very active, pump-handle shake
4. A delicate, fingertip handshake
5. The "bruiser," or bone-crusher

Discussion

A. Did you have any trouble demonstrating these different styles of shaking hands? Have you had experience with them?

B. What other behaviors, nonverbal and verbal, would you expect to go with each kind of handshake? Did you adopt a "role" when you attempted each kind of handshake—a role that seemed appropriate for the kind of hand clasping being attempted? Is there more to a handshake than simply the hands of two people grasping each other? Are there postures, head positions, facial expressions, and verbal reinforcements for the handshakes?

C. Taking each of the five different handshakes in turn, have the class demonstrate the other nonverbal and verbal signals which would logically (for the majority of the class) accompany each handshake. Where did you learn to do that? Are your estimates of the person doing those things consistently accurate? Is a handshake one of the first contacts we may have with others?

D. Does American culture make as much use of handshaking as other cultures? At one time in our history the expression "We shook hands on it" implied a binding contract. What kind of handshake accompanies that kind of deal?

E. Another historical item: When asked if he knew a certain person, a rural American man said, "We've howdied, but we ain't shook." What level of acquaintance was signified by that response? Is that expression clear to you?

EXERCISE 9-5
HOW FAR AWAY TO SIT? (Game)

Using chairs set up in front of the class, have two or more students locate them in relation to each other according to the suggested situations. (You may want to develop some sample situations of your own.) As the class observes, the "actors" adjust the arrangement of the chairs to fit the following cases:

1. There are four chairs available. Two people who don't know each other come into the waiting room of a dentist.
2. Two good friends come into the same waiting room.
3. A mother and her worried 10-year-old child come into the same waiting room.
4. There are six stools at the counter of an eating establishment. Four people come in and take their places at the counter. Two strangers, a woman and a man, enter first. Then two people enter together who are obviously friends going to have lunch together.
5. A boss has called in a secretary to complain about consistently smudged and crooked letters. Arrange the two chairs in relation to a desk showing where each would sit.
6. A boss has called in a shipping clerk to say that the last few orders were very carefully dispatched and the customers have already telephoned compliments. There are four available seats and a desk in the room; arrange the furniture.
7. You have asked for an appointment with your boss in order to request a transfer to another department. When you enter the room the boss is at the desk and invites you to sit anywhere. There are three chairs available to you. Locate them for distance and direction.

Discussion

A. As the actors adjust the chairs, the audience may be consulted and some consensus developed on the placement of the persons in relation to one another. At the end of each skit the audience should be asked to comment on the location of the actors and their furniture, and also to comment on the reason for any lack of agreement with the actors' arrangements.

B. Status has some effect on where people sit. Does placement confer status, or do people of status take over a group from any position? A Scottish chieftain — Macdonald — was attending a dinner at a lord's castle and was asked, "Don't you want to sit at the head of the table?" To which he replied, "Wherever Macdonald sits, there is the head of the table."

C. Even in public places do you feel strongly about how you are seated? Is this a cultural factor as well as a personal matter? Do some cultures enourage closer seating at public events?

D. Where did you learn how far away to sit from someone else? How do you know what others are telling you by their location when they are talking to you? Are there predictable distances and arrangements? Do you see them yourself, or do you just have them used on you?

EXERCISE 9-6
HOW CLOSE SHOULD YOU STAND? (Game; Role Playing)
This exercise can be done by pairs of students acting out the situations and reporting to each other their feelings and experiences. It also should be demonstrated by one pair of students in front of the class so that the advice of all the class members can be used in establishing distances.

Dyads: Working in pairs. At a signal from the instructor the members of each pair stand up and place themselves at a distance which both can agree is comfortable to meet the assignment. If you and your partner cannot agree, make a specific note of which parts of the exercise caused the most difficulty in agreeing.

Simulate the following situations:

1. You want to tell the other person a secret. How close do you get?
2. You want the other person to check a list of items for you; no talk is needed.
3. You want to ask the other person to help you decide which necktie or scarf to wear.
4. The purpose of this exercise is to imagine what it is like to be a small child in a world of adults. Each dyad consists of an "adult" and a "child." The adults stand on chairs or in some other way elevate themselves about 1½ feet above the children. The children ask permission to have a friend over to dinner, or to go to the movies, or to buy some popcorn. The children try their best to be heard and to politely get what they want. After a few minutes, the members of the dyads exchange roles and repeat the exercise.

Demonstration in front of the class. Two persons from the class should be selected to role-play the appropriate distances for the situations listed below and for others suggested by class members. When the pair is ready to perform, the class can call out their ideas.

Sample situations follow:

1. A boy and a girl talking about class assignments
2. A boy and girl deciding where to go to eat
3. A boy and girl with a secret between them
4. Two women talking business
5. Two men talking sports
6. Two men conspiring to get another man fired
7. Two women who are doctor and patient talking
8. A man patient and a woman doctor talking

If the distance is not agreed on by the class members, ask the actors what they think. Clarification of the relationships, and additional data about the content of what is being exchanged, may affect the distance.

Discussion
A. Ask the dyads to tell how they feel when another person is encroaching on their space. Were any of the situations difficult to understand?
B. How did the "child" feel when trying to talk with the "adults"?
C. When dyads disagree about how far apart to stand in any of the sample situations, ask the class to guess why the differences exist. Do the dyad members come from different cultures? Is there a predictable difference between men and women? Does content make the most difference? (In other words, does what people are talking about establish how far apart they should be?)

ASSIGNMENT 9-1
ADJUST YOUR TELEVISION SET

A. Watch a television show with the sound turned down. Are you able to follow much of what is happening? If you are watching a comedy, do most of the gags depend on sight rather than sound? Write a paragraph about your reactions to this experience, and estimate what percentage of the meaning of the program you were able to understand by only seeing it.

B. Try the opposite experience. With the sound turned on normally, either close your eyes or turn your back on the television set. Besides the content of the show, with the information provided by your hearing, are there elements of paralanguage which help you interpret the action? Write another paragraph about your reactions to this experience, and estimate what percentage of the meaning of the program you were able to get by only hearing it.

C. In a final paragraph, speculate on how the two systems of seeing and hearing reinforce each other. Are there instances in which they do not? (One classic example is the play-by-play narration of a football game which accompanies the television action. The pictures may not be accurately describing what is happening, and the same narration on radio has no picture to be compared with.)

ASSIGNMENT 9-2
LOGGING SILENCES

During the course of a day keep a record of the times when you experienced silence. Arrange the incidents by these categories:

1. Silences which occurred because nobody was around to talk to
2. Silences which represented indecision — not knowing what to say
3. Silences which were deliberate retreats into privacy
4. Silences of some emotion — sadness, awe, etc.
5. Silences of difficult thinking, or problem solving
6. Other categories

Write your reactions to these various silences. Were you aware before this exercise how much time was spent in silence? Or how little? Are silences useful to you? Do you enjoy them? Do they bother you?

ASSIGNMENT 9-3
SPACE DESIGN

How may the way a house is designed affect the nature of family relationships? Use examples from your own experience to answer this question.

ASSIGNMENT 9-4
GROUP OBSERVATION

Select any small group (not more than twelve members) on the campus holding its regular meeting. Secure permission to attend the meeting and observe the group. Make a chart representing the seating arrangement and observe only the nonverbal behavior of the group members. Observe their postures, facial expressions, who they look at, how they look at each other, etc. Take notes, and later summarize your findings in a short paper or an oral report to the class.

ASSIGNMENT 9-5
INTERVIEW

If you are able to meet one or more architects, interview them and ask them how they see spatial relationships, space design, and the effects of design on communicative behavior. Use the notes you take during your interview to make a report.

ASSIGNMENT 9-6
YOUR OWN NONVERBAL SIGNALS

Make a list of the gestures, moves, actions, etc., which you use to communicate with others (nodding your head to encourage someone to speak more, waving your arms to attract attention) in your everyday speaking encounters. Ask the class members, or other people who know you, if they have noticed these moves and if the moves meant anything to them.

Write a description of your nonverbal moves as you have observed them and had them checked by someone else. Analyze the moves to determine which are so characteristic of you that they may be considered a trademark, or a means of identifying you to your friends. Speculate on why people develop characteristic moves or nonverbal devices. Speculate on how communication effectiveness relates to use of nonverbal behaviors.

PERSONAL IMPROVEMENT BLANK (Chapter 9)

1. Watch a group sitting together some distance from you in a restaurant, a waiting room, a committee room, or some other place. Describe what behaviors you noticed and—because you were not listening to what was said but were only observing the nonverbal—tell why you think the group members were together. Did they work well together? What was their general mood?

2. As you watch others' nonverbal behavior, do you pay more attention to the (1) head signals, (2) moves of the body, or (3) actions of the arms and legs? Is it possible to isolate each part and its messages? Do you make better evaluations of the messages when you watch for the total context of nonverbal messages as they combine to form a total picture?

3. What have you learned in this unit on nonverbal communication and silences which will be of immediate use to you in your communication? Be specific.

Your name _____

Chapter 10

INTERPERSONAL TRANSACTIONS: THE RULES OF THE GAME

FEEDBACK BLANK

EXERCISES

ASSIGNMENTS

PERSONAL IMPROVEMENT BLANK

FEEDBACK BLANK (Chapter 10)   DO NOT SIGN

1. Rate the productivity of this session's work for you.

    1   2   3   4   5   6   7   8   9   10

Not productive   Very productive

2. Rate how you think the rest of the class felt about the productivity of this session's work.

    1   2   3   4   5   6   7   8   9   10

Not productive   Very productive

Comments:

3. In relation to this week's lecture, were you assigned a role you did not like in your group activity? If people assign ''identities'' to you, what effect does this have on your reactions?

4. Did you enjoy working with your group? Why or why not?

5. Add other comments, criticisms, questions, suggestions, etc.

EXERCISE 10-1
CHARACTERISTICS OF MEN AND WOMEN (Group Project)

This exercise is based on a number of studies which have investigated the attitudes of American society about men and women and their roles. It can provide an interesting study of sex stereotyping if the class members can remain open-minded and avoid having their feelings hurt by what must inevitably be sexist statements or categories.

Divide the class into groups, men on one side and women on the other. Ask each group, working independently of the other, (1) the chief characteristics of men in our society and (2) the chief characteristics of women in our society. When both groups have finished, members of the groups should put all four lists of characteristics on the chalkboard or write them with felt markers on large sheets of paper in big letters.

Each group will be allowed three additions and three subtractions as preemptory challenges if either group feels that the other group's lists have particularly unfairly characterized that sex. For example, the women may insist that a total of three items be removed from the men's lists and that a total of three items be included on the men's lists.

After this period of adjustment, have the students compare lists. Lead a discussion on the implications for roles and communication.

Discussion

A. In comparing the lists, ask if the men see their own characteristics better than they see those of women. Ask if the women are more perceptive about men's characteristics or their own. Ask for specific comparisons of those lists to make sure there is a careful examination for accuracy.

B. Select those items in each of the four lists which are positive in their relation to the society's values and those which are negative. Some items on the lists may be neutral or may so depend on circumstances that their positive or negative value cannot be determined in the abstract. Are there more positive items about men than about women? What implications does that have for self-concept and for assuming roles?

C. What kinds of items did the women and the men ask to have either removed from or added to the opposite group's list? Was there a pattern to those objections? How did the participants feel when they were challenged by the other group? Was there any reason given for the omission or the inclusion of these objectionable items?

D. Ask each group to rank its characteristics by selecting the five most important characteristics from the lists. (Each sex group may use any of the items from any of the lists.) The women will select those five items they most prize as characteristics for women; men will select the five most prized items for men. This should be done individually, unless there is a substantial amount of time for the segregated groups to spend in reaching an agreement on the top five characteristics. After all individuals have ranked their choices, ask for a discussion on what prevents all persons of the same sex from agreeing on items. Would you think that the opposite sexes would agree on items?

EXERCISE 10-2
WRITING A JOB DESCRIPTION (Group Project)

Divide the class into groups of five to seven persons each. Each group should have paper on which to write a job description and display it for the rest of the class. (Or the job descriptions may be written on the chalkboard.)

Identify in the group one or more persons who have a title for which a brief job description can be written (letter carrier, waiter, accountant, clerk-typist, swimming teacher, etc.). Working together, construct a job description for that position or job, including those items which distinguish performance of that task from other activities. Display your job description for the rest of the class.

Discussion

A. Are there adequate mentions of the needed skills so that only qualified people would apply for the job? Is the description so vague that many applicants would be misled into thinking they could do the job?

B. This is a verbal map of a real territory (the job itself) and, like most maps, is subject to loss of detail. What kinds of details were left out which might prove very important when an applicant comes in for an interview?

C. Are there more items mentioned having to do with skills than with other qualities of a personal or social character? Can you specify some special qualities which you expect a person to have?

D. Are there items in the job description which might give an applicant a feeling of rejection? An overstated or exaggerated sense of importance? What would potential applicants have to believe about themselves before applying?

EXERCISE 10-3
ROLE PLAYING WITH ALTER EGOS (Role Playing)

This exercise is a skit of two people talking to each other, but six people must work together to perform the skit.

First there are the primary characters — call them Joe and Jill. Joe and Jill are planning to go out to dinner. Joe wants Chinese food; Jill wants Mexican food.

Behind Joe and Jill are their respective alter egos, representing metacommunication levels which will speak up for the inner voices and will tell Joe what Jill thinks and Jill what Joe thinks. In this case Jill understands that Joe wants to go to a Chinese restaurant, but Joe is not sure what Jill wants.

A third level of communication is meta-metacommunication, and thus a third set of speakers will represent the alter egos of the alter egos. These are the characters of Joe's thinking that Jill understands that he wants Chinese food and Jill's thinking that Joe has heard her say she wants Mexican food, while that was not actually the case.

In groups of six, plan role-playing situations for the class in which all three levels of communication are represented. Actors or actresses may speak in turn, being interrupted for comments by alter egos who place a hand on the speaker's shoulder or otherwise signal to get a turn to speak.

Each speaker should interpret only his or her own level; that is, no one should anticipate the interpretation of the alter egos, and certainly no one should appear to overhear what the other alter egos are saying.

Topics which might prove interesting include:

1. Roommates discussing hours to study or to be quiet
2. Parent and child discussing completing some chores around the house
3. A pair of friends ordering from a menu
4. A pair of friends deciding which movie to see
5. A salesperson and a customer buying shoes, batteries, cameras, etc.
6. A teacher and a student discussing a grade

Discussion

A. The confusion in these skits may be analogous to the confused state of your communication as you try to understand your own metacommunication levels and take into account those of other people. Ask how participants felt when they were (1) planning the skit and (2) actually taking part in it.
B. Were the outcomes of these role-playing situations likely to be the same as the outcomes in "real life"? Ask for specific reasons for the other students' answers to this question.
C. Are there more chances of misunderstanding in the direct communication between the primary actors and actresses, or between the metacommunication and meta-metacommunication levels? Discuss why.
D. Did any of the role players develop better ways of talking about your communication? In other words, how do you apply metacommunication in a practical way to reduce misunderstanding?

EXERCISE 10-4
THE BOB LEE CASE (Discussion)

Bob Lee was taking a difficult, required course during his junior year at Strivemore University. Bob needed a B average to keep his scholarship, but no matter how hard he studied, he could only get C's and D's on the weekly tests that would form the major part of his grade in the course. The professor curved the grades of the thirty students in the class, and Bob just could not seem to come out on the top of the curve.

After the fourth test, Bob was complaining about the situation to a fraternity brother who also was in the class. The brother sized him up and decided that since Bob was a good guy and part of the group, he'd give him the inside dope on the course. He swore Bob to secrecy and then told him the whole story. It seemed that the professor didn't correct her own papers but used a graduate student grader. The grader had found a new way to work his way through college. He had arranged, through a star football player in the class, to provide cram sessions before each test based on the key the professor gave him. He "tutored" nine of Bob's classmates at the rate of $5 per test or $10 if the student wanted the answers to memorize. For just "five or ten bucks" a week, Bob could join the group, and his problem would be solved.

Bob had a little money from his summer job, but he wasn't immediately ready to invest it in an A. Wasn't the whole thing unethical? Shouldn't the professor be told? But then again, what if his fraternity brother or the football player were expelled? Still, what about the students at the bottom of the curve?

All these questions and more went through Bob's mind. He had to decide soon, or it would be too late to save his grade.

If you were Bob, what would you do? Why? Try to get a consensus from your group. Have one member report your decision to the rest of the class.

Discussion

A. If more than one group in the class came to a consensus, did all groups come up with the same answer? What are the implications of that?

B. Was there a role conflict as well as a question of ethics? What did Bob want to be? How did he see himself? Which of many roles did he give a priority to?

C. In your analysis of the case, you placed yourself in Bob's role and made some assumptions about how you would act. Were you also conscious of the role you play as a member of a group discussing this case? Did the others in the group you are with have an effect on how you responded to Bob's dilemma? What are the implications of belonging to different groups who can influence you in different ways, even on a single issue?

EXERCISE 10-5
BREAKING THE RULES (Role Playing)

Members of the class should volunteer to demonstrate how to break the rules of looking and talking as discussed in Chapter 9.

One pair takes the front of the room and demonstrates the principle "If you talk, you're supposed to look at the other person." The class members observe the reactions of the speakers and also watch their own reactions to the exchange. (Note: The principle may be demonstrated either by following the rule or by breaking it.)

Another pair should demonstrate the principle of how long to hold eye contact. This episode can be expected to become quite involving for the members of the class.

Still another pair can demonstrate the third principle, "If you don't talk, you're not permitted to look." There is a culturally acceptable distance from which you are permitted to look and not talk. It is especially applied in sidewalk cafe society, where the imbibers watch the strollers.

Discussion

A. Are the ways you apply these rules so universal that you can relate to the actors even if you are only a member of the audience? Have you had some experiences of your own which have sensitized you to these "principles"?

B. Do you get confirmed or disconfirmed by these actions from others? How do you tell people you like them or do not like them? Where did you learn how to do that?

EXERCISE 10-6
WHAT PROFESSIONS DO YOU ADMIRE?[1] (Group Project)

The list of professions below is part of the exercise explained in the following paragraphs:

_____Novelist

_____Newspaper columnist

_____Police officer

_____Banker

_____U.S. Supreme Court justice

_____Lawyer

_____Undertaker

_____State governor

_____Sociologist

_____Scientist

_____Public school teacher

_____Dentist

_____Psychologist

_____College professor

_____Physician

_____(Your own if not included) _____

Above are fifteen occupations listed at random, with a blank for you to fill in your own choice of a career or occupation if it is not included. Rank these fifteen or sixteen professions according to your opinion of their prestige in the United States. Place a number 1 next to the occupation you think most people would consider most prestigious, and so on. It may be easier for you to rank the highest as 1, then the lowest as 15 or 16, then next highest, then next lowest, working toward the middle.

After you have finished working alone to get your own rankings, you will work together with other members of a small group (four to six members) to arrive at a consensus on your choices. Try to discuss the items thoroughly and get others to agree rather than voting too quickly, "horse-trading," or browbeating others into agreement.

All groups should report to the entire class by putting their rankings on the chalkboard or on large sheets of paper for all to see and discuss.

[1]This exercise is adapted from data gathered by the National Opinion Research Center and reported to R. Bendix and S. M. Lipset (eds.), _Class, Status, and Power_ (2d ed., New York: The Free Press, 1966). Although the preferences and prestige may have changed in the time since the test was first administered, the principle is more important than the normative data on rankings.

Discussion

A. Do all groups generally agree? If not, is there a reason or a logic which can explain the disagreements? Was it easy to get consensus? How did some groups manage to arrive at agreement by other means?

B. If your own career or occupation is not on the printed list, did you have much difficulty having it included by others? How did you feel if someone ranked it lower than you did?

C. How does someone who chooses one of the low-ranked occupations feel about himself or herself? Is prestige a value for most people? Is it a major one for you? Do you care? Are there more important values in your choice of an occupation which makes prestige not very significant to you? What do parents say about their children's choices of occupations? How do children talk about their parent's occupations?

D. Do we try to euphemize our occupations? Is an undertaker sometimes called a "funeral director" or a "mortician"? Is a janitor called a "sanitary engineer"? If we pay so much attention to what our jobs are called, does that mean we identify with their role assignment?

E. Look in the help-wanted sections of the newspaper to find how jobs are described on the basis of their labels.

ASSIGNMENT 10-1
HOW TO BEHAVE

Find some passages in a book of etiquette or a manual of manners which tell you how you should behave in a certain situation. Does this advice fit all occasions? If your etiquette book is not up to date, maybe the advice is not too good. Copy down and hand in:

1. A brief passage giving advice on how to behave which you believe would help a reader reduce role ambiguity or role conflict.
2. A brief passage which gives advice which would make you feel out of place rather than helping to reduce your role ambiguity.

ASSIGNMENT 10-2
SELF-CONCEPT

It was said in Chapter 3 that in arriving at a conception of self, every person sees himself or herself in relation to others. Can you explain in brief what is meant by that statement? What other factors play a part in helping a person arrive at a self-concept?

In a dyad with someone you know, tell the other person things about yourself which you like. These can be characteristics, things you do, etc. Then have the other person help you develop a list of behaviors which demonstrate or show up those characteristics you like about yourself — things which allow others to react to your behaviors and reinforce your self-concept. After you have worked on your own list, work with your partner on a list of his or her qualities and behaviors.

ASSIGNMENT 10-3
CHANGING SELF-CONCEPT

What aspects of the self-concept are particularly difficult to change? How do you protect your self-concepts? What do you protect them from? Why do you feel the need to protect them? Rather than answering these questions in the abstract, use yourself as a concrete example. Write your comments. Ask volunteers from the class to read their comments. Do most of the students seem to have the same lists of items? Discuss similarities or differences in lists.

ASSIGNMENT 10-4
REFERENCE GROUPS

Reference groups help us determine whether or not we are performing our roles successfully. Can you give examples from your own experience that would support this statement?

Make a list of the reference groups you can identify that have an influence on you. After you have made the list, rank the groups in order of their importance to you. After the most important ones write a brief comment on (1) why the group is important to you and (2) how much time or energy you spend in keeping a relationship going with that reference group.

As a class exercise, it is interesting to compare lists of highest-ranking reference groups for the entire class. Are there consistent patterns among the students which indicate a similarity of role relationships?

ASSIGNMENT 10-5
TEACHER EVALUATION

1. What would you like your instructor to know about you in order to evaluate you fairly? Write a list.
2. Look at what you just wrote, and try to figure out how much of it you said because you thought your instructor would want to read it, or because it would look good, and how much of it represents a real and honest expression of what you believe is important for the instructor to know in order to evaluate you fairly.

In class get together with another student or two to compare lists. Make an oral summary of results from your dyad or triad after you have picked out the important features you would like known. Consider how those characteristics would affect the evaluation you would get from an instructor. The instructor may comment on what must be known about students in order to give them accurate evaluations. Do the lists seem alike?

PERSONAL IMPROVEMENT BLANK (Chapter 10)

1. On the basis of material in this chapter, identify briefly a relationship you have with a person whom you consider to be in a role very much like yours. Without using names, describe how you act toward each other. What is your communication like?

2. Identify a relationship you have with someone whose role you consider very different from yours. Without using names, describe how you talk and act toward each other.

3. Briefly list a recent example of a "double message" which you either experienced or observed.

Your name _____

Chapter 11

INTERPERSONAL CONFLICT: HOW THE GAME IS PLAYED

FEEDBACK BLANK (CHAPTER 11)   DO NOT SIGN

1. Rate the productivity of this session's work for you.

    1   2   3   4   5   6   7   8   9   10
Not productive   Very productive

2. Rate how you think the class felt about the productivity of this session's work.

    1   2   3   4   5   6   7   8   9   10
Not productive   Very productive

Comments:

3. List those members of the class or of your group with whom communication is easy for you. Can you speculate why?

4. List those members of the class or of your group with whom you find it difficult to communicate. Why?

5. At this point, how comfortable or at ease do you feel in this class?

EXERCISE 11-1
THE FAIR HOUSING CASE (Discussion)

The Problem

You are the local community advisory and investigatory board which determines whether or not a specific case involving alleged racial discrimination should be brought to court under the Fair Housing Act in your state. The board employs its own investigator.

The section of the act with which you are presently concerned reads: "It shall be an unlawful discriminatory practice . . . for any person to . . . refuse to sell, transfer, assign, rent, lease, sublease, finance, or otherwise deny or withhold commercial housing from any person because of race, color, religion, ancestry, or national origin of any prospective owner, occupant, or user of such commercial housing."

Greg Stephen and John Moore have filed a case with your board alleging that Mr. Genove has unlawfully discriminated against them. They state they they are students at the university. They are black. They arranged by telephone, answering an ad in the local paper, to rent an apartment owned by Mr. Genove. The apartment is part of a four-unit apartment house. They sent a check for the first month's rent on an upstairs apartment. The check was cashed by Mr. Genove. He wrote them a letter which stated they could rent the apartment for a full year if they so desired. Mr. Genove did not know that the men were black.

The men stated that they arrived at the university on the day before registration for the fall semester. They called Mr. Genove, and he delivered the keys to the apartment. Mr. Genove seemed "surprised" that the men were black. He gave them the keys, however, and stated at the time that he hoped they would find the apartment comfortable and that they would "decide to stay."

One week later, the men were served notice by registered mail that Mr. Genove was starting evicition proceedings and that they had two weeks to vacate the apartment. They phoned Mr. Genove to ask him why they were being evicted. Mr. Genove replied, "My attorney advised me not to discuss the case."

Additional Information

The board's investigation disclosed the following:

1. Mr. Genove and his attorney, in conference with the board, claimed that there was absolutely no discrimination involved in asking the men to move.
2. Mr. Genove showed the board a note from one of his renters in the apartment units, complaining that the men had staged a "wild party the night they moved in, with people tramping up and down the stairs until 3 A.M. and noise like a wild orgy or something."

In talking with the men, the board discovered:

1. They claim not to have had a "wild" or noisy party. They state that on the night in question they had asked two of their friends over and that they had watched television and played cards until 12:30 A.M.
2. The men claim that while they were moving in, they overheard the complaining renter say to another occupant: "I am going to do something about them."

3. The complaining renter refused to talk to the board, stating that he did not want to be bothered by a lot of "silly" questions.
4. The only other occupant of the building who was home on the night in question stated that she had heard the men "laughing" late in the evening but did not consider it "excessive noise."
5. Mr. Genove has stated that the complaining renter was an old, retired man who had been renting from Mr. Genove for fourteen years.

What should the board do? One very effective way of analyzing this case is to divide the class into small groups and ask them to come up with a consensus on what the board should do.

Discussion
A. In analyzing the possible actions by the board, it would be useful to apply the principles of Chapter 10 of the text. First, try to analyze the types of conflict involved: personal, needs, etc. Identification of the basic nature of the conflict will be helpful in determining the course of action for the board.
B. Conflict among the participants must be managed either by directive of the board or by some other means. How possible do you think it is for the board to impress on the participants the need to manage their conflict?
  1. Should the board attempt to have participants avoid the conflict?
  2. Should the board attempt to defuse conflict by its own actions?
  3. If the board attempts to confront the conflict, should it work from the basic situations of win-lose, lose-lose, and win-win?
  4. Is it too idealistic to anticipate that the participants (as well as those who are not directly involved but who add to the conflict) will integrate their conflict rather than be subject to power or compromise? What are the possiblilities?
C. If all the class were to be divided into separate small groups and each group given the responsibility for deciding what to do, would all groups come up with the same answers? What does that say about negotiating conflict? Is it always subject to the same "one right and correct answer"? On what do the various answers depend?

EXERCISE 11-2
WIN AS MUCH AS YOU CAN[1] (Game)
The instructor will give details on how the game is to be played. The class is divided into groups of eight. Students not finding a place in a group will be assigned roles of observers and help monitor the activities. Groups of eight will be known as "clusters." Each group of eight, or cluster, will be further divided into dyads.

Each round is directed by the instructor. Time for working on a choice will be monitored, and payoff scoring will be quickly entered in the tally form (Table 11). When the round specifies that all the group (or cluster) will talk, it is possible for all members to talk with one another by teams. Otherwise only partners will discuss their strategies, as indicated. Strategies are shown in Table 12.

[1]Adapted from an exercise developed by William Gellerman. In J. William Pfeiffer and John E. Jones, (eds.). *A Handbook of Structured Experiences for Human Relations Training,* vol. 3 (rev.), Universities Associates, La Jolla, Calif., 1974.

TABLE 11. **Tally Sheet**

Directions. For ten successive rounds, you and your partner will choose either an X or a Y. The payoff for each round is dependent upon the pattern of choices made in your cluster:

	4 X's:	Lose $1 each
	3 X's 1 Y:	Win $1 each Lose $3
	2 X's: 2 Y's:	Win $2 each Lose $2 each
	1 X: 3 Y's:	Win $3 Lose $1 each
	4 Y's:	Win $1 each

TABLE 12. **Strategy**

Directions. You are to confer with your partner on each round and make a *joint decision.* Before rounds 5, 8, and 10, confer with the other dyads in your cluster.

Round	Strategy		Choice	$ Won	$ Lost	$ Balance	
	Time allowed	**Confer with**					
1	2 min.	Partner					
2	1 min.	Partner					
3	1 min.	Partner					
4	1 min.	Partner					
5	3 min. +1 min.	Cluster Partner					Bonus round: Payoff is multiplied by 3
6	1 min.	Partner					
7	1 min.	Partner					
8	3 min. +1 min.	Cluster Partner					Bonus round: Payoff is multiplied by 5
9	1 min.	Partner					
10	3 min. +1 min.	Cluster Partner					Bonus round: Payoff is multiplied by 10

Discussion

A. If this is an exercise in conflict, how do participants deal with the choices of win-win and win-lose?

B. In the title "Win as Much as You Can," who is the "you" referred to? The entire group? A set of partners?

C. In developing strategies, did communication within the cluster have any advantage? When only partners were talking together, did you want to add the others to your conversation?

D. This is also an exercise in trust. What happened when the issue of integrity and honesty came up in the cluster communication?

E. How much could a cluster (the group of eight students) win if it were to maximize its wins and mimimize its losses as a cluster? Did any groups come close to the maximum? Why not? Trace the negotiating efforts of those groups which had the highest scores — not just partners, but the entire cluster — to see whether there is anything special in what they did.

F. Would more frequent communciation have been an advantage?

EXERCISE 11-3
ALLOCATION OF RESOURCES AND FAVORS (Role Playing)

Role-play some of the situations below to demonstrate how conflict arises from the scarcity of some commodity — whether a real thing like dollars, or a subjective concept like love or attention. It might be interesting to have small groups in the class work out role-playing skits from these items and present them in two acts: the first act to set the scene for the problem and the second act to present a potential solution or resolution of the conflict.

1. A roommate borrows your sweater very often and has begun to use it even without asking. You go to the closet for the sweater; it's not there. You wait, ready to start an argument as soon as your roommate comes in.

2. A brother and sister both want to use the car on the same night. Should they settle the conflict with or without parental help? Look at it both ways.

3. You want to buy a motorbike. Your father wants you to save the money for college.

4. A new typewriter is purchased for the office where you work. You and two other employees have old models, and each hopes to get the new machine. The boss has said that the three of you must decide who gets it. The boss refuses to participate in the discussion.

5. Four members of the history department are up for promotion to full professor from associate professor. Only one can be awarded that promotion this year. The other six members of the department are given the responsibility of deciding which member of the department gets promoted.

Hint. Managing conflict in these situations may involve avoiding, defusing, or confronting. Try some solutions from each of these options to see which may be most dramatic to role-play for the class. Identify the kind of conflict management you are working with. Ask the class for comments on that method of handling the conflict.

Discussion

A. In applying the skills recommended in the chapter did you tend to get stopped at the stage of identifying the nature of the conflict? Do you find it easy to just sit and blame each other?

B. The steps recommended in the chapter have a certain logic to them and a recommended sequence. Did you have difficulty following the sequence? Was it hard to stay on the topic of conflict management?

C. Does this set of role-playing skits demonstrate why we are insisting on the terminology "management of conflict" instead of "avoidance"?

D. Can you identify the types of conflict you are dealing with? Personal conflict? Interpersonal conflict? Organizational conflict? Why is it useful to identify the type? Is it important therefore to understand that not all conflict is the same in its origin, and therefore that not all conflict may be amenable to the same kinds of solutions or management?

EXERCISE 11-4
HOW YOU SOLVED YOUR OWN PROBLEMS (Discussion; Role Playing)

Each of us has occasions when managing conflict has worked well. Can you recall an incident in which you properly identified a conflict situation and then proceeded to manage it appropriately?

In a small group of four to six members, share such experiences. This is a chance, also, to check out with others how they might have solved the same problem. When you tell your "managing conflict" anecdote, ask others to suggest some alternatives you may or may not have considered. After all group members have told their stories, select one as a role-playing situation for the class. Develop the characters. You may want to present more than one act — the conflict arising in the first act, the management of it in the second act. Each group in turn will present its drama of real-life conflict.

Discussion

A. In the general discussion make sure all members of the class have understood the nature of the conflict. It should be phrased in the nomenclature of Chapter 11. Once the class members agree on the kind of conflict, then discussion can proceed to alternative methods of resolving the conflict.

B. Much of the disagreement that occurs at the stage of finding solutions can be traced back to lack of agreement on the nature of the conflict. Did any groups find themselves in that situation?

C. Did the process for managing conflict (or skills as set forth in the text) help the group to arrive at a better conclusion than was possible in the actual situation?

D. Identify the forces working for win-win, lose-lose, and win-lose. Which seem to be more typical of your interactions? Is there a tradition in American culture for one of these forms of confronting?

EXERCISE 11-5
NEGOTIATION CASE (Role Playing)

This exercise may include more than one person on a side — that is, the seller and a friend may be negotiating with the potential buyer and that buyer's friend, parent, etc. The important thing is to establish for yourself before you start negotiating the minimum you will accept if you are the seller and the maximum you will pay if you are the buyer. An appointed observer will monitor the negotiation, help determine when the negotiation has ended, and lead a discussion later.

Seller. You have a hi-fi set for sale. You have had it less than a year, and originally paid $750 for it including amplifier, tuner, two speakers, tape deck, and turntable. Although you bought it new, the fact that you got it as a matched set meant you paid less than the components would have cost you individually — you estimate that at about $900 if each component had been bought by itself. You are graduating next month and want to sell the hi-fi rather than pack it and take it with you, since you are not sure where you will be living. Several people have asked to buy components separately but don't want to pay much, and you are hoping to find one person to take the whole outfit for a more reasonable figure. A similar outfit was advertised in the campus paper for $500. Another outfit by a different manufacturer was listed on a bulletin board for $400, but there was some question of its age. Yours is in excellent condition and still under warranty. (Without telling the buyer, write down on a piece of paper to give to the observer what is the lowest figure you will take for the outfit.)

Buyer. This is the kind of matched set you have been looking for, and this particular brand is difficult to find in a balanced outfit like this one. You can probably sell one you have for around $150, which can help offset what you would pay for the newer one. Unless you sell yours, however, you don't want to buy another one. You know what other sets are being sold for, but your intention is to upgrade your hi-fi system when you can. Although you have something over $400 in savings for the purpose of getting better components, you aren't anxious to spend it all right now without some hope of building up more savings in the near future — maybe by selling your old set. (Without telling the seller, you should decide what is the most you will pay. Do this before you start negotiating and write it down to give to the observer.)

Observer. Obtain from both buyer and seller a piece of paper which will have on it the figure each has set. You will use it later to check on how each managed to work within his or her minimum and maximum. During the negotiation, pay particular attention to any devices used by the sellers and buyers which helped move the negotiation to a conclusion. If it turned out well for both, ask how they thought it happened. If it did not turn out well, try to find out how each thought he or she tried to get a satisfactory solution, and also how each thought the other contributed to the efforts. Share your observations with the rest of the class and invite comments from the buyers and sellers.

ASSIGNMENT 11-1
A WEEK OF CONFLICTS

A. Keep a diary for a week on the conflicts you experience, whether they are trivial or of grave importance. At the end of the week categorize each conflict as "personal," "interpersonal," or "organizational." Speculate in a brief paragraph on which category seems to be most prevalent and why.

B. From the same list, put the conflicts into three time categories: (1) already taken care of, no carry-over, (2) being worked on and capable of imminent solution, and (3) very long term and possibly insoluble. How do you feel about each of those categories? Which take most of your time each day?

C. Place each conflict in one of the following categories: (1) conflicts you have avoided or will attempt to avoid, (2) conflicts you have defused or are attempting to defuse, and (3) conflicts you have confronted or will confront.

D. Finally, estimate how many of your conflicts could have been treated or managed with the skills of conflict management discussed in Chapter 11.

ASSIGNMENT 11-2
CONFLICT FROM FICTION

Much of dramatic literature involves the presence of conflict and its ultimate resolution. From your own recent reading or viewing identify a story (novel, movie, television drama, etc.) which depended on conflict to maintain your interest. Analyze that study in conflict for the existence of destructive outcomes and positive outcomes. Would the story have been as interesting if the ending had been different? Write your analysis of the conflict and its resolution.

ASSIGNMENT 11-3
WHAT DO YOU HAVE TO KNOW?

Two friends of yours are sitting with you and talking about the outcome of a recent city election. You discover that the two supported opposing candidates. Even though the election is over, your friends are still bitter about the conduct of the campaign and the outcome of the election. What do you have to know about them and their positions — and what can you communicate to them — that will help them manage their conflict? Which option should you select: avoid, defuse, or confront? What would be the advantage of each of those options in this situation?

Assuming you want at least to bring some harmony into the present discussion, and perhaps to help the two friends manage their conflict better over a longer period of time, write a brief paper answering the above questions.

ASSIGNMENT 11-4
EITHER-OR

Identify as many examples as you can of "allness" or polarization of statements in radio or television advertising. Include them in your scrapbook.

Think of either-or slogans such as "My country — right or wrong," "America — love it or leave it," "You're either for me or against me." Write a short paper in which you explain other possible alternatives to the choices suggested by the slogans. Try to recall other either-or slogans that you are familiar with.

List the either-or slogans you can find. Each slogan will have a group or some identifiable representatives behind it. What is the purpose of the group which promotes such a slogan? Write down the potential sides which would be drawn if the slogans were translated into legislation or brought up for public debate.

You may be asked to give a brief statement in class about what you think is the reason a group supports such slogans. (Who is behind the "Better Red than dead" slogan? What political or social philosophy is involved? Who is the slogan attacking?) The class may be asked to divide up in dyads to discuss the slogans. A common way to do this is for each person who believes one way to try to find another person who believes the opposite. The first step in trying to discuss the slogan is to find out what the words "mean" to each of the members of the discussion dyad. A discussion of the "meanings" may be as far as you get.

ASSIGNMENT 11-5
HONESTY

How do you feel about the advantages and potential dangers of honesty about interpersonal relationships in group situations?

Write a report on a situation in which one person insists on being honest about everything. Does it complicate communication? Is there a pure form of honesty which people can determine for themselves and always depend on using with others, or does what is "honest" sometimes vary with the situation or with how much information is available?

PERSONAL IMPROVEMENT BLANK (Chapter 11)

1. Recount briefly here a recent conflict situation in which you won, lost, or came out even. What contributed to the outcome? Did you have any control over the outcome? Could you have applied the skills suggested in this chapter?

2. Write out a recent case or incident that required conflict management over the allocation of scarce resources. Describe the parties who were contending for the resources, their methods of confronting, and the outcome.

Your name _____

Chapter 12

INTERPERSONAL SKILLS: MAKING IT WORK

FEEDBACK BLANK

EXERCISES

ASSIGNMENTS

FEEDBACK BLANK (Chapter 12)   DO NOT SIGN
This feedback blank is designed to provide you with an opportunity to evaluate the course as a whole.

1. Rate on a ten-point scale how productive this course has been for you.
      1   2   3   4   5   6   7   8   9   10
      Unproductive   Very productive

      Comments:

2. What aspects of the class seemed of *most* value to you? Why?

3. What aspects of the class seemed of *least* value to you? Why?

4. Did you feel free to participate in class? Why or why not?

5. Did you feel that the class was interesting and challenging? Why or why not?

EXERCISE 12-1
NASA, OR LOST ON THE MOON (Group Project; Game)

Instructions

This is an exercise in group decision making about survival in outer space. Your group is to employ the method of *group consensus* in reaching its decision about the relative survival values of the items listed below. This means that the ranking for each of the fifteen items *must* be agreed upon by each group member before it becomes a part of the group decision. Consensus is difficult to reach. Therefore not every ranking will meet with everyone's complete approval. Try as a group to make each ranking one with which all group members can at least *partially* agree.

   Here are some guides to use in reaching consensus:

1. Avoid *arguing* for your own individual judgments. Approach the task on the basis of logic.
2. Avoid changing your mind *only* in order to reach agreement and avoid conflict. Support only solutions with which you are able to agree at least somewhat.
3. Avoid ''conflict-reducing'' techniques such as majority votes and trading.
4. View differences of opinion as helpful rather than as a hindrance in decision making.

   Here are the items:

_____Box of matches

_____Food concentrate

_____50 feet of nylon rope

_____Parachute silk

_____Portable heating unit

_____Two 45-caliber pistols

_____One case of dehydrated Pet milk

_____Two 100-pound tanks of oxygen

_____Stellar map (of moon's constellation)

_____Life raft

_____Magnetic compass

_____5 gallons of water

_____Signal flares

_____First-aid kit containing injection needles

_____Solar-powered FM receiver-transmitter

Direction Sheet for Scoring

A group member will assume the responsibility for directing the scoring.

1. Score the net difference between your answers and the correct answers given by the instructor. For example, if your answer was 9 and the correct answer was 12, the net difference is 3. Therefore 3 becomes the score for that particular item. If your answer is 12 and the correct answer is 9, your score for that item will be 3.
2. Total all item scores to obtain your individual score.
3. The member responsible for directing the scoring will then total all individual scores and divide that number by the number of participants to obtain the average of individual scores.
4. The member in charge of the group worksheet will then score the group worksheet in the same way that individual scores were obtained.
5. The group consensus score and the average of individual scores will then be given to the instructor, who will record them on the board. The range of individual scores in the group, consisting of the lowest and the highest individual scores, will also be given to the instructor.

Ratings

0–20	Excellent
20–30	Good
30–40	Average
40–50	Fair
Over 50	Poor

Discussion

A. Was it easy to follow the instructions for conducting the discussion (the four points listed on the previous page)? Could you avoid arguing for the answer you had put down, and could you open up your mind to various logics? Having committed yourself to an answer, were you eager to change?
B. What devices did the group use to arrive at consensus?
C. In scoring the results, did the individual answers to the problem seen to be more "accurate" than the groups' answers, compared with the expert opinion of space personnel? What can you conclude about group decisions? Do they take more time? Are they more accurate? Are there occasions when time and accuracy are balanced and a group decision process may not be important? How do you decide when to use a group discussion method and when not?

EXERCISE 12-2
A MAN BOUGHT A HORSE (Problem-Solving Game)

A man bought a horse for $60 and sold it for $70. He then bought that same horse back again for $80 and sold it for $90. How much money did the man make in the horse-trading business?

1. Solve the above problem *individually* first. Record your answer in the space provided below.
2. Your instructor will then have you break up into groups of six or seven students. You will then

try to arrive at a consensus on the right answer. Record the group answer in the space provided below.

Individual answer   *Group Answer*

Discussion

A. When the instructor gives the right answer at the end of the project, compare the accuracy of the individual replies and the group replies. Did the groups come up with more correct answers? Why?

B. Did the groups take sufficiently more time to work out the answer to make the group process a slow method of arriving at a decision? Do you sacrifice time for accuracy (especially if you multiply the time spent by the number of people in the group to arrive at the person-hours involved)?

C. What logic kept the group members from arriving quickly at the correct answer? Did they fail to see some feature of the problem which could have helped them work it out more quickly?

D. What techniques of argument did group members use to support their own ideas of the correct answer? How did the group members handle one person who may have disagreed for a long time? Did they bully the person? Plead with the person? Use logic? Use force or decision? How much of the group's time and attention was directed to only one person who may have been on an opposing side?

E. Did the fact that you had to write down an answer before the group began its discussion affect your attitude about how strongly to argue for ''your answer''? Was that a hidden agenda for you?

EXERCISE 12-3
DESCRIBE THE STYLES (Role Playing)

This is a role-playing exercise for at least two persons at a time; pick a partner with whom you can work out a believable ''script'' to fit the styles described in the text.

Situation. You and a friend are discussing the possibility of taking a summer vacation together. While you are very much interested in the outdoors, your friend is much more interested in historical events and would like nothing better than to tour museums, battlefields, and visit library collections of historical significance. Role-play the conversation you would have if your friend were to act in a consistent way in each of the following styles:

Blaming, or aggressive

Placating, or nonassertive

Computing, or intellectual

Distracting, or manipulative

Leveling, or assertive

EXERCISE 12-4
CASES; TRUST AND DEFENSIVENESS (Role Playing)
Select people from the class to take various roles.

Situation. A new plan for city revenue has just been proposed by the city council in the city your college is in. The plan involves taxing students for use of the city streets; it will apply only to those students who do not live in the city, and therefore it sounds like an equitable way to get "transients" to help pay for the upkeep of the streets they use. A special ordinance will require each college or university in the city to assist in the fee collection by reporting all registered automobiles owned or operated by students. Local automobiles will, of course, not be taxed, as it is assumed that the people owning them are already supporting the local government's projects by paying some taxes. (If there are other items of concern to the actors, make up some reasonable extensions of this ordinance.) The scene is a meeting of the city council where various witnesses and other interested people are in attendance. The mayor is presiding and has asked certain people to speak (they will be so indicated in the cast of characters); others may want to be heard and will volunteer. The parts to be played include:

The mayor (who is in favor of the ordinance)

A city council member who is in favor of the issue

A city council member who is against the issue

The president of one of the local colleges (invited by the mayor, even though he or she is opposed to the ordinance)

A student from out of town

A student from within the city

Observers. Several observers should be appointed. Watch for the signs of defensiveness, and mark them down to report later. Other observers should watch for the ways in which defensive communication was either avoided or introduced and what effect it seemed to have on the flow of communication. Still other observers should watch for signs of developing trust, or for symptoms that trust did not develop.

EXERCISE 12-5
TAKING RISKS (Discussion)
In a small group (four to six persons) develop a list of disclosure situations or communication occasions for which you believe there is a risk involved (talking to a salesperson, asking support for a political candidate, discussing your religious views, asking for a date, etc.). Be prepared to write these on the chalkboard or on large sheets of paper for a discussion by the class.

When you have set up your list, ask group members to speculate on what would be the most serious thing that could happen in the situation. In other words, when people say they are taking a risk, what is it they are risking? If disclosing yourselves to others is a risky business, then what would be the worst consequences?

Add the list of consequences of taking risks to the list of risky situations, and discuss, either in small group or in class session, the relationship between disclosing and risking.

Discussion

A. If self-disclosure means taking risks, just what kind of risks are involved? Is disclosing worth the risks involved? Can you get hurt physically or emotionally?

B. Was it easy to find a list of occasions on which disclosing would possibly involve some risk? Do you find yourself in those situations very often? How do you deal with them?

C. If you avoid situations of disclosure, how do you manage that? Are your patterns different from those of the person who actively seeks situations for self-disclosure?

D. In the class discussion were there some situations which everyone seems to be involved in? Some which were very unusual? Do coping patterns differ?

EXERCISE 12-6
WHEN TO TRUST AND WHEN NOT TO TRUST (Role Playing)

Remember the picture of a political candidate and the legend under it which asked "Would you buy a used car from this man?" If that means we judge a person at least somewhat by physical appearance, what other factors do we also use to make sure we can trust someone?

In a small group develop a skit or drama of a communication situation in which the question of trust is central. The situation may be personal or general, and it may be quite trivial or of larger significance. The best kinds of role-playing material come from the experiences of the students themselves, but newspapers provide a wealth of examples. (The famous "pigeon drop" swindle is a classic, and reports of that con game appear almost weekly in the newspapers. In this trick, the victim is offered a part of money which was "found in an envelope." But to establish "good faith" the victim must put up some personal funds, usually placing them in an envelope with the original money. The victim even gets to hold the envelope while the con artists go to check just one more time on who lost the envelope. They never come back. The victim has an envelope full of cut-up paper and no money. This is a recurring example of greed balanced against trust.)

It must be emphasized that you can trust others with your feelings as well as with material goods. Your role-playing situation can make use of the fact that people can develop trust by words, looks, actions, and a past history of comparing those. Husband and wife, child and parent, teacher and student, customer and salesperson are all relationships in which development of trust is important. These are only a few suggestions for the role-playing situation you will plan and produce.

At the end of your skit, ask the class for an evaluation of whether or not the people in the drama should have trusted each other. Ask the class to estimate what would be the outcome of the situation.

Discussion

A. Besides the questions you ask the class after the skit is finished, there are some general ideas which can be developed. For example, are people more careless about the smaller items of trust than the larger ones?

B. In looking back on the skits, discuss which kinds of information — verbal, nonverbal, etc. — were most influential in establishing trust. Do you believe what you hear or see or "know" from past experience? Which trust-producing devices did the actors use? Are they familiar ones to you in your real life?

C. If there are differing opinions in the class on the outcome of the skits and on who should have trusted whom, how do you account for the differences? Do you start out to trust or not to trust at a different level from others in the class? Where did you learn about trust? Do you rely primarily upon your own experience? Do the media and literature influence you also?

EXERCISE 12-7
PRISONER'S DILEMMA (Game)

Exercises like "Win as Much as You Can" (Exercise 11-2) are known as the "prisoner's dilemma." They are logical problems developed from a win-win, win-lose, zero-sum game. Such games are also very important exercises in looking at trust and taking risks. If you did not do Exercise 11-2 earlier, this may be a good time to try it — concentrating on the risk-taking and trust nature of the game.

Discussion

A. Whether or not you did Exercise 11-2 as a laboratory experience, the principles of trust and risk can be discussed. Review the outcomes of the game and ask for opinions on how trust was developed or held back.

B. Once a partnership agreed to call for an X or a Y and then did not live up to the agreement, what happened to the relationship with other partners? Was there a warm relationship operating among the partners? Was there distrust?

C. Even during those times when the partners were permitted to consult only with one another (not talking in the cluster among various sets of partners) was there some information exchanged? Did the whispering between partners make others question their intentions and potential actions? Do you always depend only on verbal instructions or agreements to take risks? Are there nonverbal cues also which serve to make you trust or not?

EXERCISE 12-8
THE CITIZEN OF THE YEAR (Role Playing)

"Well, friends," said the chairperson of the Community Club, "That does it! We've selected our 'Citizen of the Year.'"

"And a close race it was, too," said Al Martin. "People were saying it was going to be close, but I never figured . . ."

"By the way, Al," the committee chairperson broke in, "I want to see that all three candidates are at the Community Club dinner Thursday night. I don't care how you get them there, but they all should come."

"You mean you want all three candidates rather than just the winner?"

"That's right, Al. I've been thinking. With the selection being as close as it was, I really think we ought to mention all three candidates — even though, of course, only one will receive the award.'' The other committee members nodded in agreement. ''We've never done this before, but it will be good to have a change in format.''

The committee began to break up, and Al sighed. Well, he would see what he could do.

Al's job is to see each candidate and convince each to be in attendance without telling which one is to be the Citizen of the Year. The candidates are Jim Farnsworth, Bill Nichols, and Anne Rollins. Al has a note in his pocket from the committee listing the name of the winner. He knows the winner's name but must not disclose it. At the dinner there will be a skit, and after the skit is completed, the class will be asked to guess which of the three was elected. Al will then share the note with the entire class.

One by one, Al approaches the candidates and tries to convince them that they should be present as finalists. None of the candidates, however, is anxious to come to that dinner and be presented only as a ''runner-up.'' The candidates want to find out as much as possible about their chance of being the winner before agreeing to be there. The actor selected for Al's role should be persuasive but able to keep a secret without ever lying — a difficult combination.

Al may choose to see the three candidates together (more difficult) or one by one in a series of short scenes; use no more than five minutes each if possible.

Discussion
A. Watch especially for the devices used by the three candidates to get information out of Al without directly pinning him down. How does he avoid answering their questions? Are these familiar devices to you?
B. How would each of the candidates feel about going to the dinner after having the conversation with Al? How high would each person's expectations be about receiving the award? When the announcement comes, are all the candidates going to be preparing to rise and be recognized?
C. What does Al risk in disclosing too much? In disclosing too little?
D. What do the candidates risk in demanding to know too much? In not knowing enough?
E. How can trust be maintained between Al and his committee if he lets the candidates know which is to be given the award, and then the runners-up do not appear at the dinner? How can Al maintain the trust of the candidates when they ask him about their chances of receiving the award? What would you do in Al's position?

EXERCISE 12-9
LEVELING OR ASSERTIVE STYLES (Role Playing; Discussion)
This is an exercise in examining the ways in which four unhealthy styles can be replaced by a more healthy one. The text lists the following styles as categories on which to base responses to communicative incidents: (1) blaming or aggressive, (2) placating or nonassertive, (3) computing or intellectual, (4) distracting or manipulative, and (5) leveling or assertive. Of these, the last seems to be most effective.

Working in small groups, make up cases of threatening communication (which normally would result in a defensive response from the person involved) or situations in which you would normally respond defensively. Role-play in two acts. The first act should show one of the ways most people respond to such a communication — aggressive, computing, placating, or distracting. The second act should demonstrate how the leveling or assertive response might be more appropriate.

If the groups do not have time to develop skits or role-playing situations in two acts, they may simply carry on a group discussion of the various responses which would be appropriate for the situation. (One situation that might be used is a teacher telling the class that because two students are suspected of cheating on the last exam, the entire class will have to take the exam over. If that is an aggressive approach, how would a placating approach handle the same situation, or a leveling approach? In another example, a friend asks to borrow your car, although he or she has not been very careful with it in the past. How do you respond? Why? Is that the only response available to you?)

Discussion

A. When you are confronted with opportunities to react to communication situations, do you tend to react much the same way most of the time? In other words, are there patterns you have adopted which you depend on? Are they always appropriate? Do you become known as a certain kind of "responder"? Do people expect you to act a certain way? Does that in turn affect how you react? (Remember how much of your behavior is related to others' expectations of you.)

B. In the situations you worked out, were some styles of response more effective than others? Why?

C. Is it easy to work out ways in which a leveling or assertive response can replace the less desirable options? Does that response take longer? Does it involve more thought?

EXERCISE 12-10
ENCOURAGING OTHERS TO TELL THE TRUTH (Role Playing; Discussion)

Asking someone to tell you the truth implies that you do not believe what is going on, or that you are sure the truth is important. The situation also has some risk for the truth-teller. The child whose father asks who broke the window is in a position of risk in the relationship. If there is an error in a set of accounting books, the question "Did you check these carefully?" is more than a simple request for data; it includes an indictment of the work and hence the worker.

In a small group develop some situations similar to the above examples in which a question is being asked with the intention of probing for a truthful answer. Either role-play the situations or discuss in the group the potential consequences of responding in various ways.

Is it possible to develop a "sandwich" situation by asking questions about the involvement of others? You give some information and at the same time take some, making layers of data.

Some additional suggestions for role playing: (1) The honor system of the military academies has come under fire in relation to the other norms of society which say that one doesn't tell on one's friends. (2) A child who breaks a lamp is promised no punishment for telling the truth, but then has privileges taken away. (3) A teacher asks a student if he or she received help on a paper, and then gives a failing grade when the student confesses.

Discussion

A. Do you make a contract with others when you ask them to tell the truth even if it is damaging to them? What immunity can be assured? In the courts of law "deals" are made in which testimony is given in exchange for a light sentence. How do you feel about such arrangements?

B. Have you ever been in a school or situation where the "honor" system was the approved way of managing relationships? How did it work? What was the reaction to it by those in authority? By those on whom the "honor system" was imposed or who pledged to follow it? This statement has been made about "honor systems": "In a college with the honor system, the faculty has the honor and the students have the system." Comment.

C. In the role playing, were you conscious of the nonverbal messages which were very much a part of the verbal communication? Do you pay attention to all the available data when you are in trusting or risking situations? Are you more attuned to what is happening than in everyday situations of simple information exchange among your friends?

EXERCISE 12-11
AGREE-DISAGREE LIST ON GROUPS (Discussion)

Groups working on the agree-disagree lists have an interesting set of activities to observe. In writing down a response to the agree-disagree choices, the student makes a personal commitment. When, following that, the student must expose the personal preference to the group, another set of factors becomes involved. Very few of you can argue from an entirely objective view — that is, you are not very good at keeping your personal feelings out of your public statements. Another way of putting it is that you seem to feel that everything you say or write is so much a part of your own self that you get uptight when somebody asks a question about what it was you wrote. Watch your own activities in ego-involving commitment to points of view as your group discusses the items about groups.

1. Agree or disagree with each statement on groups in Table 13 (page 510). In the left-hand column record A if you agree, D if you disagree. Do this first by yourself.

2. Now discuss each statement with the other members of the small group you will be placed in and reach a consensus for each of the statements. Record in the right-hand column the letter A (for agreement) or D (for disagreement) when the group has reached a consensus on the items. This means that the decision for each item *must* be agreed upon by each member before it becomes a part of the group decision. Consensus is difficult to reach. Therefore not every answer will meet with everyone's approval. Try, as a group, to make each answer one with which *all group members* can at least partially agree. Here are some guidelines to use in reaching consensus:

   a. Avoid arguing for your own individual judgments. Approach the task on the basis of logic.

   b. Avoid changing your mind only in order to reach agreement and avoid conflict. Support only solutions with which you are able to agree somewhat at least.

   c. Avoid "conflict-reducing" techniques, such as majority votes, averaging, and "trading," in reaching your decisions.

   d. View differences of opinion as helpful rather than a hindrance in decision making.

TABLE 13. **Agree-Disagree List for Exercise 12-11 (Groups)**

Individual (A)	(D)		Group consensus (A)	(D)
____	____	1. A primary concern of all group members should be to establish an atmosphere where all feel free to express their feelings.	____	____
____	____	2. In a group with a strong leader, an individual is able to achieve greater personal security than in leaderless groups.	____	____
____	____	3. There are often occasions when an individual who is part of a working group should do what he or she thinks is right regardless of what the group has decided to do.	____	____
____	____	4. It is sometimes necessary to use autocratic methods to obtain democratic objectives.	____	____
____	____	5. Generally there comes a time when a democratic group method must be abandoned in order to solve practical problems.	____	____
____	____	6. In the long run, it is more important to use democratic methods than to achieve specific results by other means.	____	____
____	____	7. Sometimes it is necessary to change people in the direction you yourself think is right, even when they object.	____	____
____	____	8. It is sometimes necessary to ignore the feelings of others in order to reach a group decision.	____	____
____	____	9. The leader who is doing his or her best should not be openly criticized or faulted.	____	____
____	____	10. Almost any job that can be done by a committee can be done better by having one individual responsible for it.	____	____
____	____	11. Democracy has no place in a military organization, an air task force, or an infantry squad, when in battle.	____	____
____	____	12. For the average mature person, it is almost impossible to increase skills in group participation.	____	____
____	____	13. Much time is wasted in talk when everybody in the group has to be considered before making the decision.	____	____
____	____	14. In a group that really wants to get something accomplished, the leader should exercise friendly but firm control.	____	____
____	____	15. Someone who does not like the way a meeting is going should say so and try to do something about it even though he or she is not the chairperson.	____	____
____	____	16. When two group members cannot seem to get along, the best thing to do is to ignore the difficulty and carry on.	____	____
____	____	17. The best atmosphere to work for in a group is one where the personal thoughts and feelings of group members are kept to themselves.	____	____

Discussion

A. Do you think you argued more strongly for your point of view after you had written down your own answer than you would have if you had not had to write down anything before discussing it in the group? Do most of you go into group discussions with a "hidden agenda" or some point of view to which you are already committed? Or do you go into group discussions completely unbiased and free from any existing inclinations?

B. What system did you use to try to arrive at consensus? Is it easy for groups to adopt ideas without voting? Are you so accustomed to voting that you will decide even inappropriate problems by voting on solutions? Was there evidence of horse-trading or logrolling behaviors to get agreement or compromise?

C. On issues where you are very deeply committed, are you willing to talk about other views? Think about some issues on which the class would have difficulty arriving at a consensus. Why would they be difficult? Are groups always effective means of arriving at answers? When are they not?

EXERCISE 12-12
AGREE-DISAGREE LIST ON LEADERSHIP AND GROUP PROCESS (Discussion)

Another agree-disagree list is provided in Table 14 (page 512)—this time focusing on the qualities of leadership. Again you can observe the group's responses to the items in the list and gain some insight into members' attitudes about leadership and human nature. You can also go one step further and observe the group as it interacts, and thus gain some additional insight into how groups operate.

1. What is your opinion on the statements listed below? Give your first reactions and check each statement indicating whether you agree or disagree. Record the letter A if you agree, D if you disagree.

2. Break up into groups of six or seven students and reach a consensus on each of the statements. Record in the right-hand column the letter A for agreement or D for disagreement when the group has reached a consensus for the item.c

Discussion

A. Did you have difficulty changing your answers after you had written them down? Would you have been more open to discussion if you had not written down your own views before starting the group discussion?

B. In your own experience how do people act with regard to leadership? Do they behave the way they talk in this exercise? Are you assuming that people will talk and act the same way? That is, are their rhetorics and their behaviors compatible?

C. Where did you get most of your ideas about leaders and leadership? Can you identify some commonly held ideas about leadership that may not be useful in the development of leadership potential? (For example, if all leaders are tall and you are only medium height, why even try to be a leader?)

TABLE 14. **Agree-Disagree List for Exercise 12-12 (Leadership and Group Process)**

Individual (A)	(D)		Group consensus (A)	(D)
____	____	1. The primary job of the leader is to bring about change in others	____	____
____	____	2. The most effective leader is the one who can maintain a pleasant emotional climate at all times	____	____
____	____	3. Discipline of the overtalkative member is the responsibility of the group leader.	____	____
____	____	4. Leadership is a set of functions which are distributed within the group.	____	____
____	____	5. Very little progress can be made unless every member of the group feels a personal responsibility for leadership.	____	____
____	____	6. Most committee assignments would be better carried out by one person with the will to act.	____	____
____	____	7. If leadership is effective, the group members will have few feelings of dependency toward the leader.	____	____
____	____	8. Unless a group is pushed by its leader, it will make little progress.	____	____
____	____	9. In discussion, it is more important for the leader to know a lot about the topic than to be skilled in discussion methods.	____	____
____	____	10. An authoritarian leader is better than one who lets the group function without any control.	____	____
____	____	11. It is impossible to be absolutely impartial in discussion.	____	____
____	____	12. Most discussion groups will make progress if given enough time.	____	____
____	____	13. The effective discussion leader should never take a stand in opposition to the group.	____	____
____	____	14. Summarizing is the most important single task of the discussion leader.	____	____

D. Your attempts to arrive at consensus for all the items may not have been consistent. Did you always poll evenly around the group and get discussion from everyone, or did you sometimes cut the process short by asking for a vote or asking "Who doesn't agree?" (which is an invitation to be pushed down by the group)? What other means did you use to arrive at consensus? Compromise? Trading off? Bullying the deviant? Ignoring the deviant? Asking for honest expressions and listening carefully and openly?

ASSIGNMENT 12-1
WHICH STYLES DO YOU RECOGNIZE AROUND YOU?

For a week watch the people around you as they interact in their normal ways. Identify (probably without using the names of the people you are observing) two or more instances of each of the five styles from the text. Note the situations in which the styles were employed, the outcome of the use of the styles, and if the styles were appropriate or not for the situations. (Remember: all styles can be appropriate under some conditions; all are useful in our communication for some purposes.) Make notes and be prepared to discuss them in class, or write a short paper describing the instances you noticed and your assessment of the effectiveness of each style use.

ASSIGNMENT 12-2
ANALYZE THE DECISION-MAKING STEPS

Observe groups you are working with or have some direct knowledge of. As the groups move to make decisions, how do they go about it? Which steps do they make use of? Which do they avoid or at the least not make good use of? Write a brief paper in which you (1) first *describe* what a group actually did in making a decision, then (2) *analyze* the process by which it made the decision, and finally (3) *evaluate* the effectiveness of that decision as best you can including a prediction of how it will work out and why.

ASSIGNMENT 12-3
LOVERS' QUARREL

You have just had a serious quarrel with your boyfriend or girlfriend. As a result, you won't be having your usual date this weekend. The quarrel was over the amount of control that your parents exert over your relationship; specific gripes were exchanged about your parents' involvement in your affairs.

You are now faced with explaining this situation to the people around you, who will probably ask why you will not be having your usual date this weekend. How will you explain the situation to:

1. Your best friend
2. His or her best friend
3. Your roommate
4. Your parents
5. Your meddling aunt or uncle

Can you make some generalizations about the levels of abstraction that you will use in your explanations to these different people? With which people do you use the most abstract language? The least abstract language? Why?

Write up your sample dialogs with the various people listed above, answering the questions in this assignment in a summary of the differences you would put into your conversations with the different people.

ASSIGNMENT 12-4
RELATIONSHIPS

Everyone is talking about "relationships." Young people are accused of jumping into relationships irresponsibly. What is a "relationship"? What role does communication play in building a relationship? How do you avoid a breakdown in communication which ultimately results in jeopardizing a relationship? Do you and those with whom you share a relationship play by rules? If so, what are some of the rules? Do you have "relationships" with friends?

Keeping your answers to the above questions in mind, what do you think are the differences in your relationships with the following people?

1. A fellow student of the opposite sex
2. A fellow student of the same sex
3. A male professor
4. A female professor
5. A dean
6. The kids you went to high school with who do not go to college
7. Your parents
8. Your rich aunt or uncle (or some other rich relative, or a rich friend of the family)
9. Your drinking aunt or uncle (or some other relative)
10. The man or woman who interviews you for a job

Why are there these differences? Can you generalize about "relationships" from these ideas? Write a brief essay on what you think is the central consideration in relationships.

ASSIGNMENT 12-5
GAMES

Games are often considered barriers to "authenthic" relationships. Do you feel that the games we play in our communication with one another are always unhealthy? Can we have authentic relationships with everyone, all the time? Should we?

Write a brief essay on games, answering the questions just posed and including your attitude about playing games.

ASSIGNMENT 12-6
CONSUMER GAMES

Do *either* 1, 2, *or* 3 below:

1. Have you ever been "had" in a business transaction by unethical advertising? Recall such instances in a written report and be prepared to share this report with the class.
2. Find another class member who has had a similar experience. The two of you make a report to the class on what happened and how you might have prevented it.

3. In a dyad or triad discuss with the others the most dishonest act of deception (one using language in advertising or personal relations) you can recall. How might it have been defended against? What motivated the deceiver to commit such an act? Did anything happen to the deceiver?

Write your own views in a brief essay on these situations. How are you affected by the activities mentioned above?

ASSIGNMENT 12-7
JUDGING OTHERS

If you are asked to say only supportive things about someone, you are then expected to give only positive statements and avoid evaluations, judgments, and criticisms. Very often the supportive comments have another side. There was the story about a 10-year-old at a dance class who had avoided all year dancing with a certain fat girl. He disliked her. He was afraid that he would be insulting to her if they started talking. Then he got instructions from the teacher to find something nice to say; "You can always find something nice to say about people, no matter how you may dislike them," the teacher said. So with that urging, the boy asked the girl to dance and struggled through several minutes of silence and awkward moving around the dance floor. Finally, the dance was over. The boy had to say something nice to the girl (he had been ordered to), so he blurted out: "For a fat girl, you sure don't sweat much!"

Write up a situation from your own experience in which evaluative or judgmental comments caused people some problems and could have been better handled by descriptive or nonjudgmental statements.

Note. There is no personal improvement blank for this final chapter. (We believe that it is important to return to the students the PIBs which they have turned in. At the end of the term, that is usually not possible; therefore, we do not ask students to complete a form on which they will get no feedback.)

INDEX